BUNNY**DROP**

yumi unita

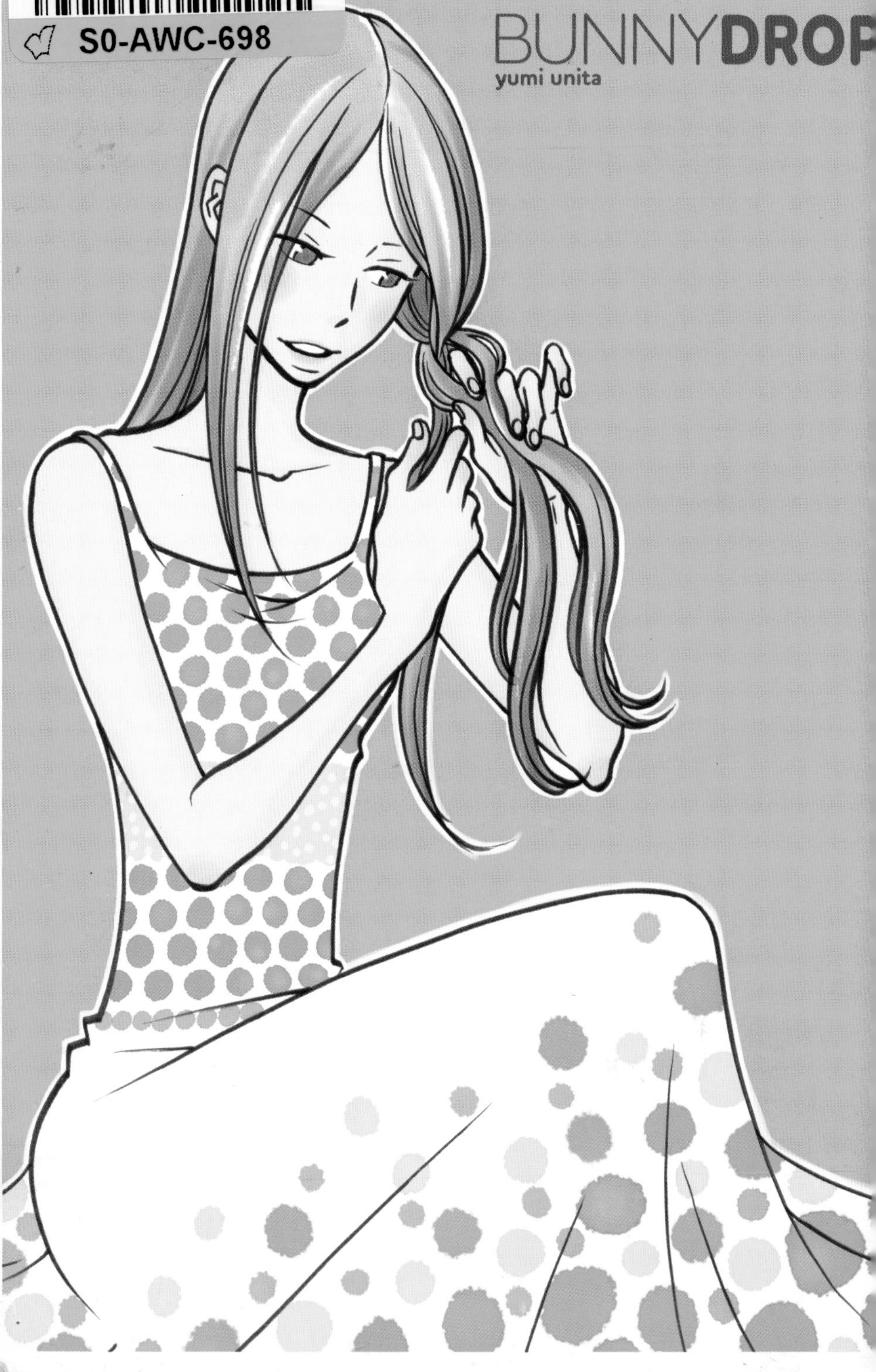

BUNNY**DROP** 8

yumi unita

STORY

Ten years have passed since Daikichi, a single guy with no experience in child-rearing, made the decision to take in Rin, his grandfather's love child, and create a family life together. Rin, now in high school, finally has the opportunity to meet her birthmother. Upon their meeting, she discovers, much to her surprise, that her mother is pregnant and about to give birth to a girl, Rin's little sister.

MAIN CHARACTERS

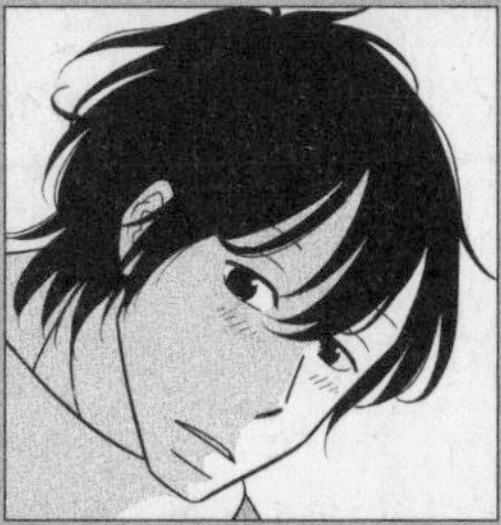

KOUKI NITANI
Rin's childhood friend from day care. High school first-year. Because of one thing after another, he was rejected by Rin.

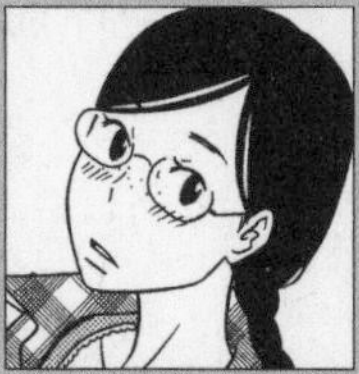

MASAKO YOSHII
Rin's birthmother. Manga artist.

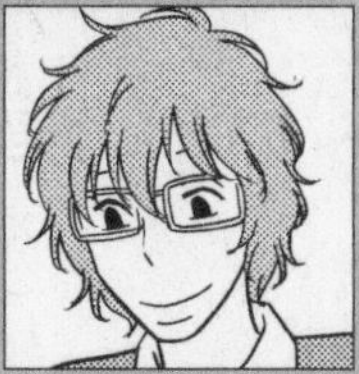

MASAKO'S HUSBAND
Also her chief assistant.

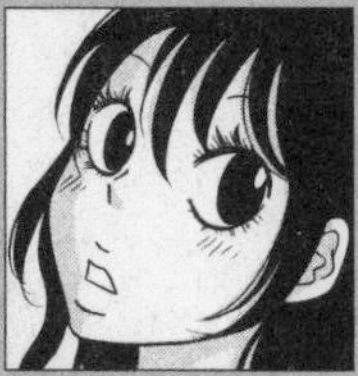

REINA
Daikichi's cousin Haruko's daughter. High school first-year.

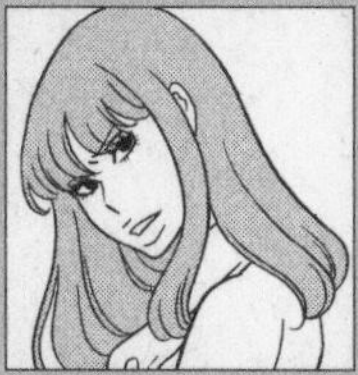

AKARI
Kouki's ex-girlfriend from middle school.

RIN KAGA
A smart and responsible high school first-year. Taken in by Daikichi when she was six.

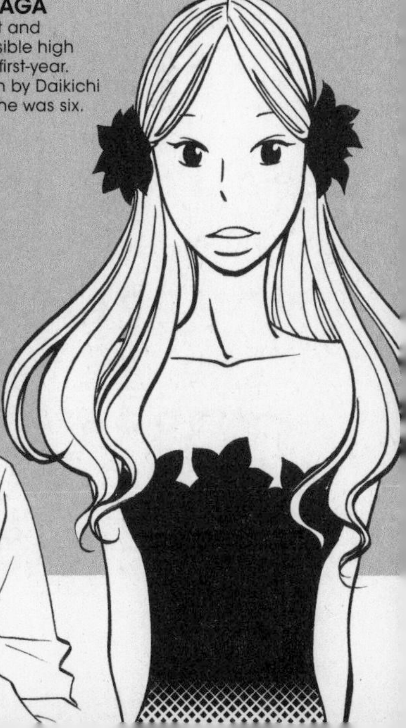

DAIKICHI KAWACHI
Forty years old and single. Has been Rin's guardian for ten years. Was hoping for a relationship with Kouki's mother, but now that has all but gone up in smoke.

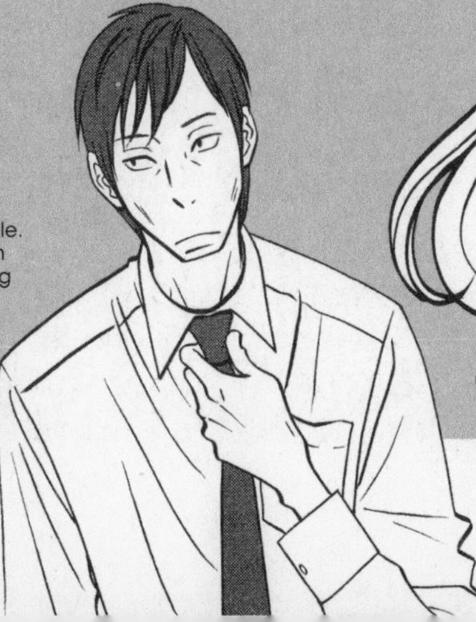

c o n t e n t s

BUNNY**DROP**

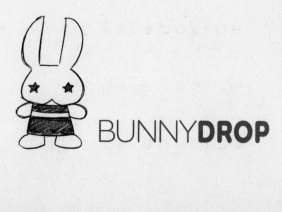

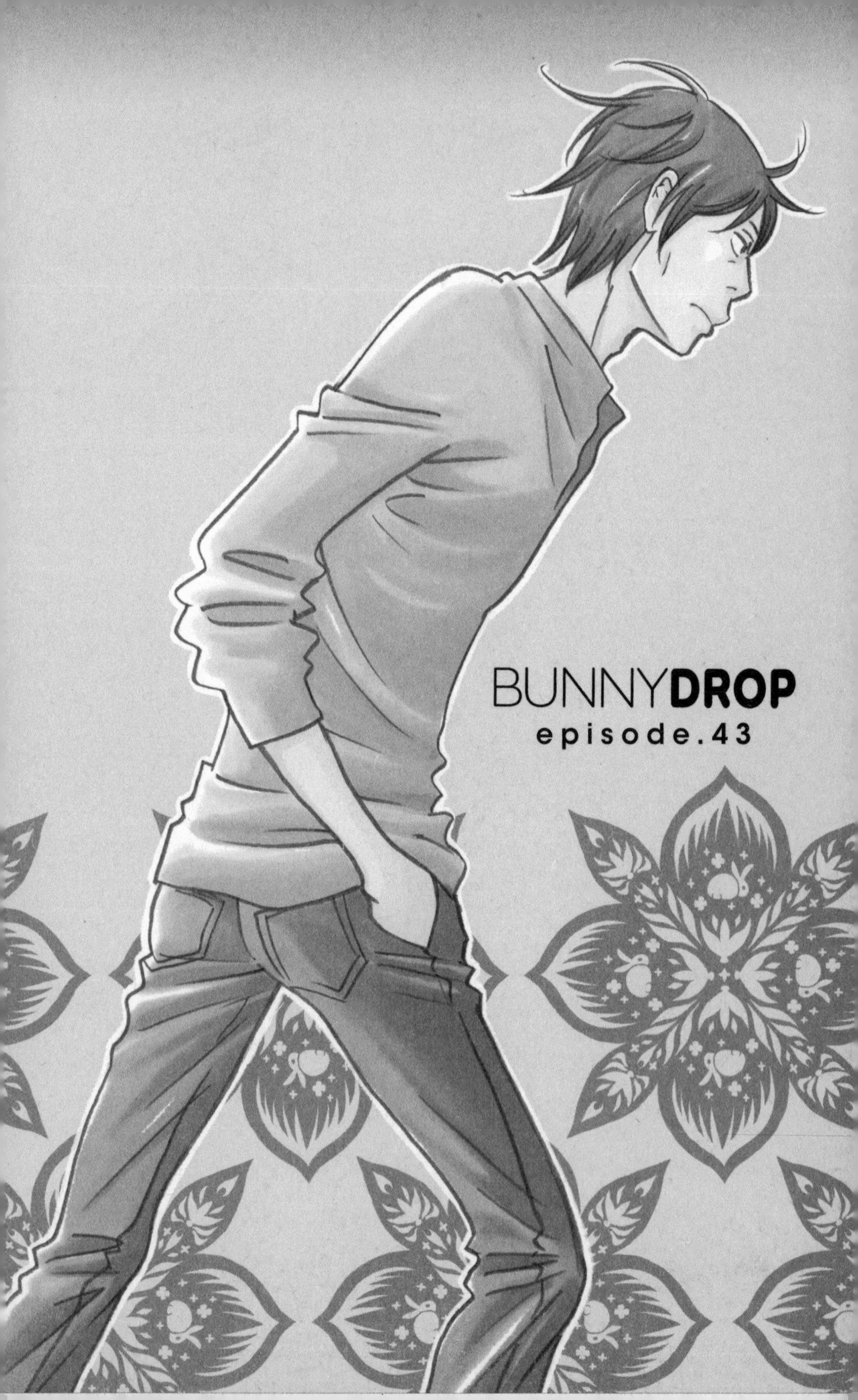
BUNNYDROP
episode.43

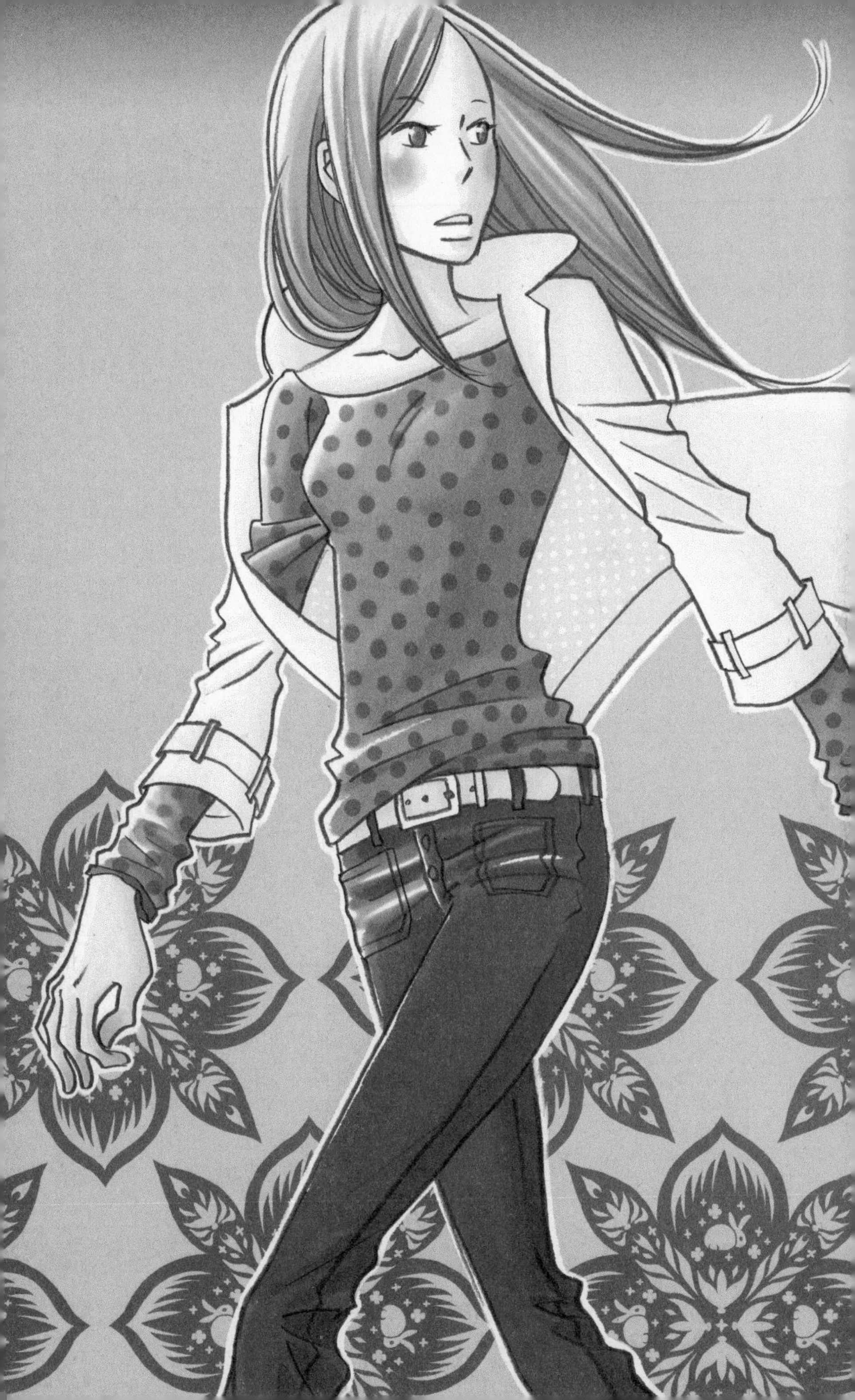

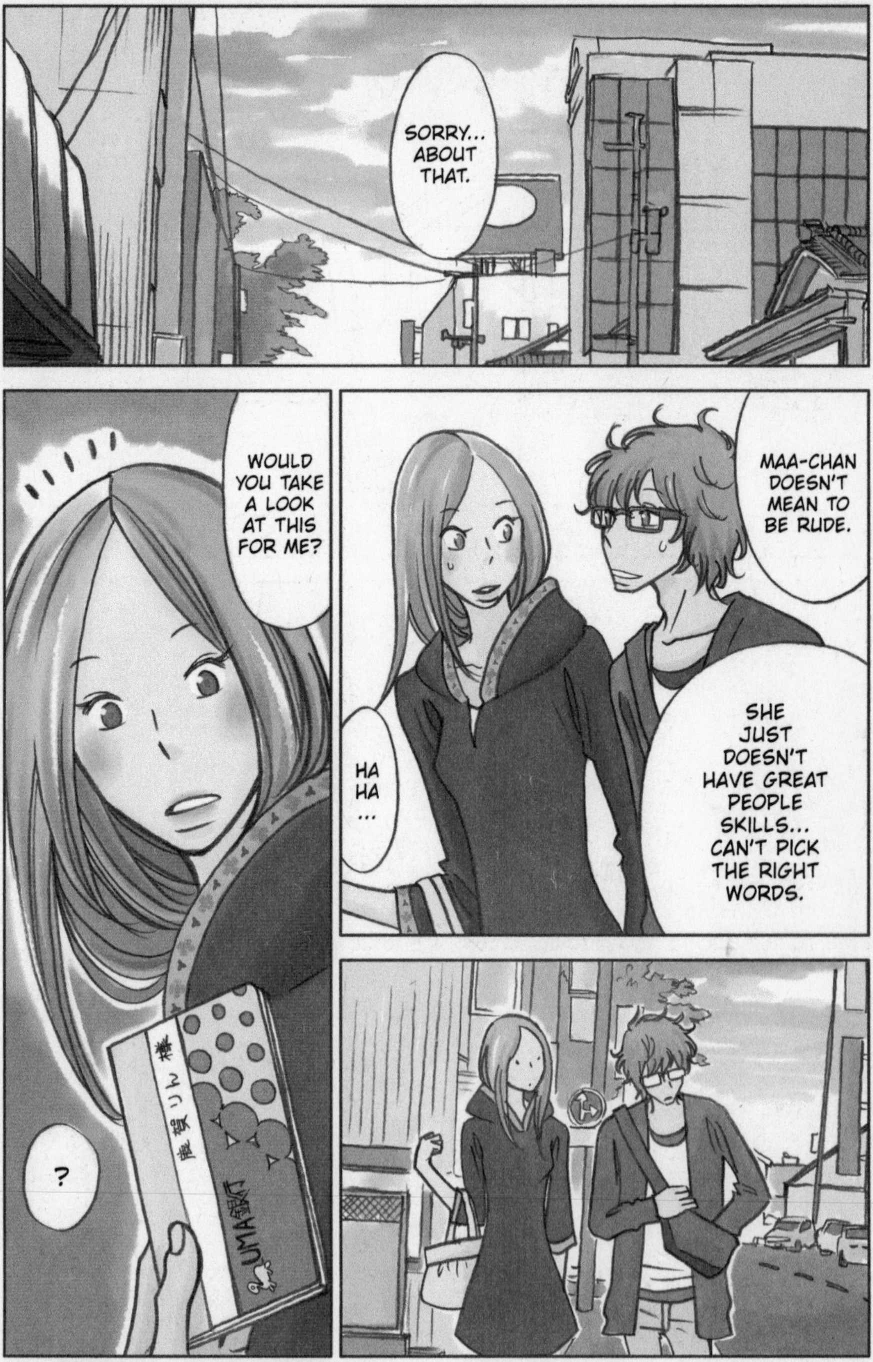
SORRY... ABOUT THAT.
MAA-CHAN DOESN'T MEAN TO BE RUDE.
SHE JUST DOESN'T HAVE GREAT PEOPLE SKILLS... CAN'T PICK THE RIGHT WORDS.
HA HA ...
WOULD YOU TAKE A LOOK AT THIS FOR ME?
?
UMA

BANK BOOK: MISS RIN KAGA / UMA BANK

PAGE: BANK BOOK

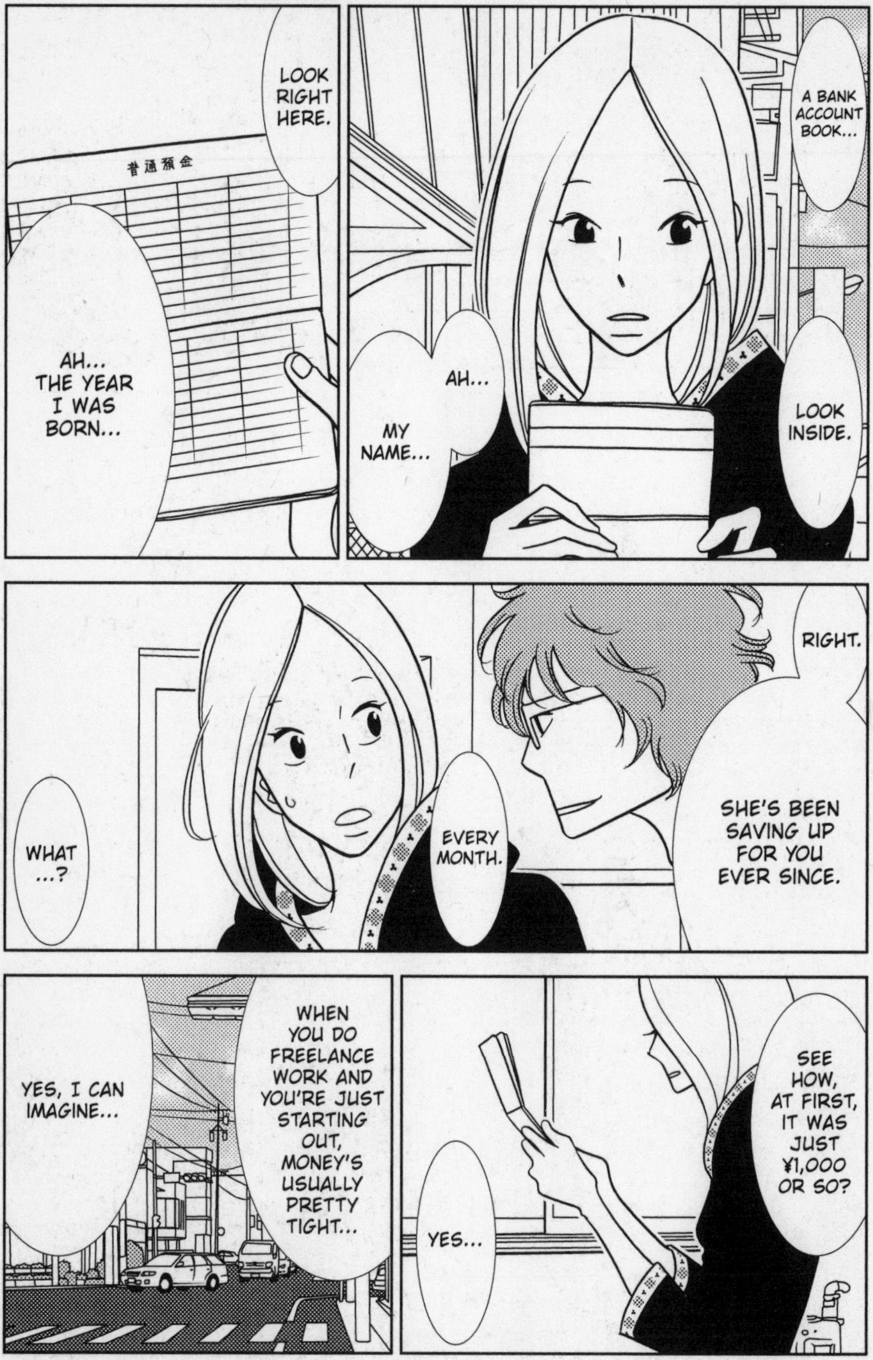

A BANK ACCOUNT BOOK...
LOOK INSIDE.
AH...
MY NAME...
LOOK RIGHT HERE.
普通預金
AH... THE YEAR I WAS BORN...
RIGHT.
SHE'S BEEN SAVING UP FOR YOU EVER SINCE.
EVERY MONTH.
WHAT ...?
SEE HOW, AT FIRST, IT WAS JUST ¥1,000 OR SO?
YES...
WHEN YOU DO FREELANCE WORK AND YOU'RE JUST STARTING OUT, MONEY'S USUALLY PRETTY TIGHT...
YES, I CAN IMAGINE...

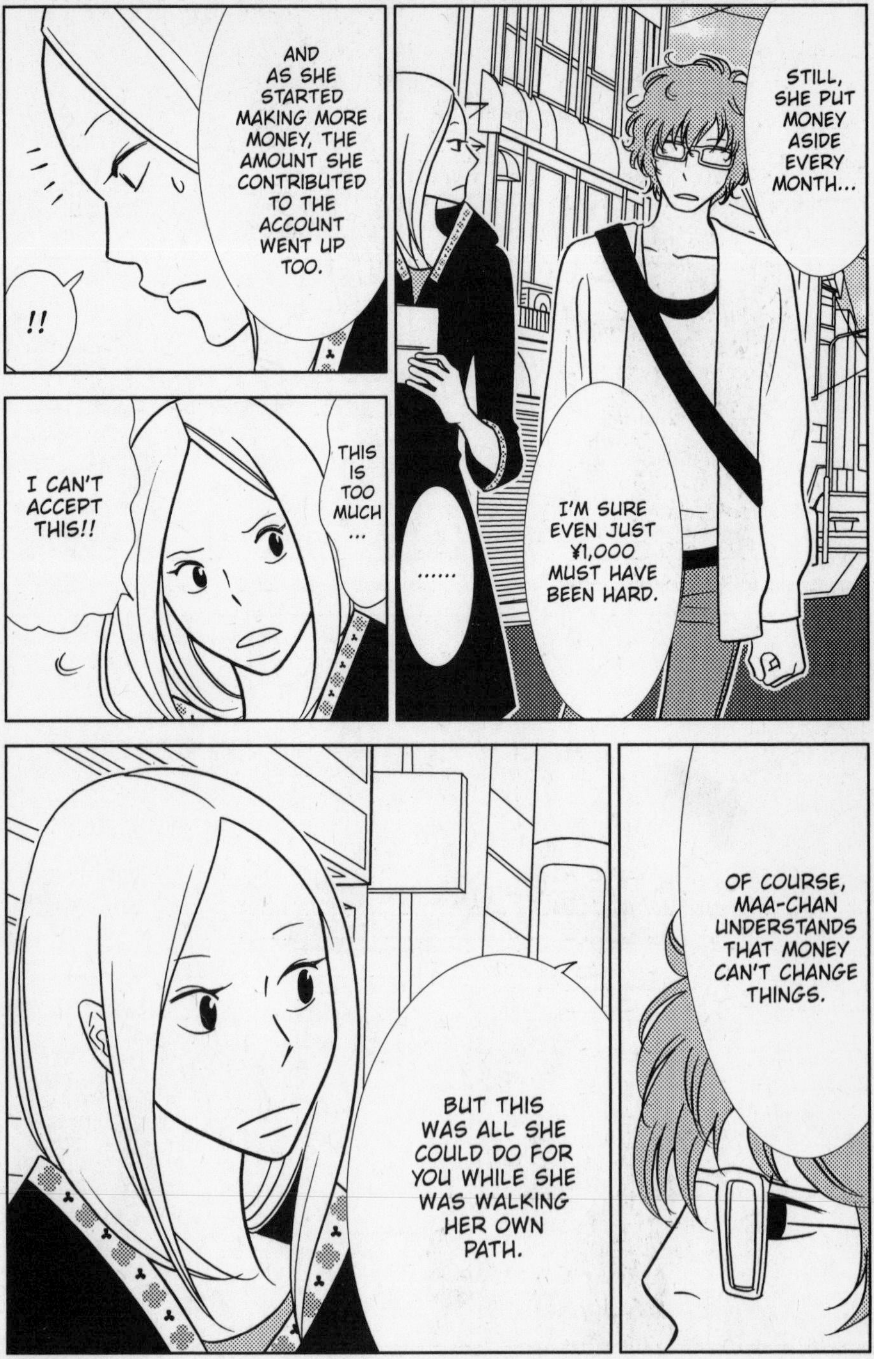
STILL, SHE PUT MONEY ASIDE EVERY MONTH...
I'M SURE EVEN JUST ¥1,000 MUST HAVE BEEN HARD.
......
AND AS SHE STARTED MAKING MORE MONEY, THE AMOUNT SHE CONTRIBUTED TO THE ACCOUNT WENT UP TOO.
!!
THIS IS TOO MUCH ...
I CAN'T ACCEPT THIS!!
OF COURSE, MAA-CHAN UNDERSTANDS THAT MONEY CAN'T CHANGE THINGS.
BUT THIS WAS ALL SHE COULD DO FOR YOU WHILE SHE WAS WALKING HER OWN PATH.

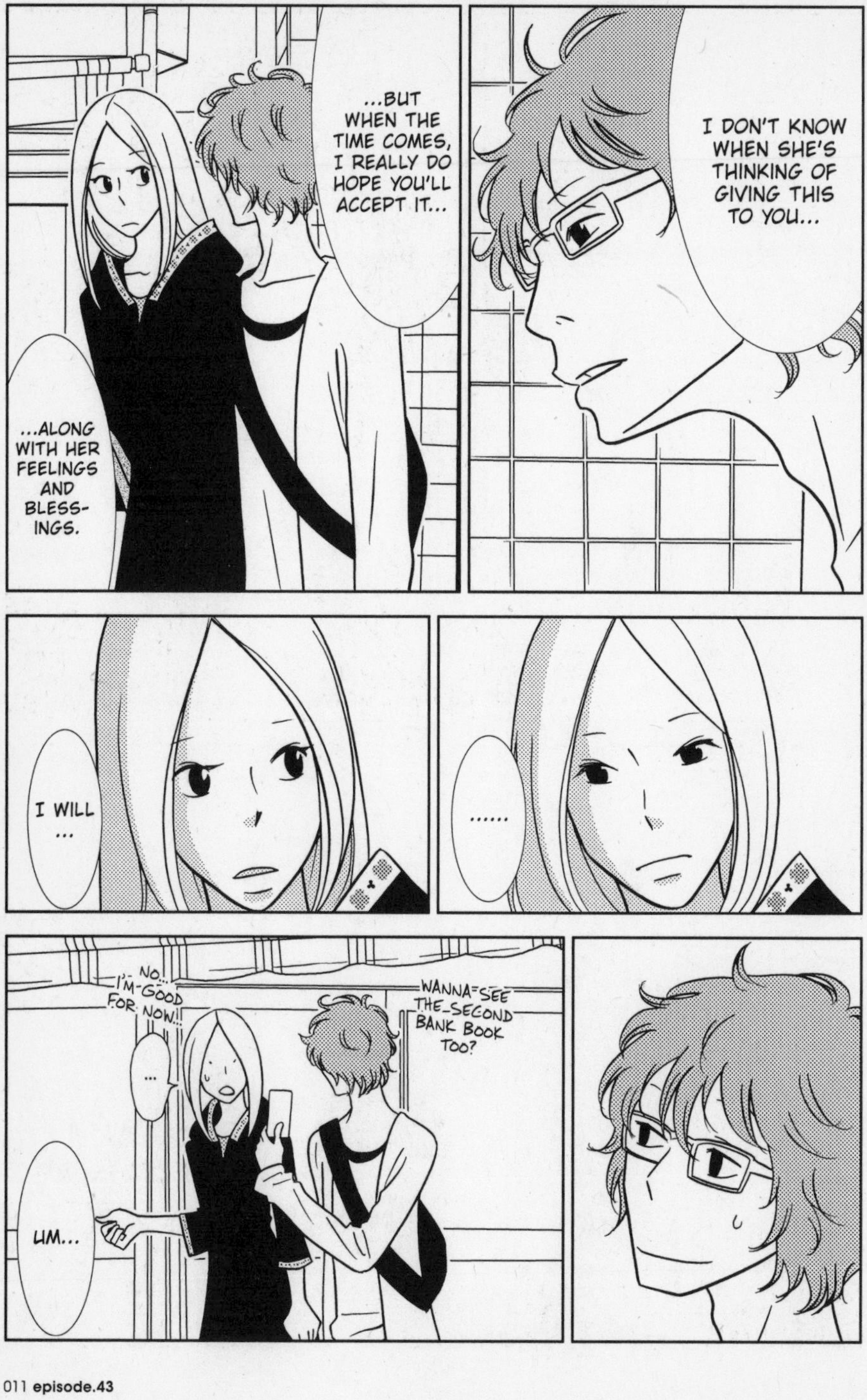
I DON'T KNOW WHEN SHE'S THINKING OF GIVING THIS TO YOU...
...BUT WHEN THE TIME COMES, I REALLY DO HOPE YOU'LL ACCEPT IT...
...ALONG WITH HER FEELINGS AND BLESS-INGS.
......
I WILL ...
WANNA SEE THE SECOND BANK BOOK TOO?
NO... I'M GOOD FOR NOW...!
...
UM...

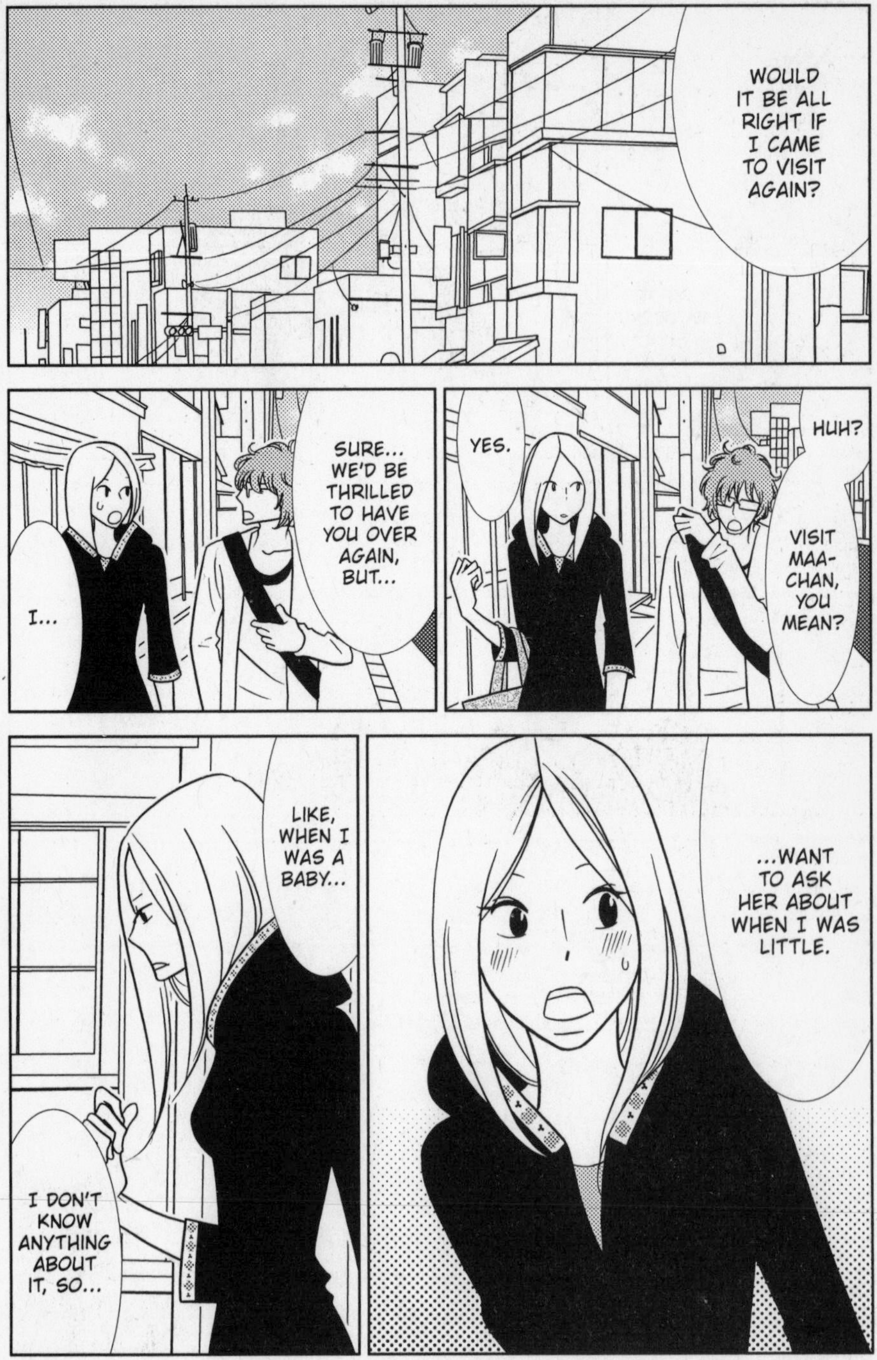
WOULD IT BE ALL RIGHT IF I CAME TO VISIT AGAIN?
HUH?
VISIT MAA-CHAN, YOU MEAN?
YES.
SURE... WE'D BE THRILLED TO HAVE YOU OVER AGAIN, BUT...
I...
...WANT TO ASK HER ABOUT WHEN I WAS LITTLE.
LIKE, WHEN I WAS A BABY...
I DON'T KNOW ANYTHING ABOUT IT, SO...

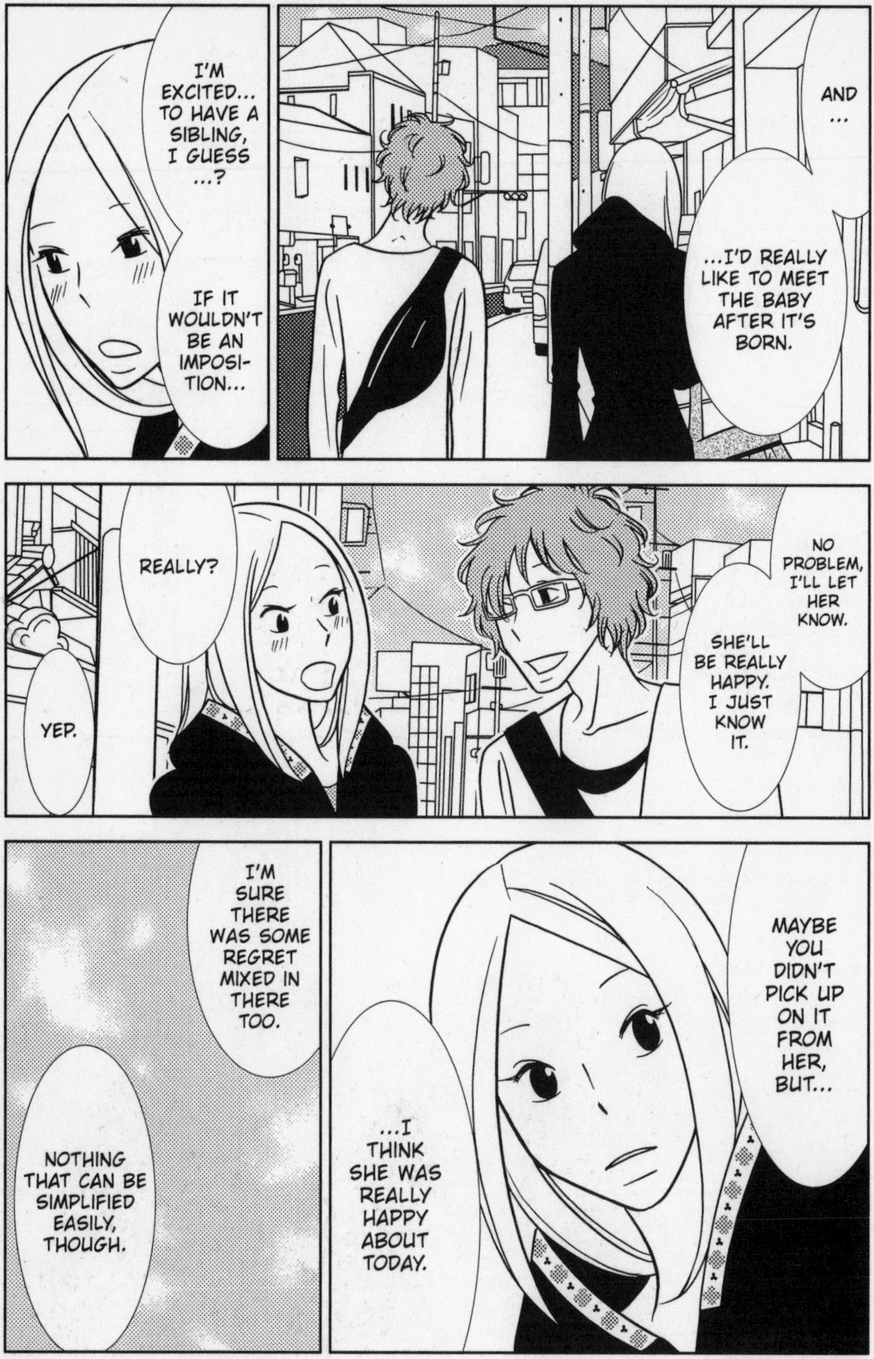
AND ...
...I'D REALLY LIKE TO MEET THE BABY AFTER IT'S BORN.
I'M EXCITED... TO HAVE A SIBLING, I GUESS ...?
IF IT WOULDN'T BE AN IMPOSITION...
NO PROBLEM, I'LL LET HER KNOW.
SHE'LL BE REALLY HAPPY. I JUST KNOW IT.
REALLY?
YEP.
MAYBE YOU DIDN'T PICK UP ON IT FROM HER, BUT...
...I THINK SHE WAS REALLY HAPPY ABOUT TODAY.
I'M SURE THERE WAS SOME REGRET MIXED IN THERE TOO.
NOTHING THAT CAN BE SIMPLIFIED EASILY, THOUGH.

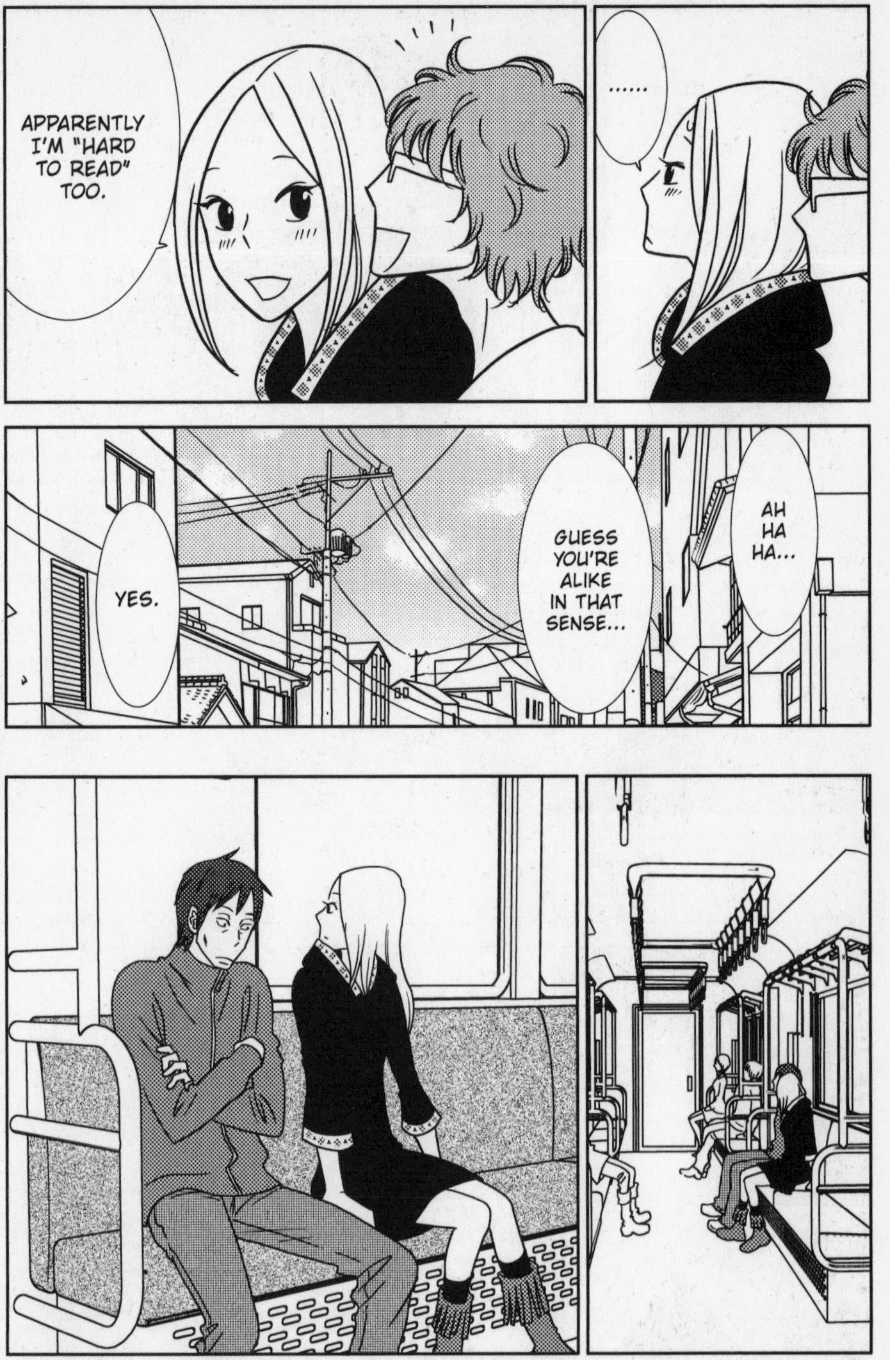
......
APPARENTLY I'M "HARD TO READ" TOO.
AH HA HA...
GUESS YOU'RE ALIKE IN THAT SENSE...
YES.

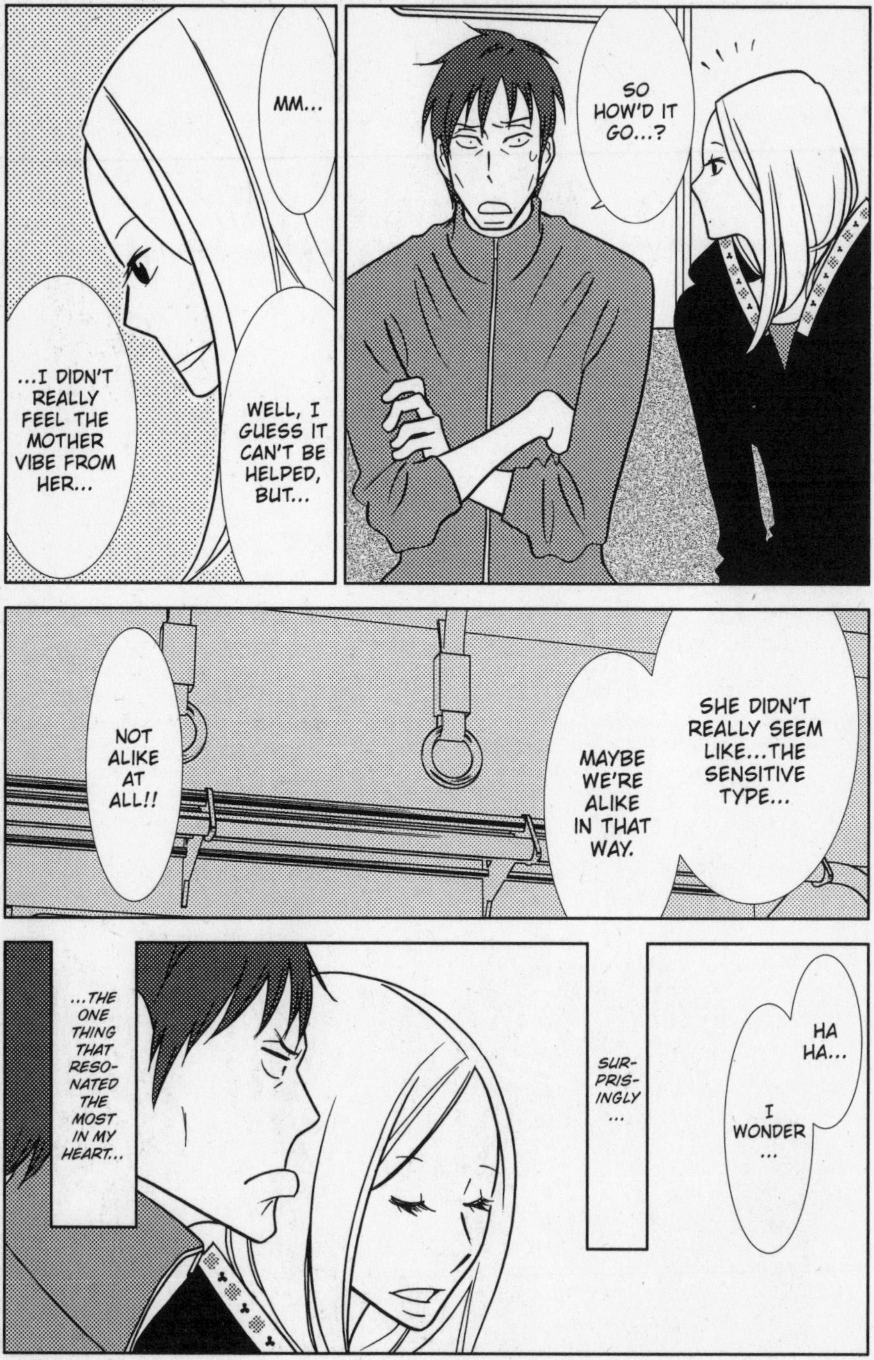
SO HOW'D IT GO...?
MM...
WELL, I GUESS IT CAN'T BE HELPED, BUT...
...I DIDN'T REALLY FEEL THE MOTHER VIBE FROM HER...
SHE DIDN'T REALLY SEEM LIKE...THE SENSITIVE TYPE...
MAYBE WE'RE ALIKE IN THAT WAY.
NOT ALIKE AT ALL!!
HA HA...
I WONDER...
SURPRISINGLY...
...THE ONE THING THAT RESONATED THE MOST IN MY HEART...

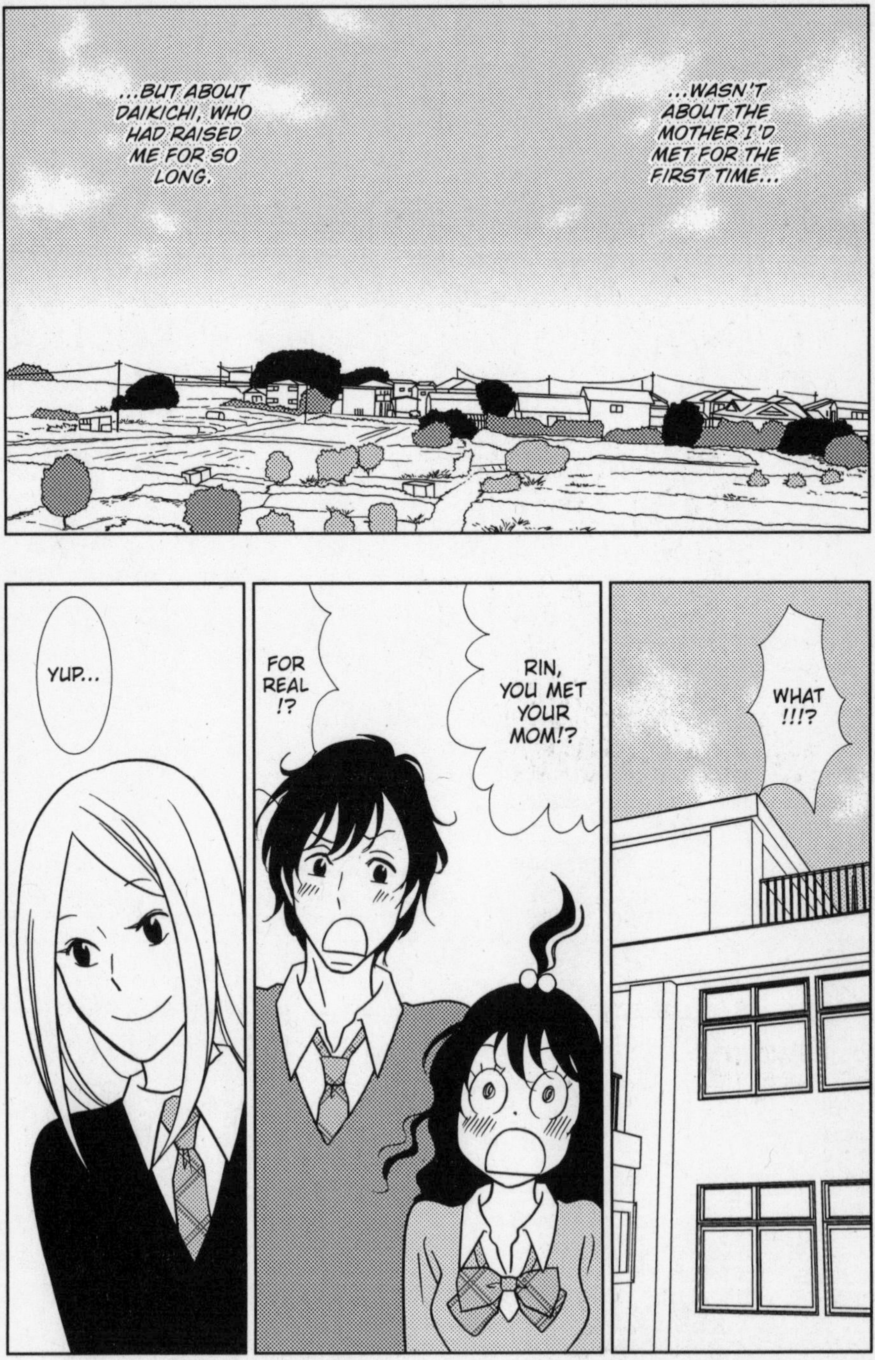
...WASN'T ABOUT THE MOTHER I'D MET FOR THE FIRST TIME...
...BUT ABOUT DAIKICHI, WHO HAD RAISED ME FOR SO LONG.
WHAT !!!?
RIN, YOU MET YOUR MOM!?
FOR REAL !?
YUP...

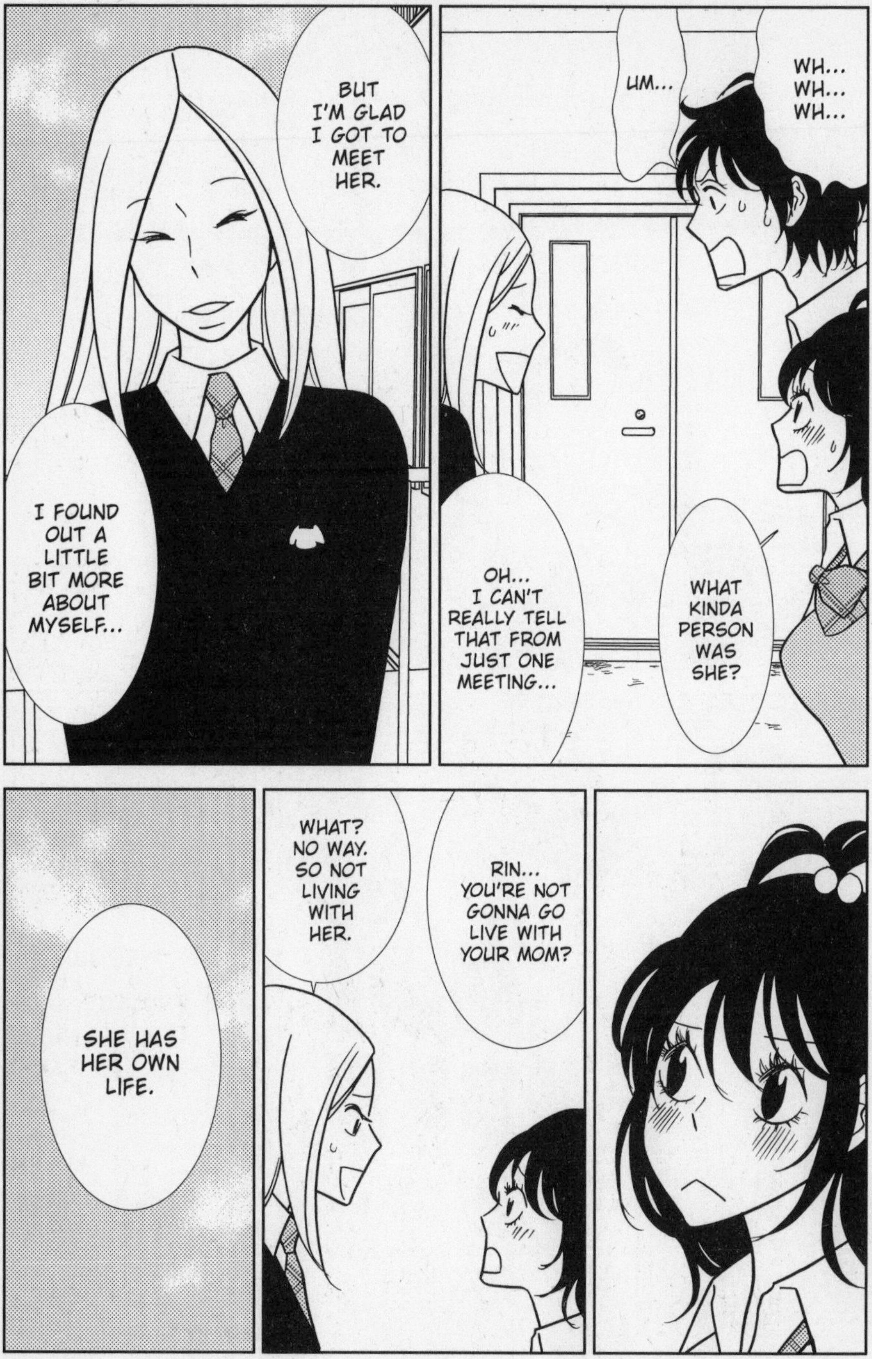
WH... WH... WH...
UM...
WHAT KINDA PERSON WAS SHE?
OH... I CAN'T REALLY TELL THAT FROM JUST ONE MEETING...
BUT I'M GLAD I GOT TO MEET HER.
I FOUND OUT A LITTLE BIT MORE ABOUT MYSELF...
RIN... YOU'RE NOT GONNA GO LIVE WITH YOUR MOM?
WHAT? NO WAY. SO NOT LIVING WITH HER.
SHE HAS HER OWN LIFE.

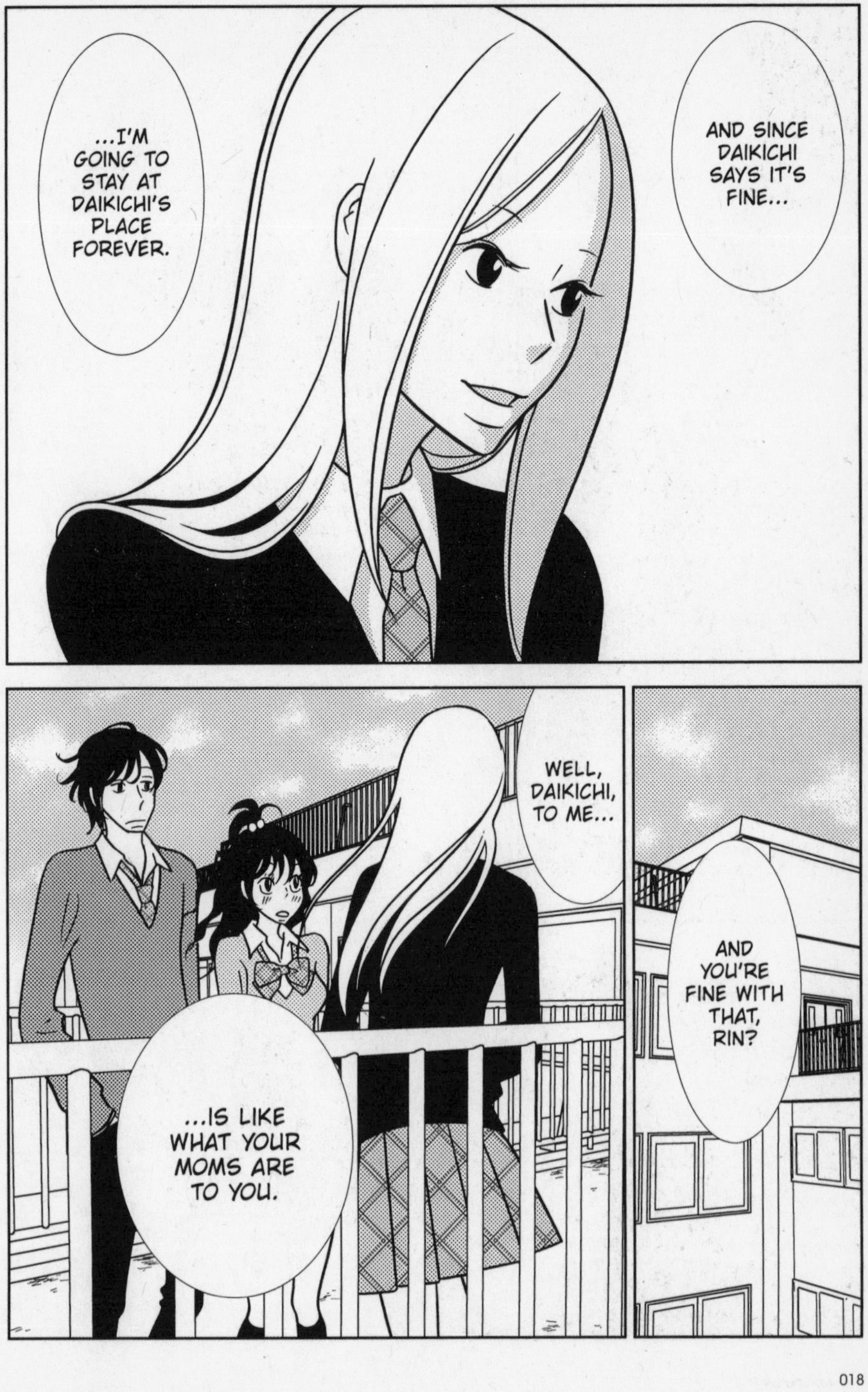
AND SINCE DAIKICHI SAYS IT'S FINE...
...I'M GOING TO STAY AT DAIKICHI'S PLACE FOREVER.
AND YOU'RE FINE WITH THAT, RIN?
WELL, DAIKICHI, TO ME...
...IS LIKE WHAT YOUR MOMS ARE TO YOU.

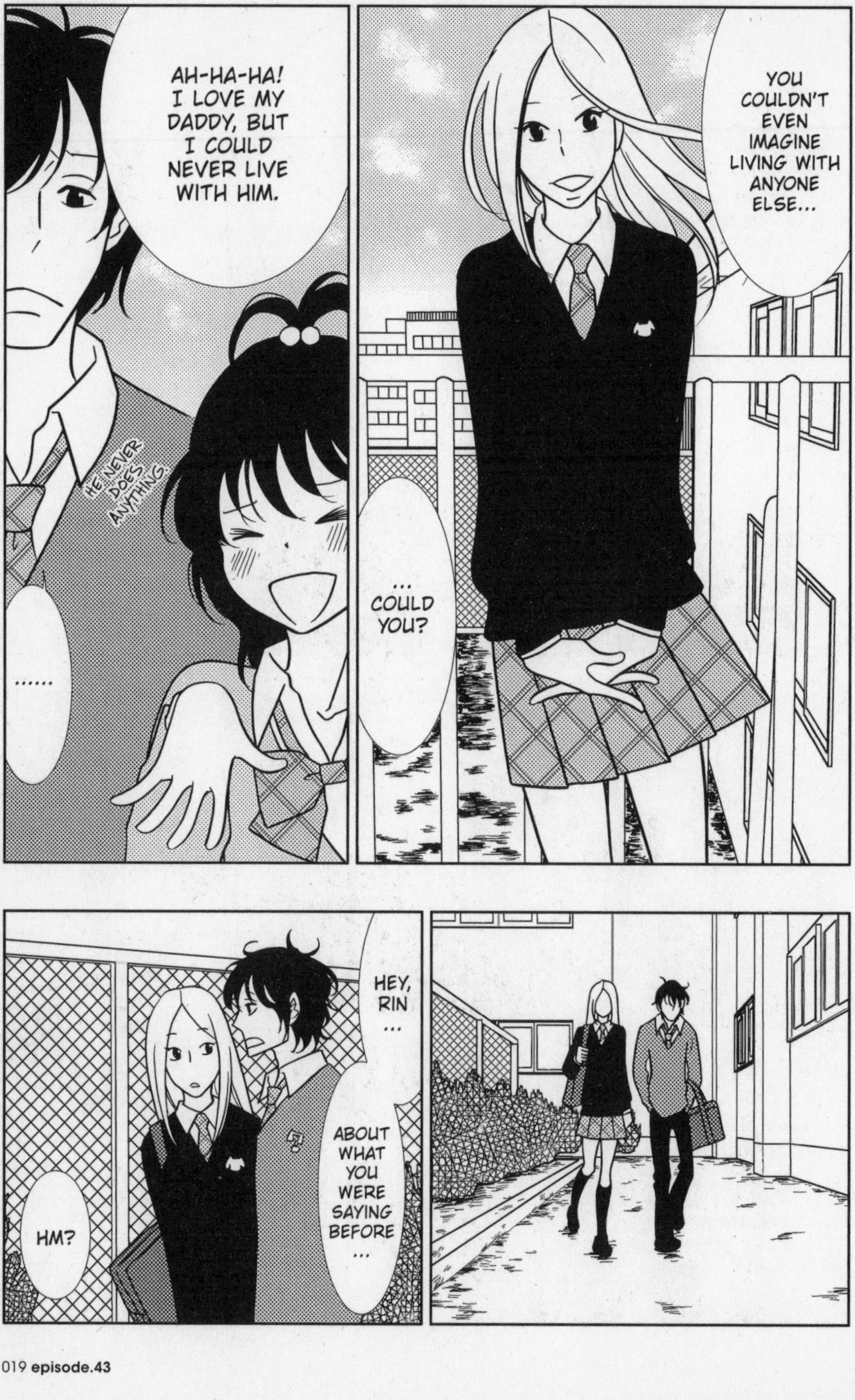

YOU COULDN'T EVEN IMAGINE LIVING WITH ANYONE ELSE...
...COULD YOU?
AH-HA-HA! I LOVE MY DADDY, BUT I COULD NEVER LIVE WITH HIM.
HE NEVER DOES ANYTHING.
......
HEY, RIN...
ABOUT WHAT YOU WERE SAYING BEFORE...
HM?

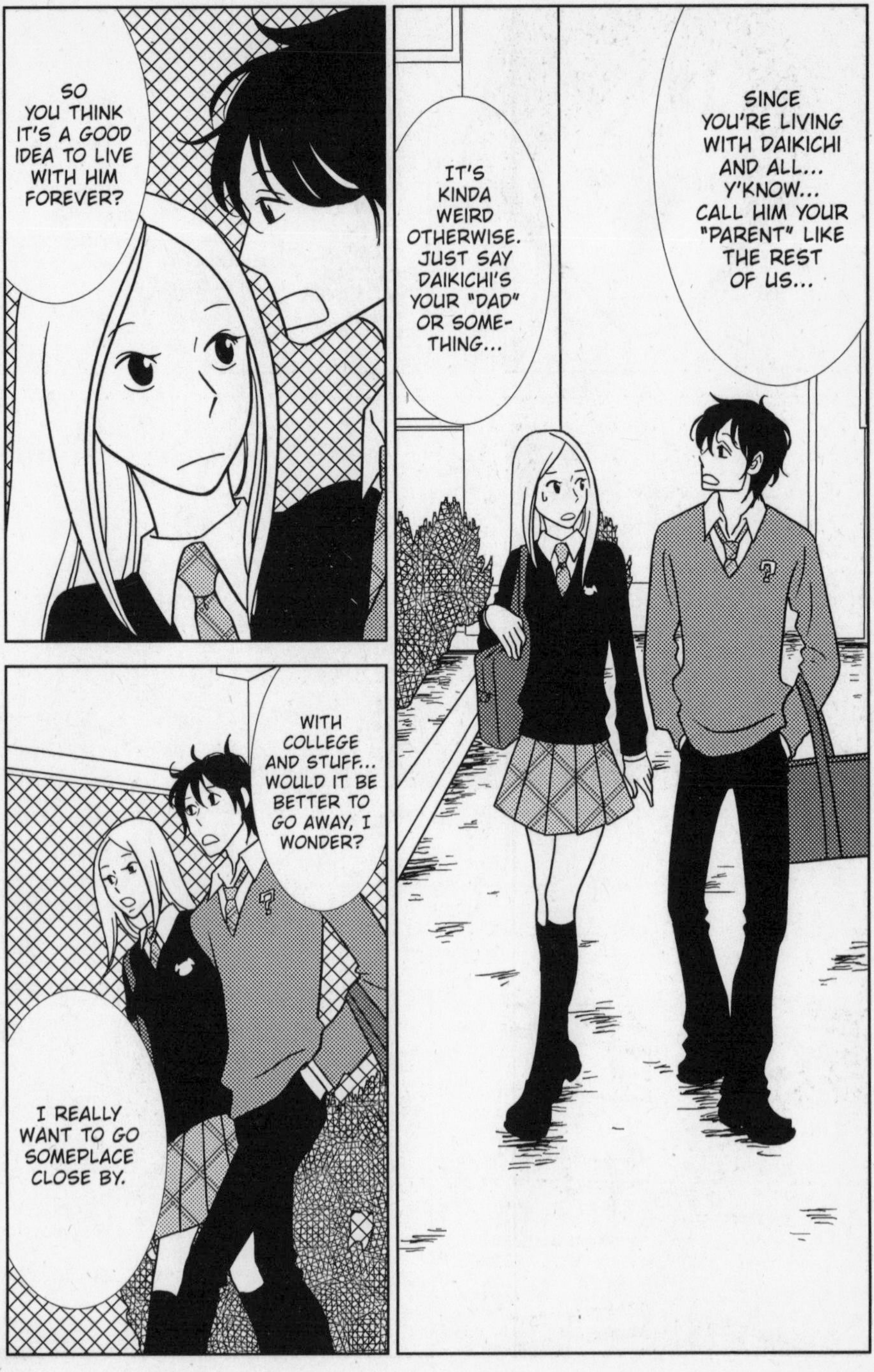
SINCE YOU'RE LIVING WITH DAIKICHI AND ALL... Y'KNOW... CALL HIM YOUR "PARENT" LIKE THE REST OF US...
IT'S KINDA WEIRD OTHERWISE. JUST SAY DAIKICHI'S YOUR "DAD" OR SOME-THING...
SO YOU THINK IT'S A GOOD IDEA TO LIVE WITH HIM FOREVER?
WITH COLLEGE AND STUFF... WOULD IT BE BETTER TO GO AWAY, I WONDER?
I REALLY WANT TO GO SOMEPLACE CLOSE BY.

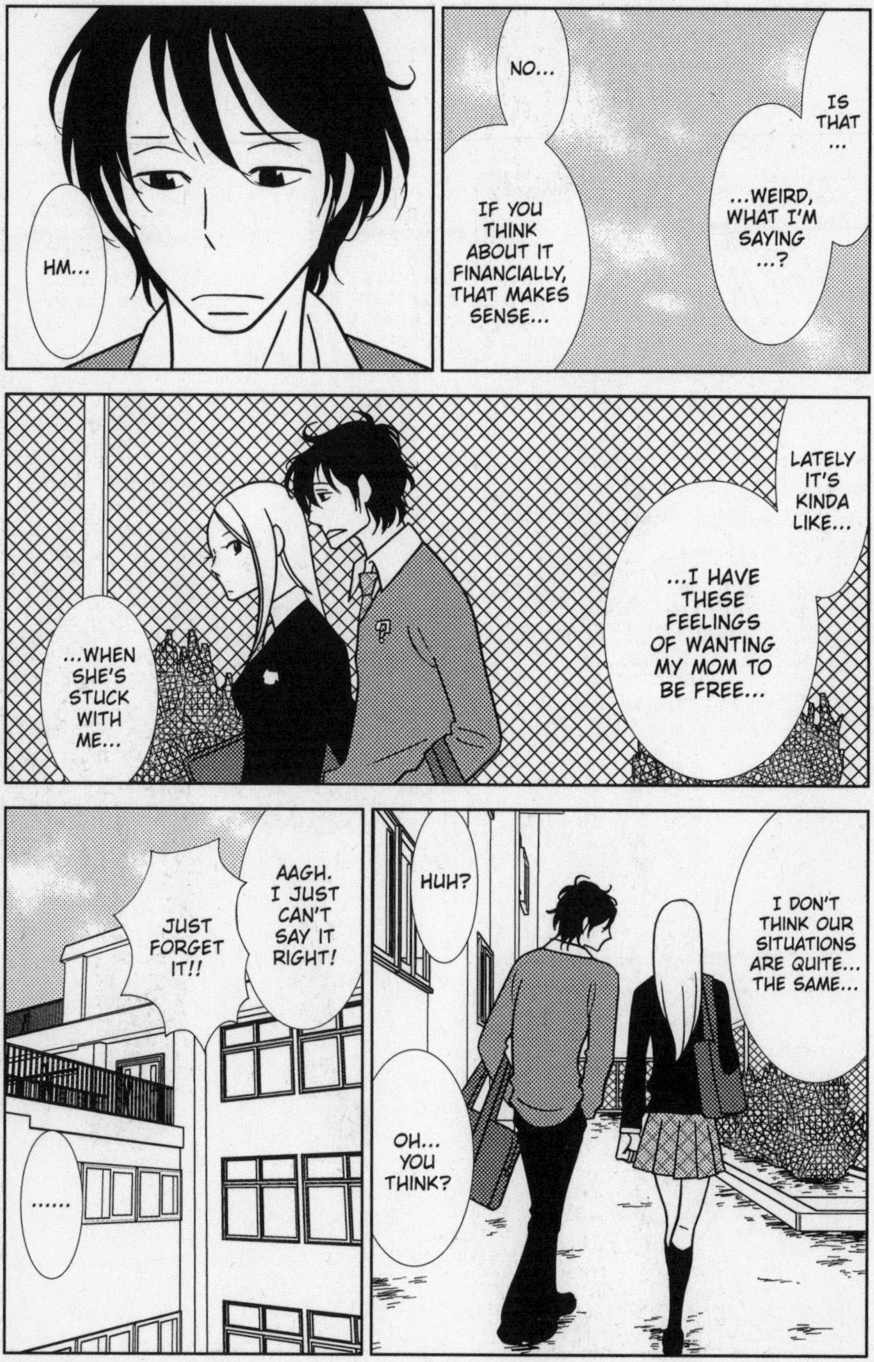
IS THAT ...
...WEIRD, WHAT I'M SAYING ...?
NO...
IF YOU THINK ABOUT IT FINANCIALLY, THAT MAKES SENSE...
HM...
LATELY IT'S KINDA LIKE...
...I HAVE THESE FEELINGS OF WANTING MY MOM TO BE FREE...
...WHEN SHE'S STUCK WITH ME...
I DON'T THINK OUR SITUATIONS ARE QUITE... THE SAME...
HUH?
OH... YOU THINK?
AAGH. I JUST CAN'T SAY IT RIGHT!
JUST FORGET IT!!
......

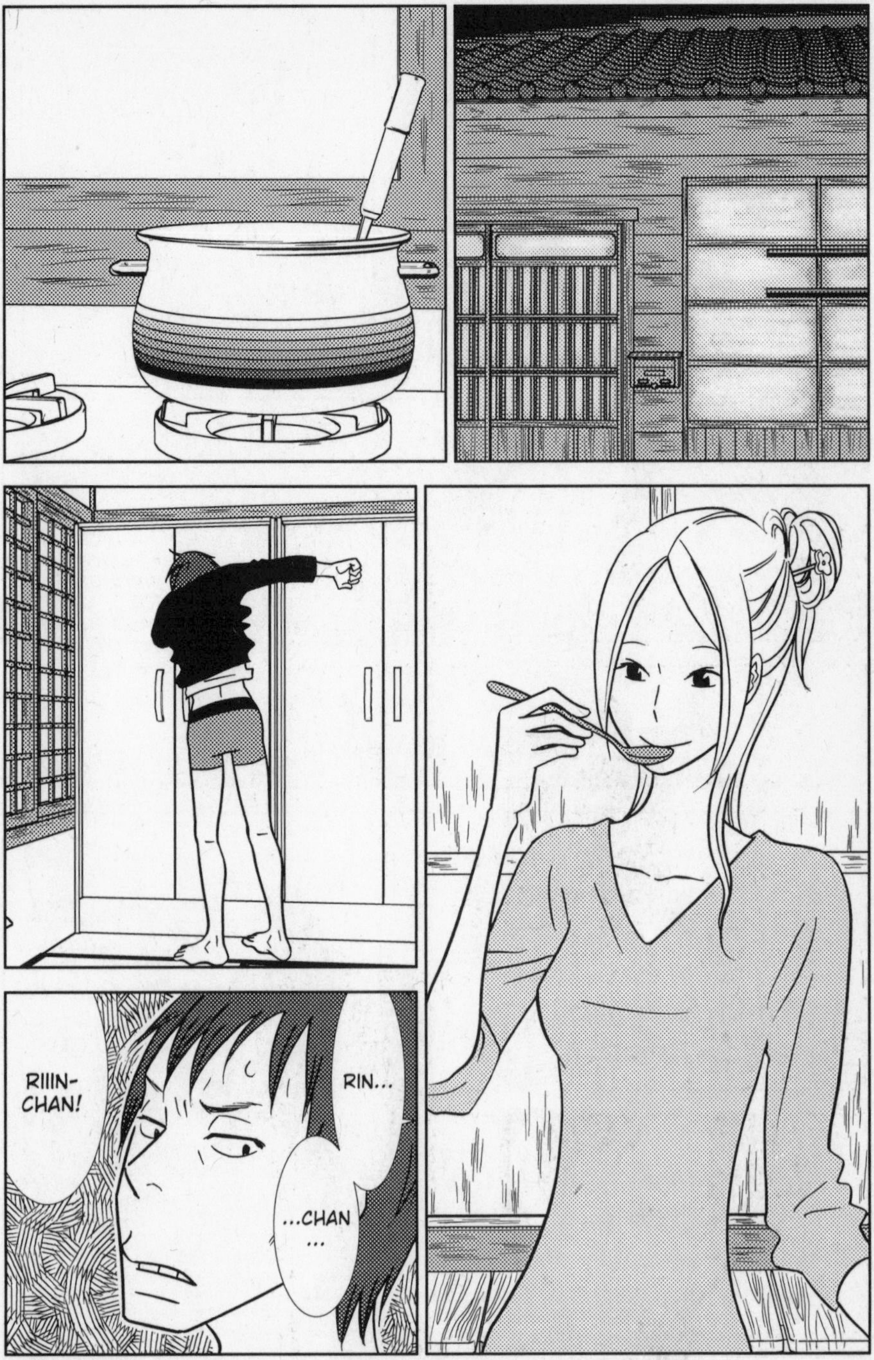
RIN...
RIIIN-CHAN!
...CHAN ...

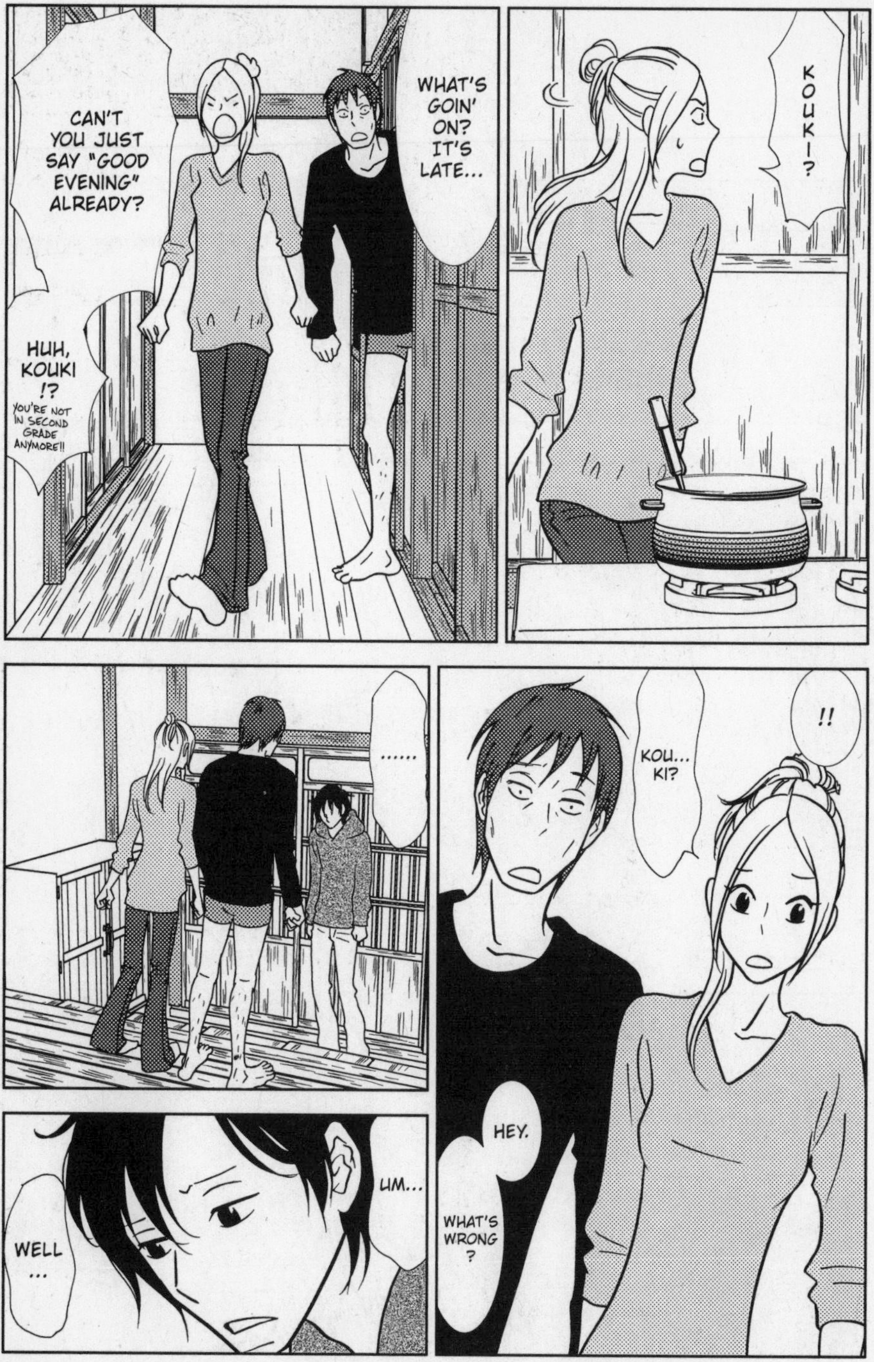
KOUKI?
WHAT'S GOIN' ON? IT'S LATE...
CAN'T YOU JUST SAY "GOOD EVENING" ALREADY?
HUH, KOUKI !?
YOU'RE NOT IN SECOND GRADE ANYMORE!!
!!
KOU... KI?
HEY.
WHAT'S WRONG ?
......
UM...
WELL ...

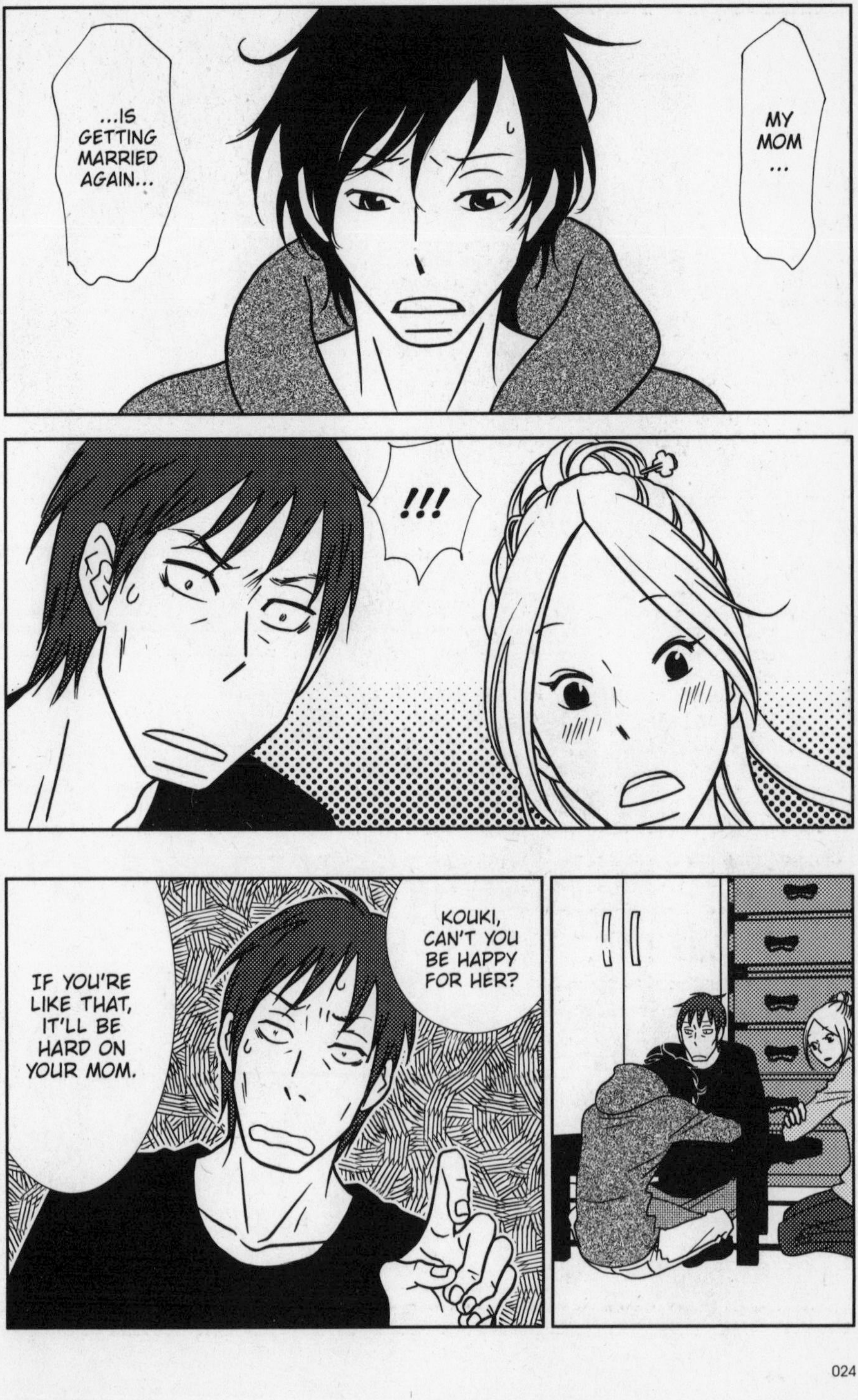
MY MOM ...
...IS GETTING MARRIED AGAIN...
!!!
KOUKI, CAN'T YOU BE HAPPY FOR HER?
IF YOU'RE LIKE THAT, IT'LL BE HARD ON YOUR MOM.

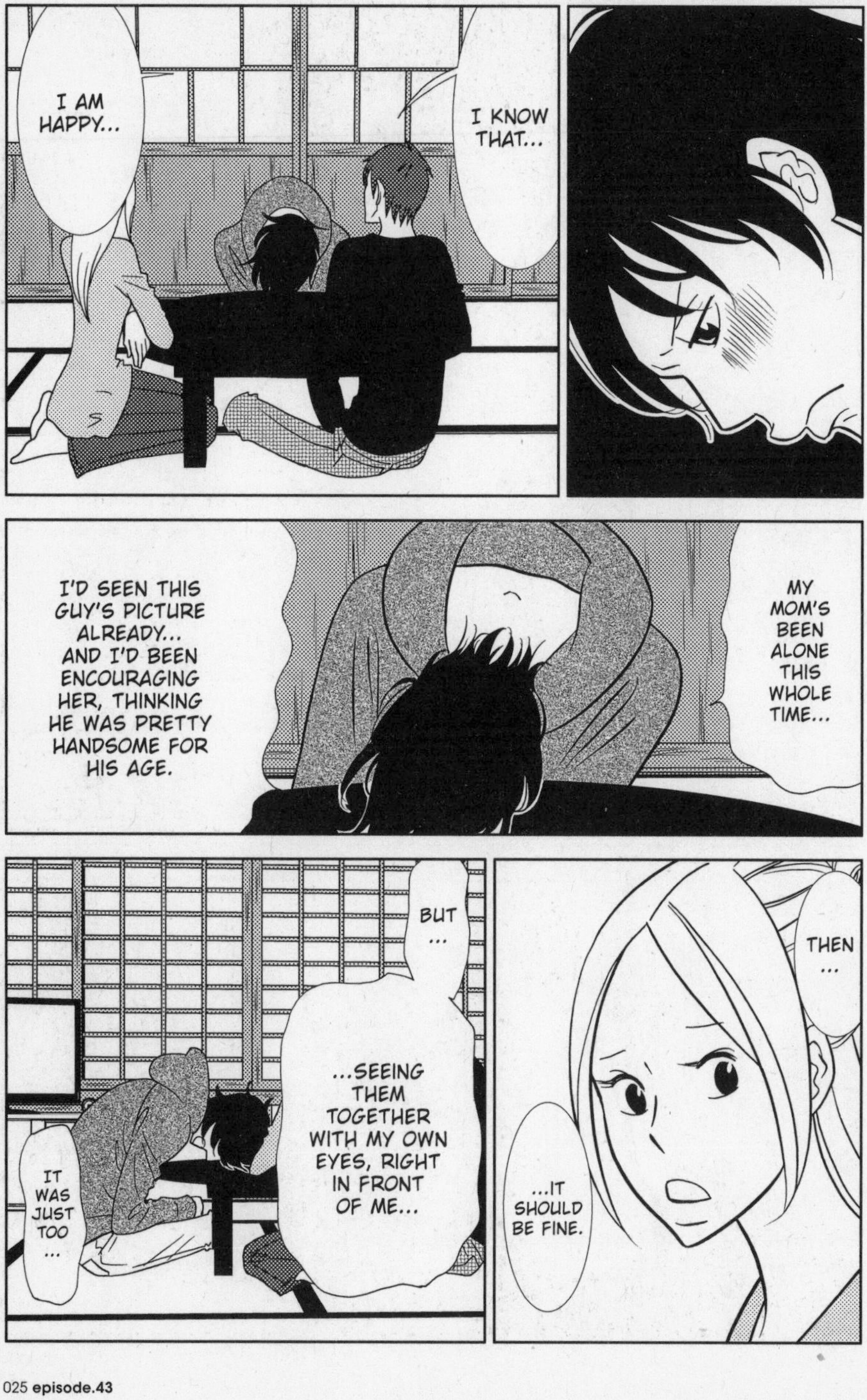
I KNOW THAT...
I AM HAPPY...
MY MOM'S BEEN ALONE THIS WHOLE TIME...
I'D SEEN THIS GUY'S PICTURE ALREADY... AND I'D BEEN ENCOURAGING HER, THINKING HE WAS PRETTY HANDSOME FOR HIS AGE.
THEN...
...IT SHOULD BE FINE.
BUT...
...SEEING THEM TOGETHER WITH MY OWN EYES, RIGHT IN FRONT OF ME...
IT WAS JUST TOO...

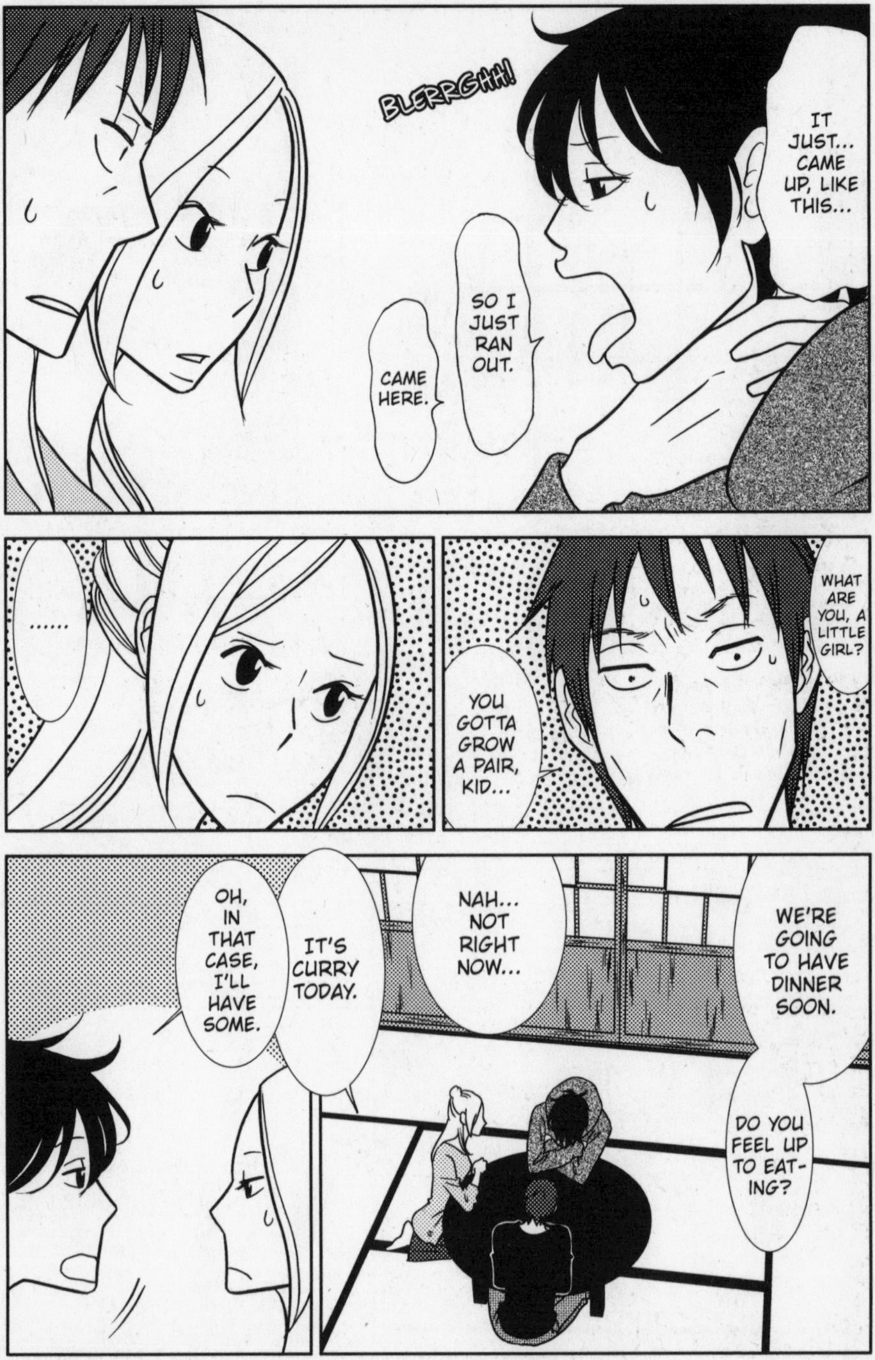
IT JUST... CAME UP, LIKE THIS...
BLERRGHH!
SO I JUST RAN OUT.
CAME HERE.
WHAT ARE YOU, A LITTLE GIRL?
YOU GOTTA GROW A PAIR, KID...
......
WE'RE GOING TO HAVE DINNER SOON.
DO YOU FEEL UP TO EAT-ING?
NAH... NOT RIGHT NOW...
IT'S CURRY TODAY.
OH, IN THAT CASE, I'LL HAVE SOME.

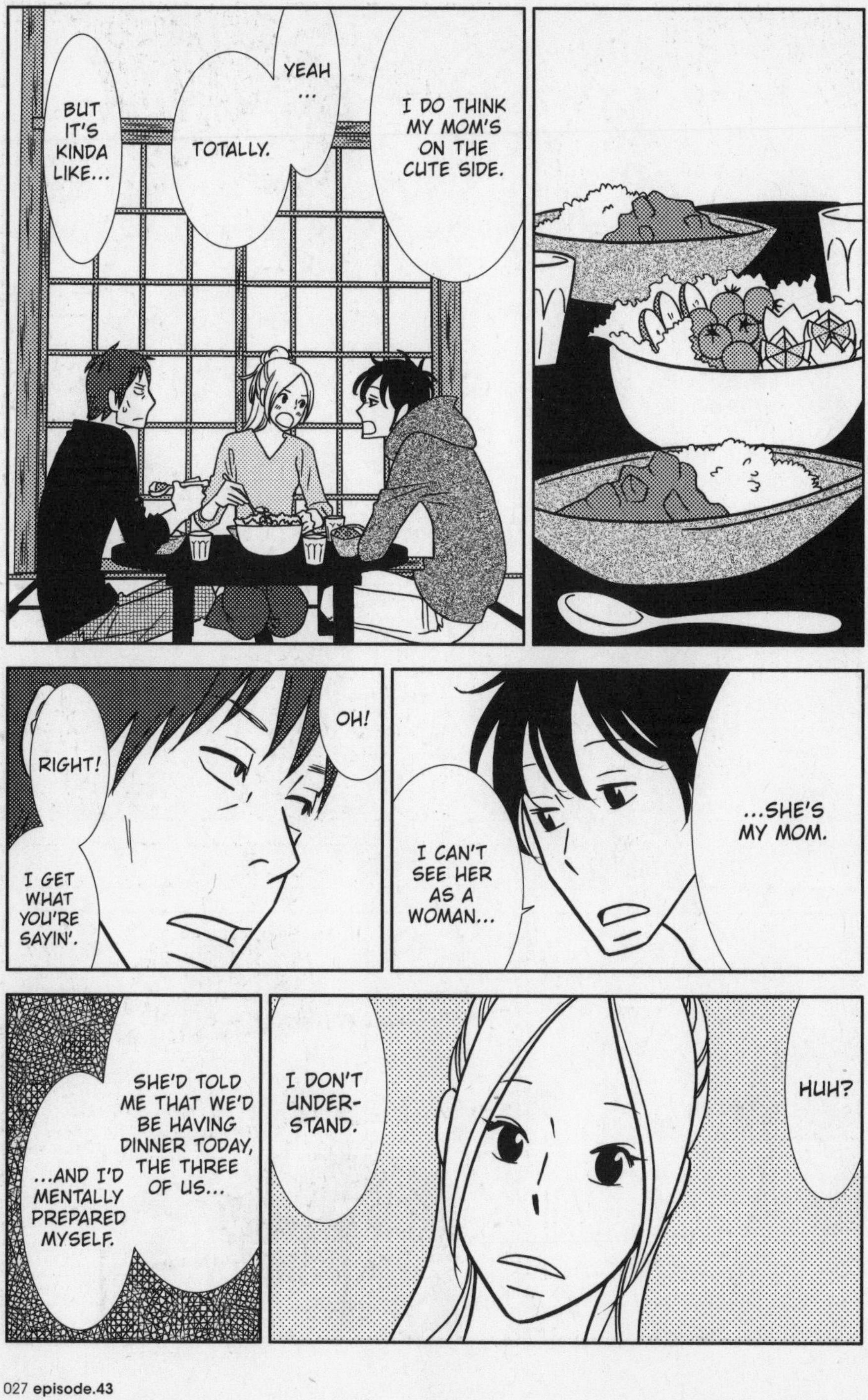
I DO THINK MY MOM'S ON THE CUTE SIDE.
YEAH ...
TOTALLY.
BUT IT'S KINDA LIKE...
...SHE'S MY MOM.
I CAN'T SEE HER AS A WOMAN...
OH!
RIGHT!
I GET WHAT YOU'RE SAYIN'.
HUH?
I DON'T UNDER-STAND.
SHE'D TOLD ME THAT WE'D BE HAVING DINNER TODAY, THE THREE OF US...
...AND I'D MENTALLY PREPARED MYSELF.

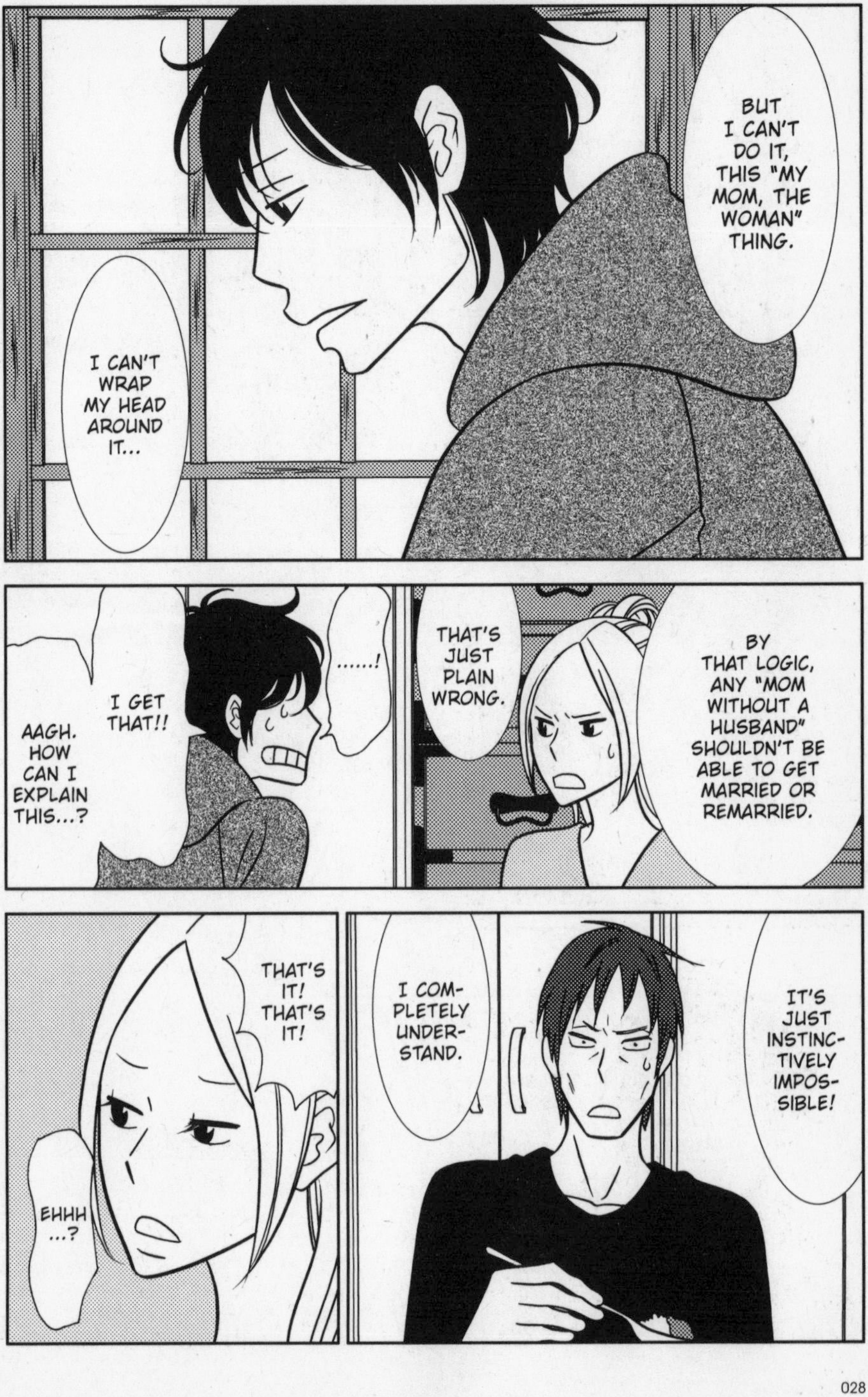
BUT I CAN'T DO IT, THIS "MY MOM, THE WOMAN" THING.
I CAN'T WRAP MY HEAD AROUND IT...
BY THAT LOGIC, ANY "MOM WITHOUT A HUSBAND" SHOULDN'T BE ABLE TO GET MARRIED OR REMARRIED.
THAT'S JUST PLAIN WRONG.
......!
I GET THAT!!
AAGH. HOW CAN I EXPLAIN THIS...?
IT'S JUST INSTINCTIVELY IMPOSSIBLE!
I COMPLETELY UNDERSTAND.
THAT'S IT! THAT'S IT!
EHHH...?

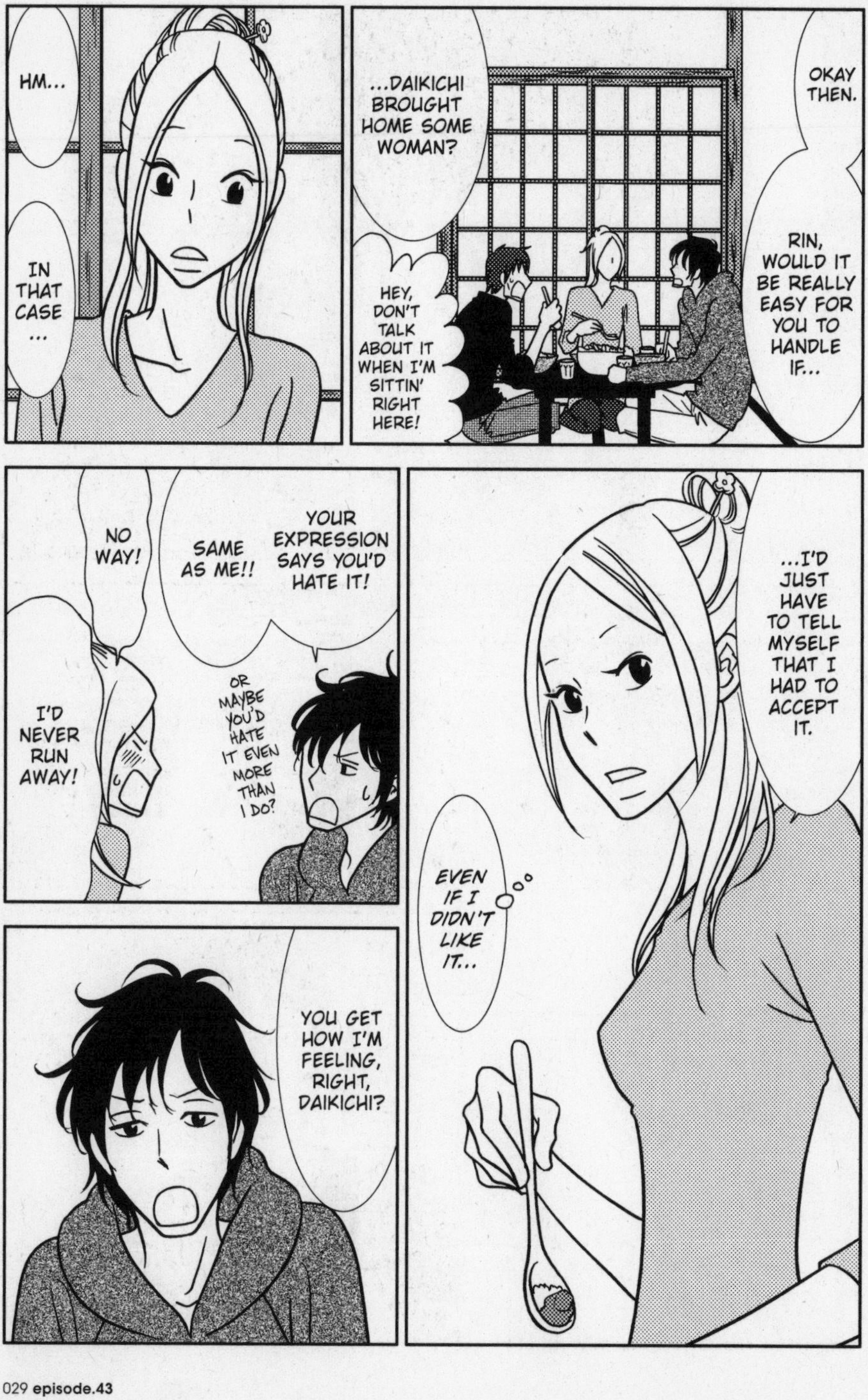
OKAY THEN.
RIN, WOULD IT BE REALLY EASY FOR YOU TO HANDLE IF...
...DAIKICHI BROUGHT HOME SOME WOMAN?
HEY, DON'T TALK ABOUT IT WHEN I'M SITTIN' RIGHT HERE!
HM...
IN THAT CASE ...
...I'D JUST HAVE TO TELL MYSELF THAT I HAD TO ACCEPT IT.
EVEN IF I DIDN'T LIKE IT...
YOUR EXPRESSION SAYS YOU'D HATE IT!
SAME AS ME!!
NO WAY!
OR MAYBE YOU'D HATE IT EVEN MORE THAN I DO?
I'D NEVER RUN AWAY!
YOU GET HOW I'M FEELING, RIGHT, DAIKICHI?

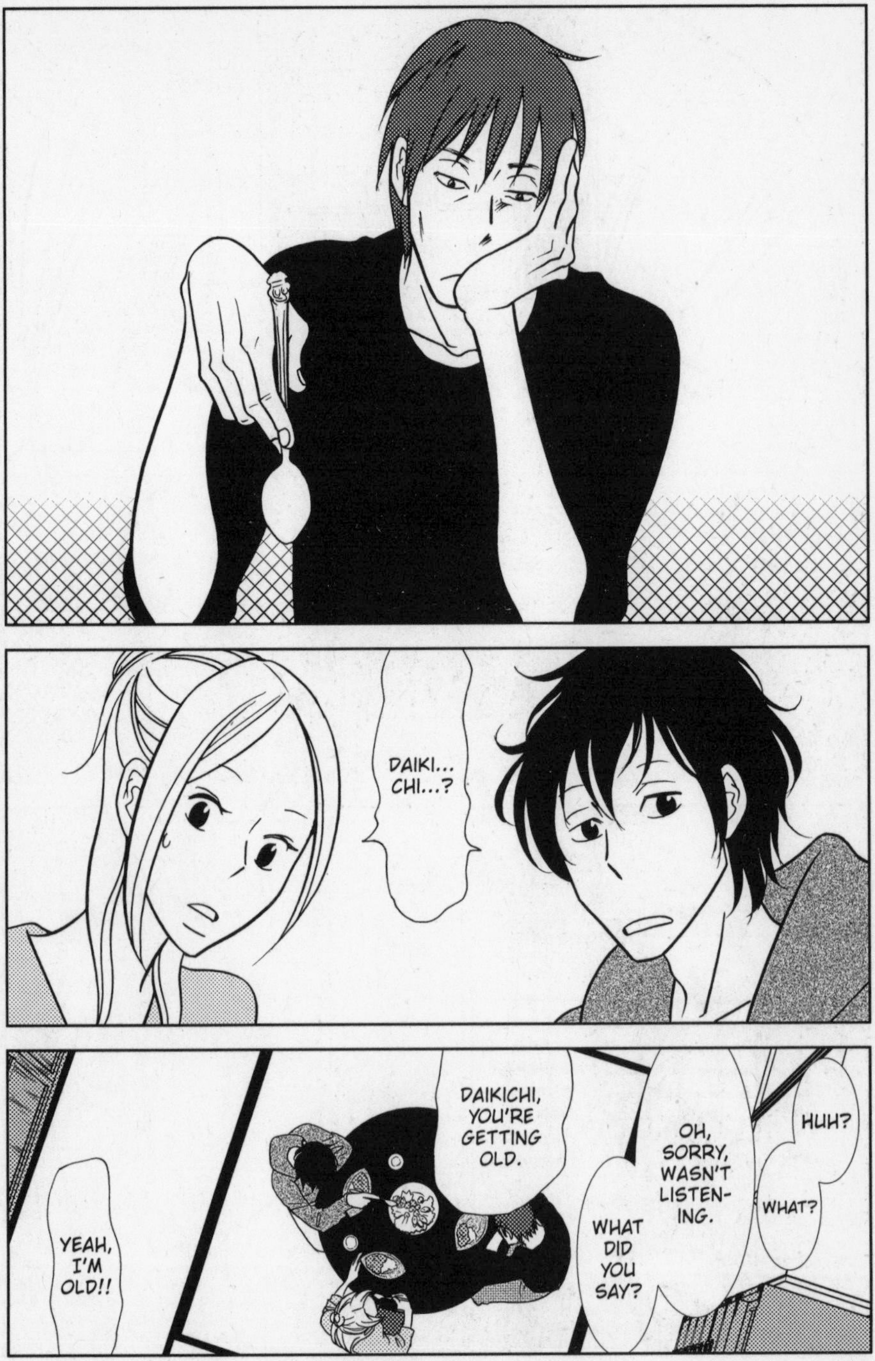
DAIKI... CHI...?
HUH?
WHAT?
OH, SORRY, WASN'T LISTEN-ING.
WHAT DID YOU SAY?
DAIKICHI, YOU'RE GETTING OLD.
YEAH, I'M OLD!!

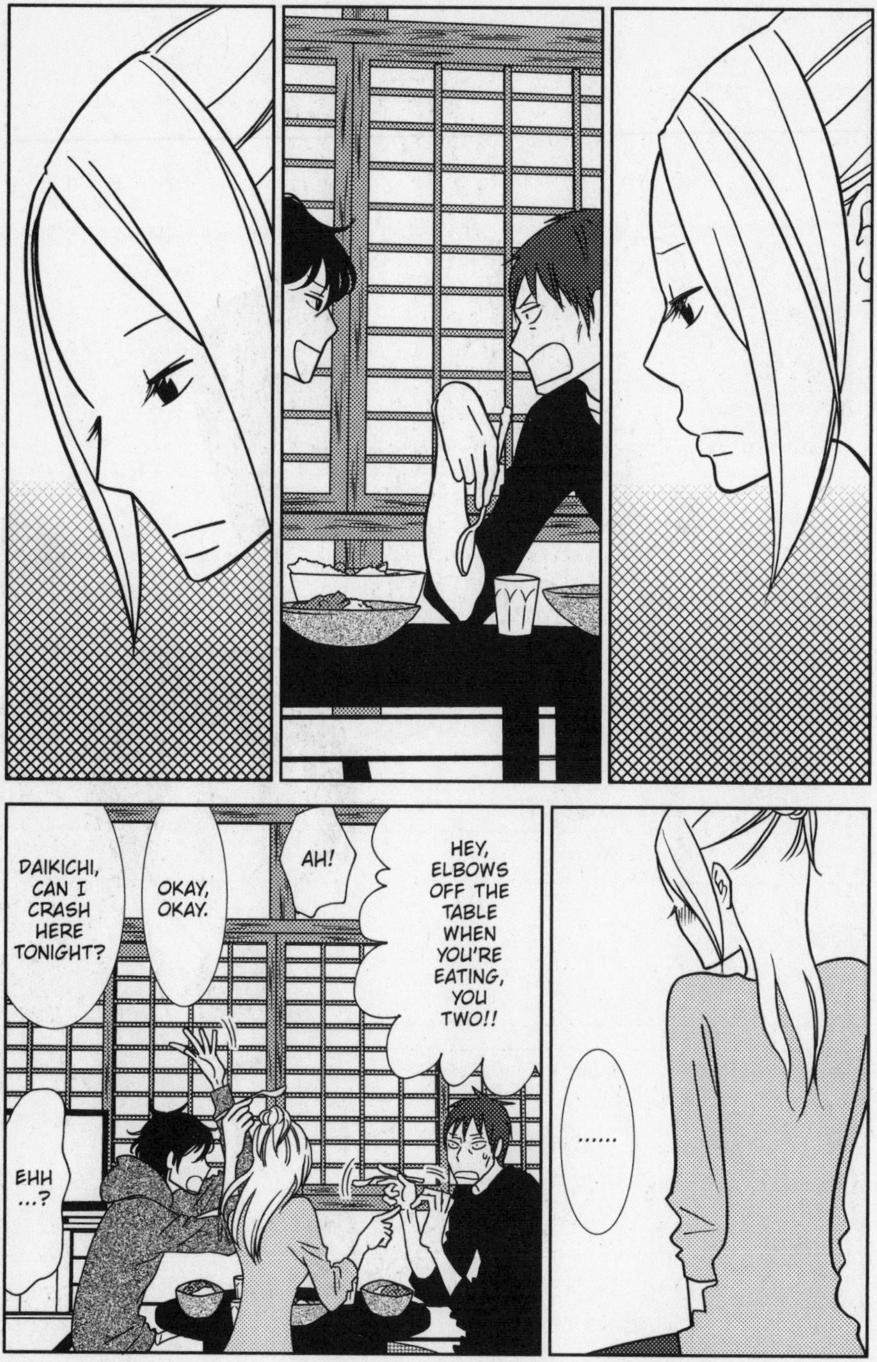
......
HEY, ELBOWS OFF THE TABLE WHEN YOU'RE EATING, YOU TWO!!
AH!
OKAY, OKAY.
DAIKICHI, CAN I CRASH HERE TONIGHT?
EHH ...?

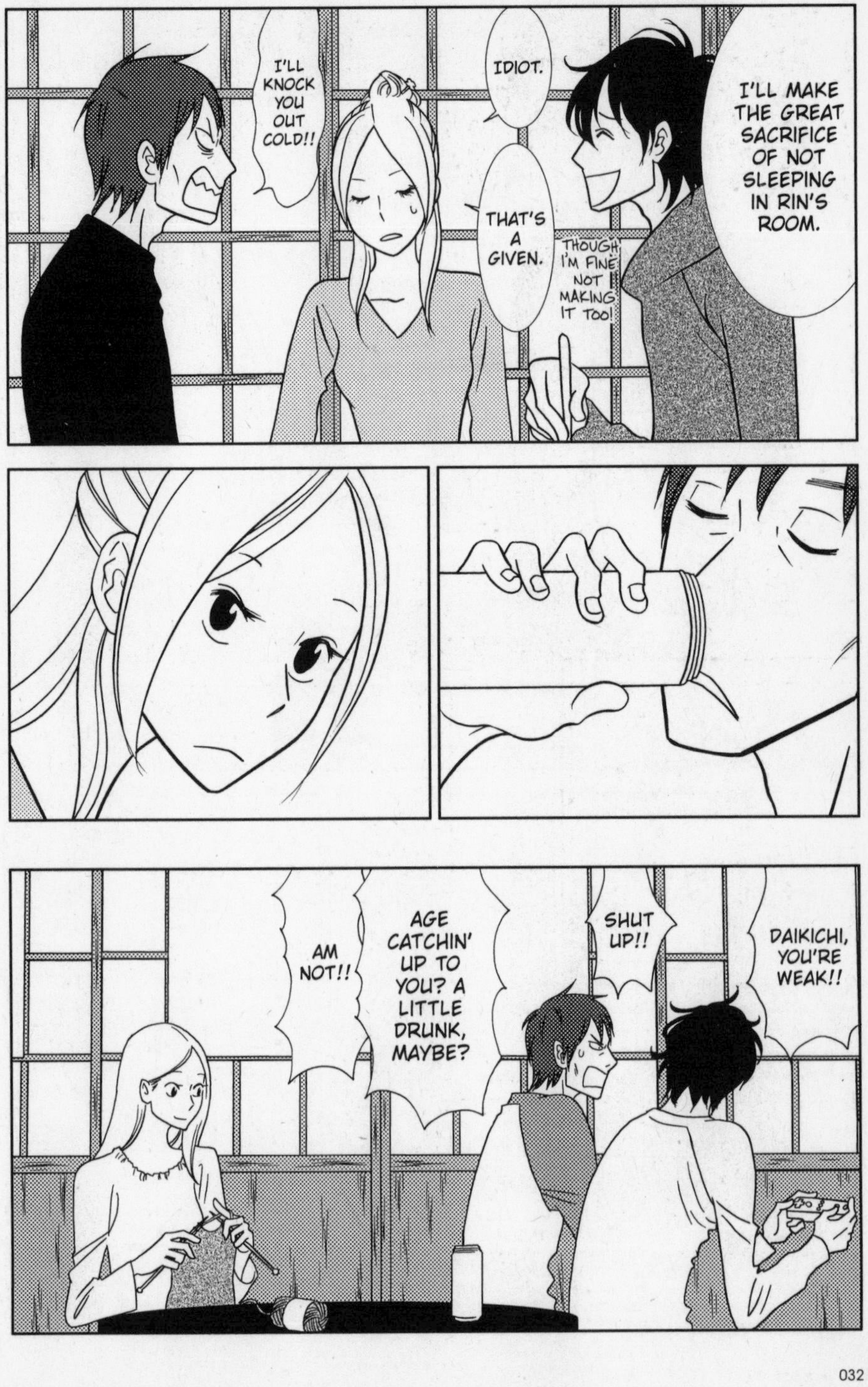
I'LL MAKE THE GREAT SACRIFICE OF NOT SLEEPING IN RIN'S ROOM.
THOUGH I'M FINE NOT MAKING IT TOO!
IDIOT.
THAT'S A GIVEN.
I'LL KNOCK YOU OUT COLD!!
DAIKICHI, YOU'RE WEAK!!
SHUT UP!!
AGE CATCHIN' UP TO YOU? A LITTLE DRUNK, MAYBE?
AM NOT!!

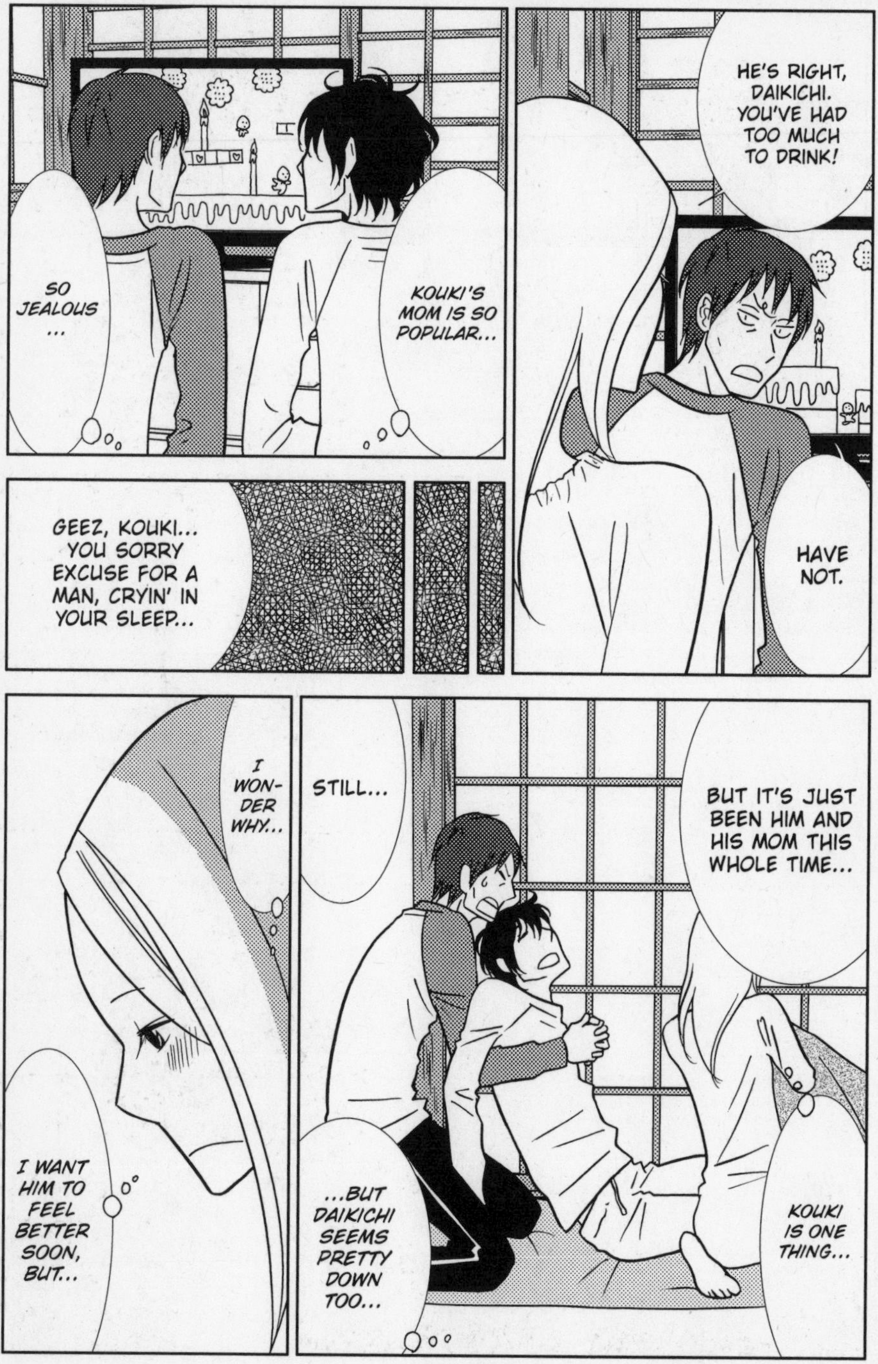
HE'S RIGHT, DAIKICHI. YOU'VE HAD TOO MUCH TO DRINK!
HAVE NOT.
KOUKI'S MOM IS SO POPULAR...
SO JEALOUS ...
GEEZ, KOUKI... YOU SORRY EXCUSE FOR A MAN, CRYIN' IN YOUR SLEEP...
BUT IT'S JUST BEEN HIM AND HIS MOM THIS WHOLE TIME...
STILL...
KOUKI IS ONE THING...
...BUT DAIKICHI SEEMS PRETTY DOWN TOO...
I WON-DER WHY...
I WANT HIM TO FEEL BETTER SOON, BUT...

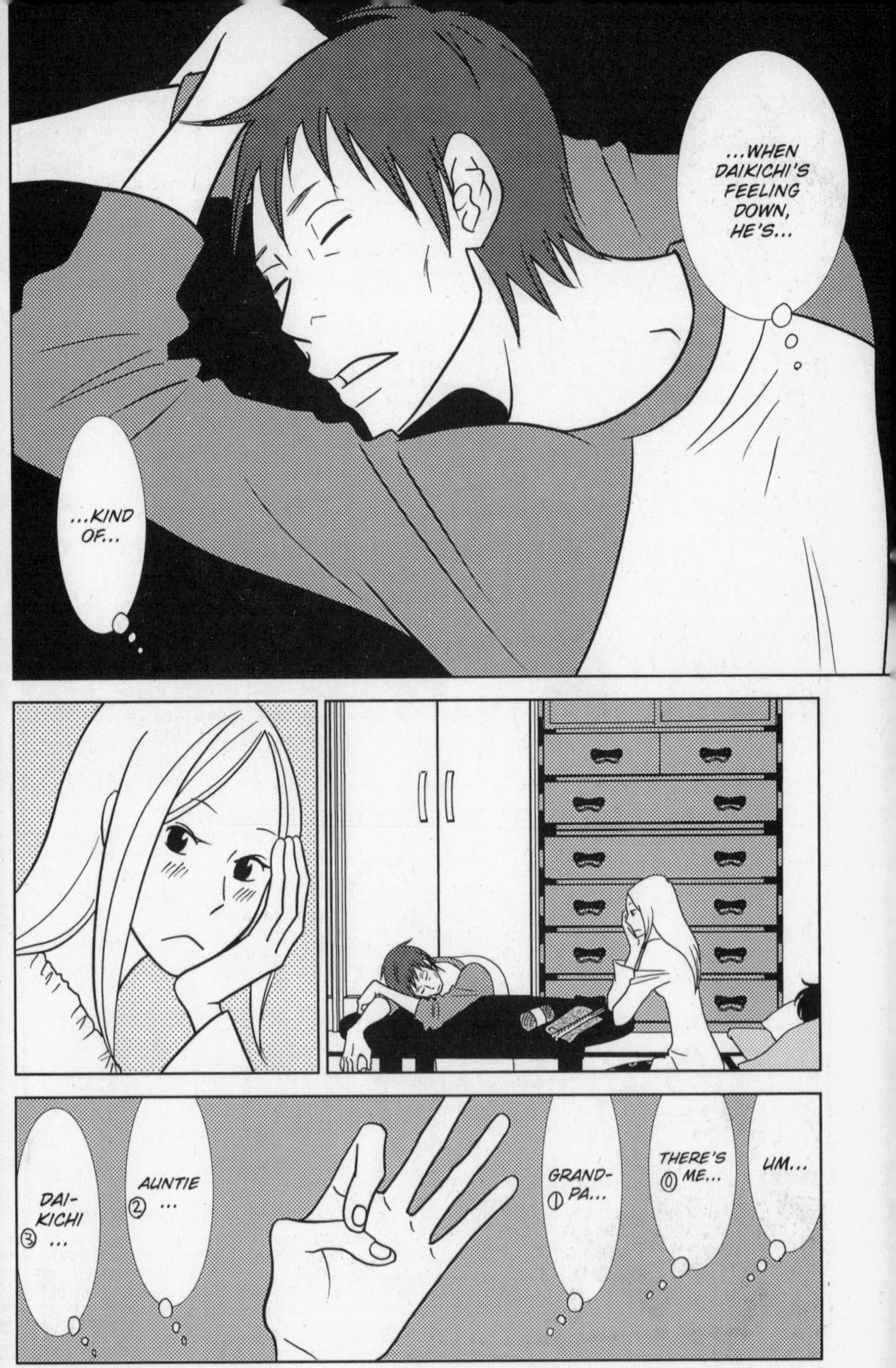
...WHEN DAIKICHI'S FEELING DOWN, HE'S...
...KIND OF...
UM...
THERE'S ⓪ ME...
GRAND-PA... ①
AUNTIE ② ...
DAI-KICHI ③ ...

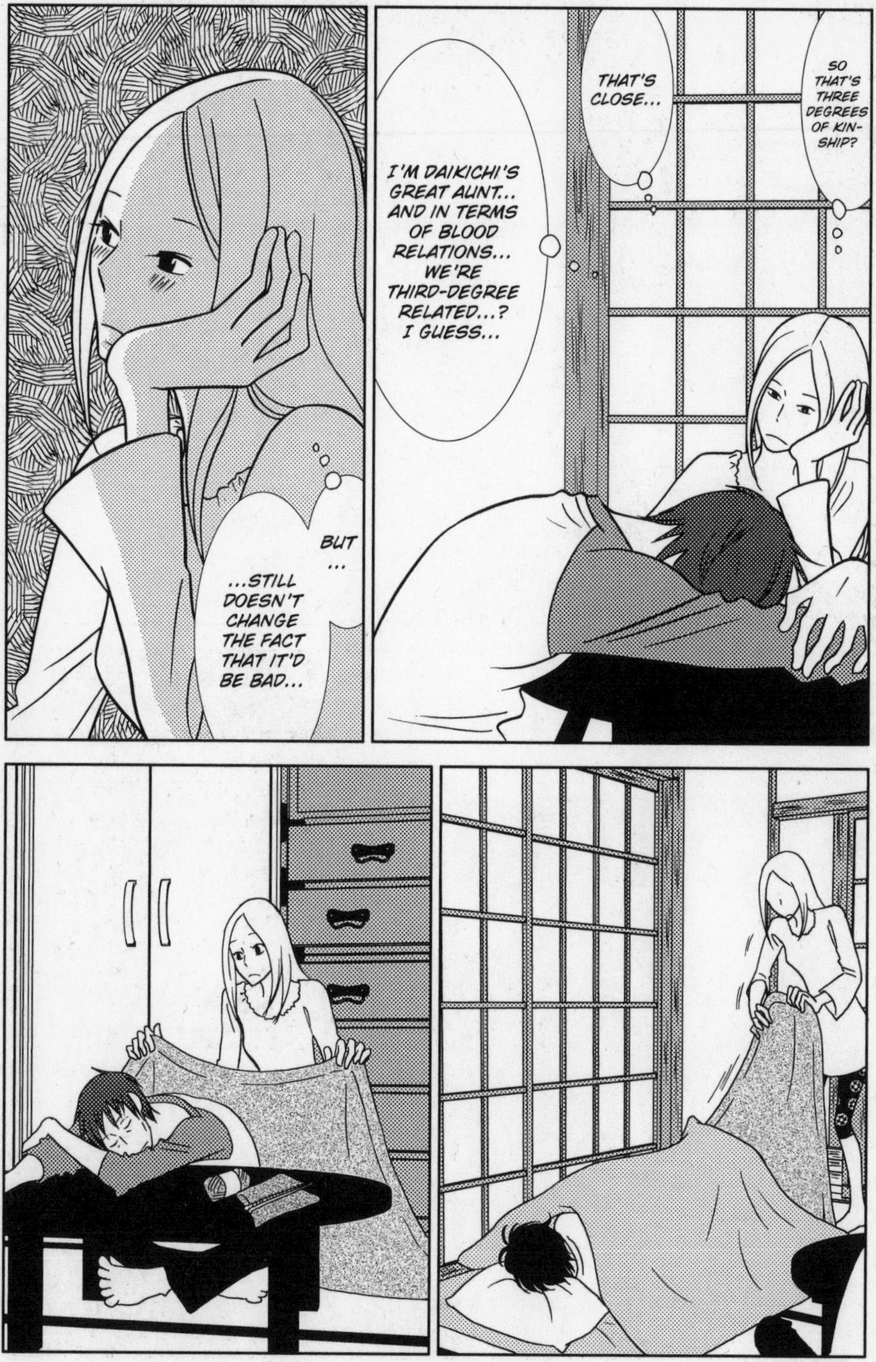
SO THAT'S THREE DEGREES OF KIN-SHIP?
THAT'S CLOSE...
I'M DAIKICHI'S GREAT AUNT... AND IN TERMS OF BLOOD RELATIONS... WE'RE THIRD-DEGREE RELATED...? I GUESS...
BUT ...
...STILL DOESN'T CHANGE THE FACT THAT IT'D BE BAD...

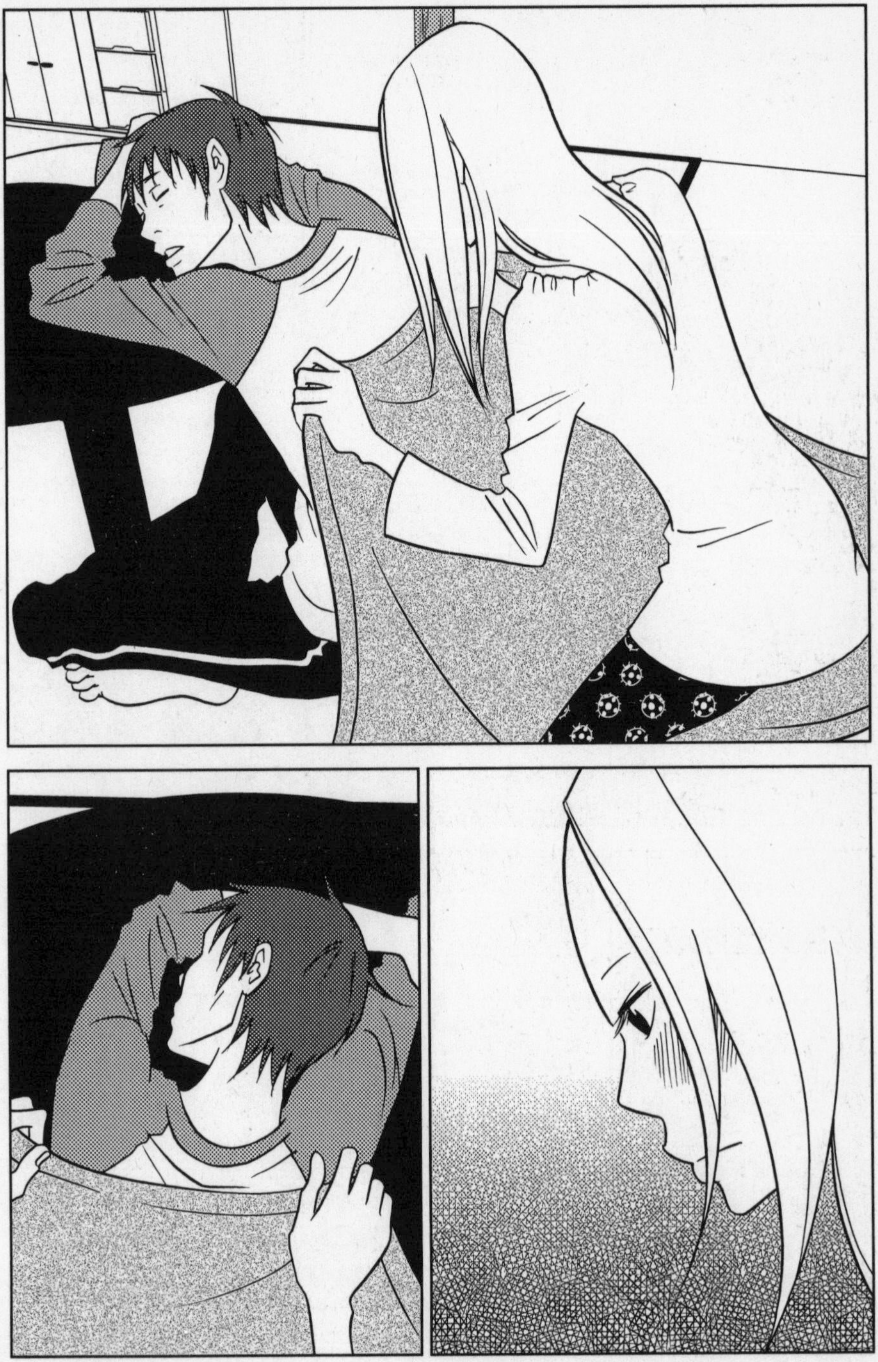

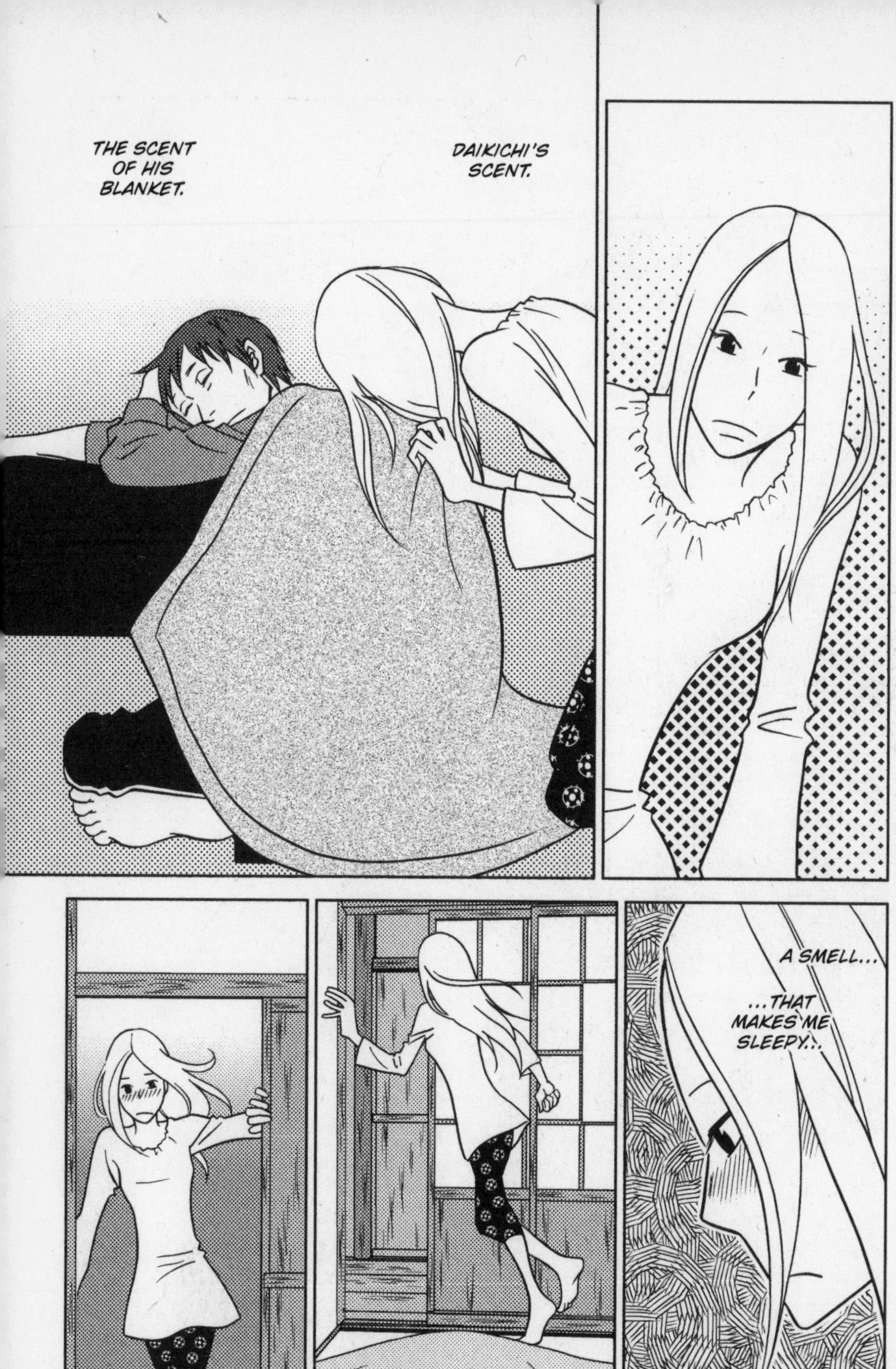
DAIKICHI'S SCENT.
THE SCENT OF HIS BLANKET.
A SMELL...
...THAT MAKES ME SLEEPY...

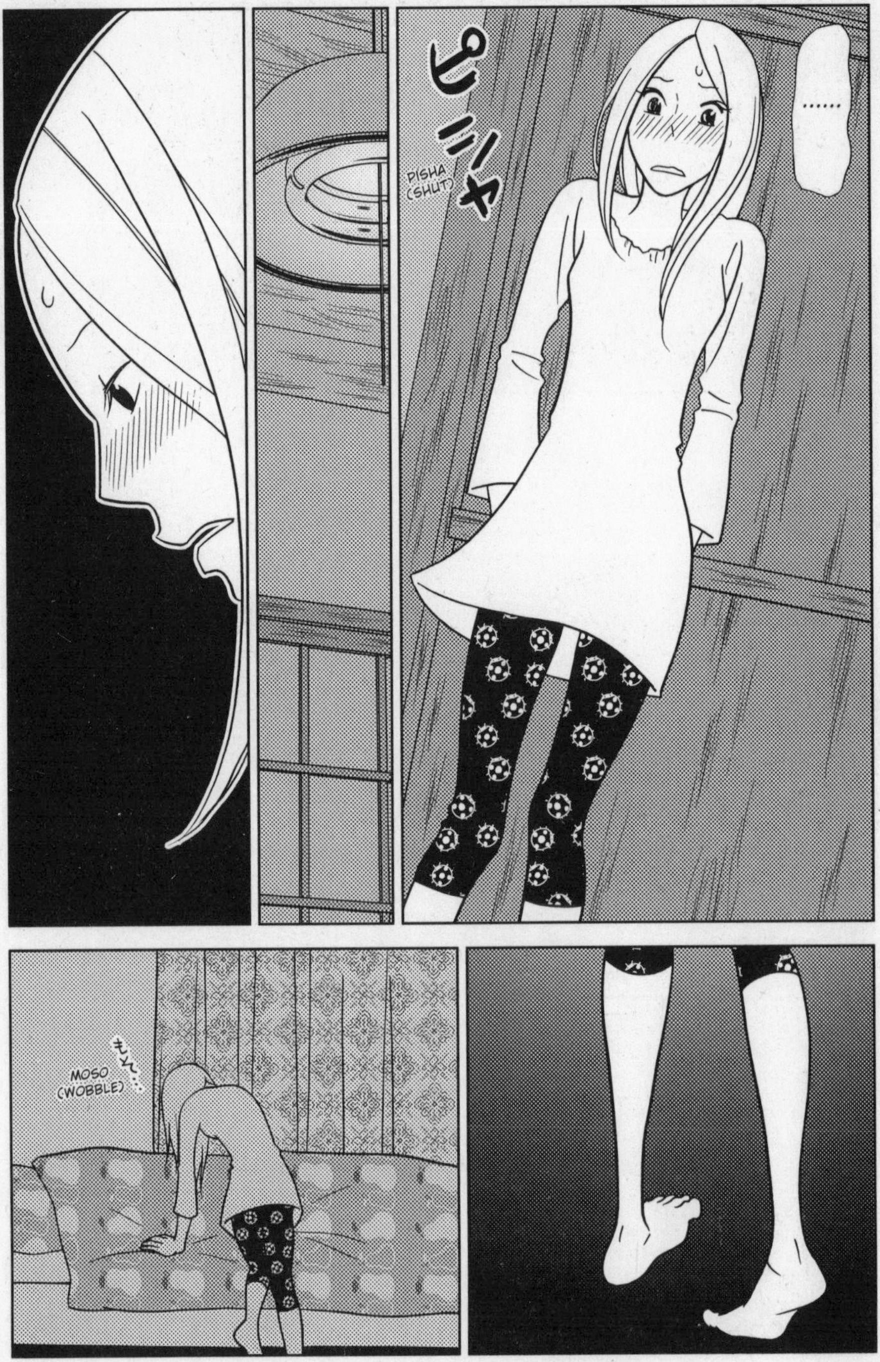
......
ピシャ
PISHA (SHUT)
もそ…
MOSO (WOBBLE)

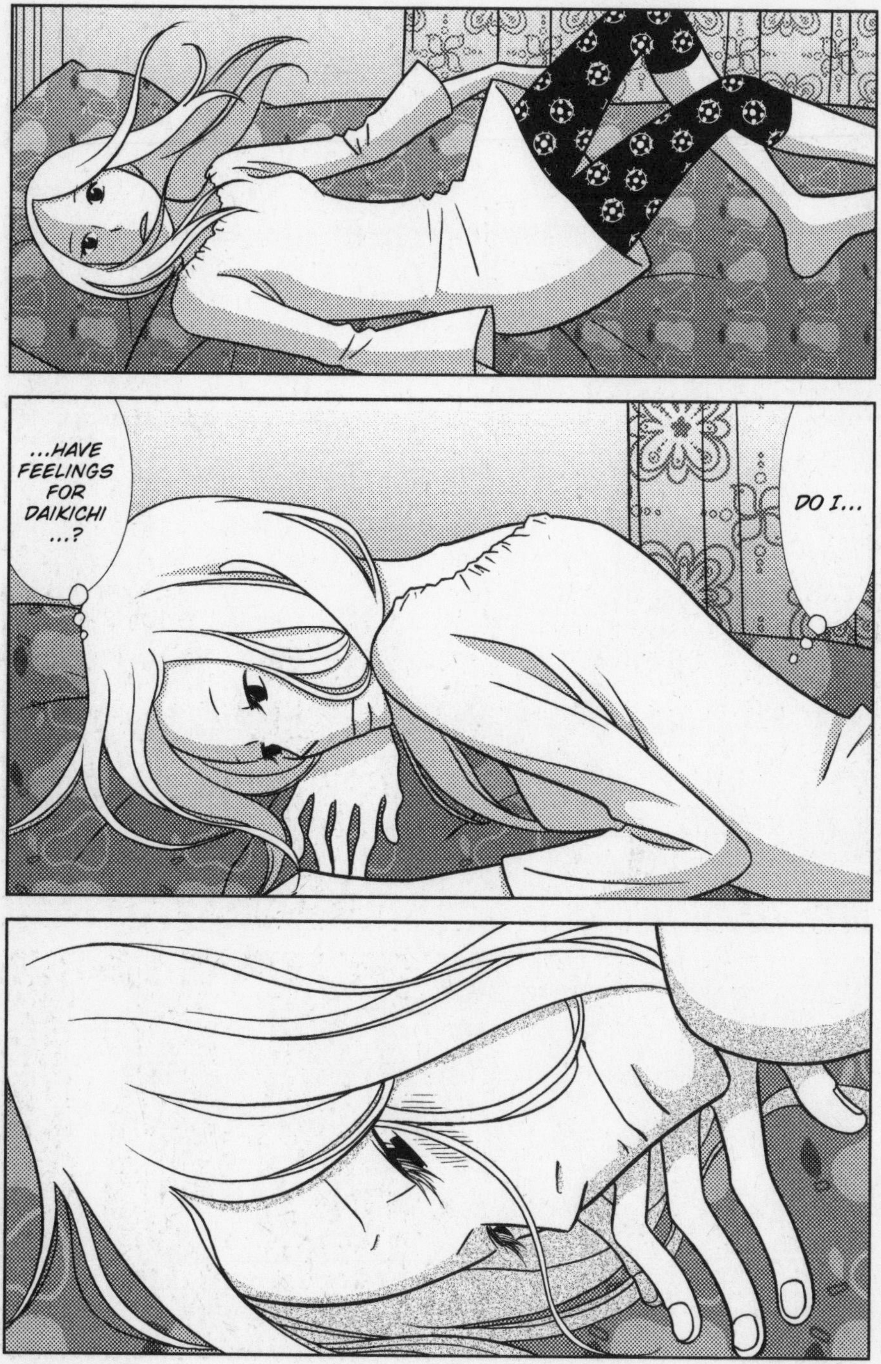
DO I...
...HAVE FEELINGS FOR DAIKICHI ...?

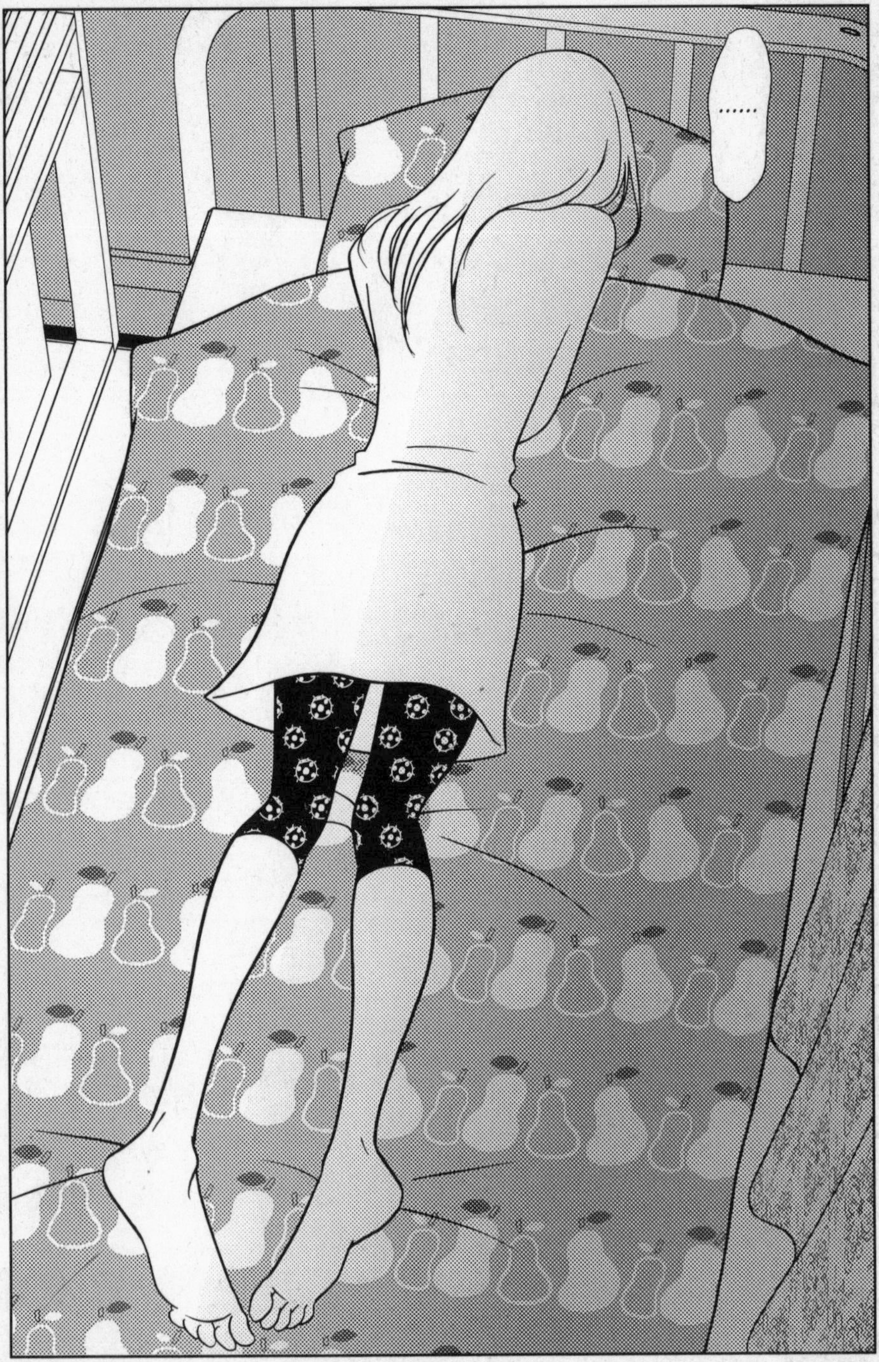
......

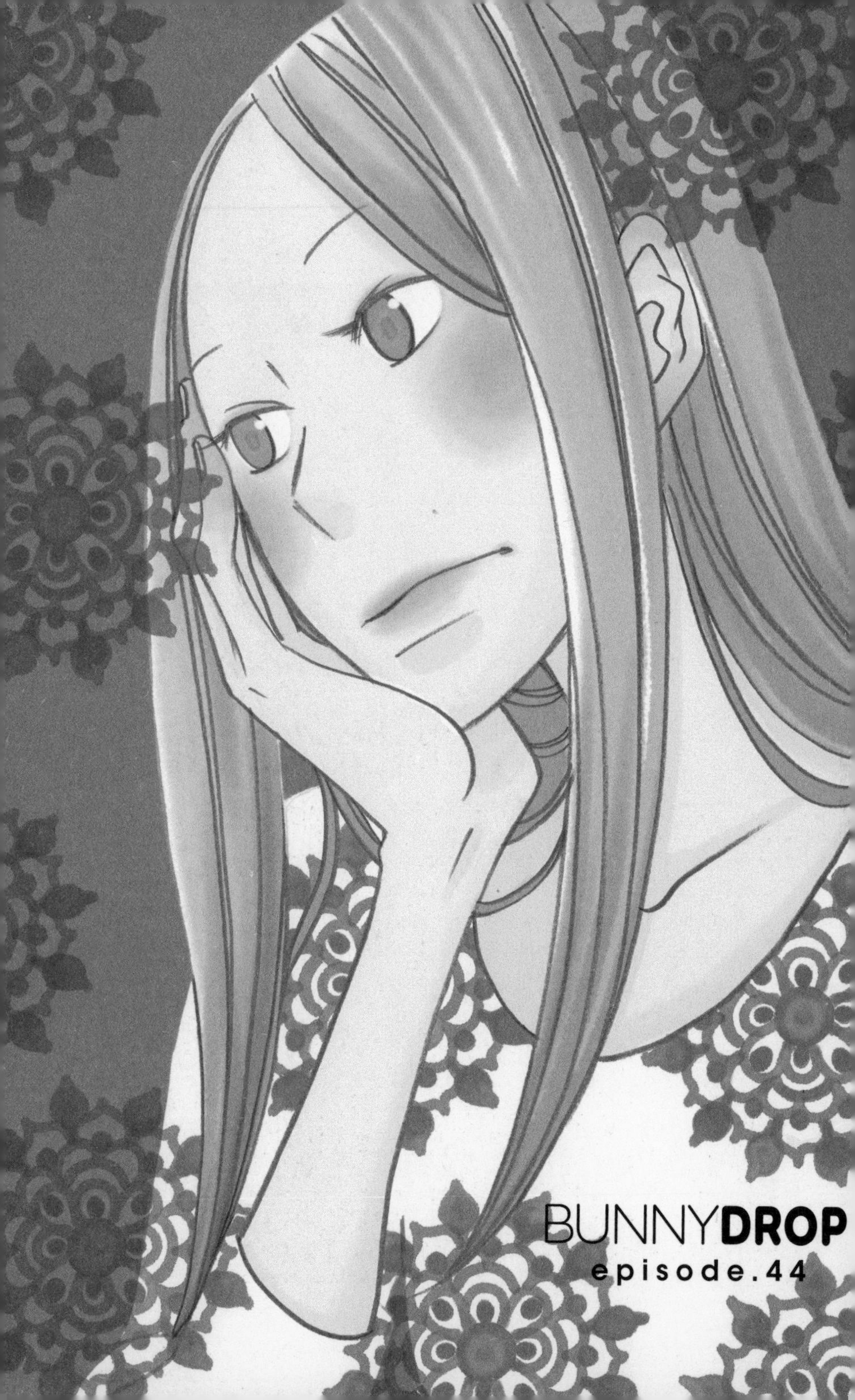

BUNNY**DROP**

episode.44

BUNNY**DROP**

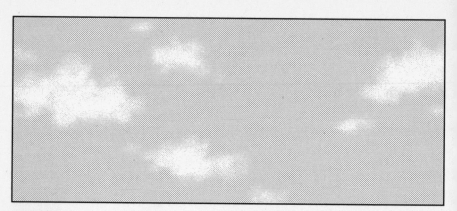

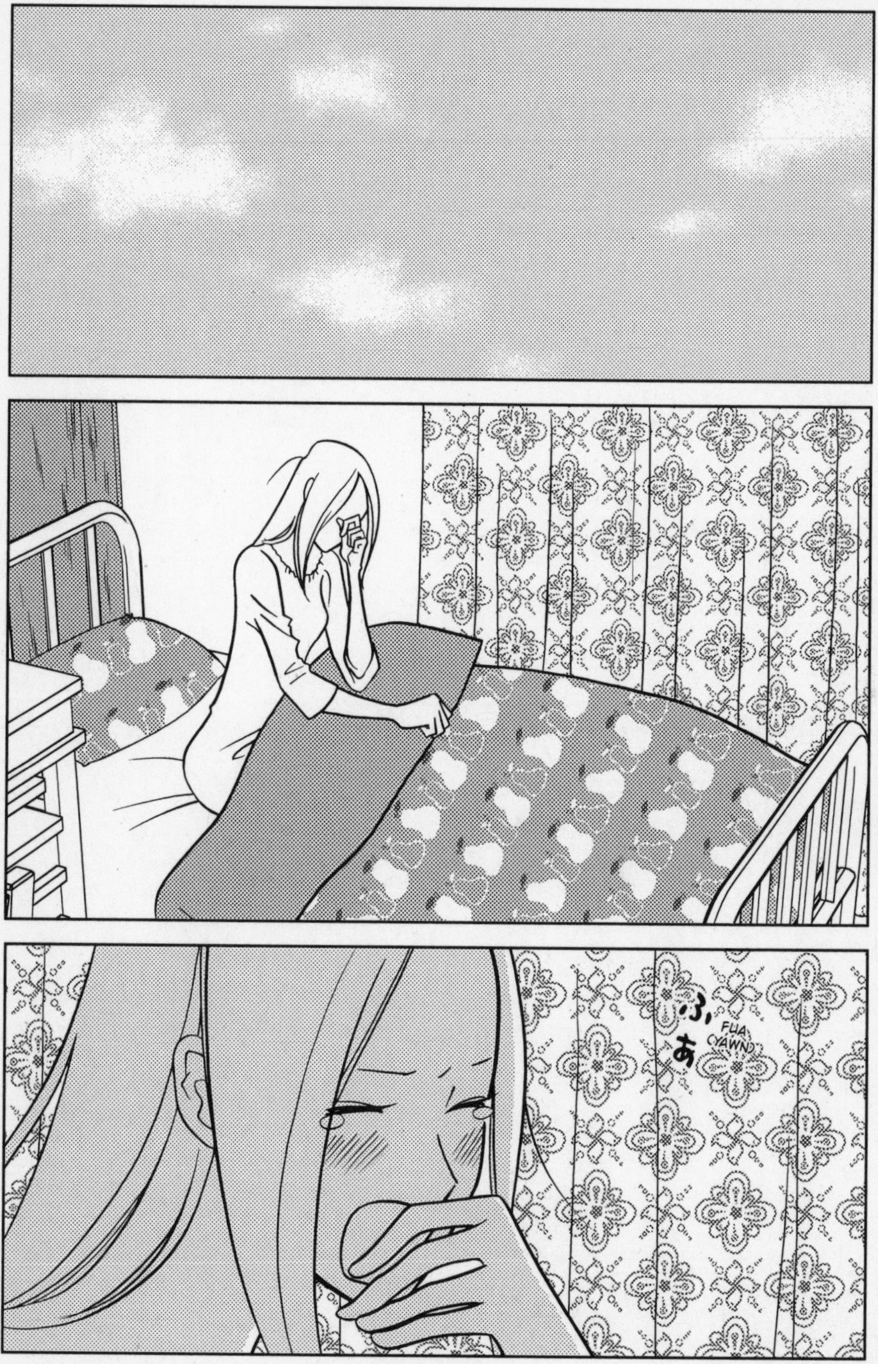
ふあ
FUA (YAWN)

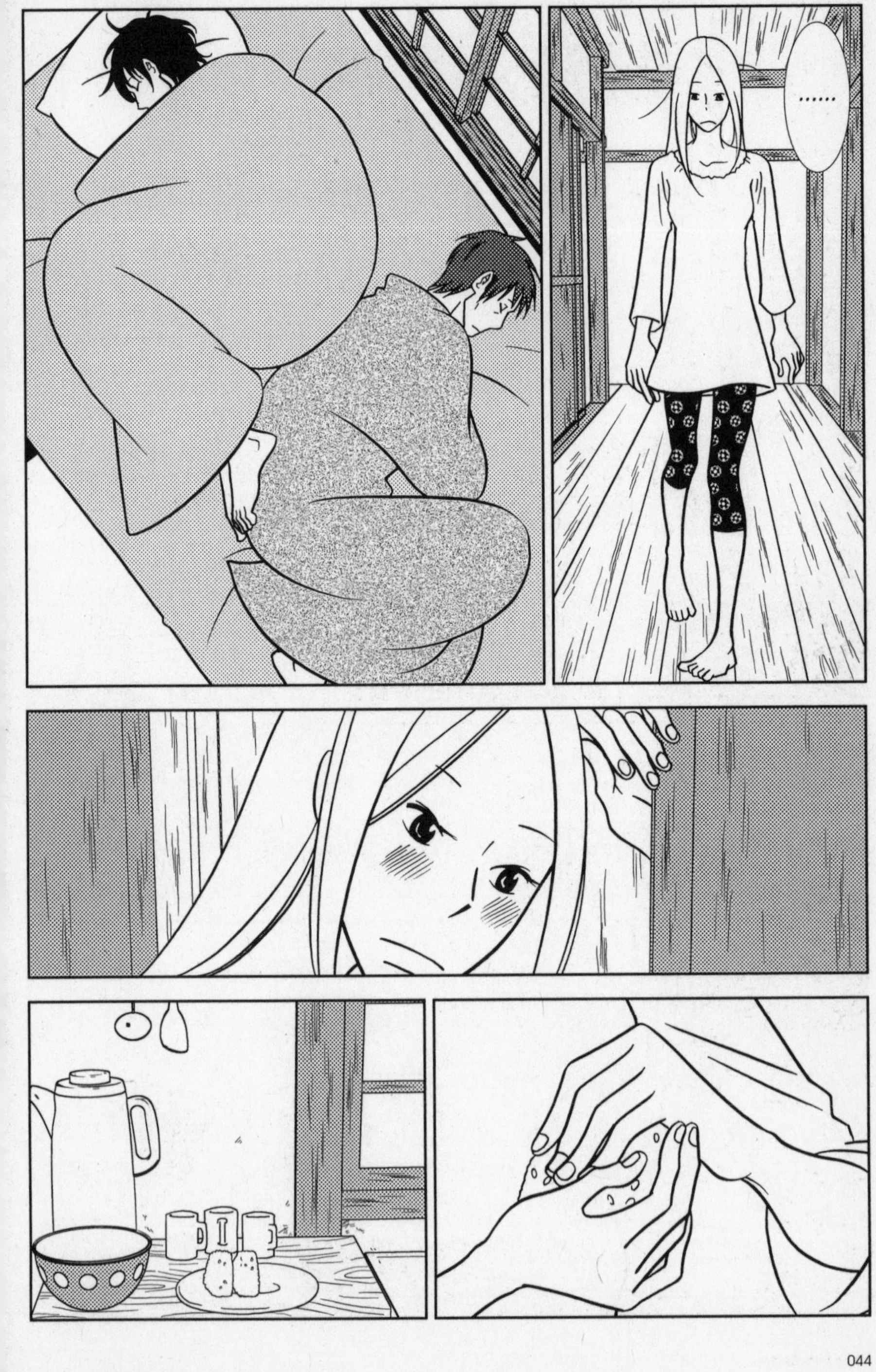
....

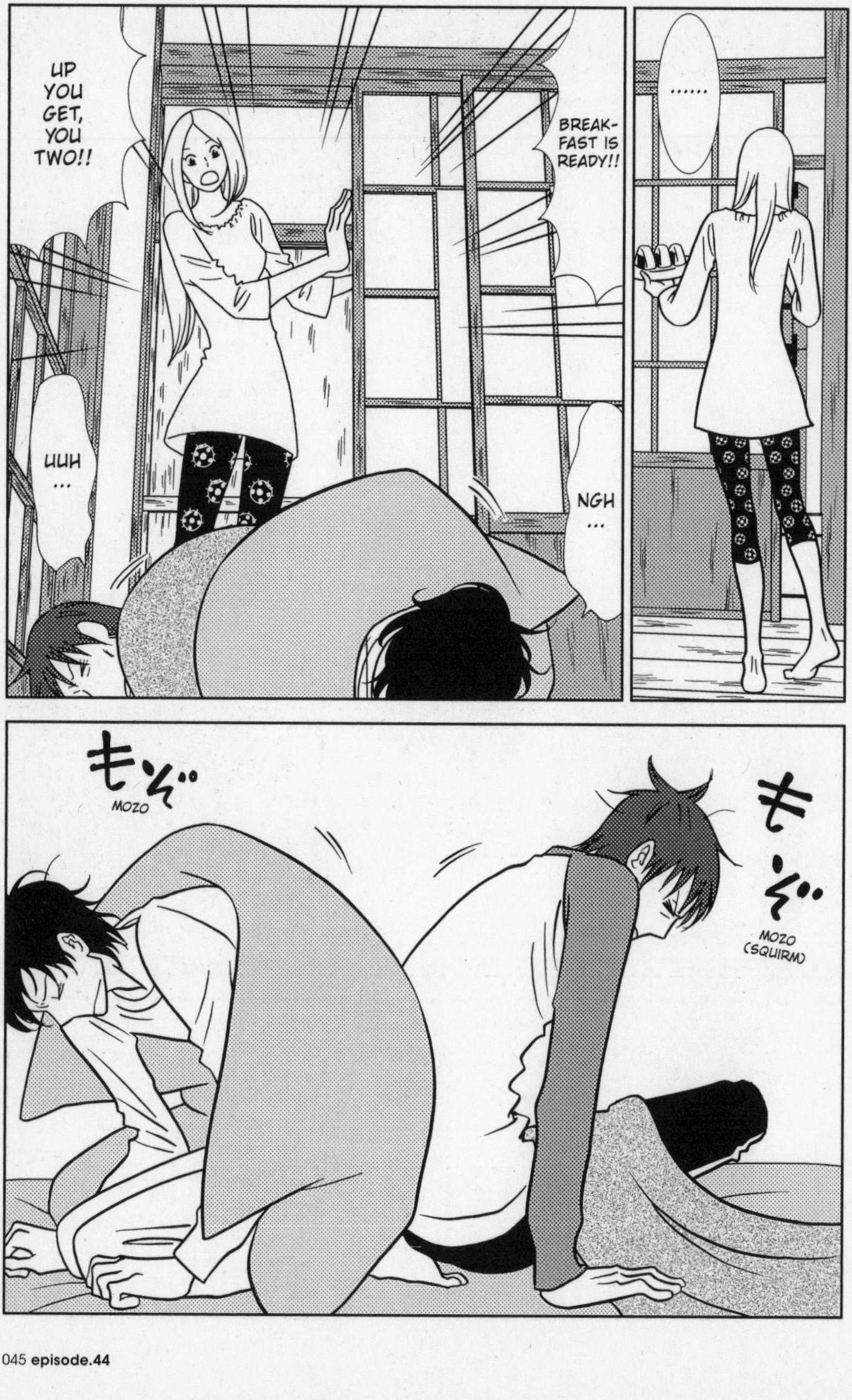
......
BREAK-FAST IS READY!!
UP YOU GET, YOU TWO!!
NGH ...
UUH ...
もぞ
MOZO (SQUIRM)
もぞ
MOZO

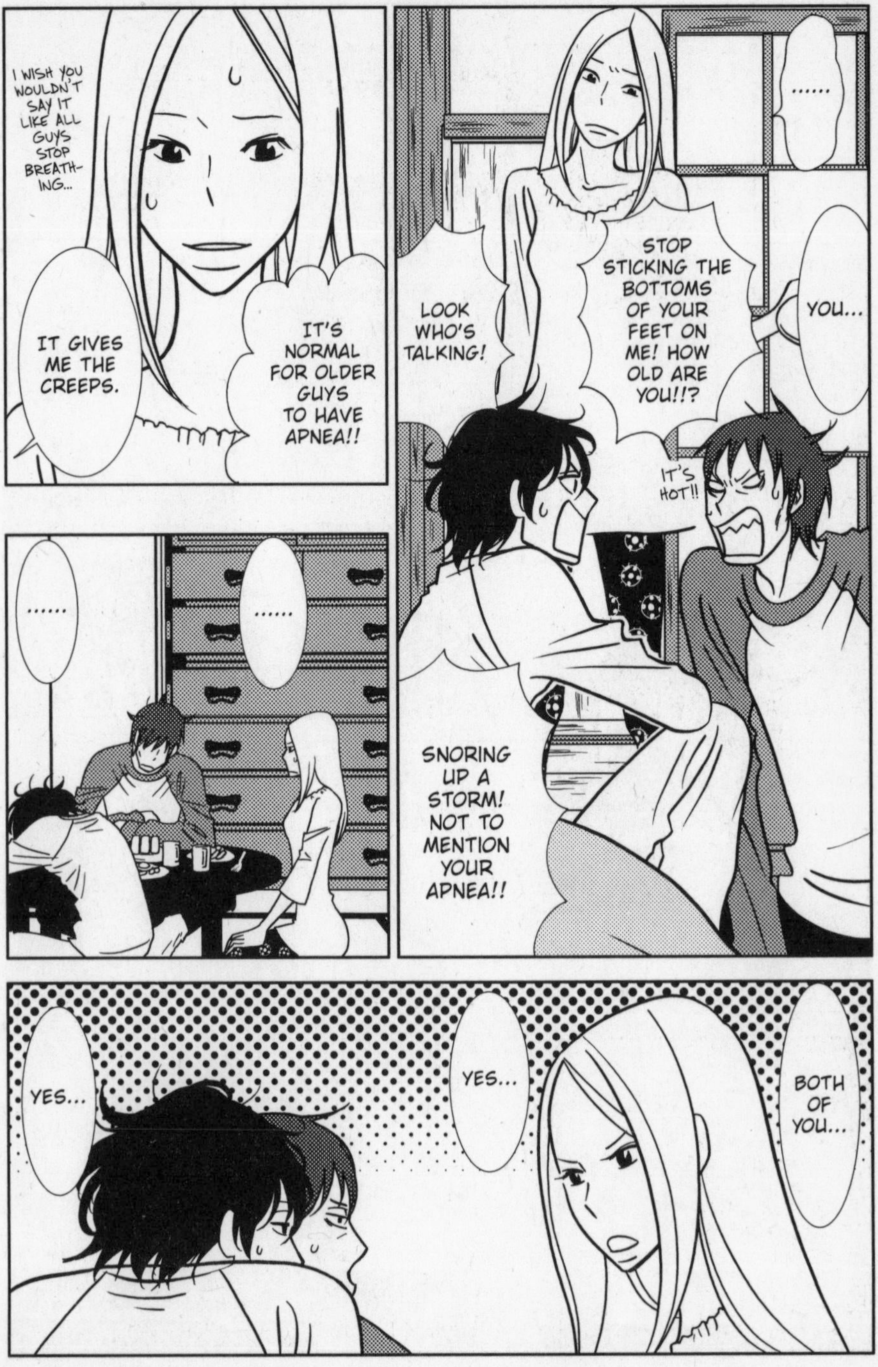
......
YOU...
STOP STICKING THE BOTTOMS OF YOUR FEET ON ME! HOW OLD ARE YOU!!?
LOOK WHO'S TALKING!
IT'S HOT!!
SNORING UP A STORM! NOT TO MENTION YOUR APNEA!!
IT'S NORMAL FOR OLDER GUYS TO HAVE APNEA!!
IT GIVES ME THE CREEPS.
I WISH YOU WOULDN'T SAY IT LIKE ALL GUYS STOP BREATHING...
......
......
BOTH OF YOU...
YES...
YES...

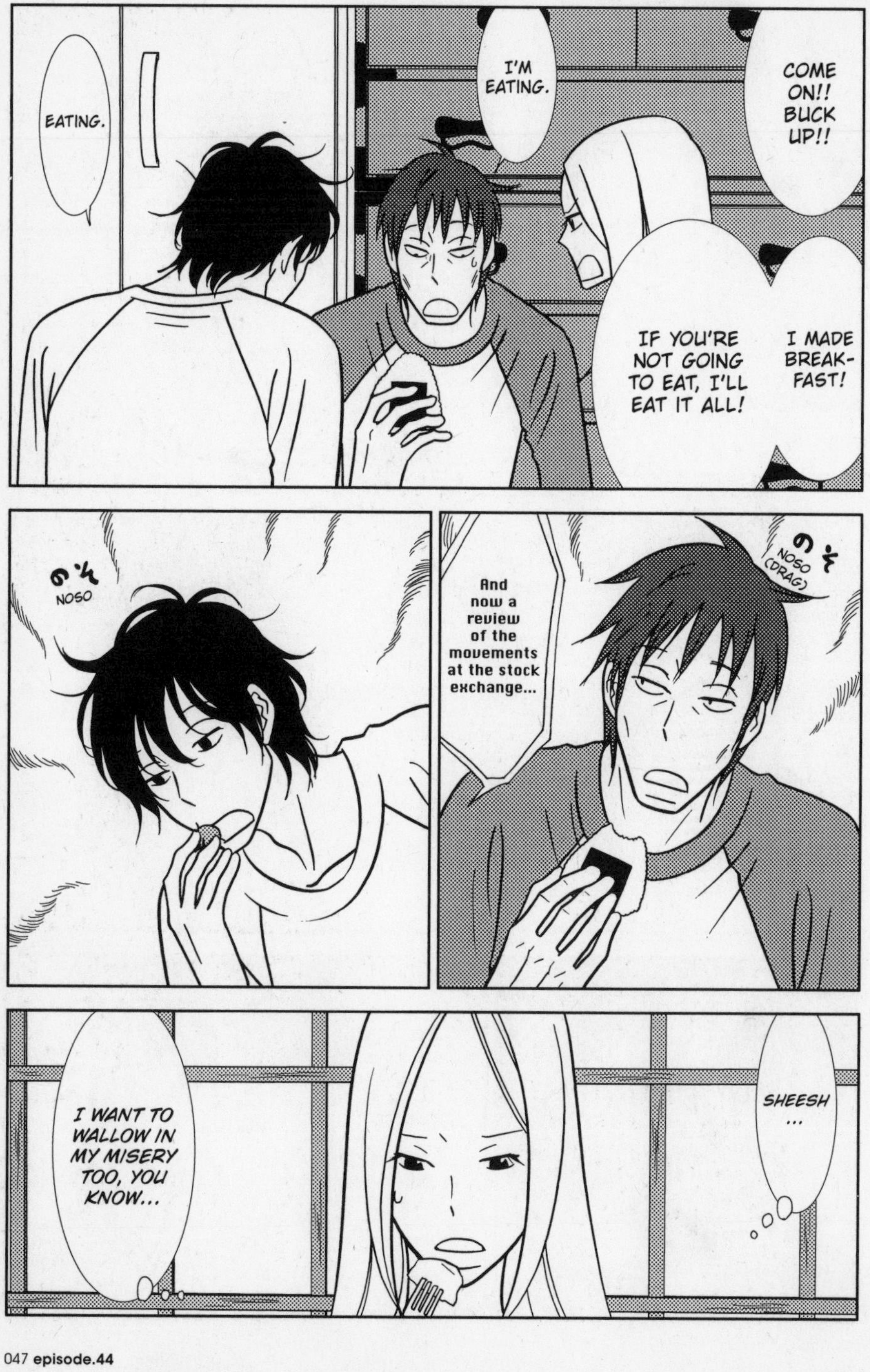
COME ON!! BUCK UP!!
I MADE BREAK-FAST!
IF YOU'RE NOT GOING TO EAT, I'LL EAT IT ALL!
I'M EATING.
EATING.
NOSO (DRAG)
And now a review of the movements at the stock exchange...
NOSO
SHEESH ...
I WANT TO WALLOW IN MY MISERY TOO, YOU KNOW...

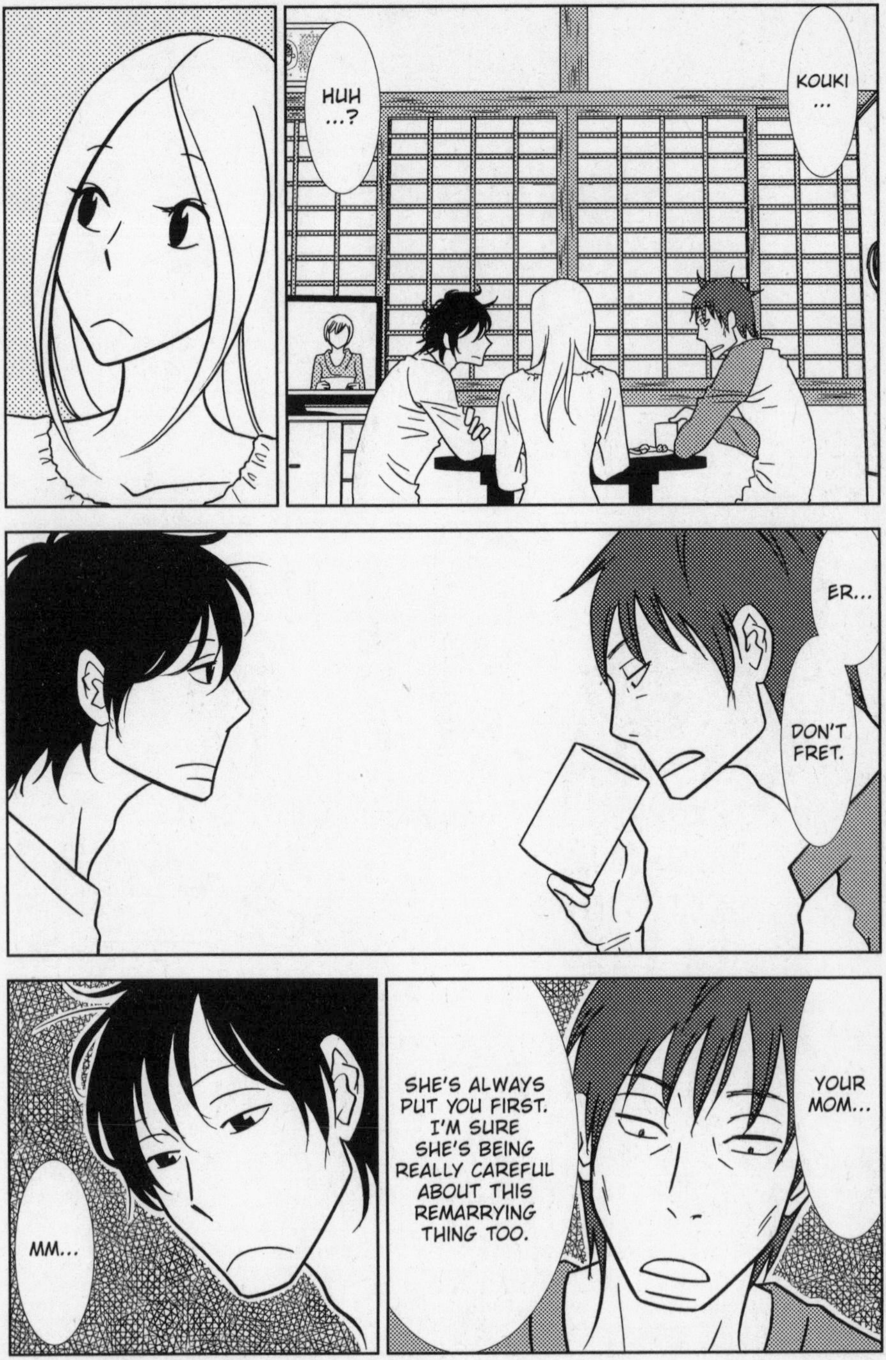
KOUKI ...
HUH ...?
ER...
DON'T FRET.
YOUR MOM...
SHE'S ALWAYS PUT YOU FIRST. I'M SURE SHE'S BEING REALLY CAREFUL ABOUT THIS REMARRYING THING TOO.
MM...

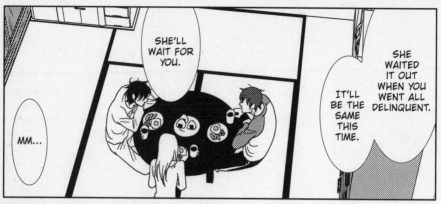

SHE WAITED IT OUT WHEN YOU WENT ALL DELINQUENT.
IT'LL BE THE SAME THIS TIME.
SHE'LL WAIT FOR YOU.
MM...
A WOMAN LIKE HER, SHE'S PROBABLY HAD A LOT OF GUYS THAT HAVE GONE AFTER HER.
YOU KNOW WHY SHE'S HELD OFF ON GETTING MARRIED UNTIL NOW, RIGHT?
MM...
......
がぶ
GABU
がぶ
GABU (SCARF)
ごぶ
GOBU (GOBBLE)
ごぶ
GOBU
ごぶ
GOBU

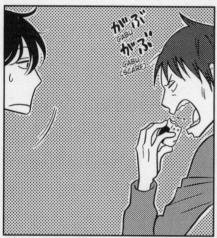

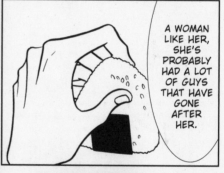

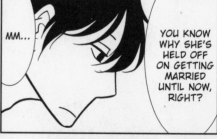

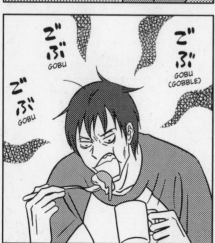

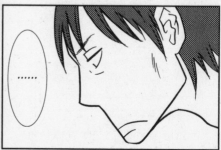

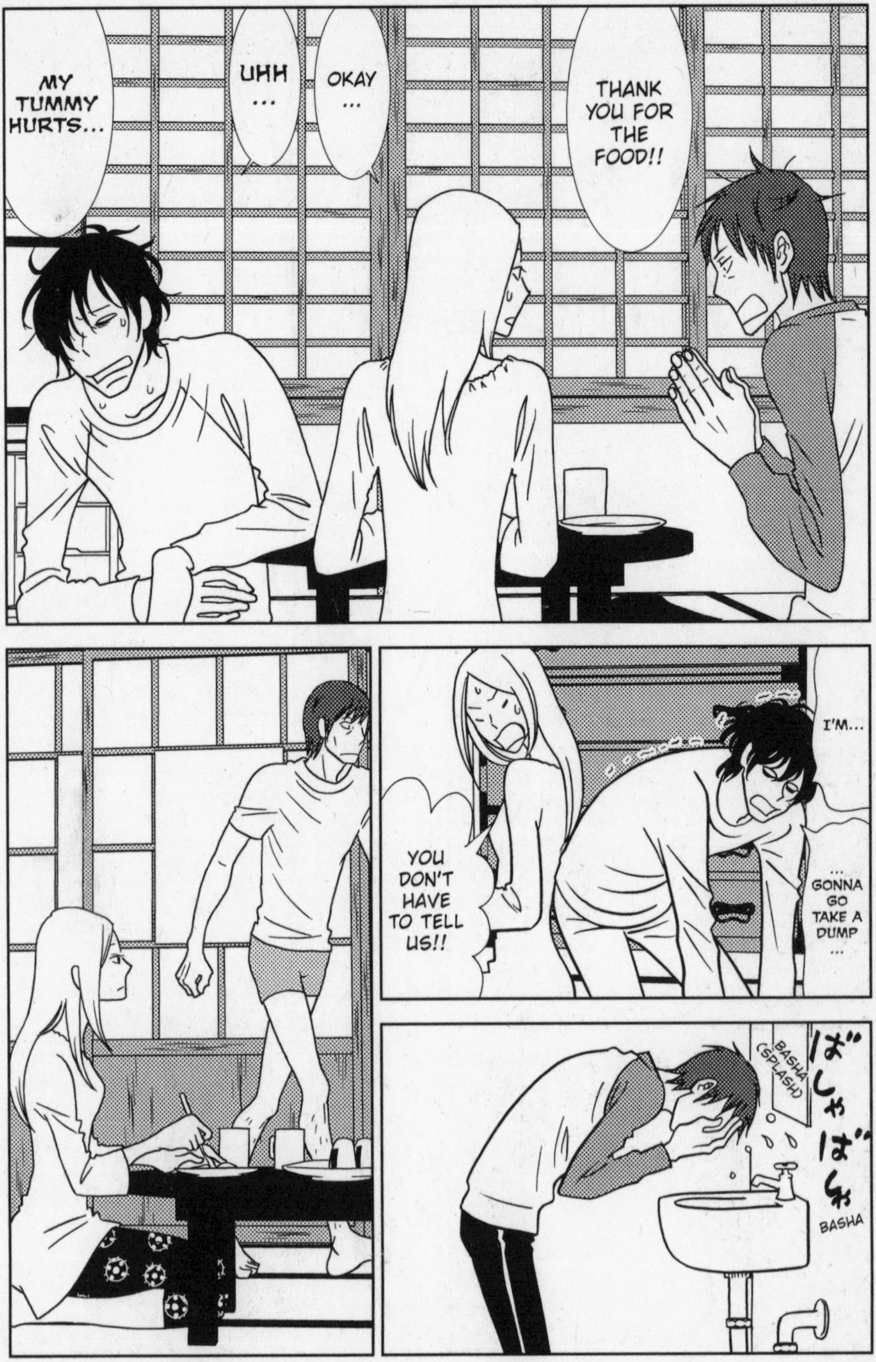
THANK YOU FOR THE FOOD!!
OKAY...
UHH...
MY TUMMY HURTS...
I'M...
...GONNA GO TAKE A DUMP...
YOU DON'T HAVE TO TELL US!!
ばしゃ
BASHA (SPLASH)
ばしゃ
BASHA

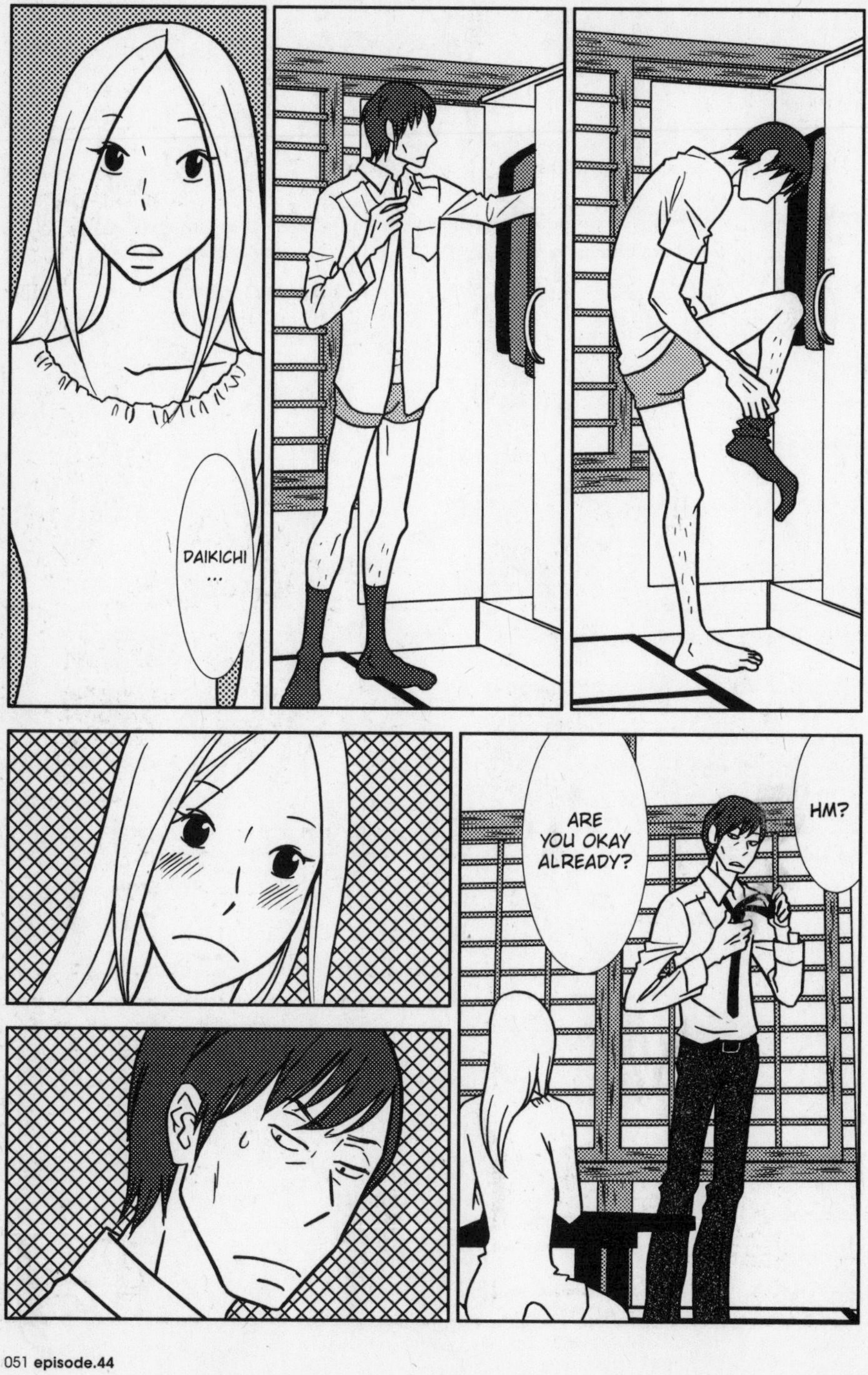
DAIKICHI ...
HM?
ARE YOU OKAY ALREADY?

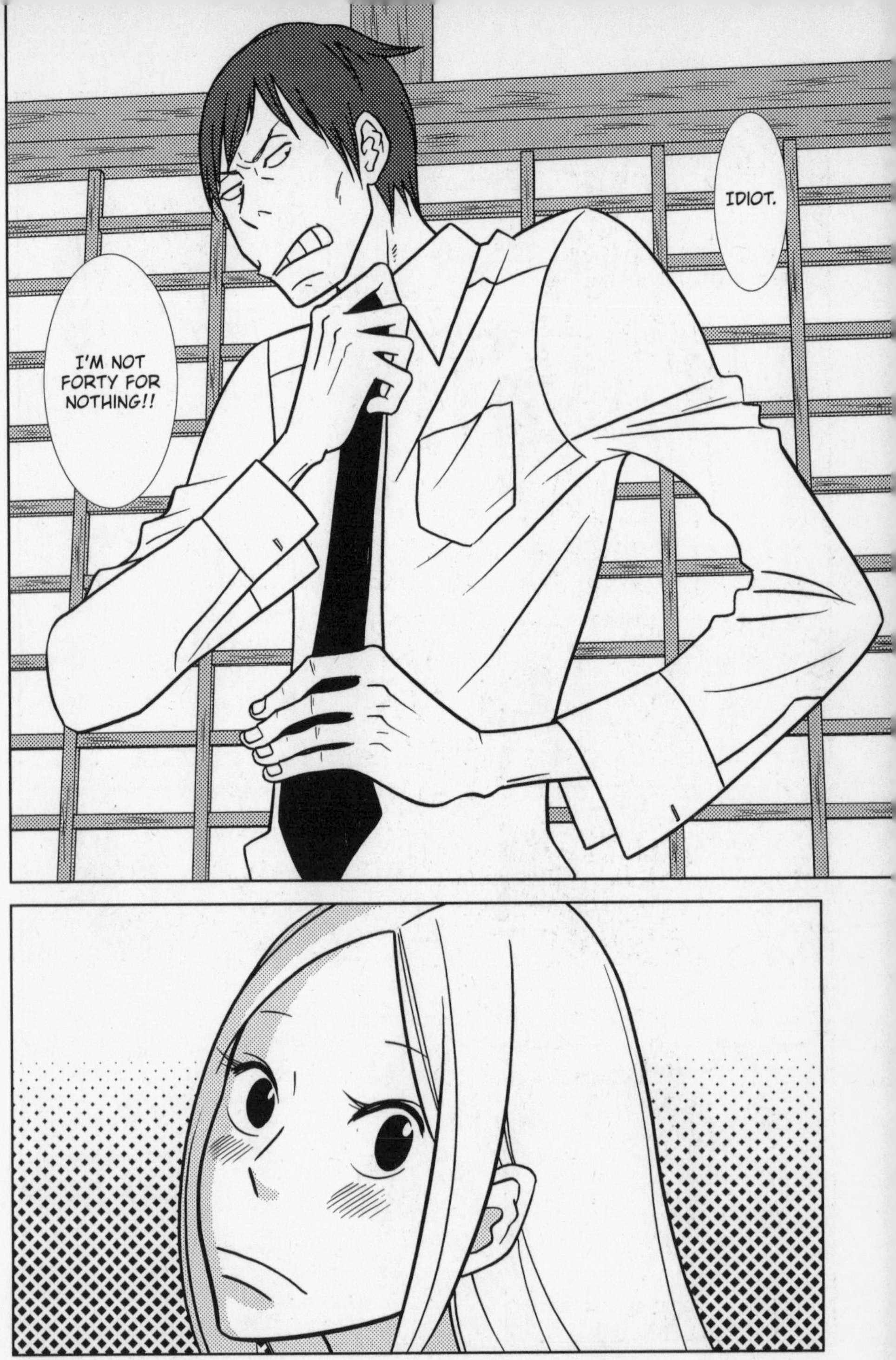
IDIOT.
I'M NOT FORTY FOR NOTHING!!

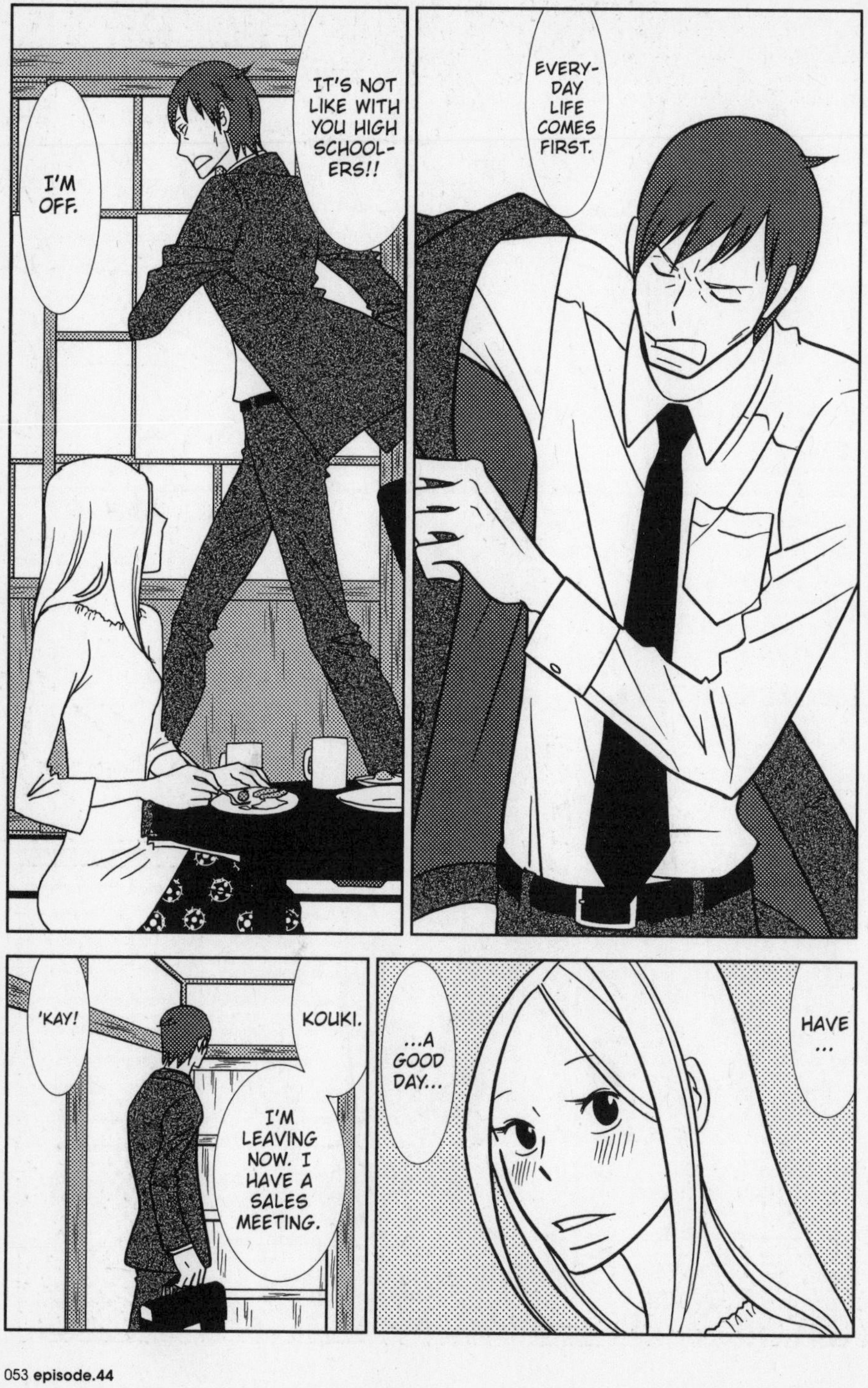
EVERY-DAY LIFE COMES FIRST.
IT'S NOT LIKE WITH YOU HIGH SCHOOL-ERS!!
I'M OFF.
HAVE...
...A GOOD DAY...
KOUKI.
I'M LEAVING NOW. I HAVE A SALES MEETING.
'KAY!

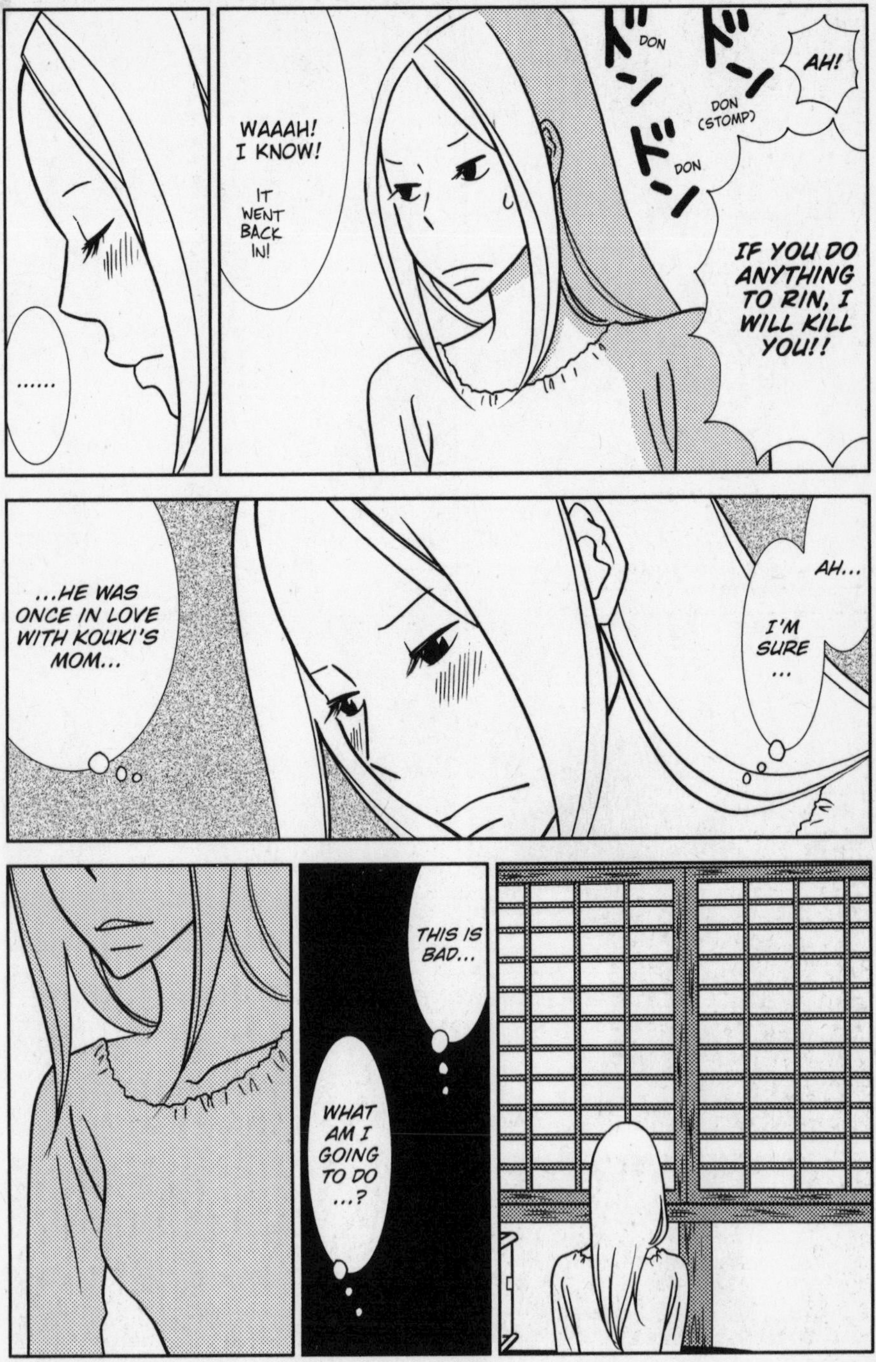
AH!
DON
DON (STOMP)
DON
IF YOU DO ANYTHING TO RIN, I WILL KILL YOU!!
WAAAH! I KNOW!
IT WENT BACK IN!
......
AH... I'M SURE ...
...HE WAS ONCE IN LOVE WITH KOUKI'S MOM...
THIS IS BAD...
WHAT AM I GOING TO DO ...?

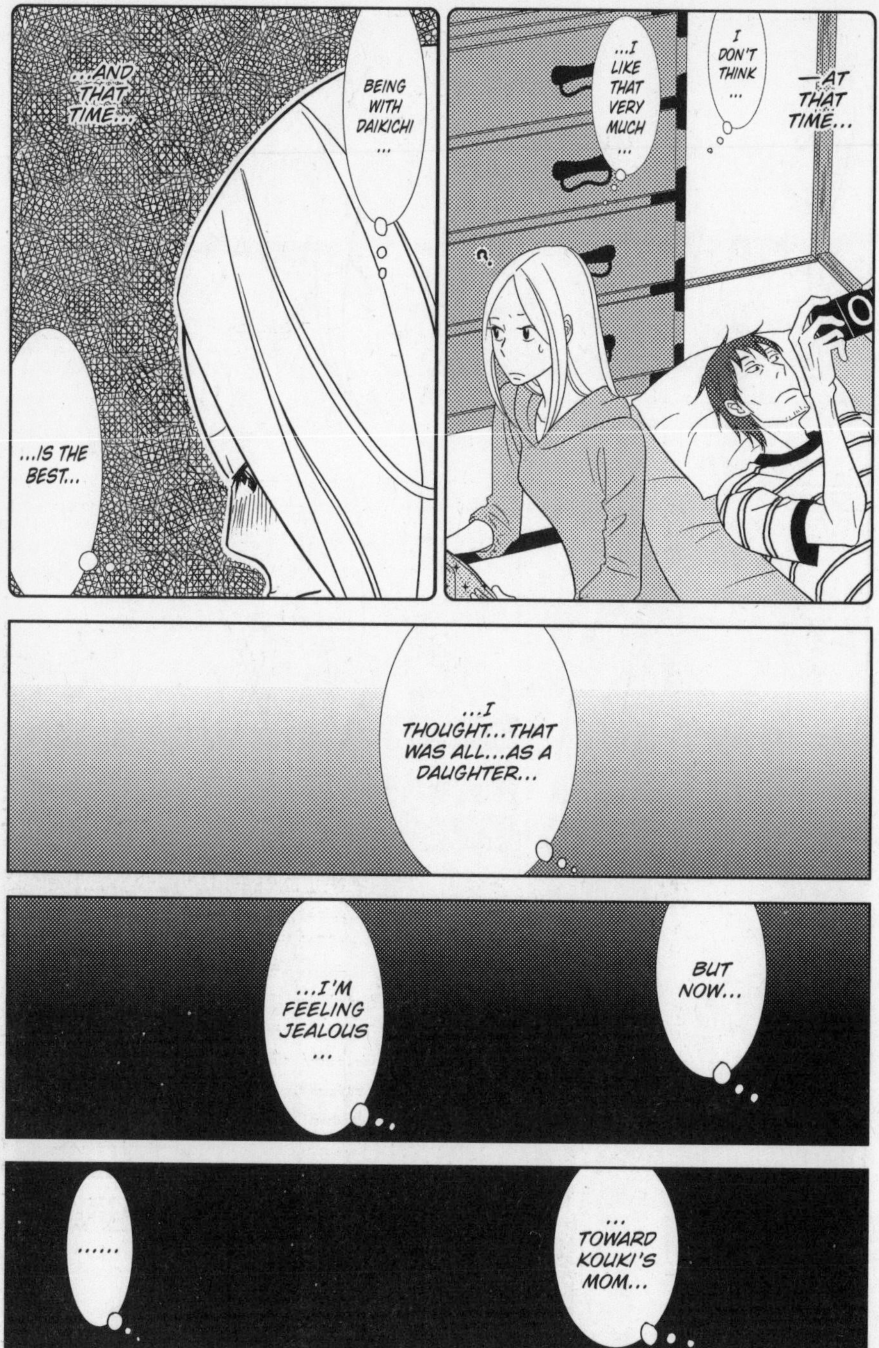
—AT THAT TIME...
I DON'T THINK...
...I LIKE THAT VERY MUCH...
...AND THAT TIME...
BEING WITH DAIKICHI...
...IS THE BEST...
...I THOUGHT...THAT WAS ALL...AS A DAUGHTER...
BUT NOW...
...I'M FEELING JEALOUS...
...TOWARD KOUKI'S MOM...
......

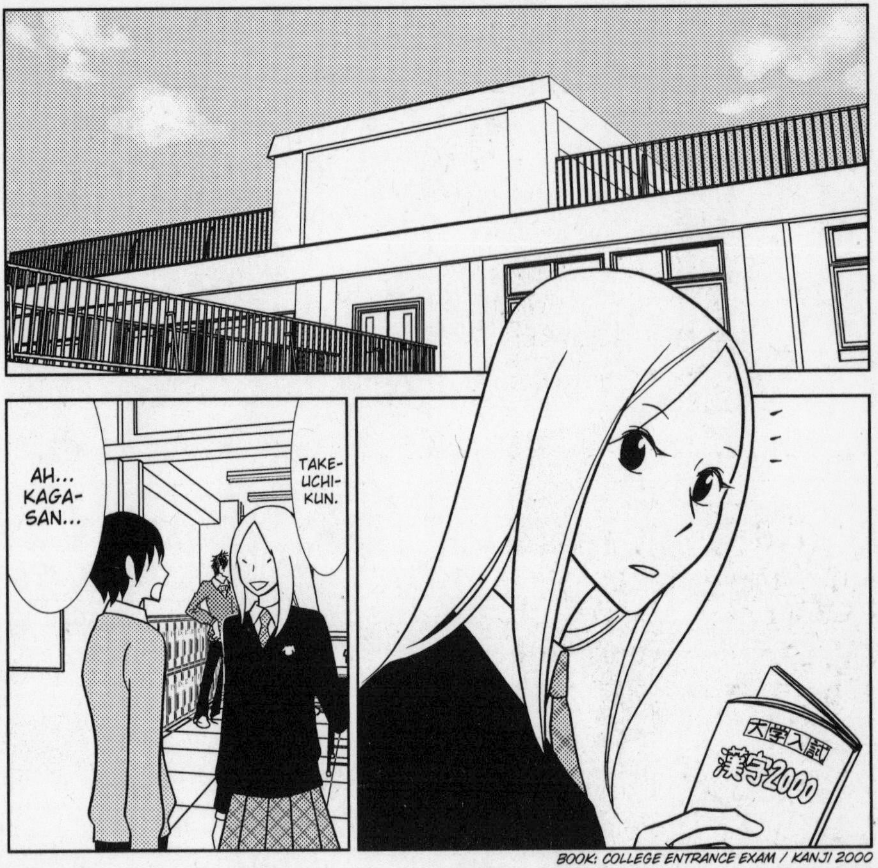
大学入試
漢字2000
TAKE-UCHI-KUN.
AH... KAGA-SAN...

BOOK: COLLEGE ENTRANCE EXAM / KANJI 2000

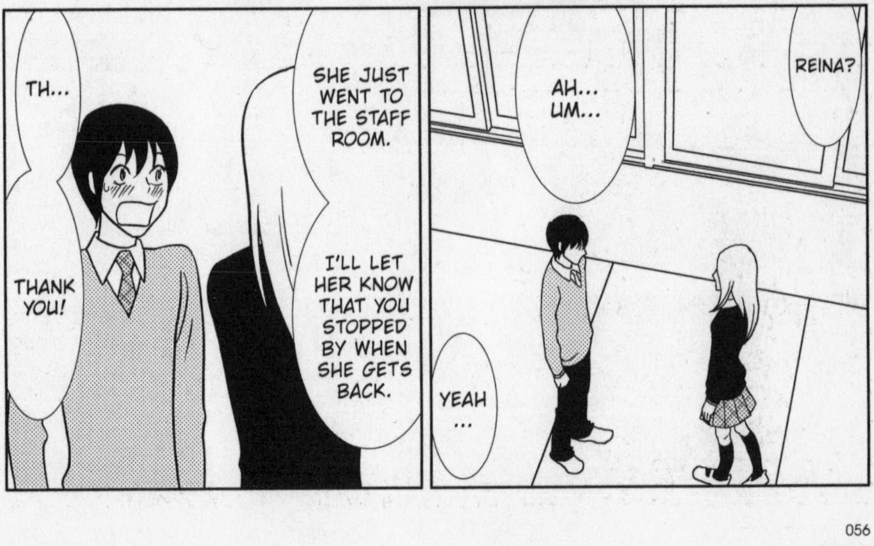
REINA?
AH... UM...
YEAH ...
SHE JUST WENT TO THE STAFF ROOM.
TH...
I'LL LET HER KNOW THAT YOU STOPPED BY WHEN SHE GETS BACK.
THANK YOU!

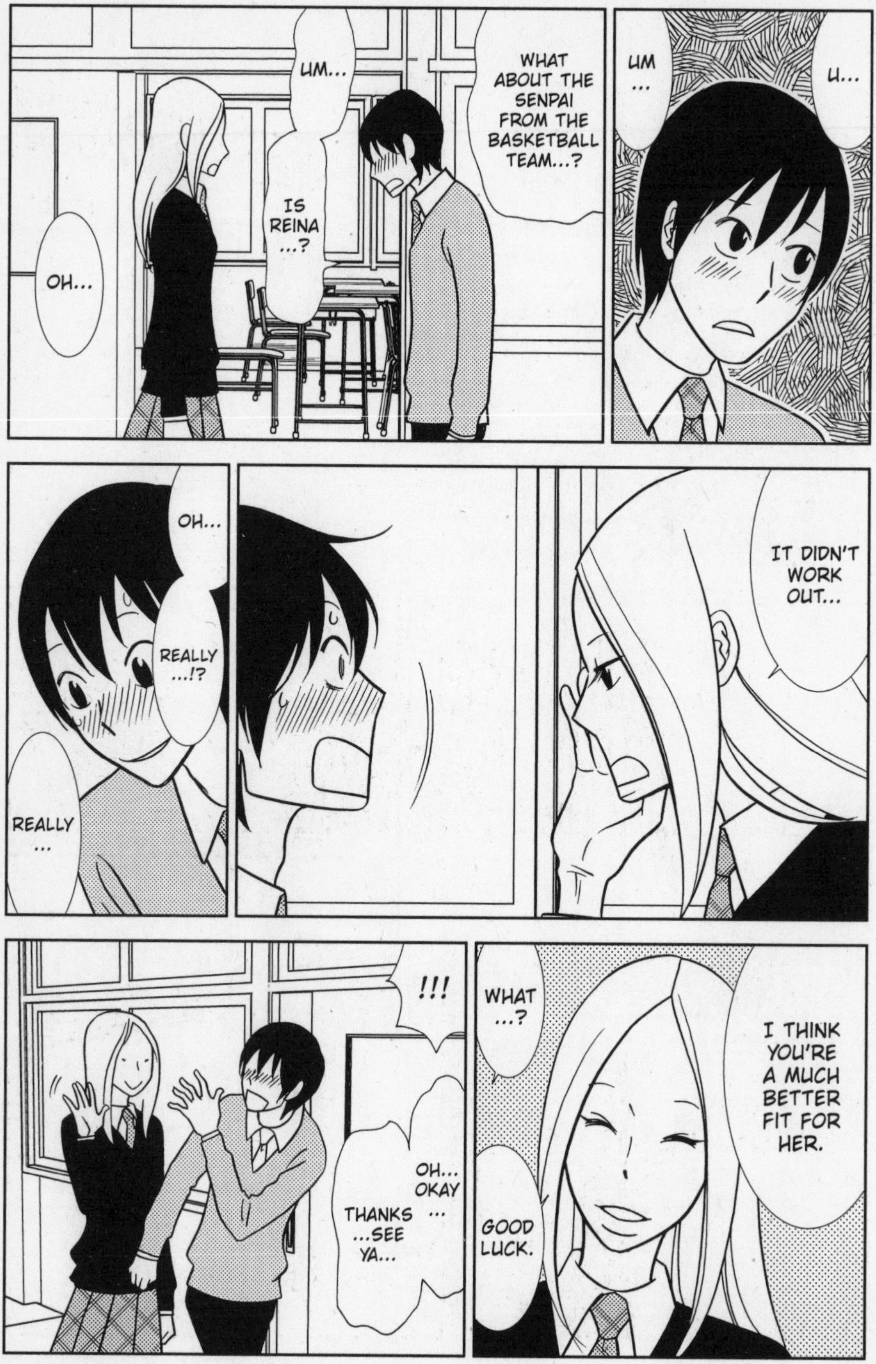
U...
UM ...
WHAT ABOUT THE SENPAI FROM THE BASKETBALL TEAM...?
UM...
IS REINA ...?
OH...
IT DIDN'T WORK OUT...
OH...
REALLY ...!?
REALLY ...
I THINK YOU'RE A MUCH BETTER FIT FOR HER.
WHAT ...?
GOOD LUCK.
!!!
OH... OKAY ...
THANKS ...SEE YA...

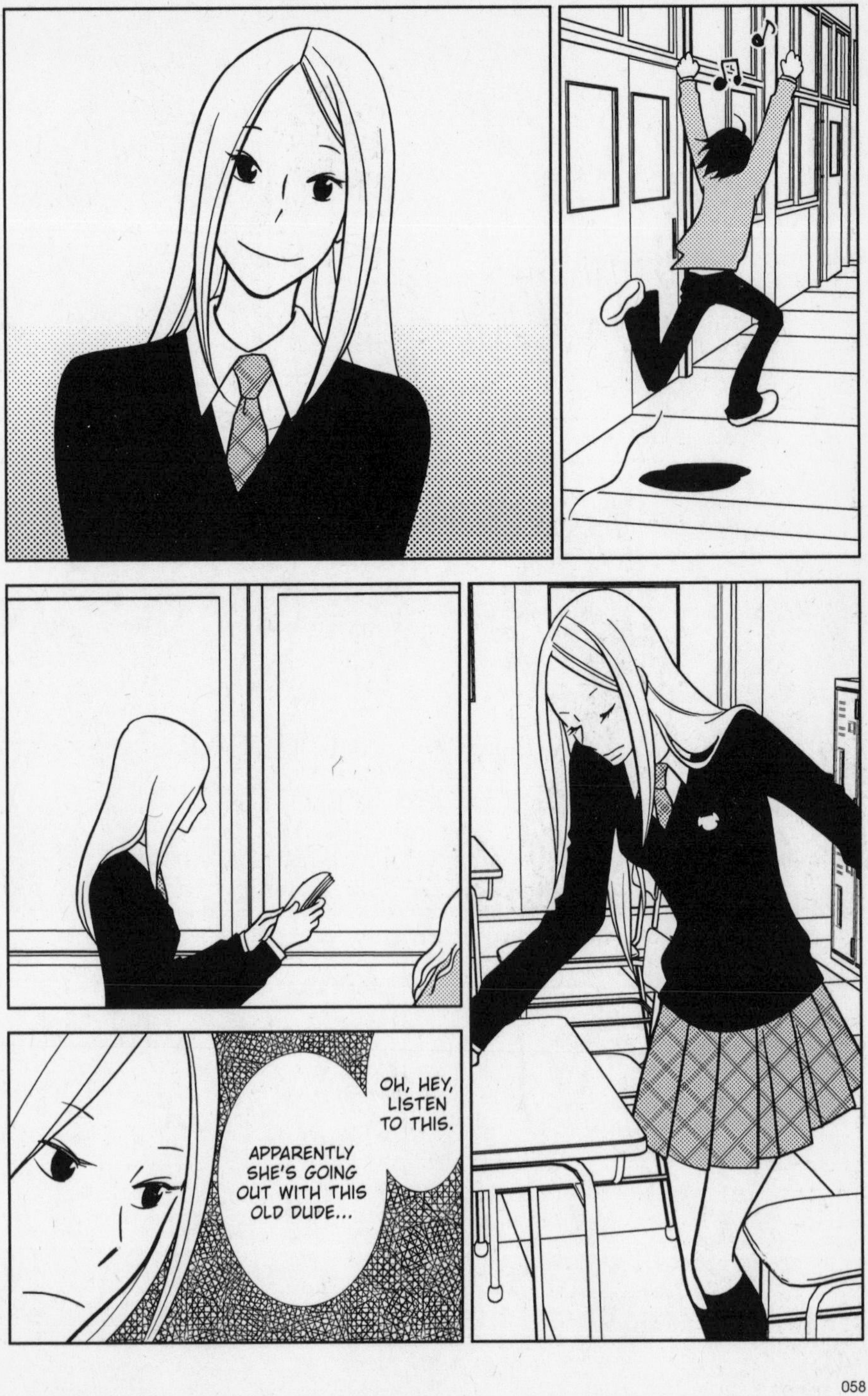
OH, HEY, LISTEN TO THIS.
APPARENTLY SHE'S GOING OUT WITH THIS OLD DUDE...

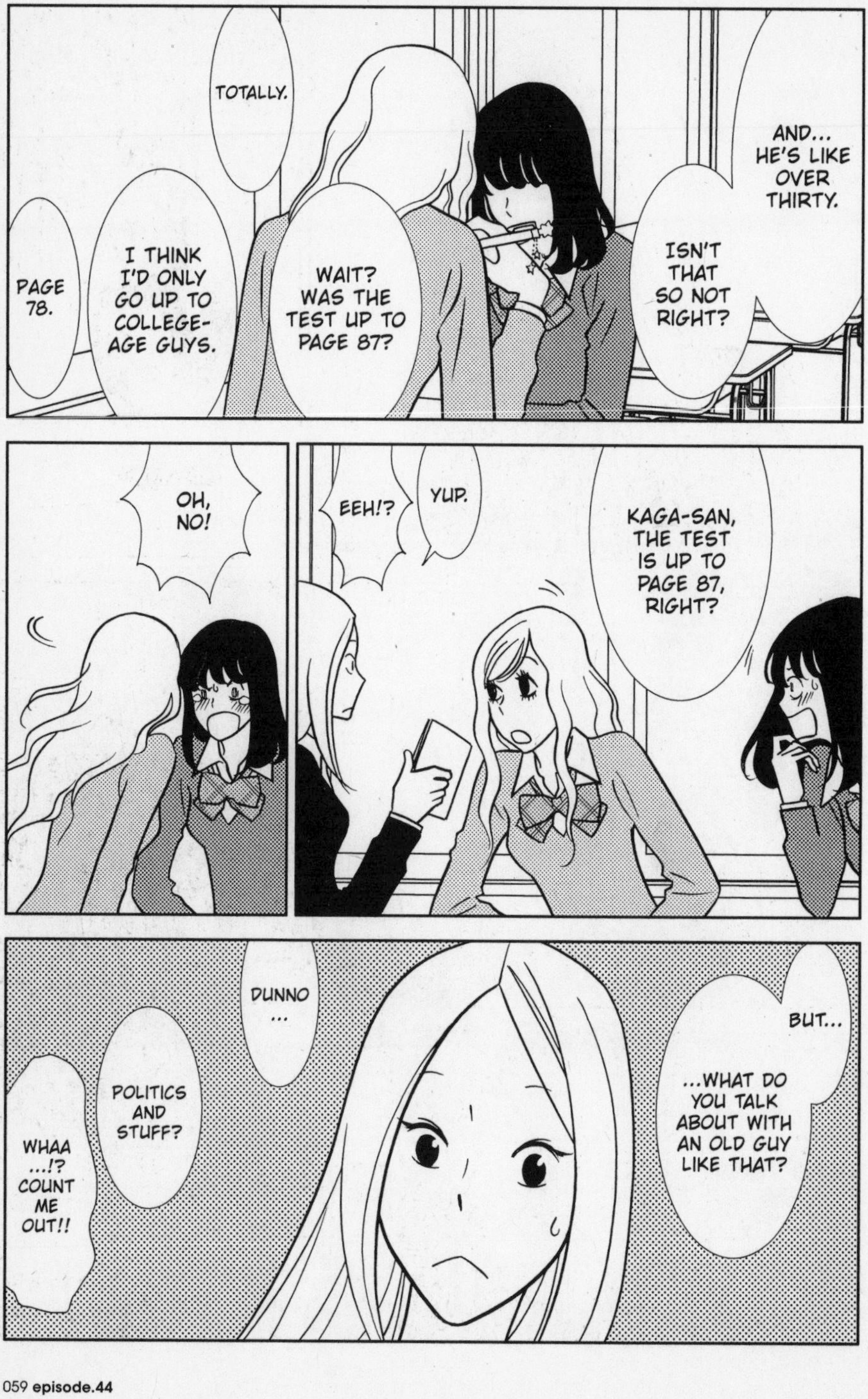
AND... HE'S LIKE OVER THIRTY.
ISN'T THAT SO NOT RIGHT?
TOTALLY.
I THINK I'D ONLY GO UP TO COLLEGE-AGE GUYS.
WAIT? WAS THE TEST UP TO PAGE 87?
PAGE 78.
KAGA-SAN, THE TEST IS UP TO PAGE 87, RIGHT?
YUP.
EEH!?
OH, NO!
BUT...
...WHAT DO YOU TALK ABOUT WITH AN OLD GUY LIKE THAT?
DUNNO...
POLITICS AND STUFF?
WHAA...!? COUNT ME OUT!!

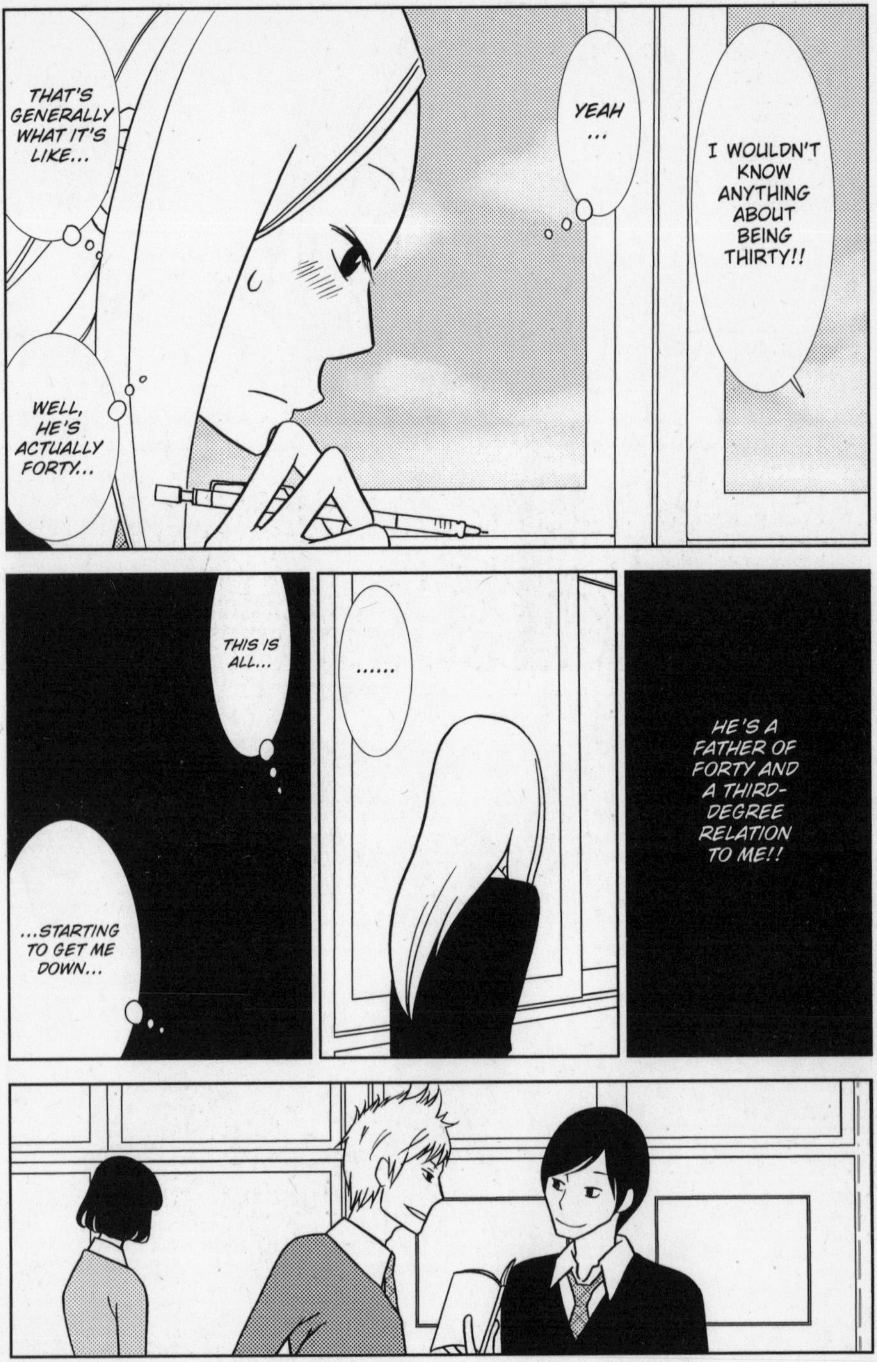
I WOULDN'T KNOW ANYTHING ABOUT BEING THIRTY!!
YEAH ...
THAT'S GENERALLY WHAT IT'S LIKE...
WELL, HE'S ACTUALLY FORTY...
HE'S A FATHER OF FORTY AND A THIRD-DEGREE RELATION TO ME!!
......
THIS IS ALL...
...STARTING TO GET ME DOWN...

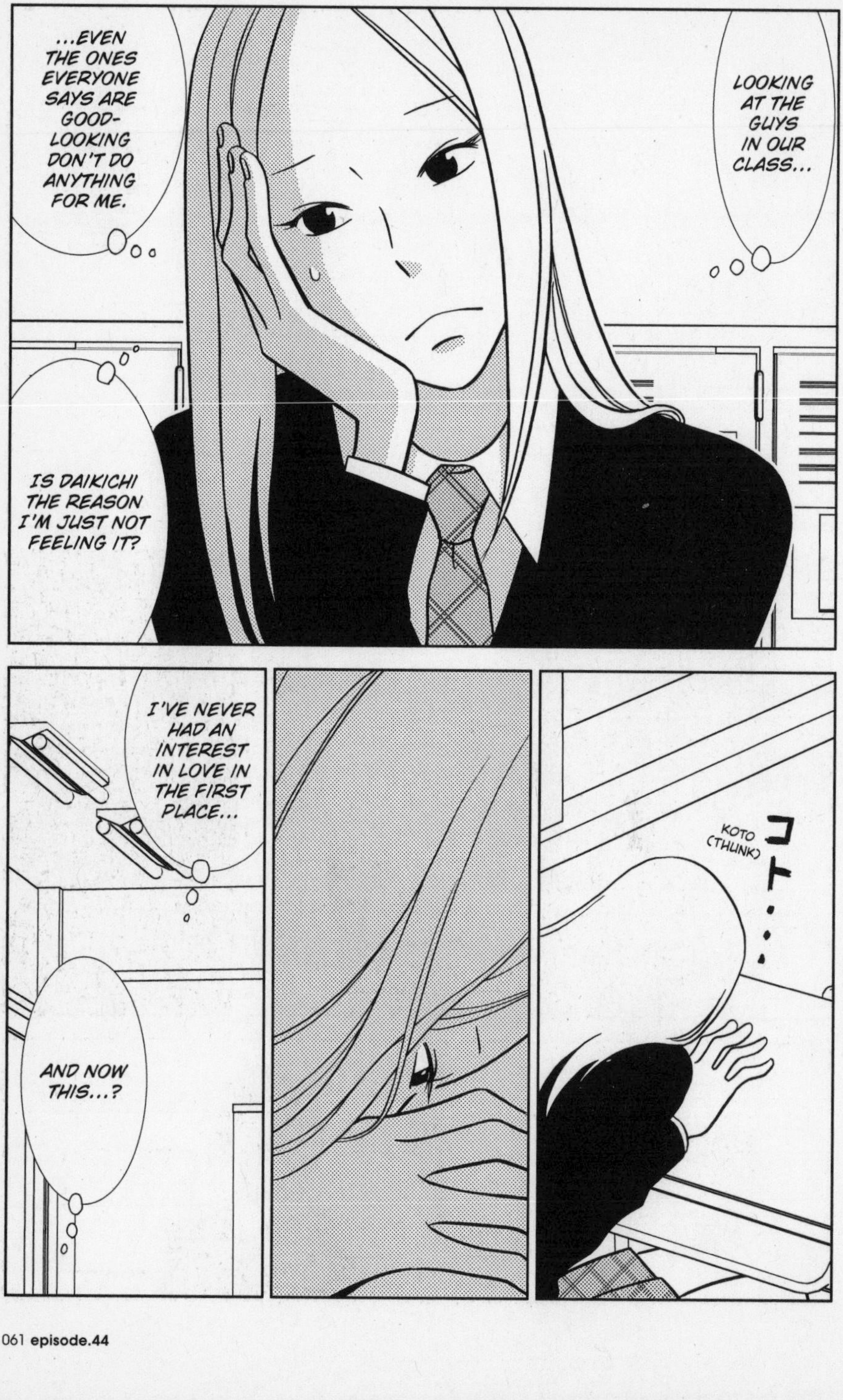
LOOKING AT THE GUYS IN OUR CLASS...
...EVEN THE ONES EVERYONE SAYS ARE GOOD-LOOKING DON'T DO ANYTHING FOR ME.
IS DAIKICHI THE REASON I'M JUST NOT FEELING IT?
コト...
KOTO (THUNK)
I'VE NEVER HAD AN INTEREST IN LOVE IN THE FIRST PLACE...
AND NOW THIS...?

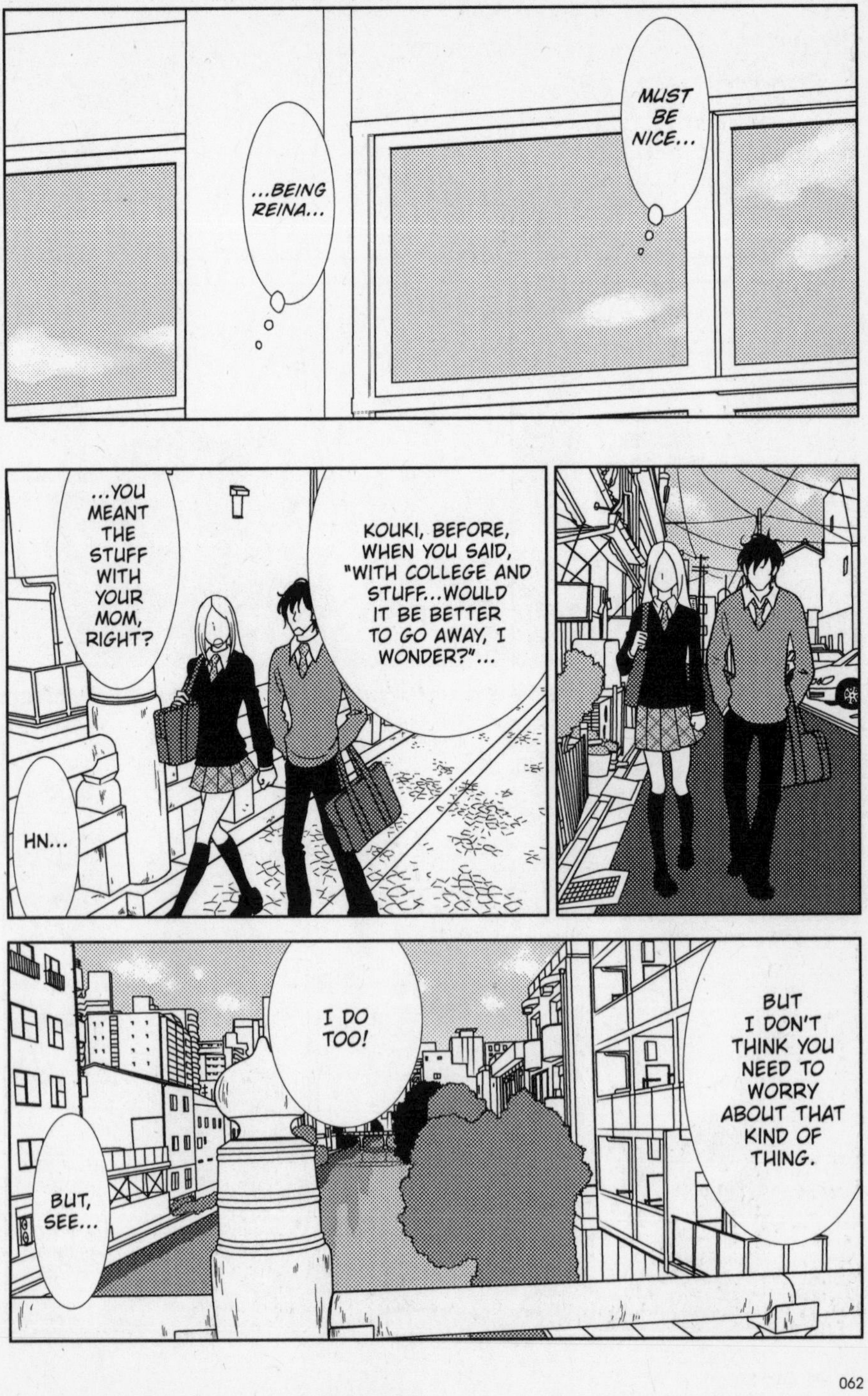
MUST BE NICE...
...BEING REINA...
KOUKI, BEFORE, WHEN YOU SAID, "WITH COLLEGE AND STUFF...WOULD IT BE BETTER TO GO AWAY, I WONDER?"...
...YOU MEANT THE STUFF WITH YOUR MOM, RIGHT?
HN...
BUT I DON'T THINK YOU NEED TO WORRY ABOUT THAT KIND OF THING.
I DO TOO!
BUT, SEE...

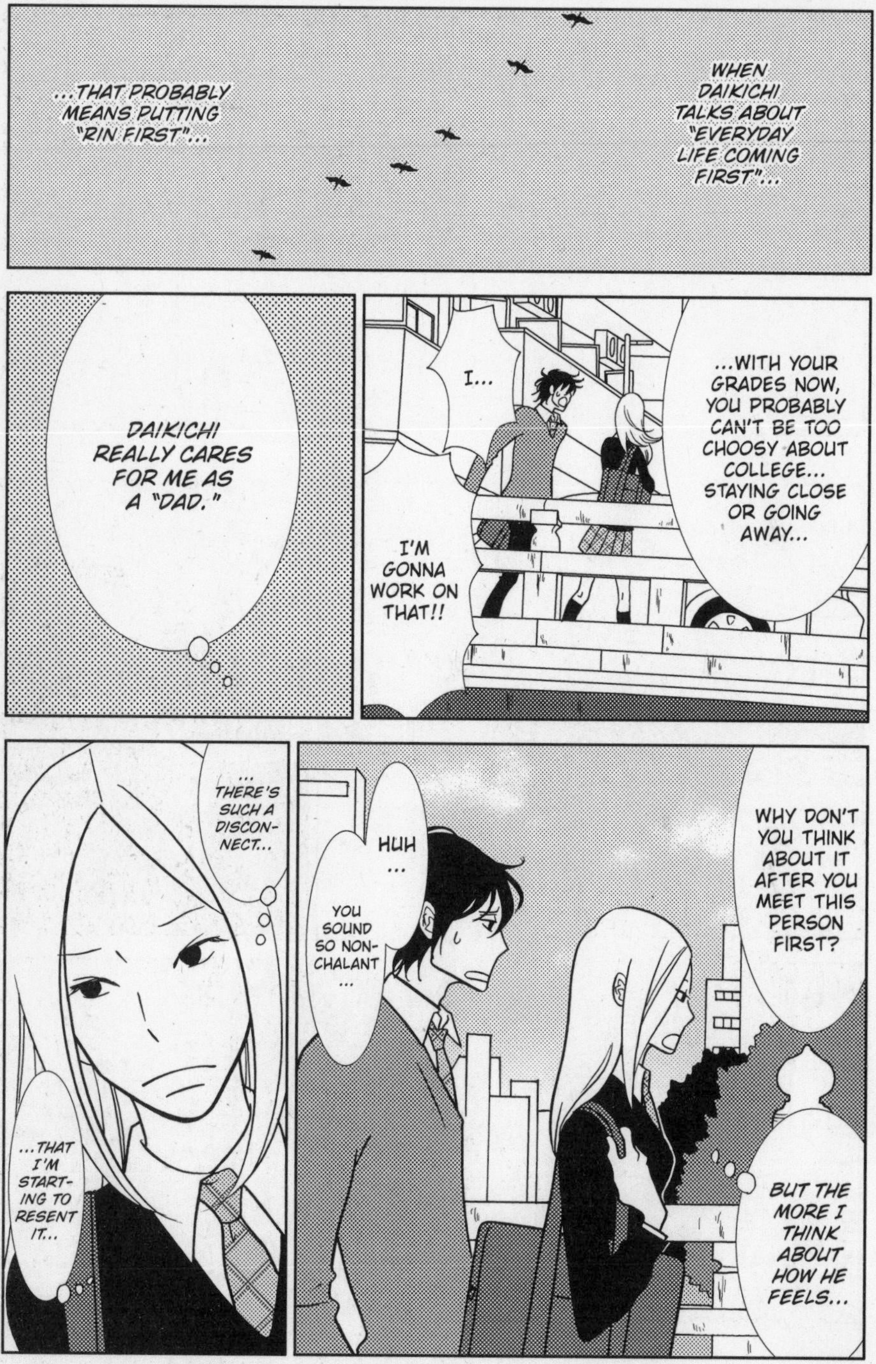
WHEN DAIKICHI TALKS ABOUT "EVERYDAY LIFE COMING FIRST"...
...THAT PROBABLY MEANS PUTTING "RIN FIRST"...
...WITH YOUR GRADES NOW, YOU PROBABLY CAN'T BE TOO CHOOSY ABOUT COLLEGE... STAYING CLOSE OR GOING AWAY...
I...
I'M GONNA WORK ON THAT!!
DAIKICHI REALLY CARES FOR ME AS A "DAD."
WHY DON'T YOU THINK ABOUT IT AFTER YOU MEET THIS PERSON FIRST?
HUH...
YOU SOUND SO NON-CHALANT...
BUT THE MORE I THINK ABOUT HOW HE FEELS...
...THERE'S SUCH A DISCON-NECT...
...THAT I'M START-ING TO RESENT IT...

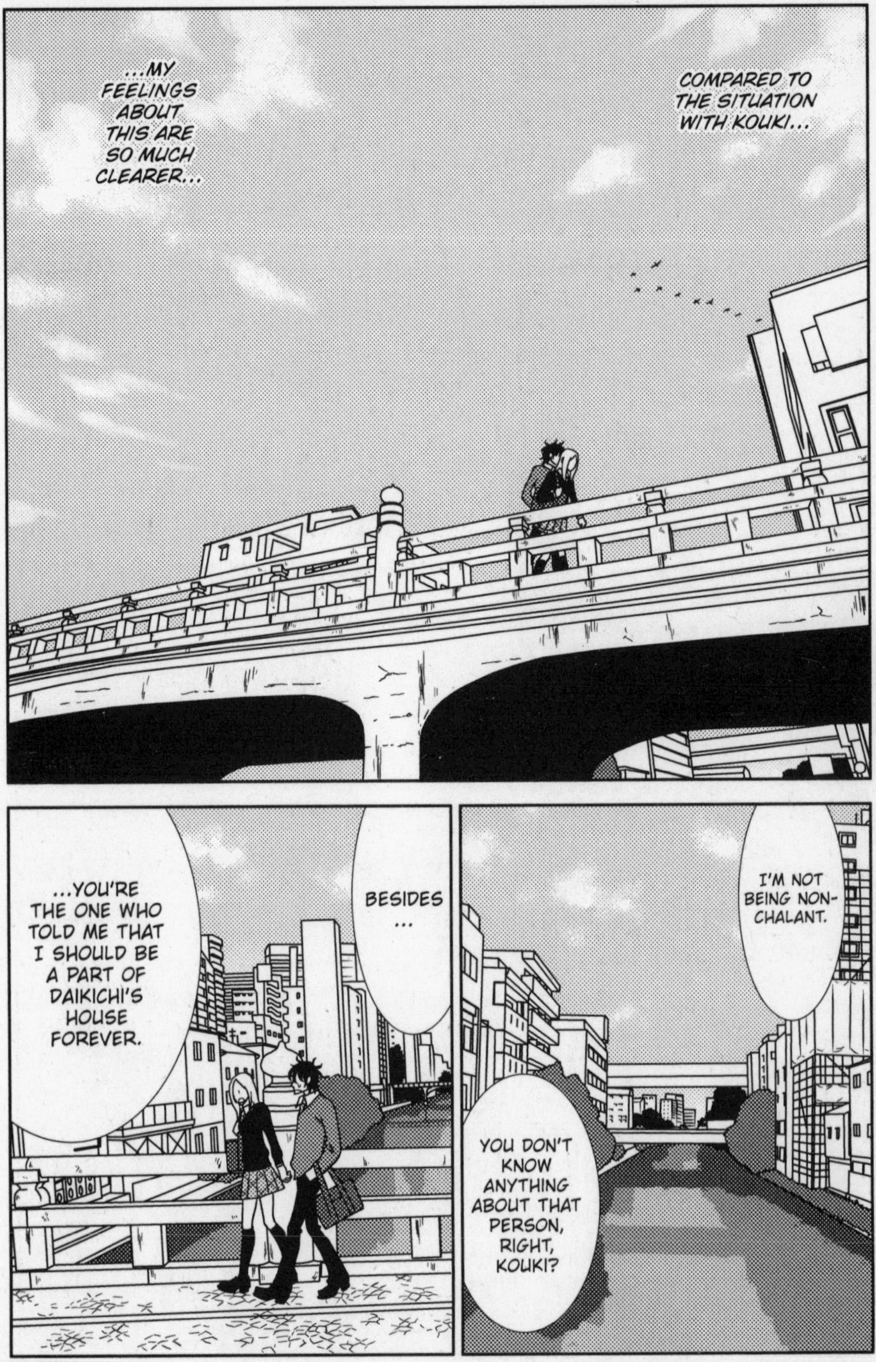
COMPARED TO THE SITUATION WITH KOUKI...
...MY FEELINGS ABOUT THIS ARE SO MUCH CLEARER...
I'M NOT BEING NON-CHALANT.
YOU DON'T KNOW ANYTHING ABOUT THAT PERSON, RIGHT, KOUKI?
BESIDES...
...YOU'RE THE ONE WHO TOLD ME THAT I SHOULD BE A PART OF DAIKICHI'S HOUSE FOREVER.

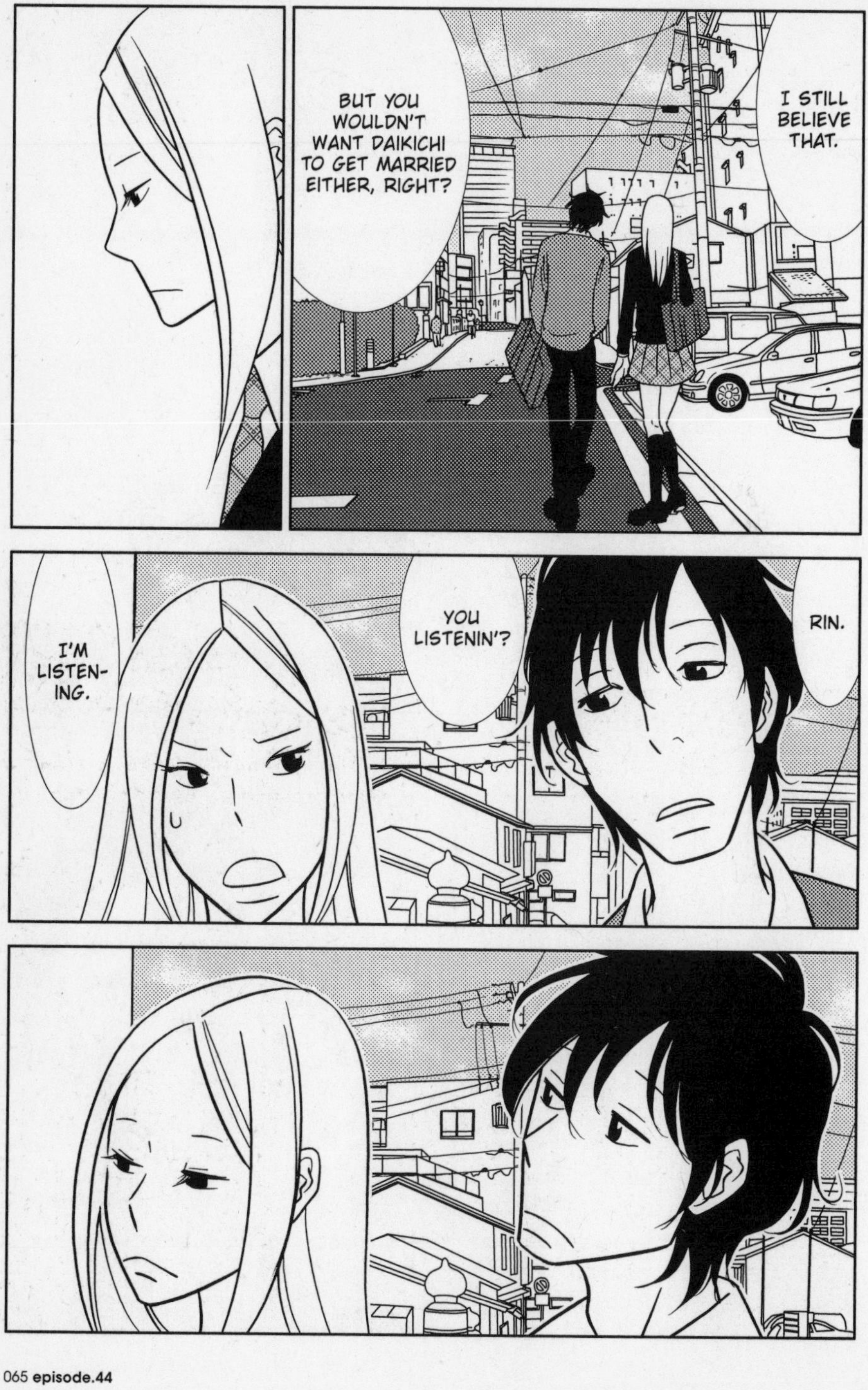
I STILL BELIEVE THAT.
BUT YOU WOULDN'T WANT DAIKICHI TO GET MARRIED EITHER, RIGHT?
RIN.
YOU LISTENIN'?
I'M LISTEN-ING.

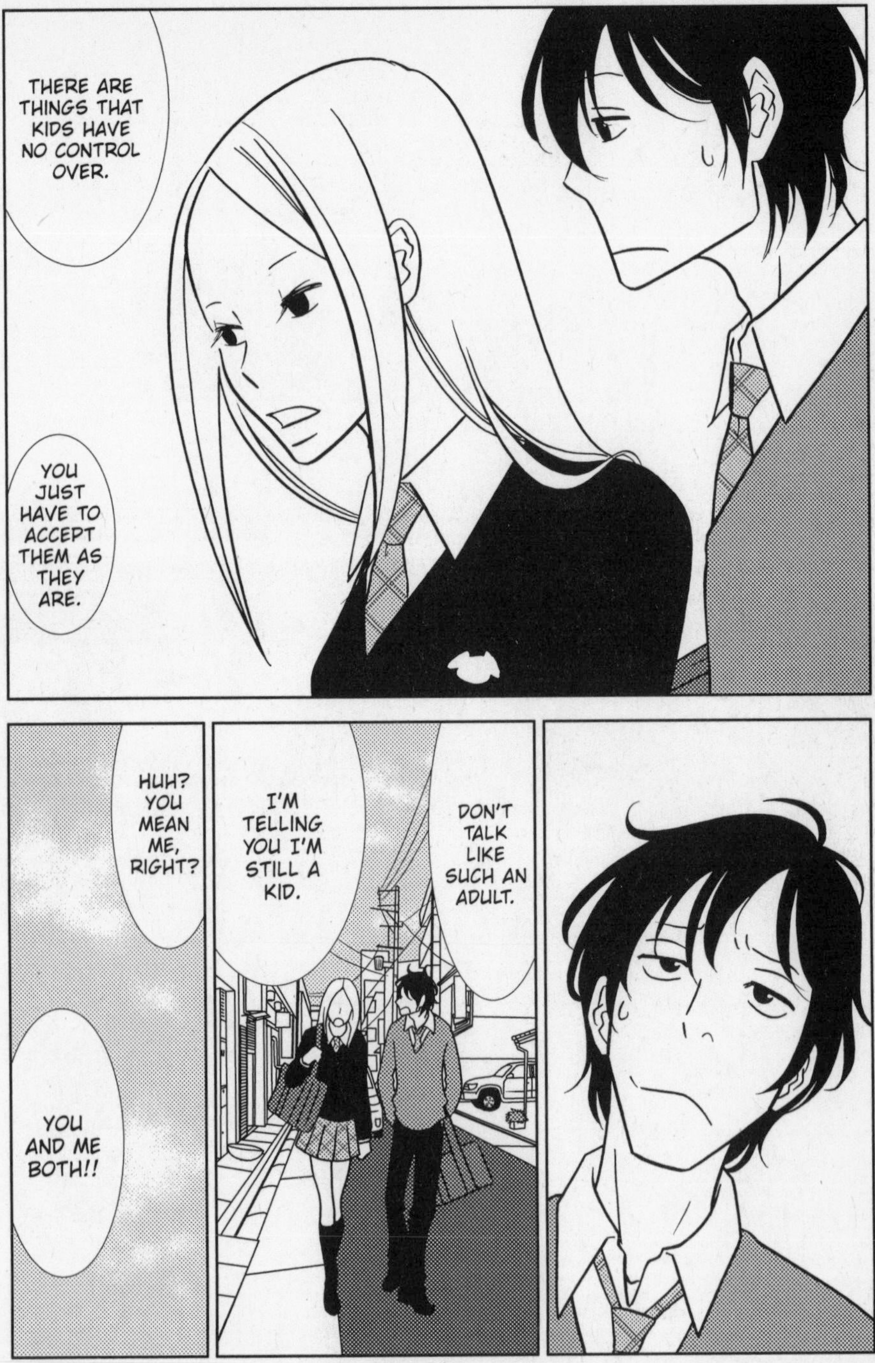
THERE ARE THINGS THAT KIDS HAVE NO CONTROL OVER.
YOU JUST HAVE TO ACCEPT THEM AS THEY ARE.
DON'T TALK LIKE SUCH AN ADULT.
I'M TELLING YOU I'M STILL A KID.
HUH? YOU MEAN ME, RIGHT?
YOU AND ME BOTH!!

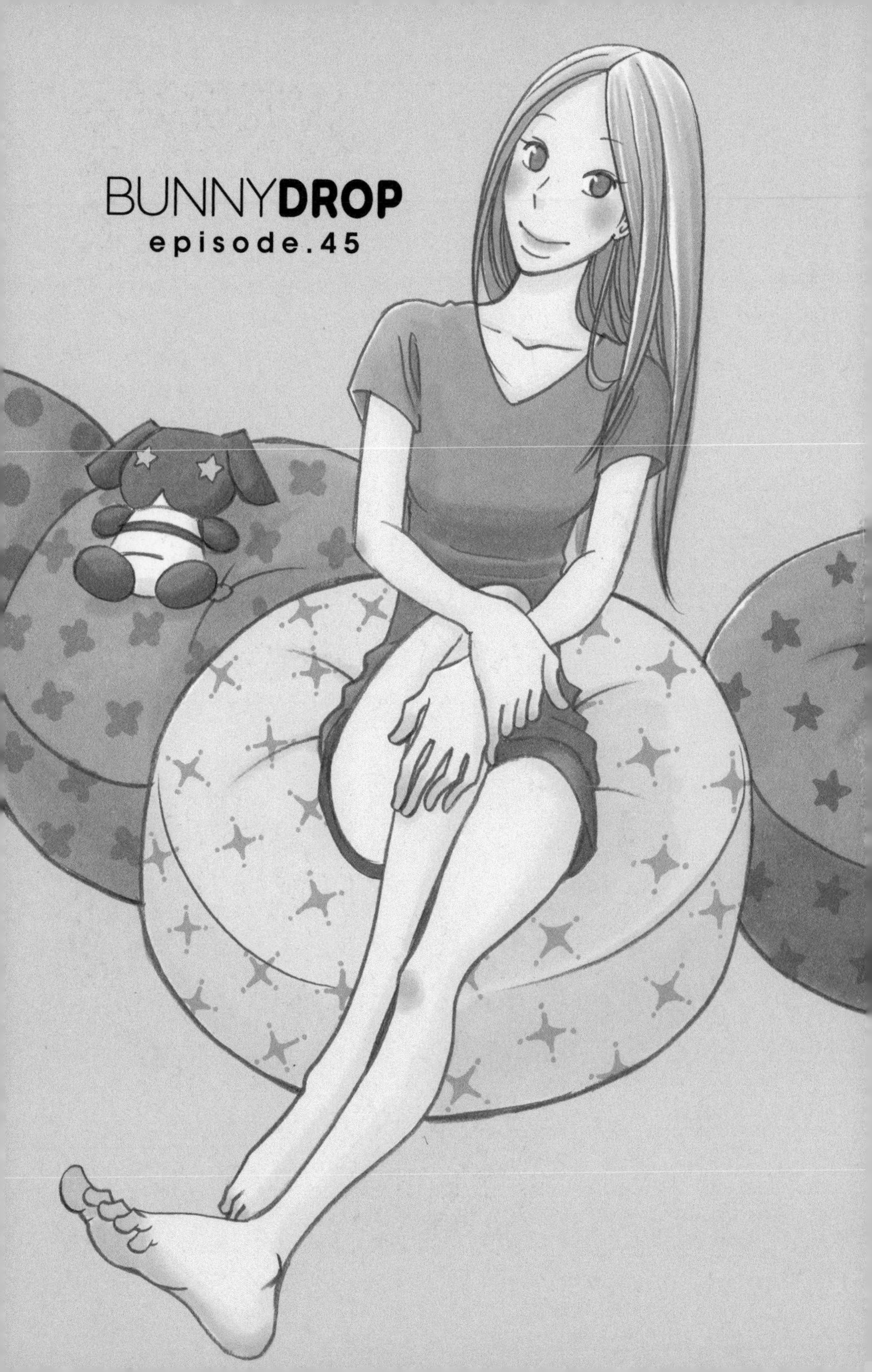
BUNNYDROP
episode.45

BUNNY**DROP**

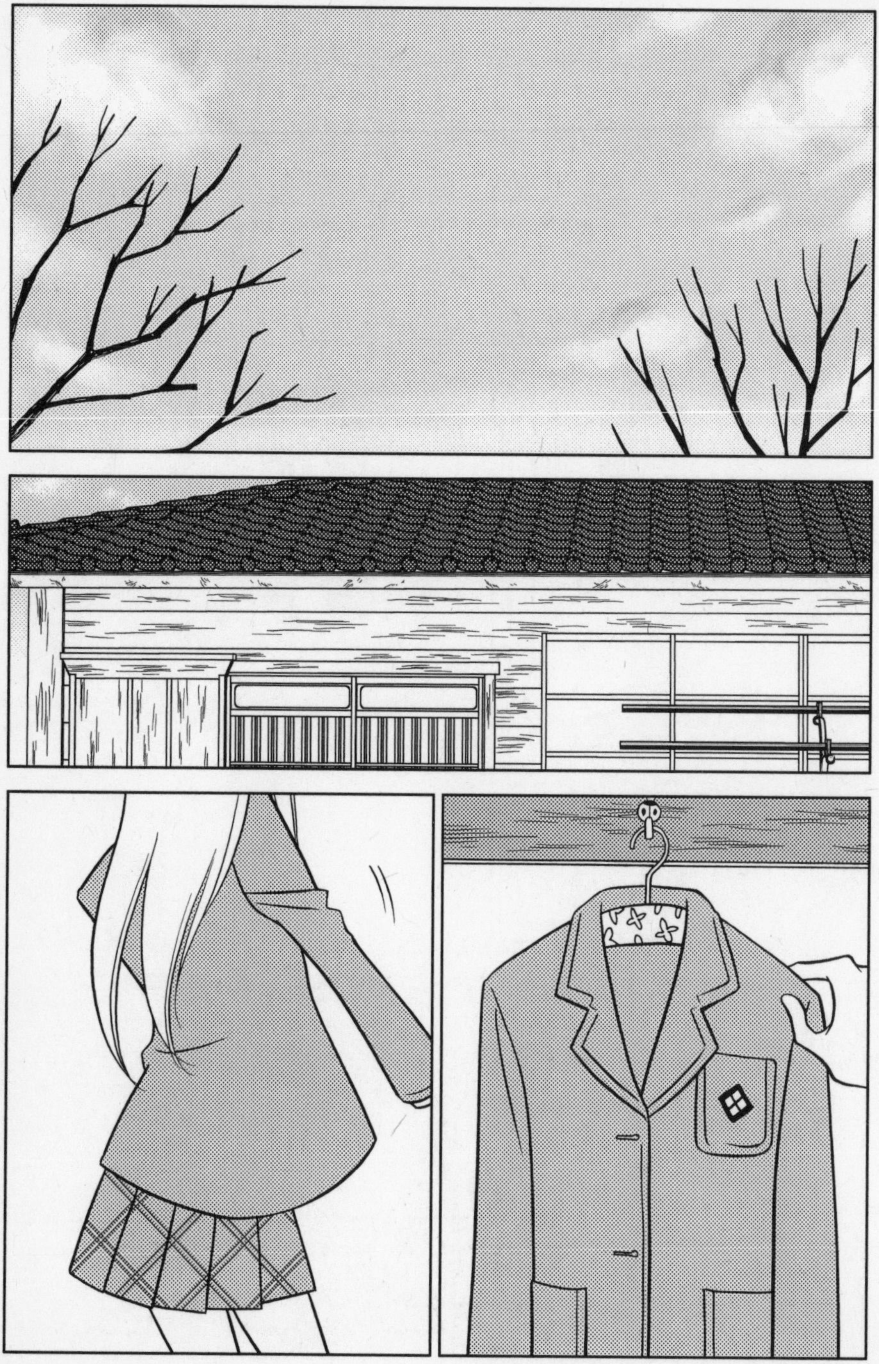

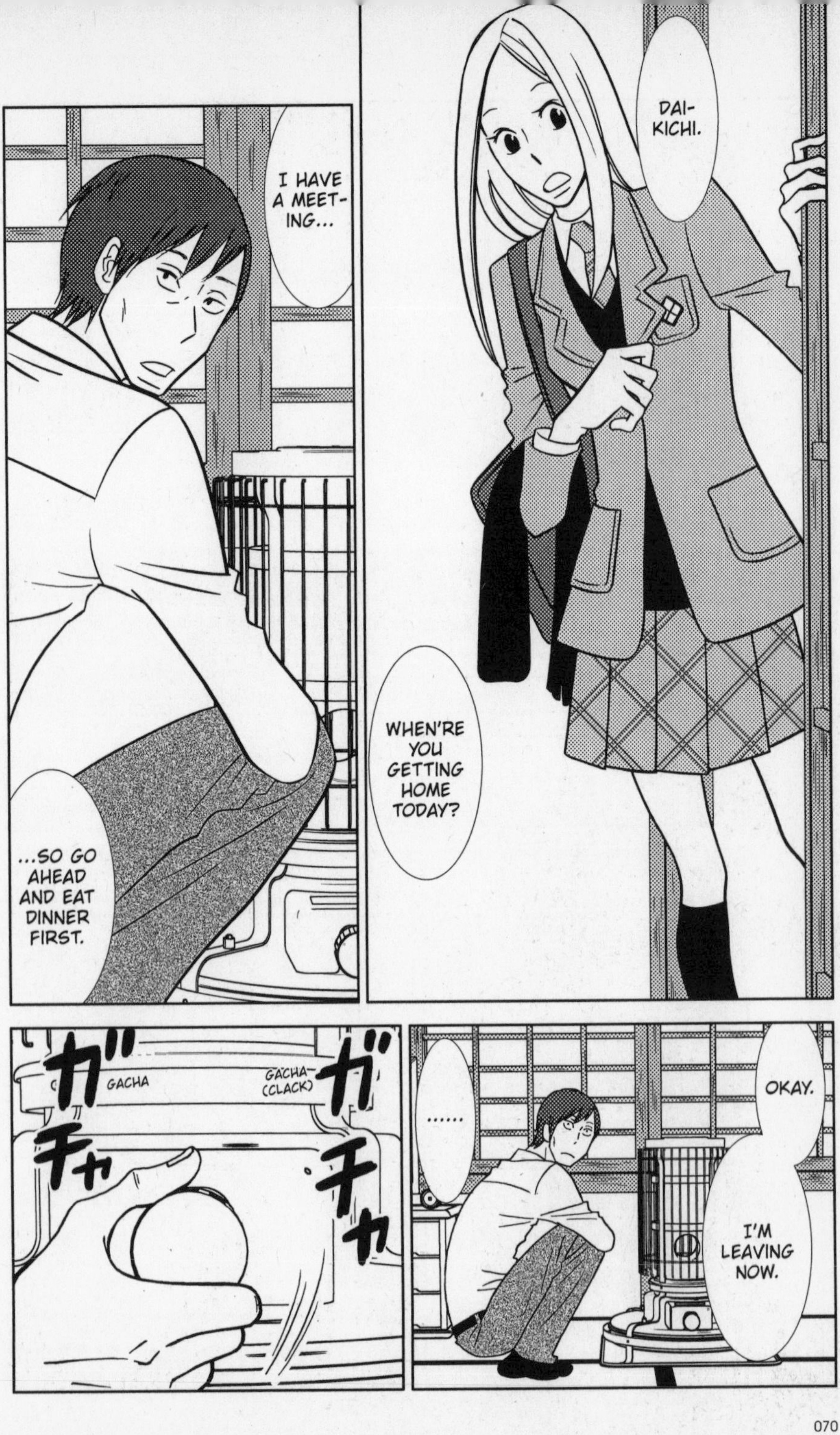
DAI-KICHI.
WHEN'RE YOU GETTING HOME TODAY?
I HAVE A MEET-ING...
...SO GO AHEAD AND EAT DINNER FIRST.
OKAY.
I'M LEAVING NOW.
......
ガチャ
GACHA (CLACK)
ガチャ
GACHA

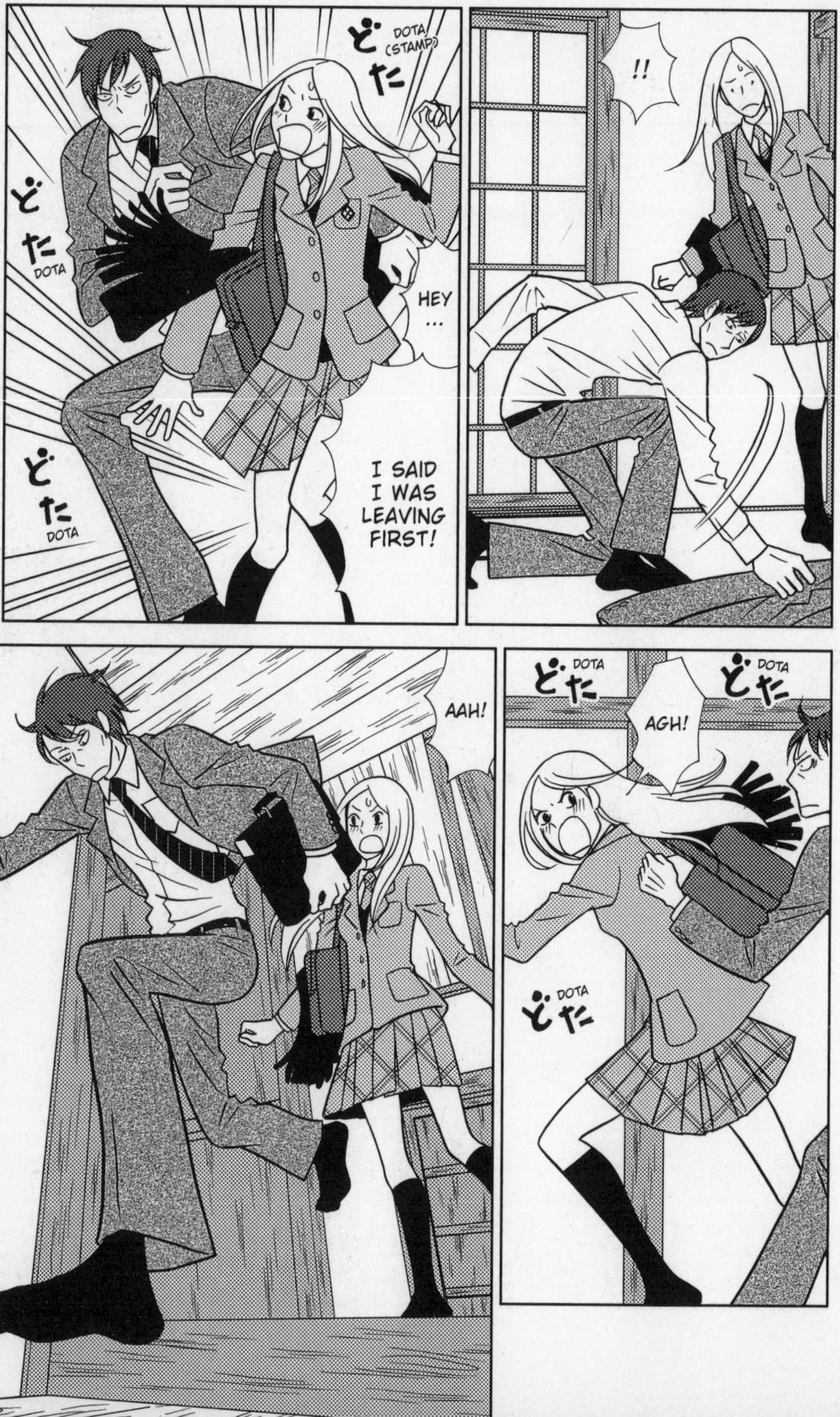
!!
どた
DOTA (STAMP)
HEY ...
I SAID I WAS LEAVING FIRST!
どた
DOTA
どた
DOTA
どた
DOTA
AGH!
どた
DOTA
どた
DOTA
AAH!

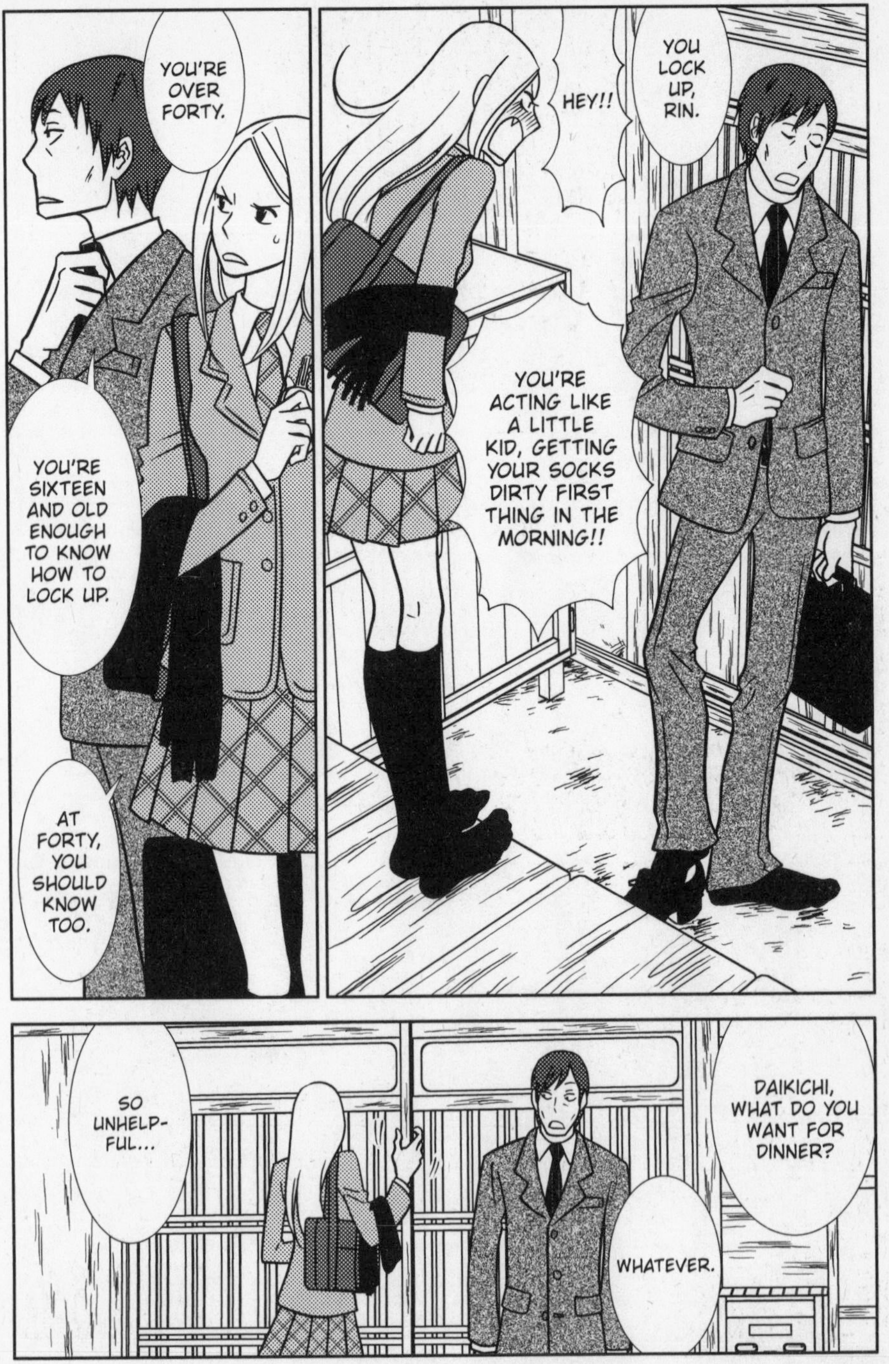
YOU LOCK UP, RIN.
HEY!!
YOU'RE ACTING LIKE A LITTLE KID, GETTING YOUR SOCKS DIRTY FIRST THING IN THE MORNING!!
YOU'RE OVER FORTY.
YOU'RE SIXTEEN AND OLD ENOUGH TO KNOW HOW TO LOCK UP.
AT FORTY, YOU SHOULD KNOW TOO.
DAIKICHI, WHAT DO YOU WANT FOR DINNER?
WHATEVER.
SO UNHELP-FUL...

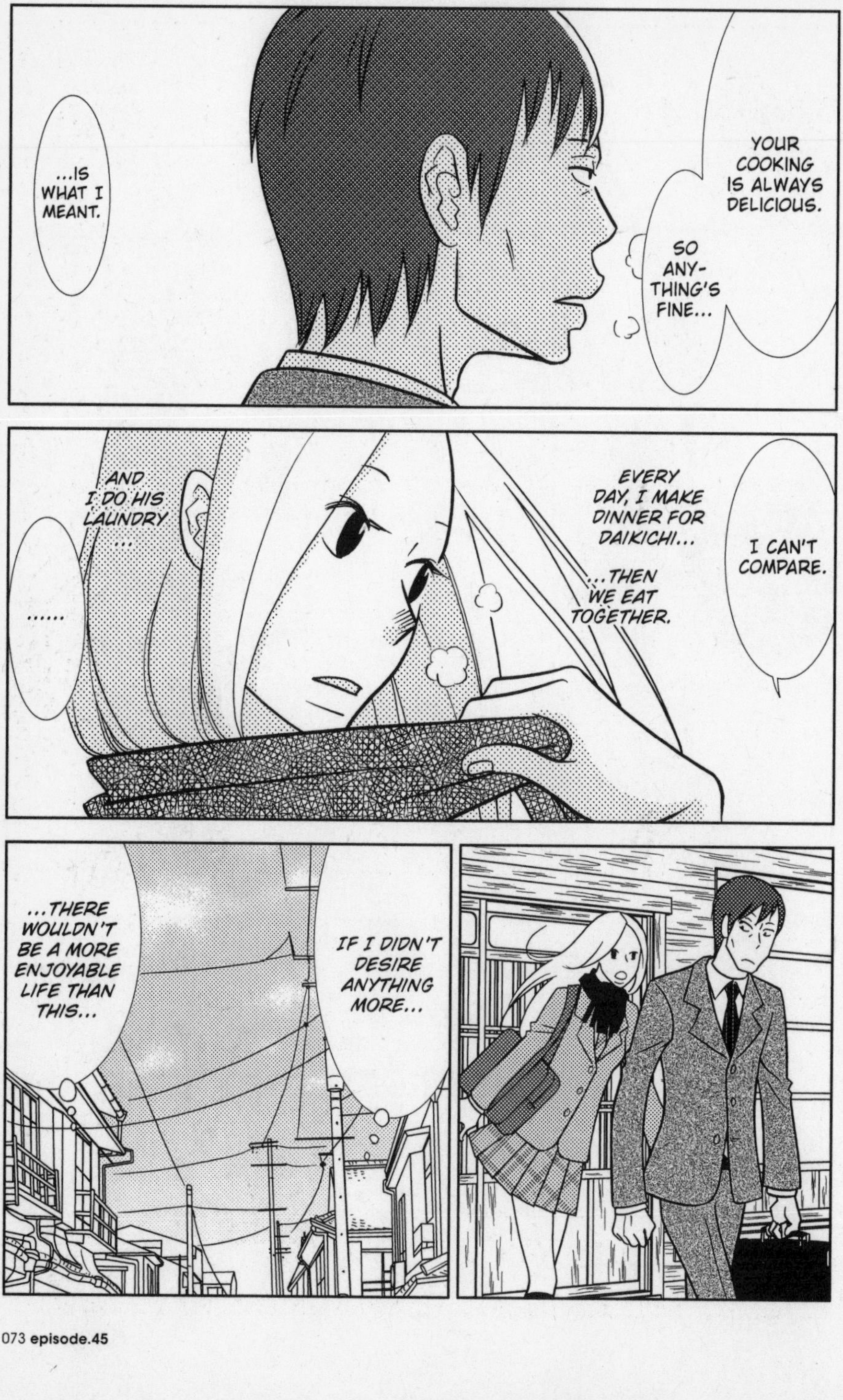
YOUR COOKING IS ALWAYS DELICIOUS.
SO ANYTHING'S FINE...
...IS WHAT I MEANT.
I CAN'T COMPARE.
EVERY DAY, I MAKE DINNER FOR DAIKICHI...
...THEN WE EAT TOGETHER.
AND I DO HIS LAUNDRY...
......
IF I DIDN'T DESIRE ANYTHING MORE...
...THERE WOULDN'T BE A MORE ENJOYABLE LIFE THAN THIS...

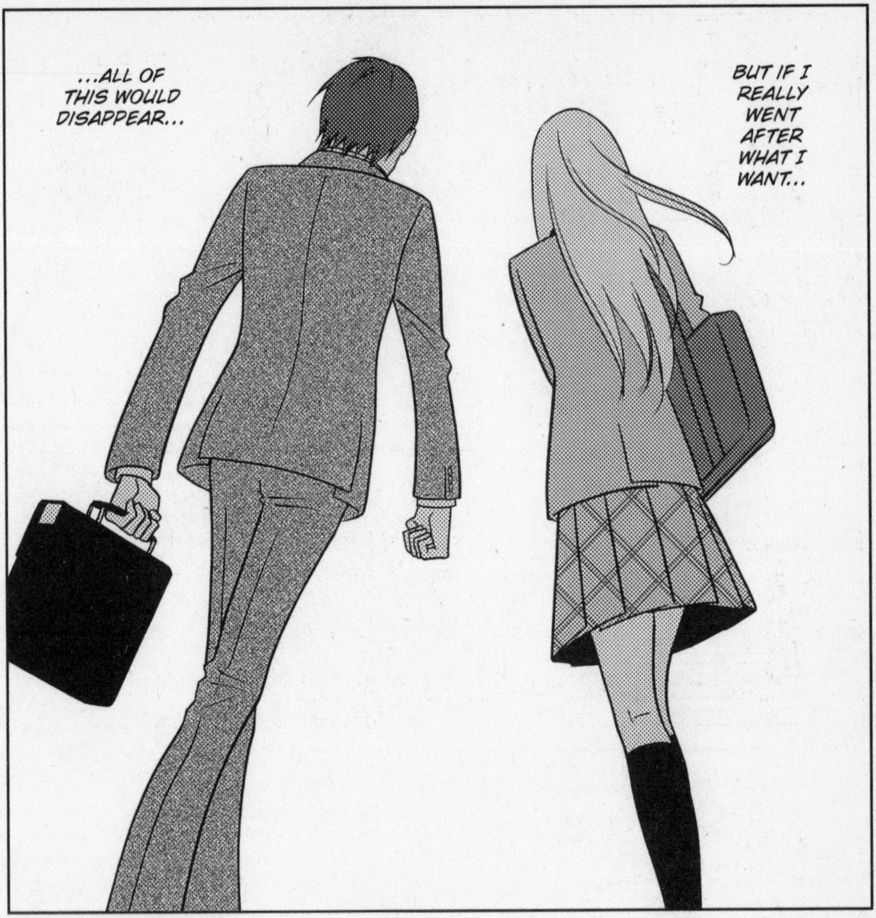
BUT IF I REALLY WENT AFTER WHAT I WANT...
...ALL OF THIS WOULD DISAPPEAR...

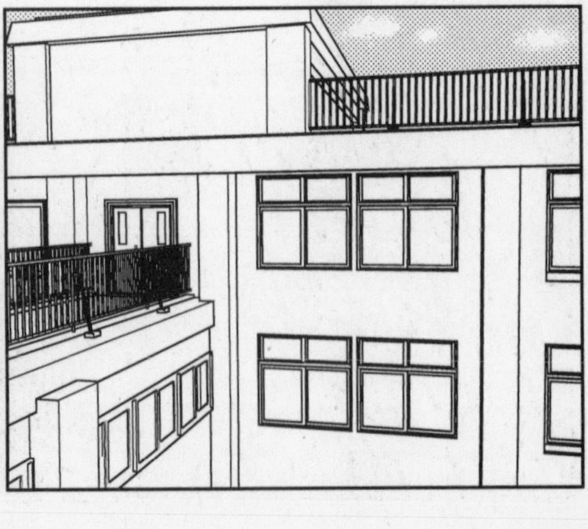

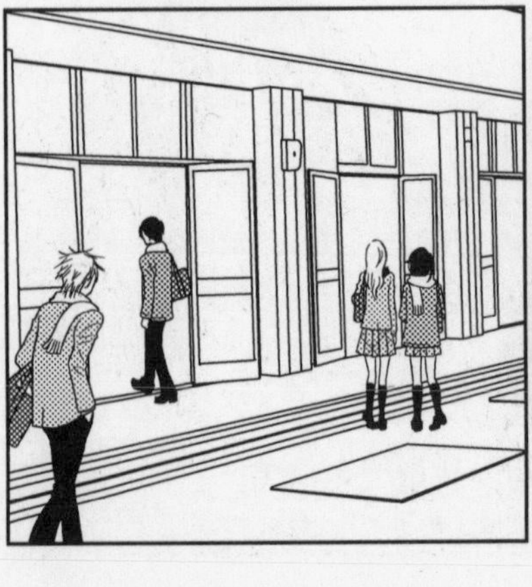

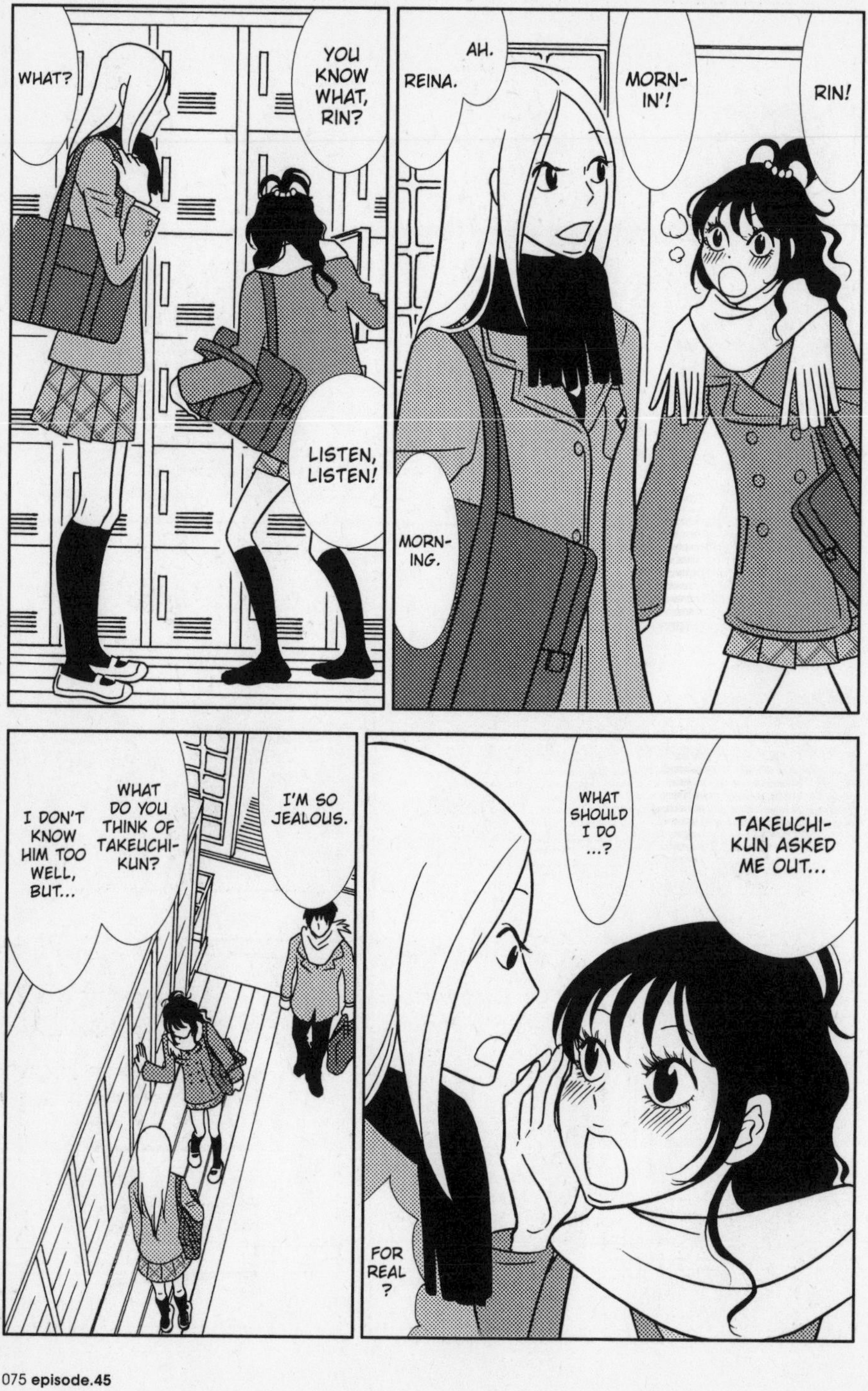
RIN!
MORN-IN'!
AH. REINA.
MORN-ING.
YOU KNOW WHAT, RIN?
WHAT?
LISTEN, LISTEN!
TAKEUCHI-KUN ASKED ME OUT...
WHAT SHOULD I DO ...?
FOR REAL ?
I'M SO JEALOUS.
WHAT DO YOU THINK OF TAKEUCHI-KUN?
I DON'T KNOW HIM TOO WELL, BUT...

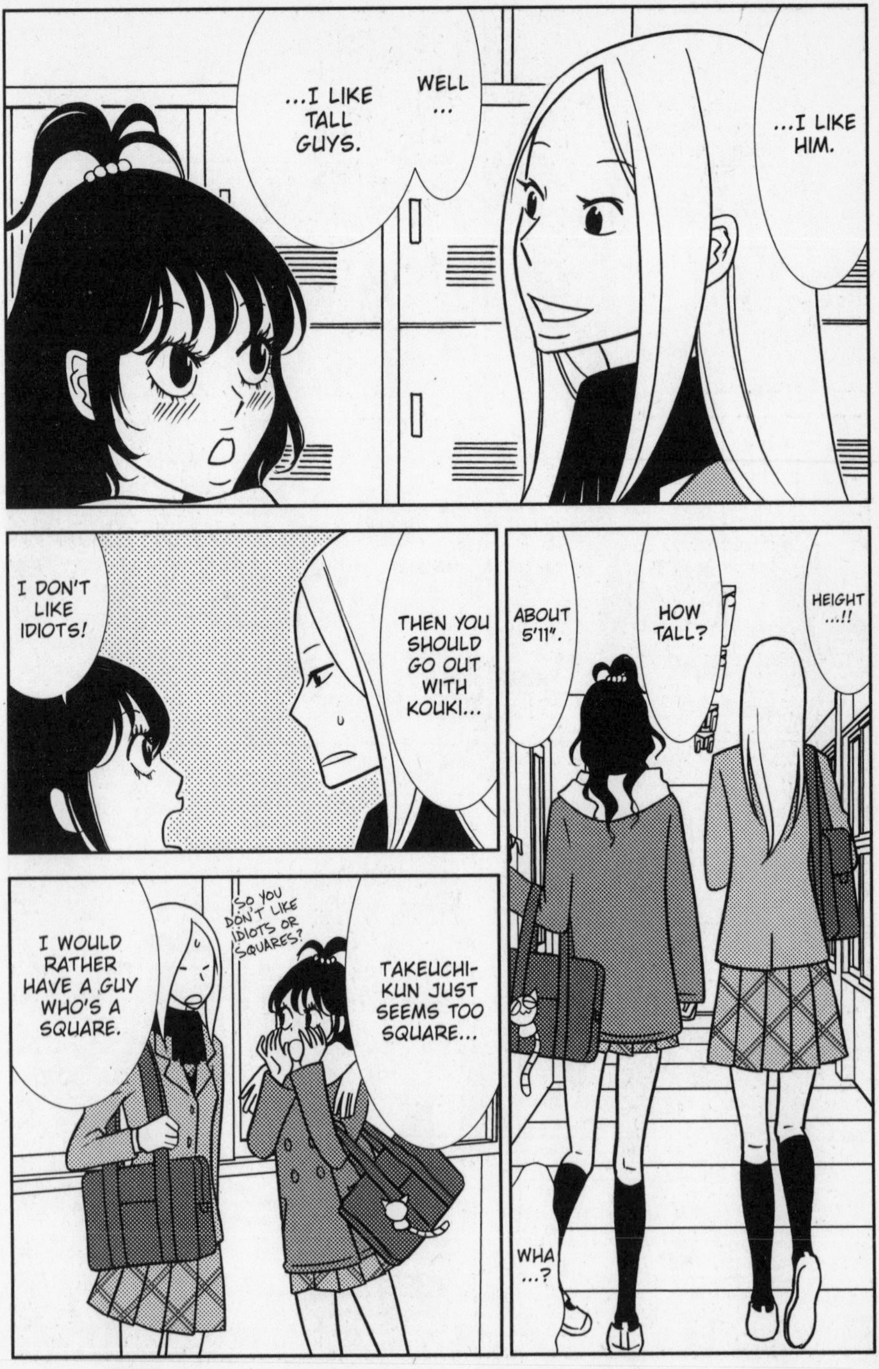
...I LIKE HIM.
WELL...
...I LIKE TALL GUYS.
HEIGHT ...!!
HOW TALL?
ABOUT 5'11".
WHA ...?
THEN YOU SHOULD GO OUT WITH KOUKI...
I DON'T LIKE IDIOTS!
TAKEUCHI-KUN JUST SEEMS TOO SQUARE...
SO YOU DON'T LIKE IDIOTS OR SQUARES?
I WOULD RATHER HAVE A GUY WHO'S A SQUARE.

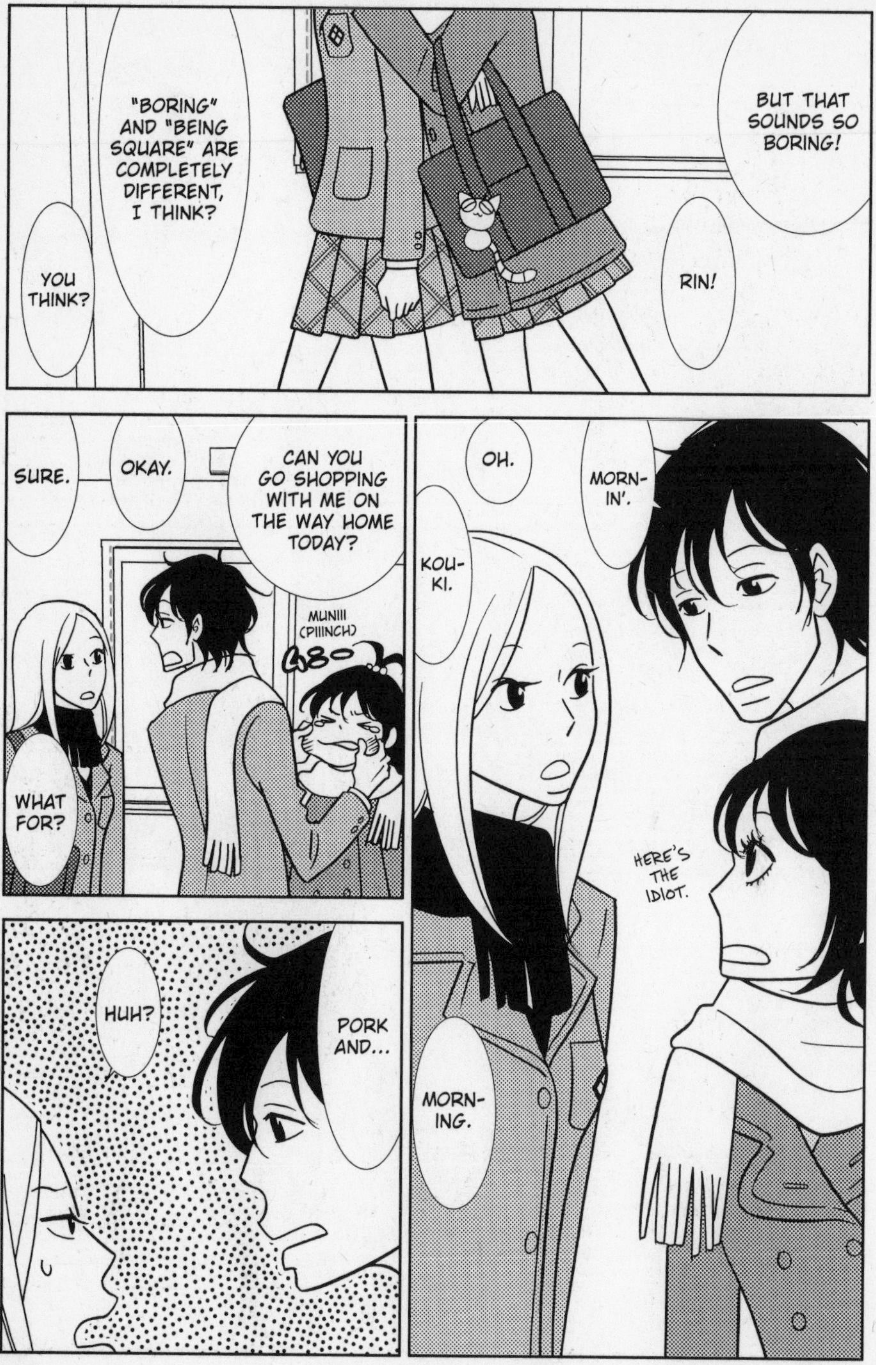
BUT THAT SOUNDS SO BORING!
RIN!
"BORING" AND "BEING SQUARE" ARE COMPLETELY DIFFERENT, I THINK?
YOU THINK?
MORN-IN'.
OH.
KOU-KI.
HERE'S THE IDIOT.
MORN-ING.
CAN YOU GO SHOPPING WITH ME ON THE WAY HOME TODAY?
OKAY.
SURE.
MUNIII (PIIINCH)
WHAT FOR?
PORK AND...
HUH?

OH...
I'LL TALK TO YOU ABOUT IT LATER.
OKAY.
OH.
KOUKI'S HERE.
SORRY, REINA.
IT'S OKAY.

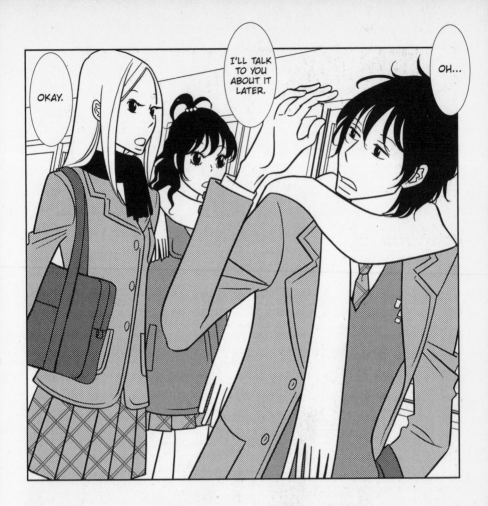

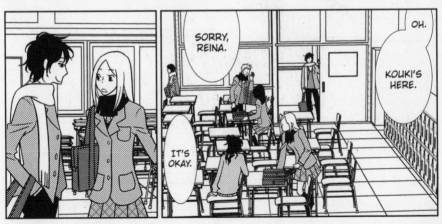

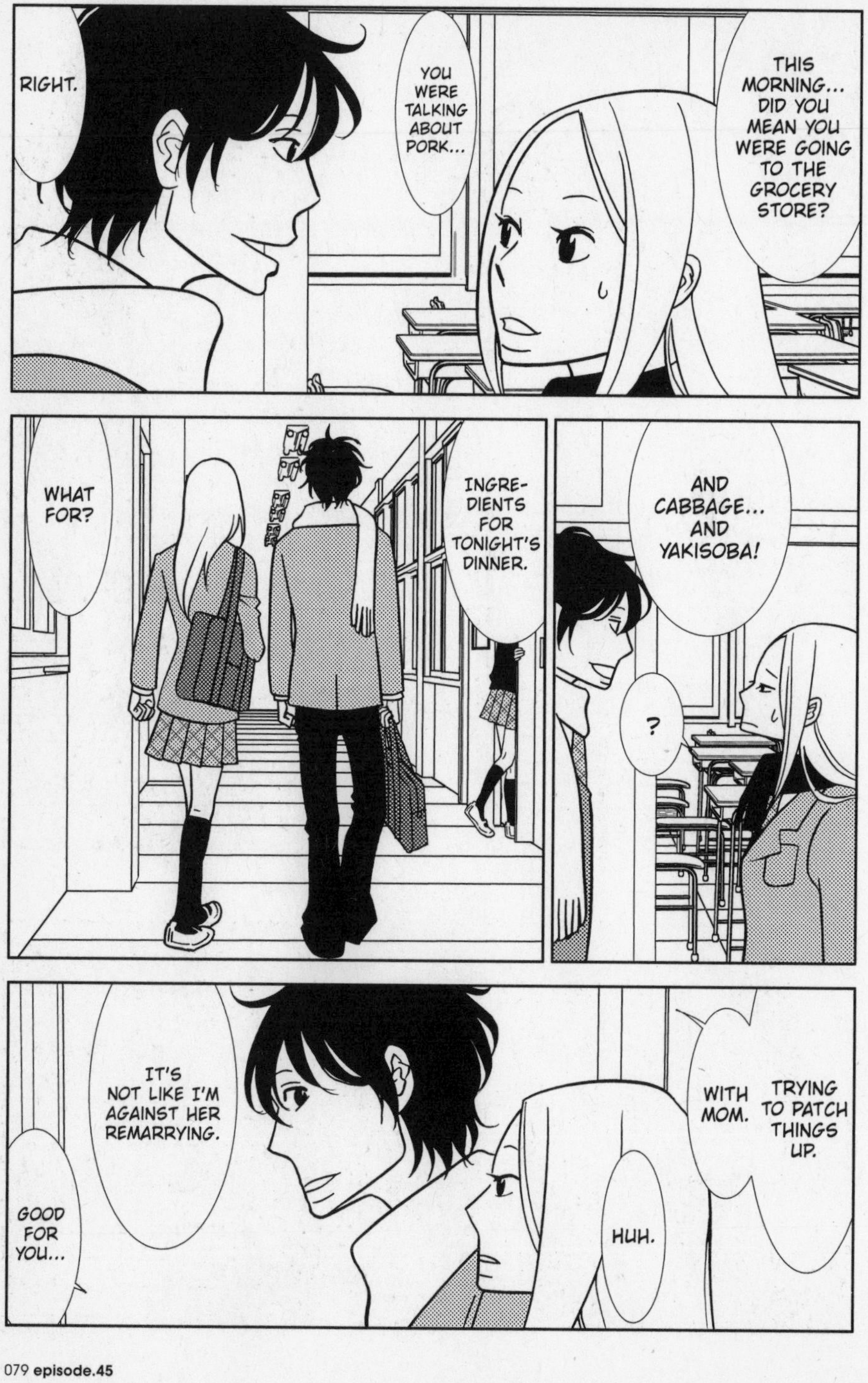
THIS MORNING... DID YOU MEAN YOU WERE GOING TO THE GROCERY STORE?
YOU WERE TALKING ABOUT PORK...
RIGHT.
AND CABBAGE... AND YAKISOBA!
?
INGRE-DIENTS FOR TONIGHT'S DINNER.
WHAT FOR?
TRYING TO PATCH THINGS UP.
WITH MOM.
HUH.
IT'S NOT LIKE I'M AGAINST HER REMARRYING.
GOOD FOR YOU...

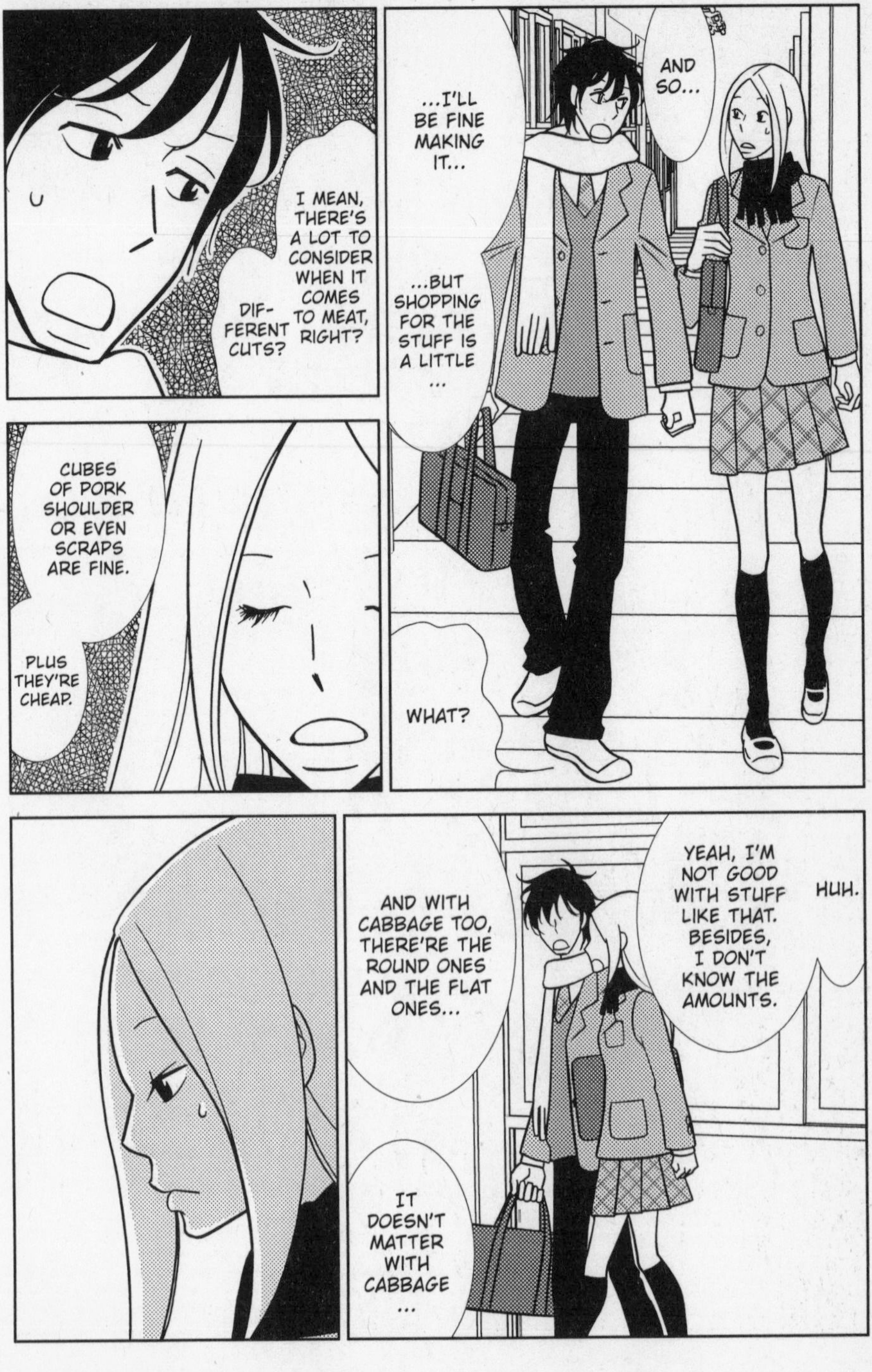
AND SO...
...I'LL BE FINE MAKING IT...
...BUT SHOPPING FOR THE STUFF IS A LITTLE ...
WHAT?
I MEAN, THERE'S A LOT TO CONSIDER WHEN IT COMES TO MEAT, RIGHT?
DIF-FERENT CUTS?
CUBES OF PORK SHOULDER OR EVEN SCRAPS ARE FINE.
PLUS THEY'RE CHEAP.
HUH.
YEAH, I'M NOT GOOD WITH STUFF LIKE THAT. BESIDES, I DON'T KNOW THE AMOUNTS.
AND WITH CABBAGE TOO, THERE'RE THE ROUND ONES AND THE FLAT ONES...
IT DOESN'T MATTER WITH CABBAGE ...

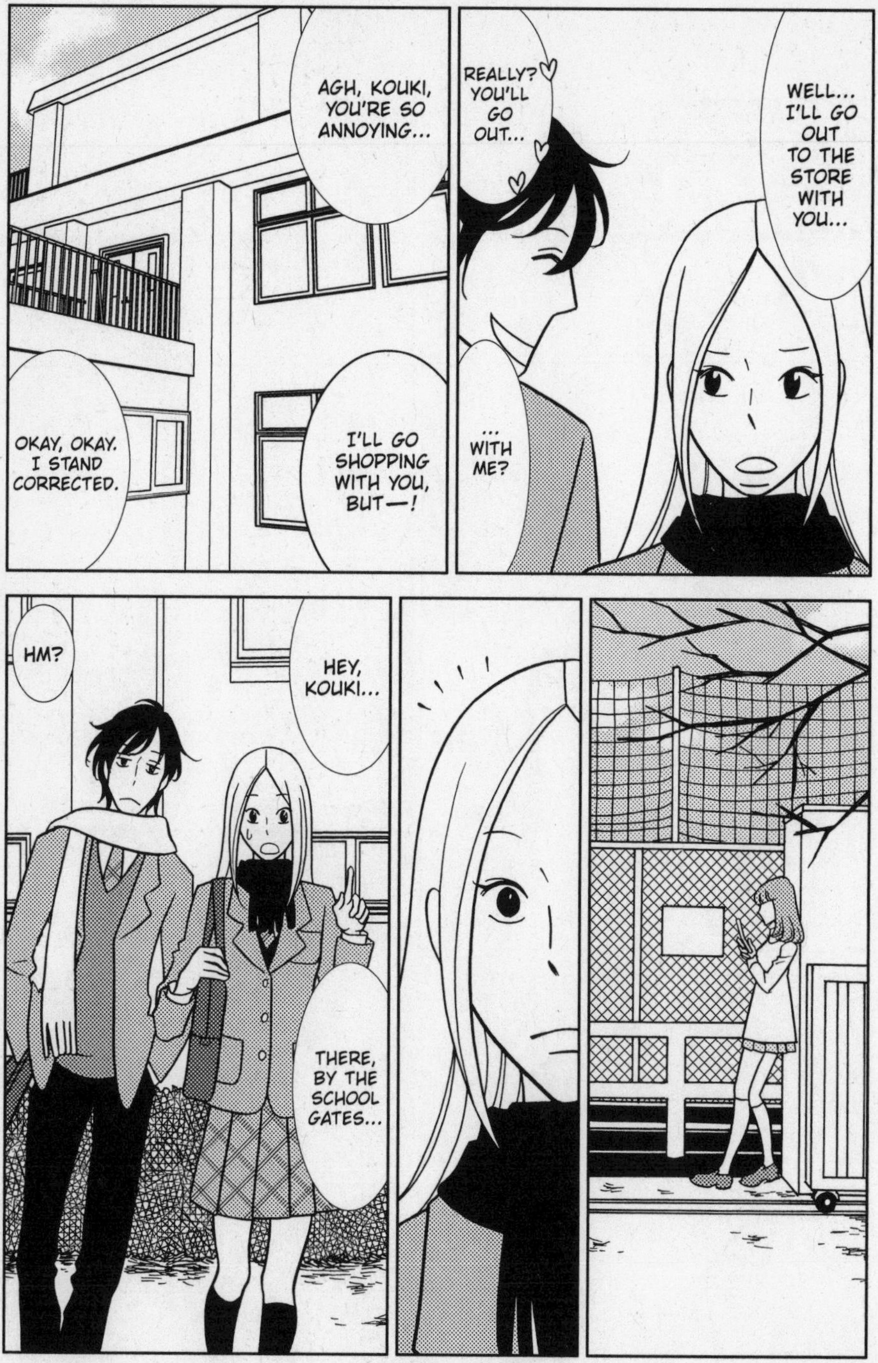
WELL... I'LL GO OUT TO THE STORE WITH YOU...
REALLY? YOU'LL GO OUT...
...WITH ME?
AGH, KOUKI, YOU'RE SO ANNOYING...
I'LL GO SHOPPING WITH YOU, BUT—!
OKAY, OKAY. I STAND CORRECTED.
HEY, KOUKI...
HM?
THERE, BY THE SCHOOL GATES...

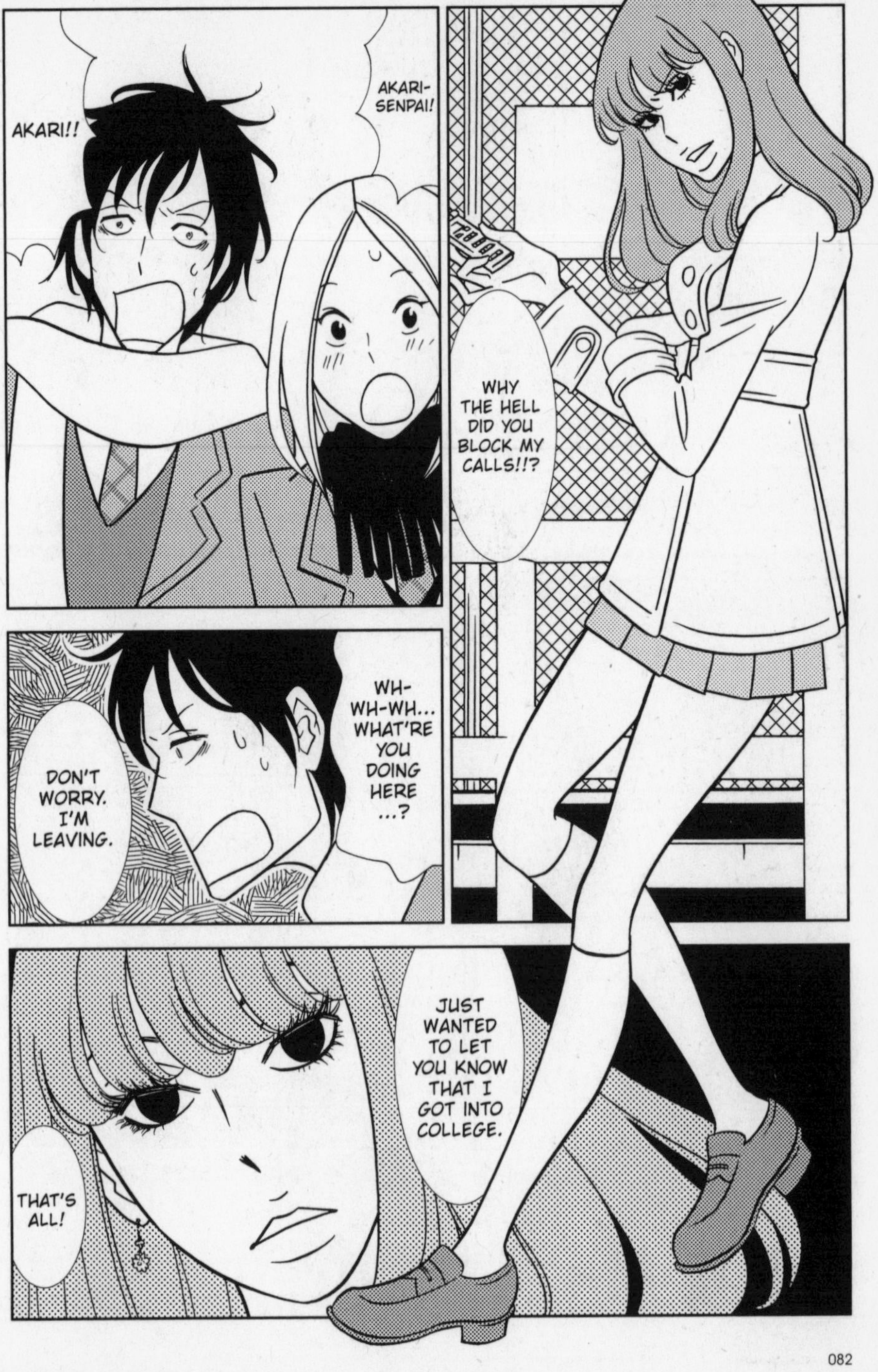
WHY THE HELL DID YOU BLOCK MY CALLS!!?
AKARI-SENPAI!
AKARI!!
WH-WH-WH... WHAT'RE YOU DOING HERE ...?
DON'T WORRY. I'M LEAVING.
JUST WANTED TO LET YOU KNOW THAT I GOT INTO COLLEGE.
THAT'S ALL!

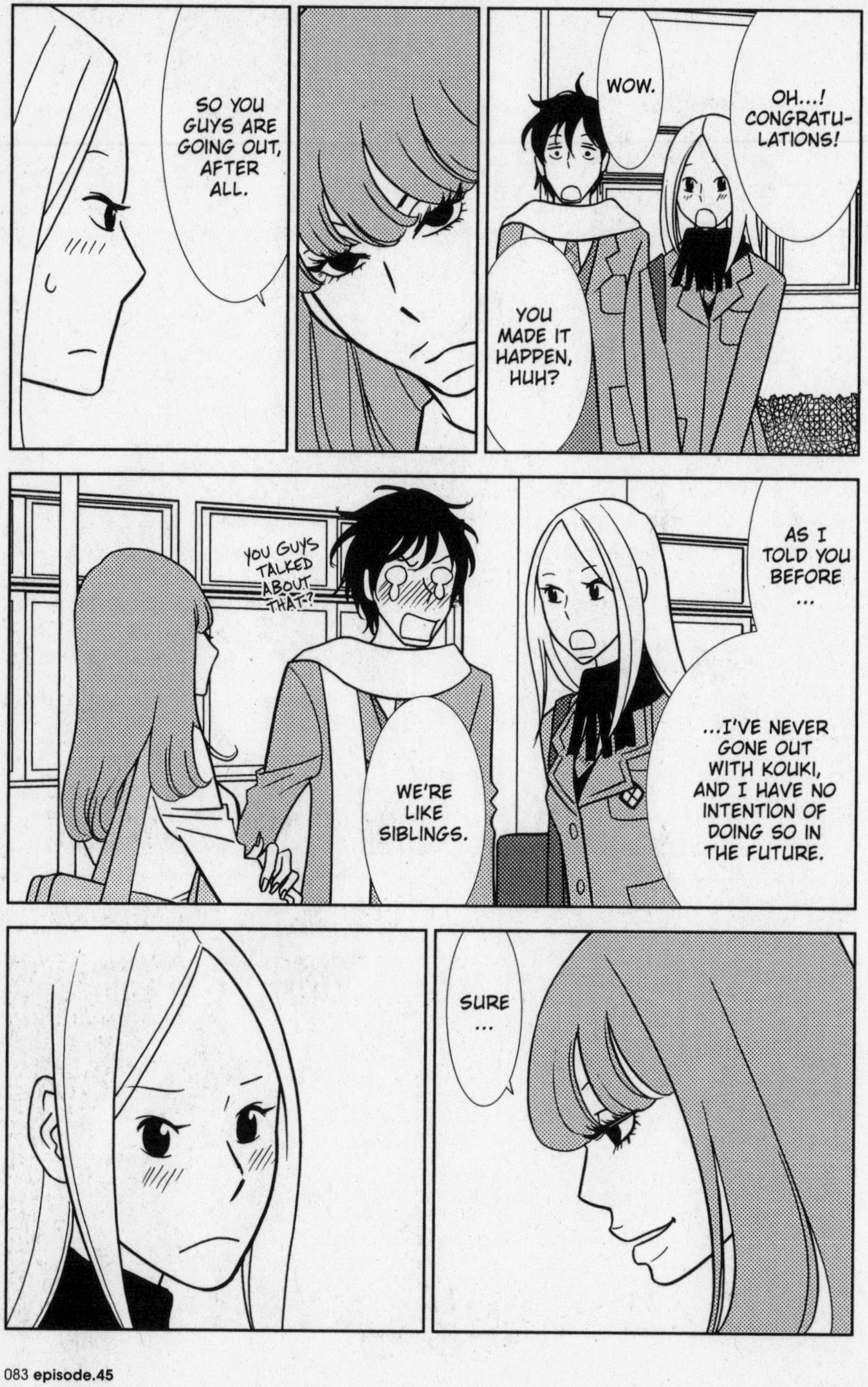
OH...! CONGRATULATIONS!
WOW.
YOU MADE IT HAPPEN, HUH?
SO YOU GUYS ARE GOING OUT, AFTER ALL.
AS I TOLD YOU BEFORE ...
...I'VE NEVER GONE OUT WITH KOUKI, AND I HAVE NO INTENTION OF DOING SO IN THE FUTURE.
YOU GUYS TALKED ABOUT THAT!?
WE'RE LIKE SIBLINGS.
SURE ...

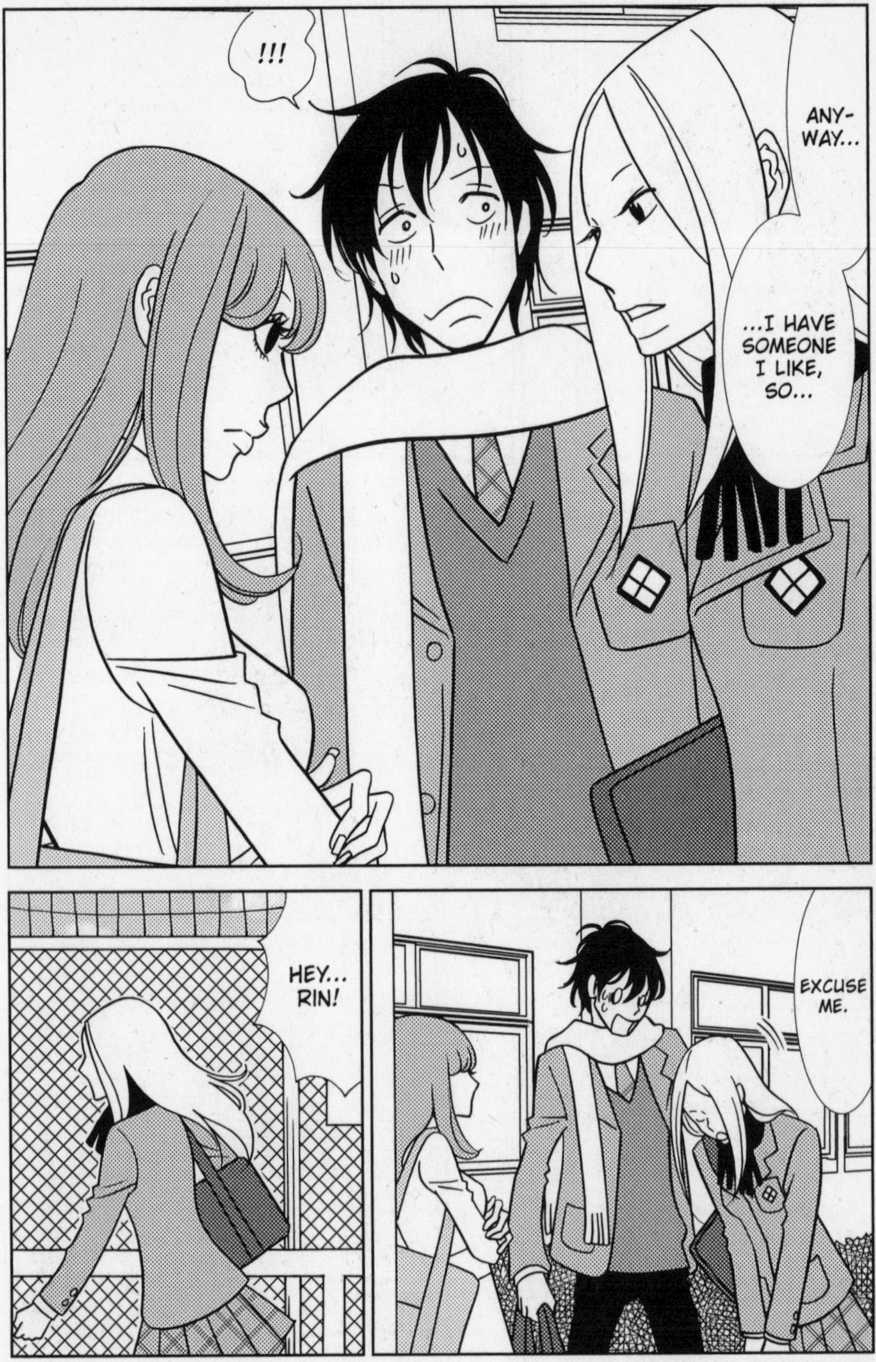
ANY-WAY...
...I HAVE SOMEONE I LIKE, SO...
!!!
EXCUSE ME.
HEY... RIN!

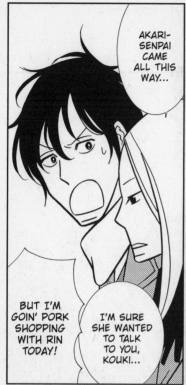

EHH?
WHAT?
RIN, THERE'S SOMEONE YOU LIKE?
WH-WHO?
AKARI-SENPAI CAME ALL THIS WAY...
I'M SURE SHE WANTED TO TALK TO YOU, KOUKI...
BUT I'M GOIN' PORK SHOPPING WITH RIN TODAY!
......
すた SUTA (STRIDE)
すた SUTA
IT...
GEEZ!
IT'S NOT ME, IS IT? THE GUY YOU LIKE?
DID YOU HEAR A WORD I SAID!?
HOW COULD IT BE YOU!?

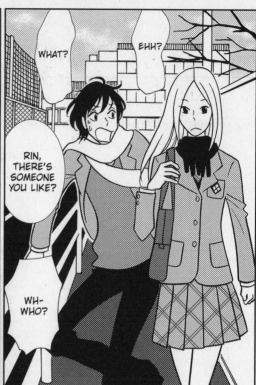

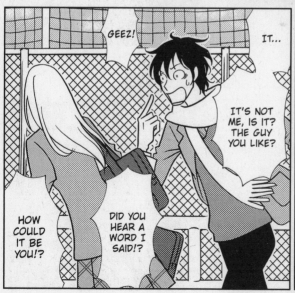

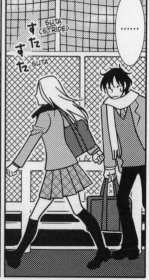

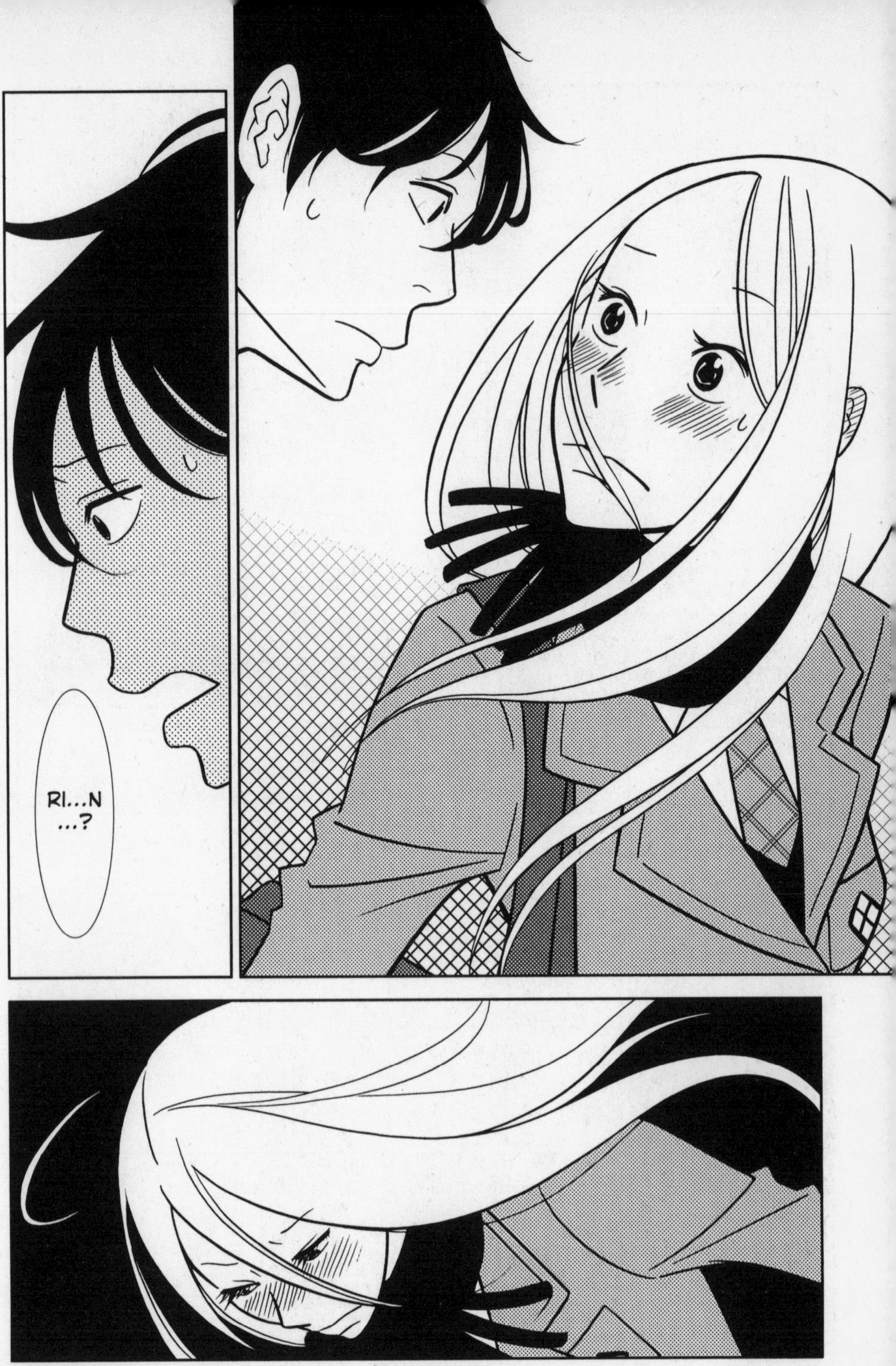
RI...N
...?

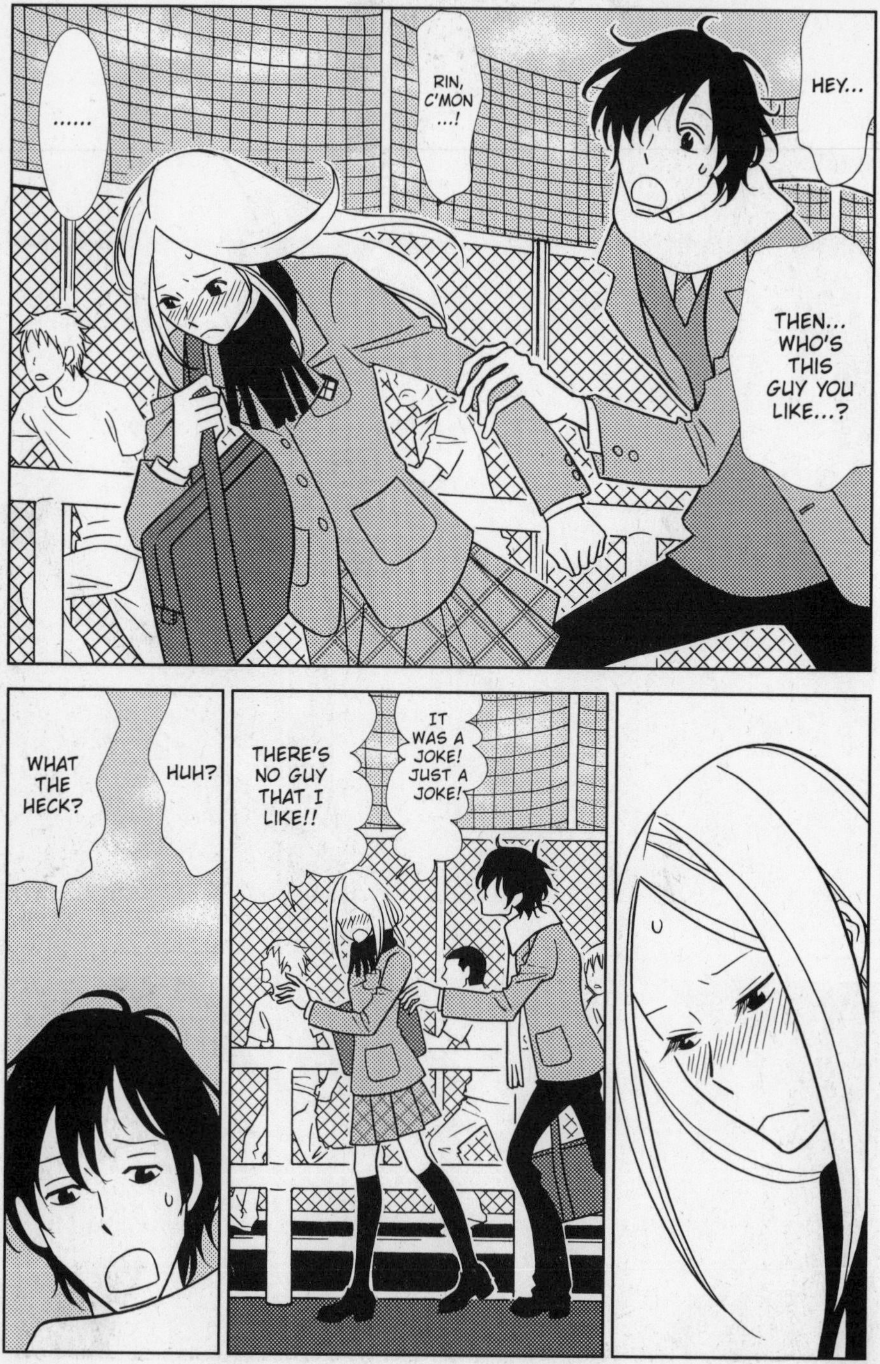
HEY...
THEN... WHO'S THIS GUY YOU LIKE...?
RIN, C'MON...!
......
IT WAS A JOKE! JUST A JOKE!
THERE'S NO GUY THAT I LIKE!!
HUH?
WHAT THE HECK?

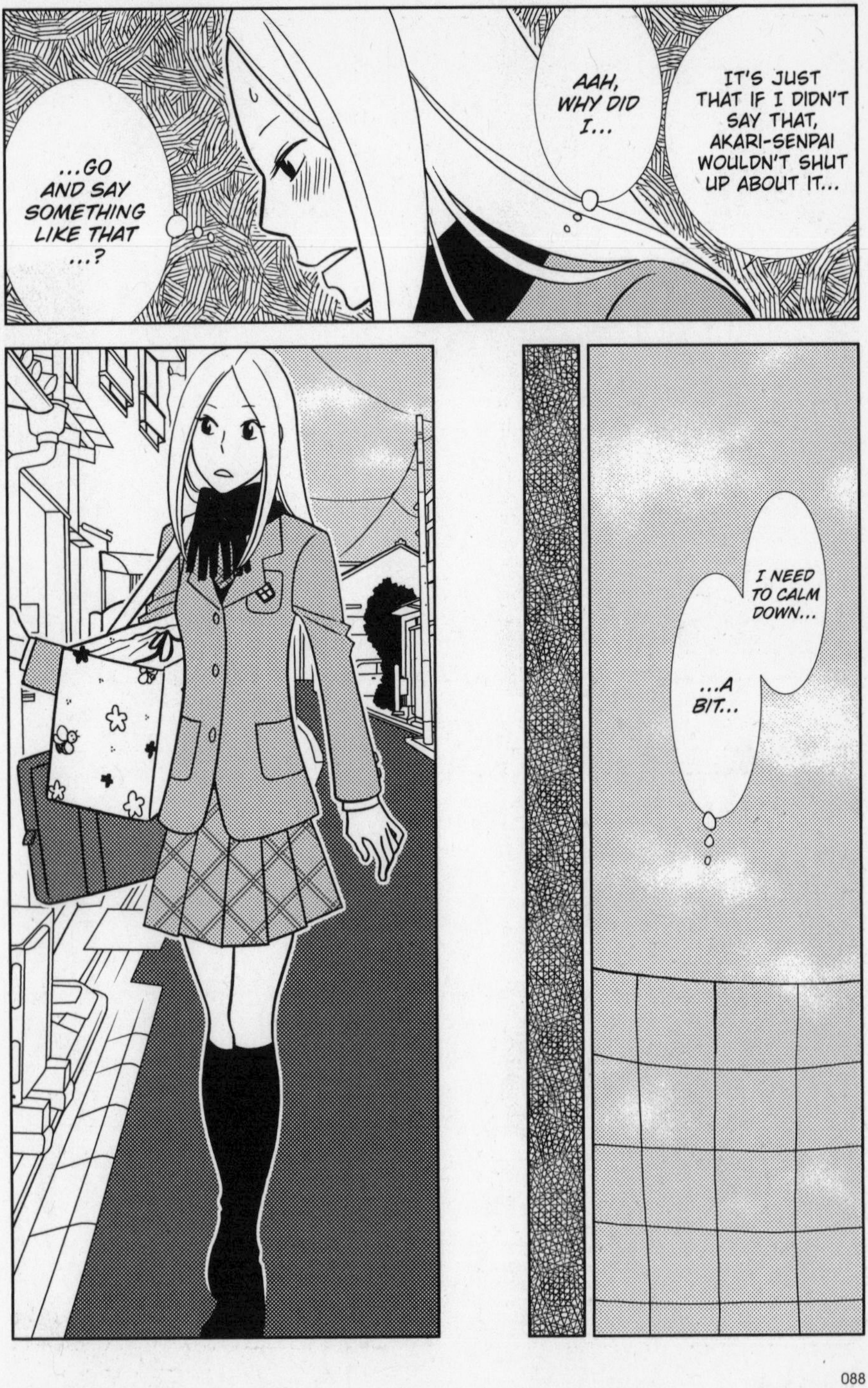
IT'S JUST THAT IF I DIDN'T SAY THAT, AKARI-SENPAI WOULDN'T SHUT UP ABOUT IT...
AAH, WHY DID I...
...GO AND SAY SOMETHING LIKE THAT ...?
I NEED TO CALM DOWN...
...A BIT...

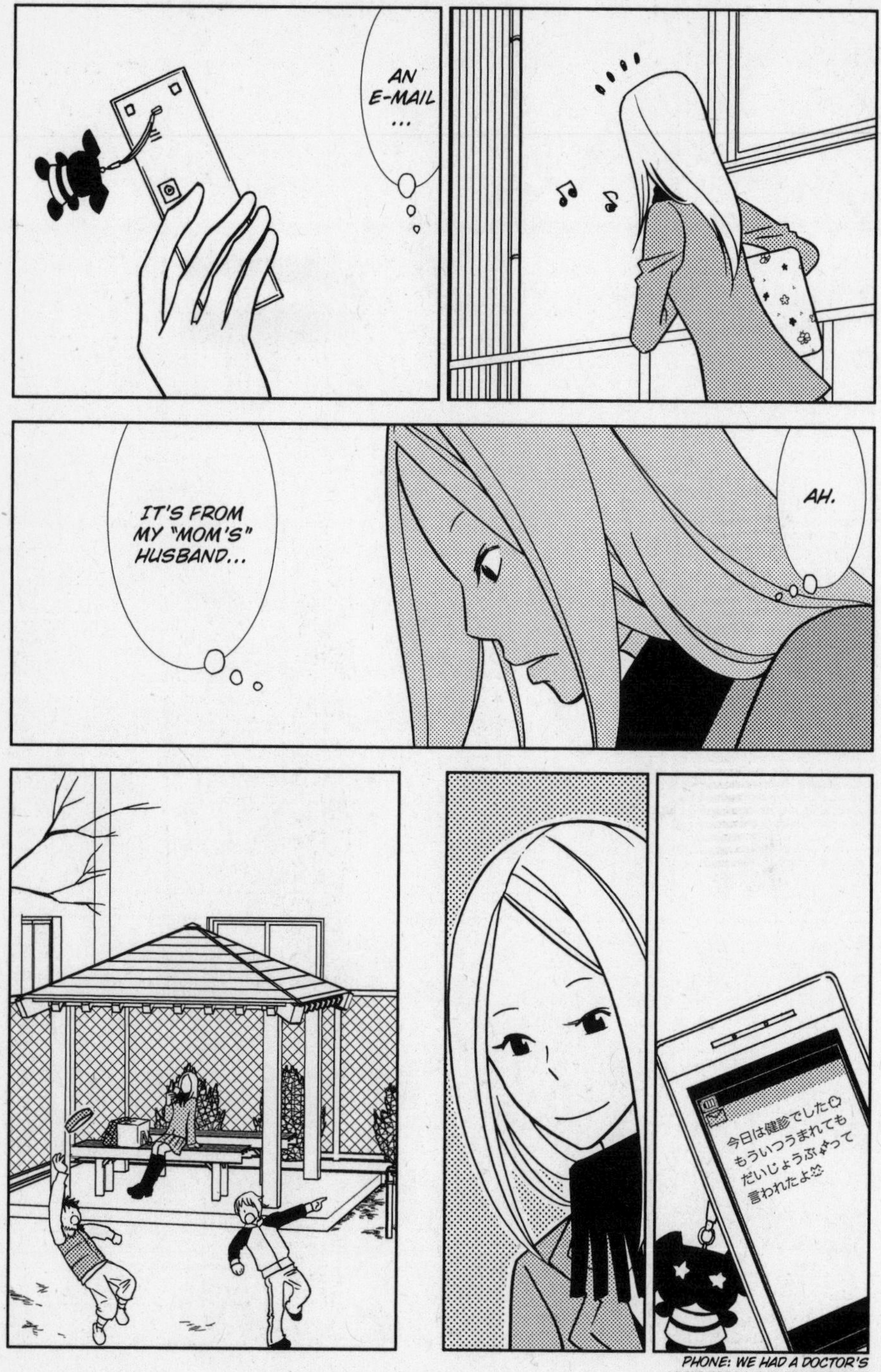
AN E-MAIL ...
AH.
IT'S FROM MY "MOM'S" HUSBAND...
今日は健診でした
もういつうまれても
だいじょうぶって
言われたよ
PHONE: WE HAD A DOCTOR'S VISIT TODAY. THE DOCTOR SAID IT MIGHT BE ANY DAY NOW.

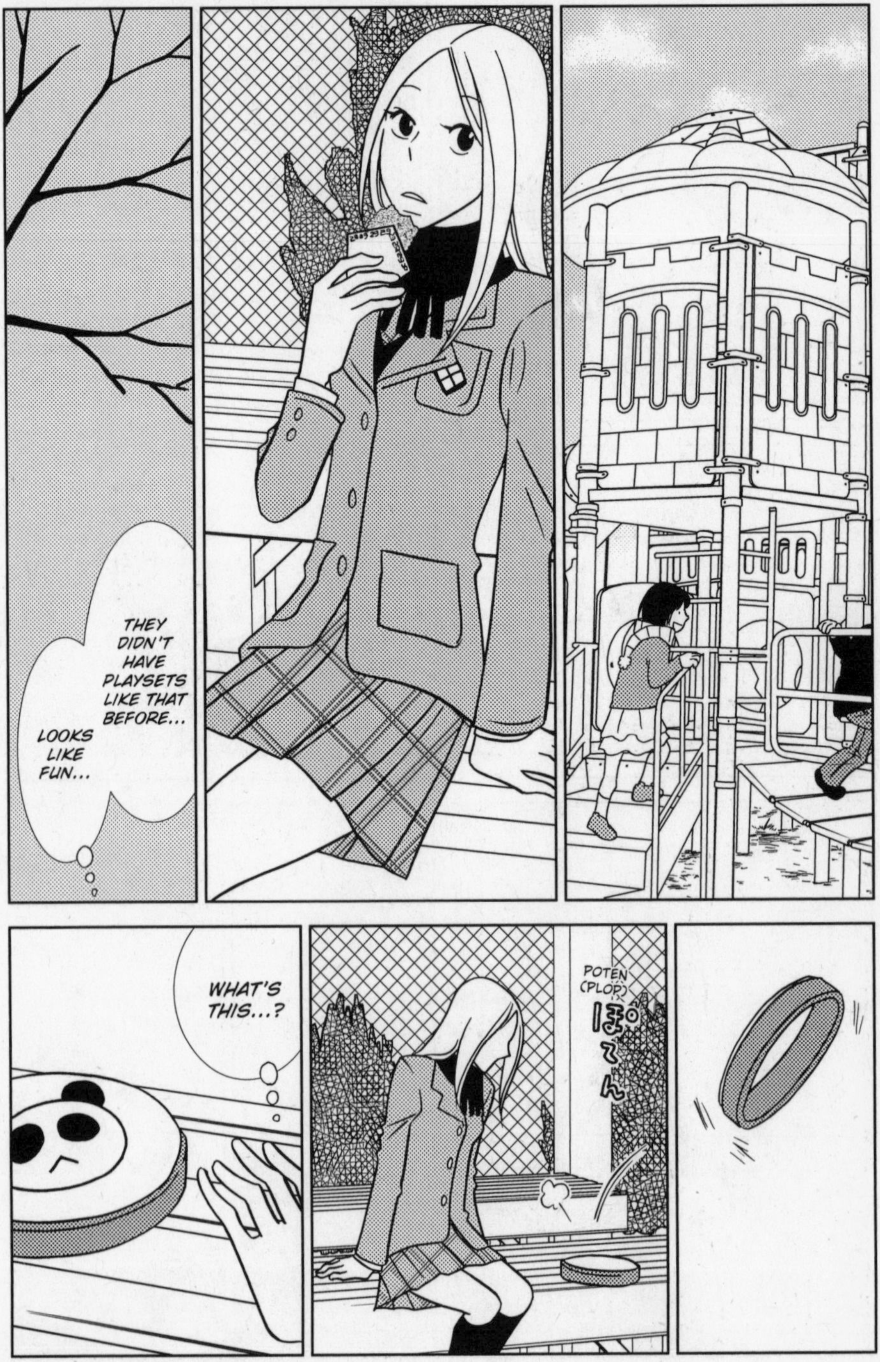
THEY DIDN'T HAVE PLAYSETS LIKE THAT BEFORE...
LOOKS LIKE FUN...
POTEN (PLOP)
ぽてん
WHAT'S THIS...?

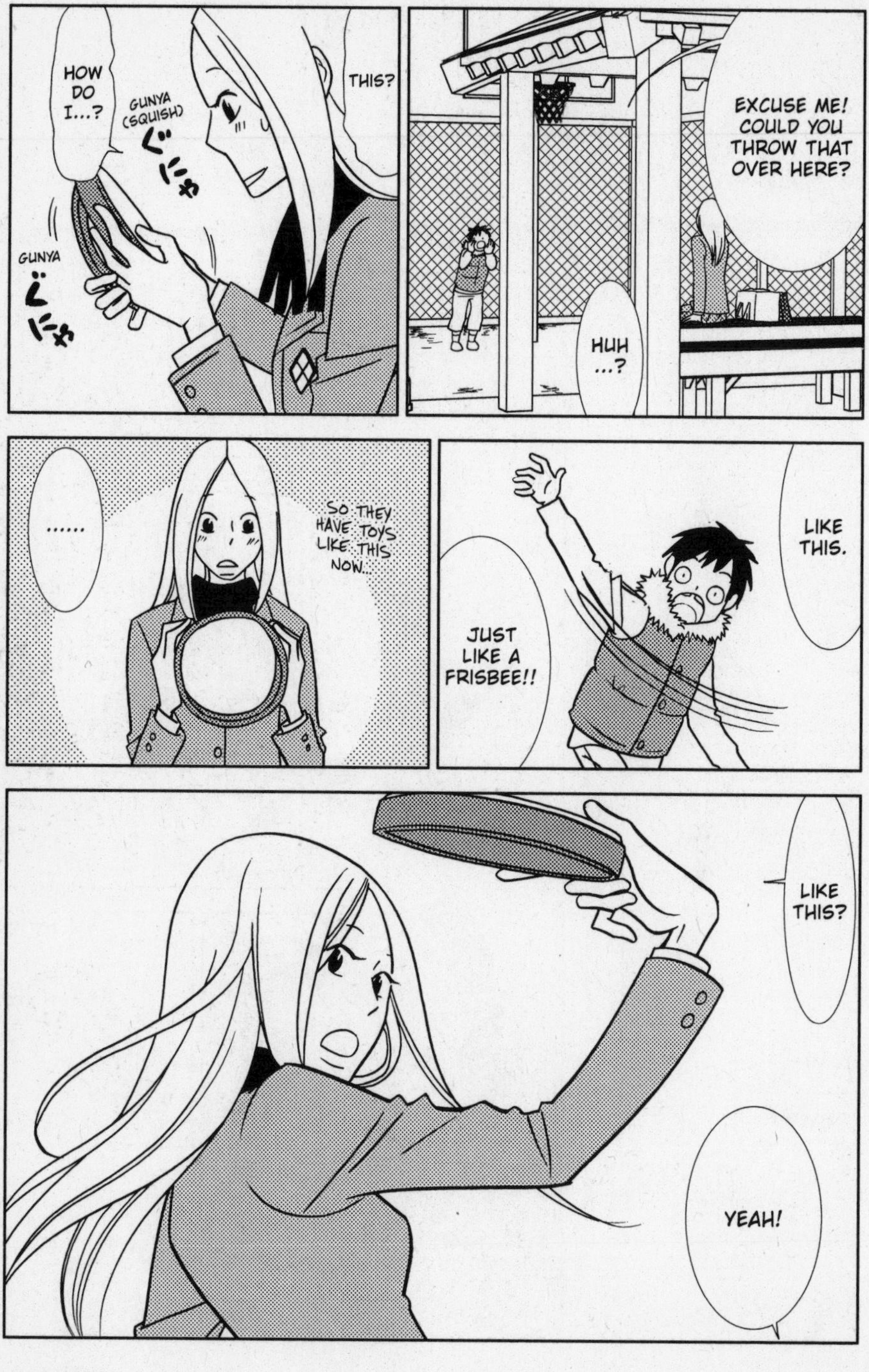
EXCUSE ME! COULD YOU THROW THAT OVER HERE?
HUH ...?
HOW DO I...?
THIS?
GUNYA (SQUISH) ぐにゃ
GUNYA ぐにゃ
LIKE THIS.
JUST LIKE A FRISBEE!!
......
SO THEY HAVE TOYS LIKE THIS NOW...
LIKE THIS?
YEAH!

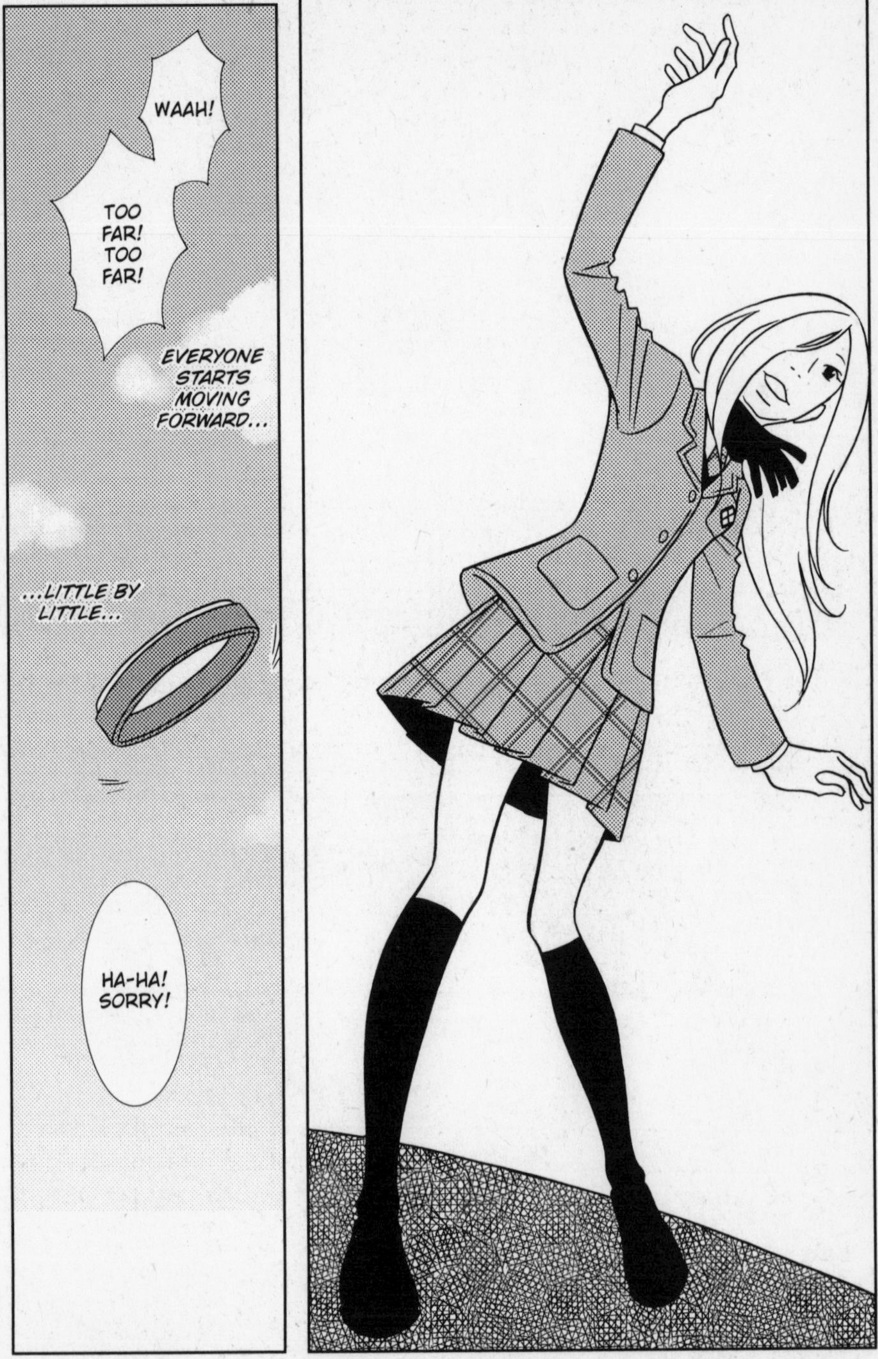
WAAH!
TOO FAR! TOO FAR!
EVERYONE STARTS MOVING FORWARD...
...LITTLE BY LITTLE...
HA-HA! SORRY!

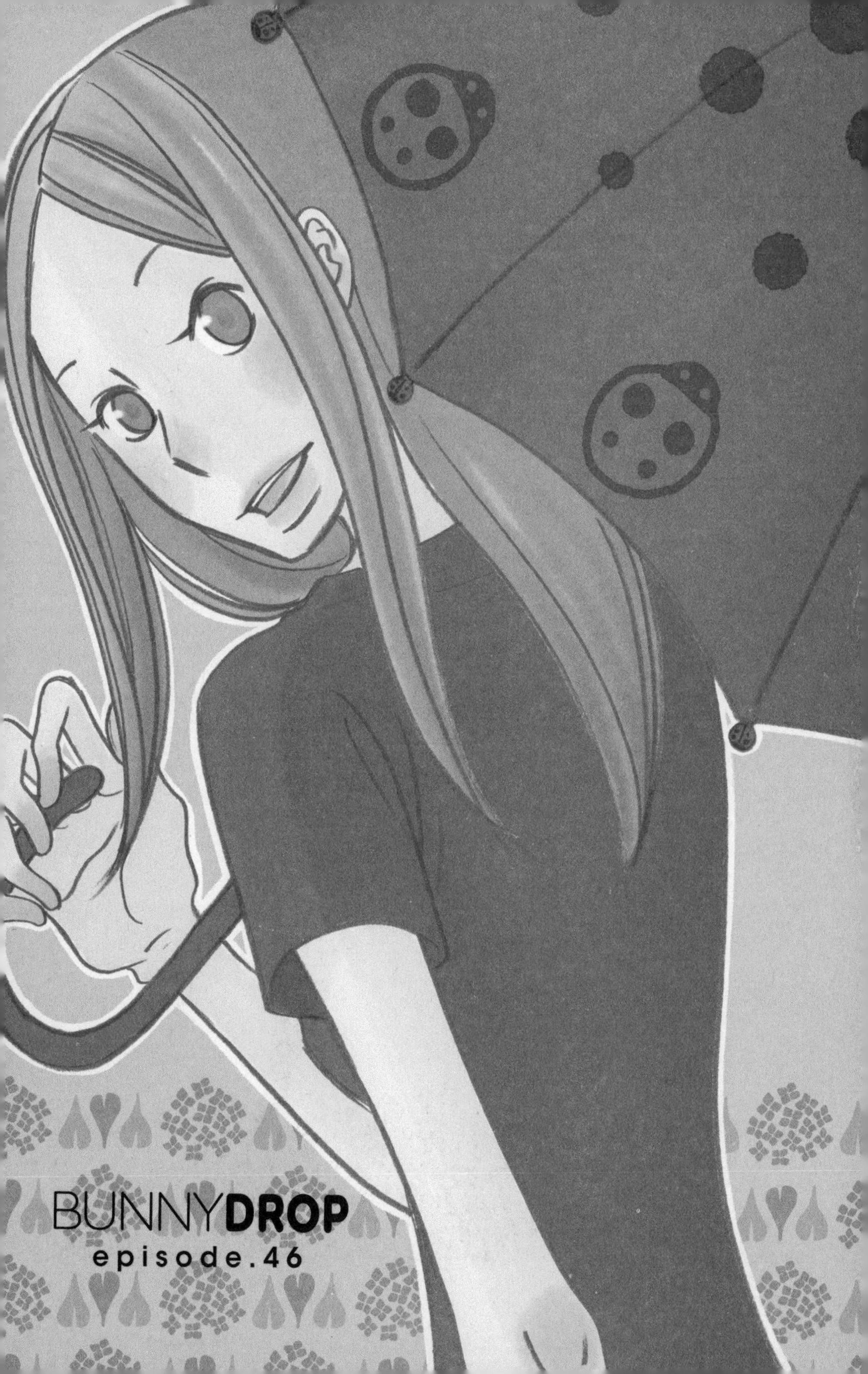
BUNNYDROP
episode.46

BUNNY**DROP**

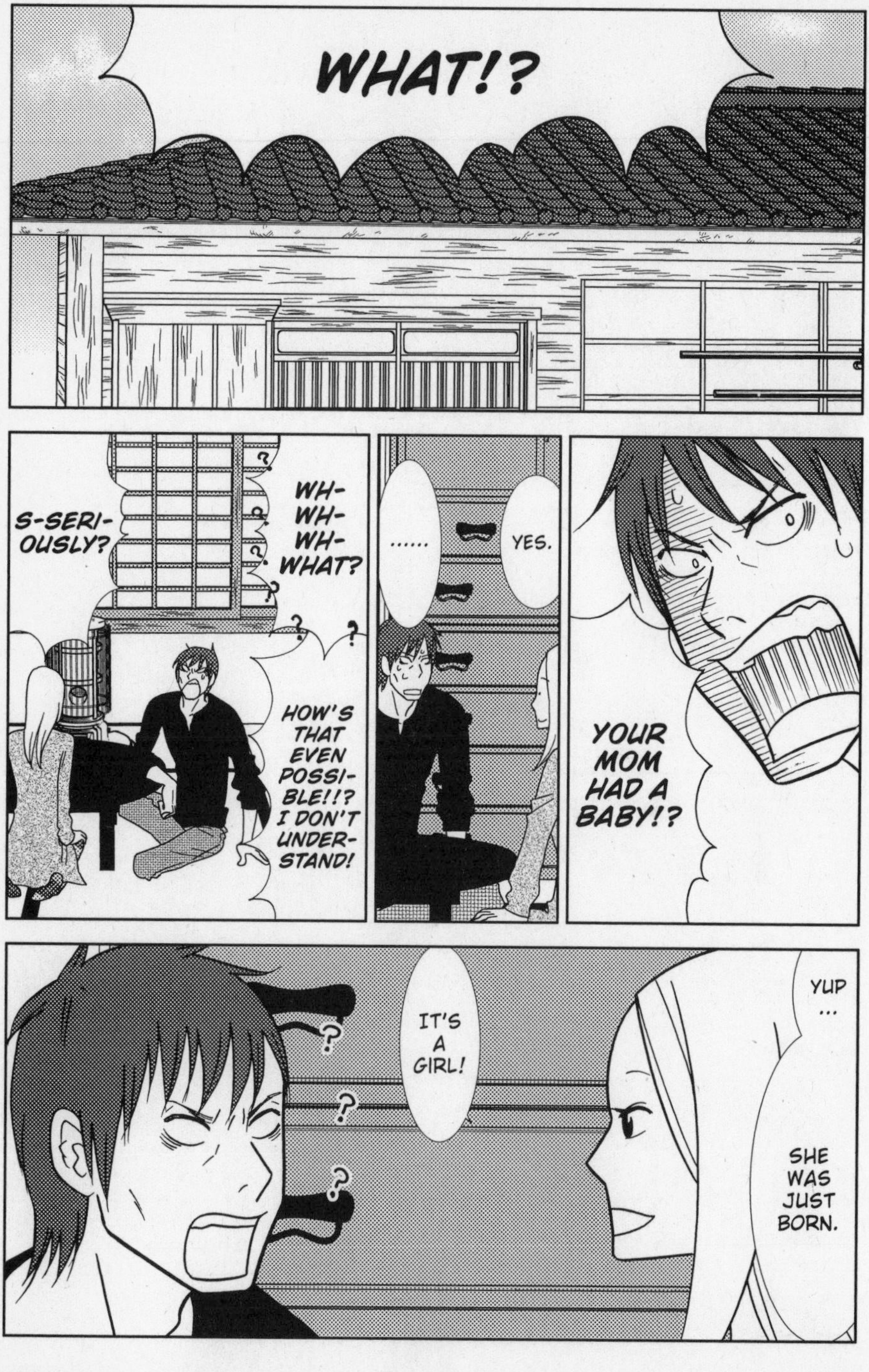
WHAT!?
YOUR MOM HAD A BABY!?
YES.
......
WH-WH-WH-WHAT?
S-SERIOUSLY?
HOW'S THAT EVEN POSSIBLE!!? I DON'T UNDERSTAND!
YUP ...
SHE WAS JUST BORN.
IT'S A GIRL!

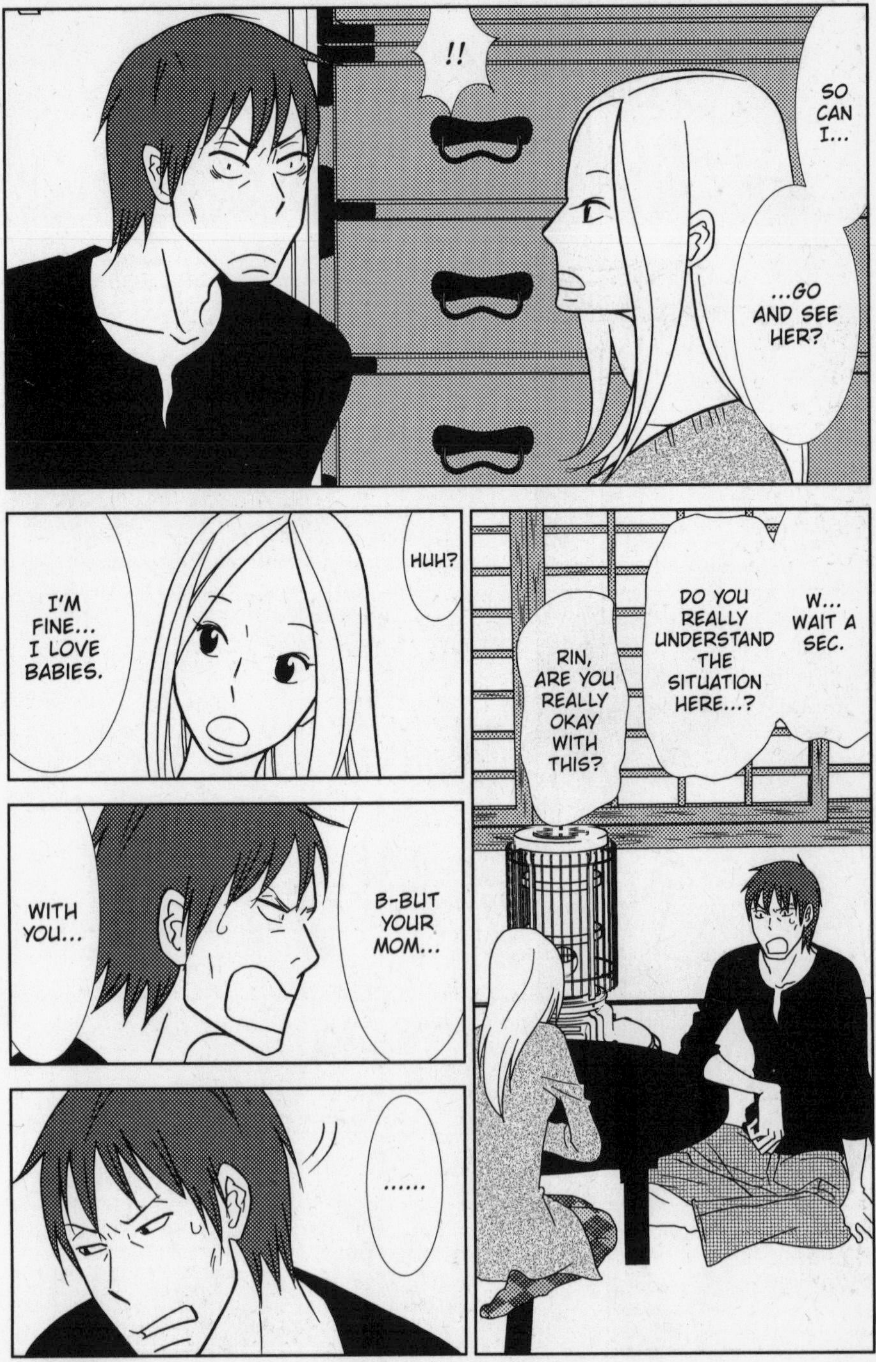
SO CAN I...
...GO AND SEE HER?
!!
W... WAIT A SEC.
DO YOU REALLY UNDERSTAND THE SITUATION HERE...?
RIN, ARE YOU REALLY OKAY WITH THIS?
HUH?
I'M FINE... I LOVE BABIES.
B-BUT YOUR MOM...
WITH YOU...
......

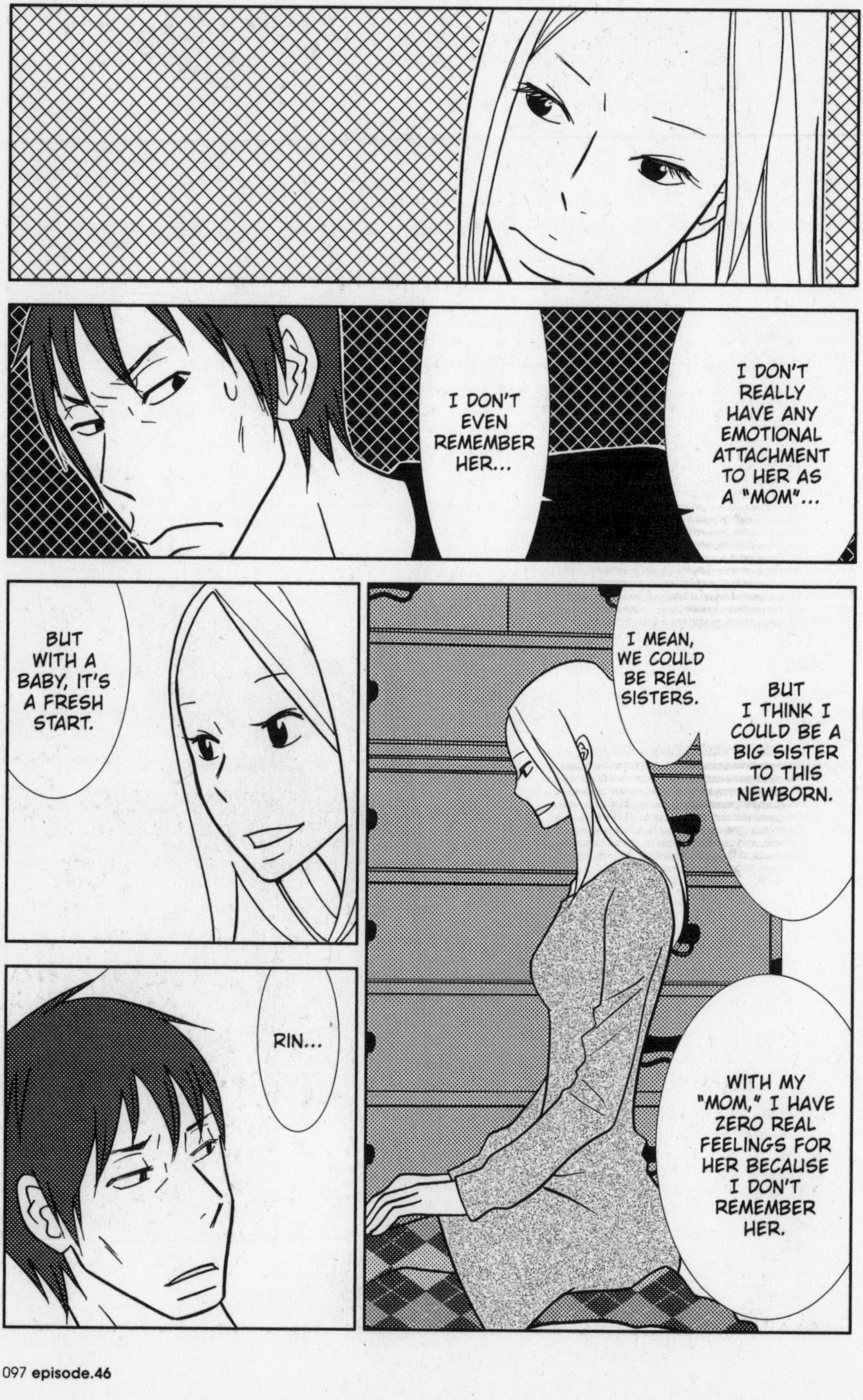
I DON'T REALLY HAVE ANY EMOTIONAL ATTACHMENT TO HER AS A "MOM"...
I DON'T EVEN REMEMBER HER...
BUT I THINK I COULD BE A BIG SISTER TO THIS NEWBORN.
I MEAN, WE COULD BE REAL SISTERS.
WITH MY "MOM," I HAVE ZERO REAL FEELINGS FOR HER BECAUSE I DON'T REMEMBER HER.
BUT WITH A BABY, IT'S A FRESH START.
RIN...

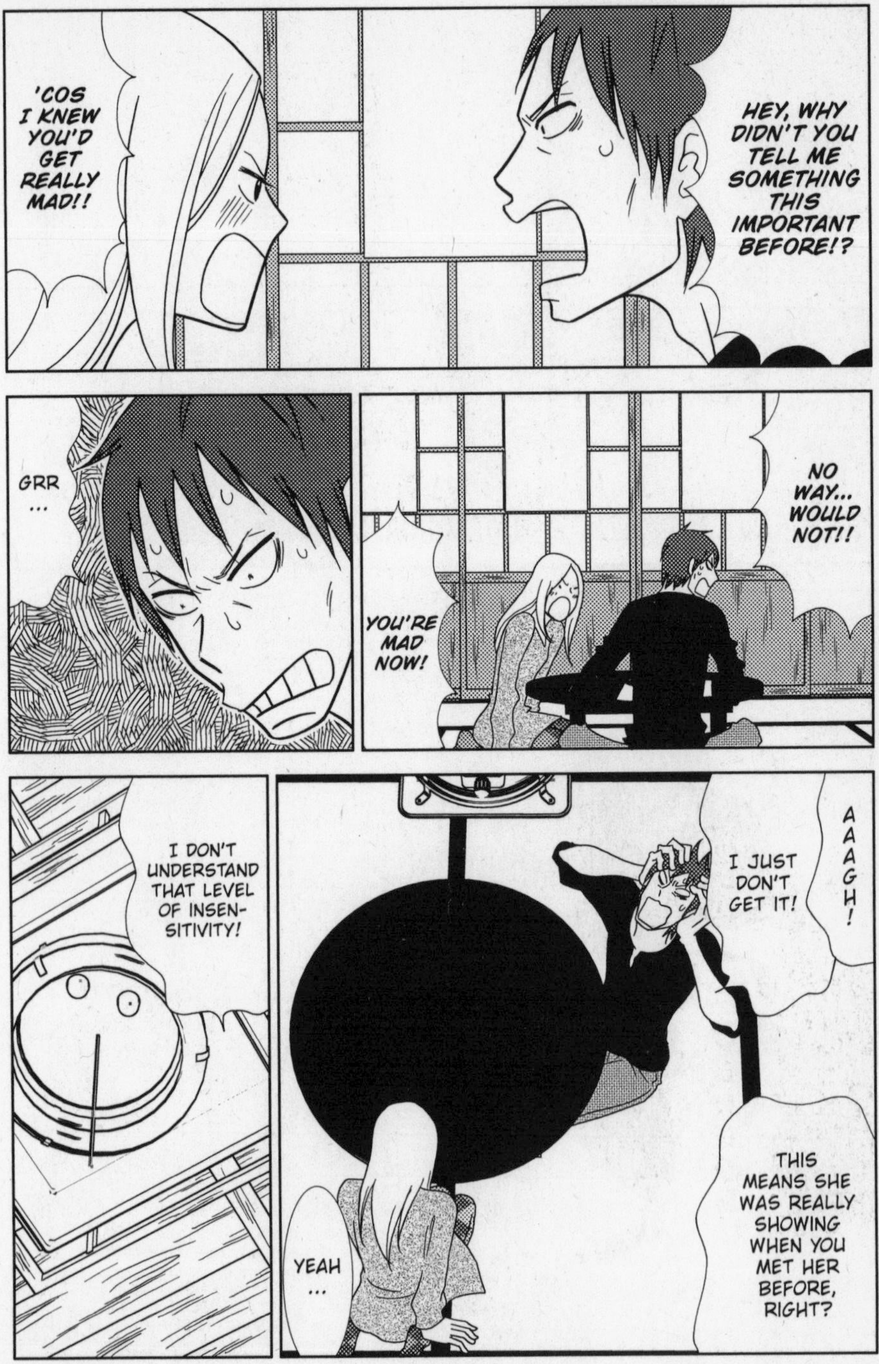
HEY, WHY DIDN'T YOU TELL ME SOMETHING THIS IMPORTANT BEFORE!?
'COS I KNEW YOU'D GET REALLY MAD!!
NO WAY... WOULD NOT!!
YOU'RE MAD NOW!
GRR ...
AAAGH!
I JUST DON'T GET IT!
THIS MEANS SHE WAS REALLY SHOWING WHEN YOU MET HER BEFORE, RIGHT?
YEAH ...
I DON'T UNDERSTAND THAT LEVEL OF INSEN-SITIVITY!

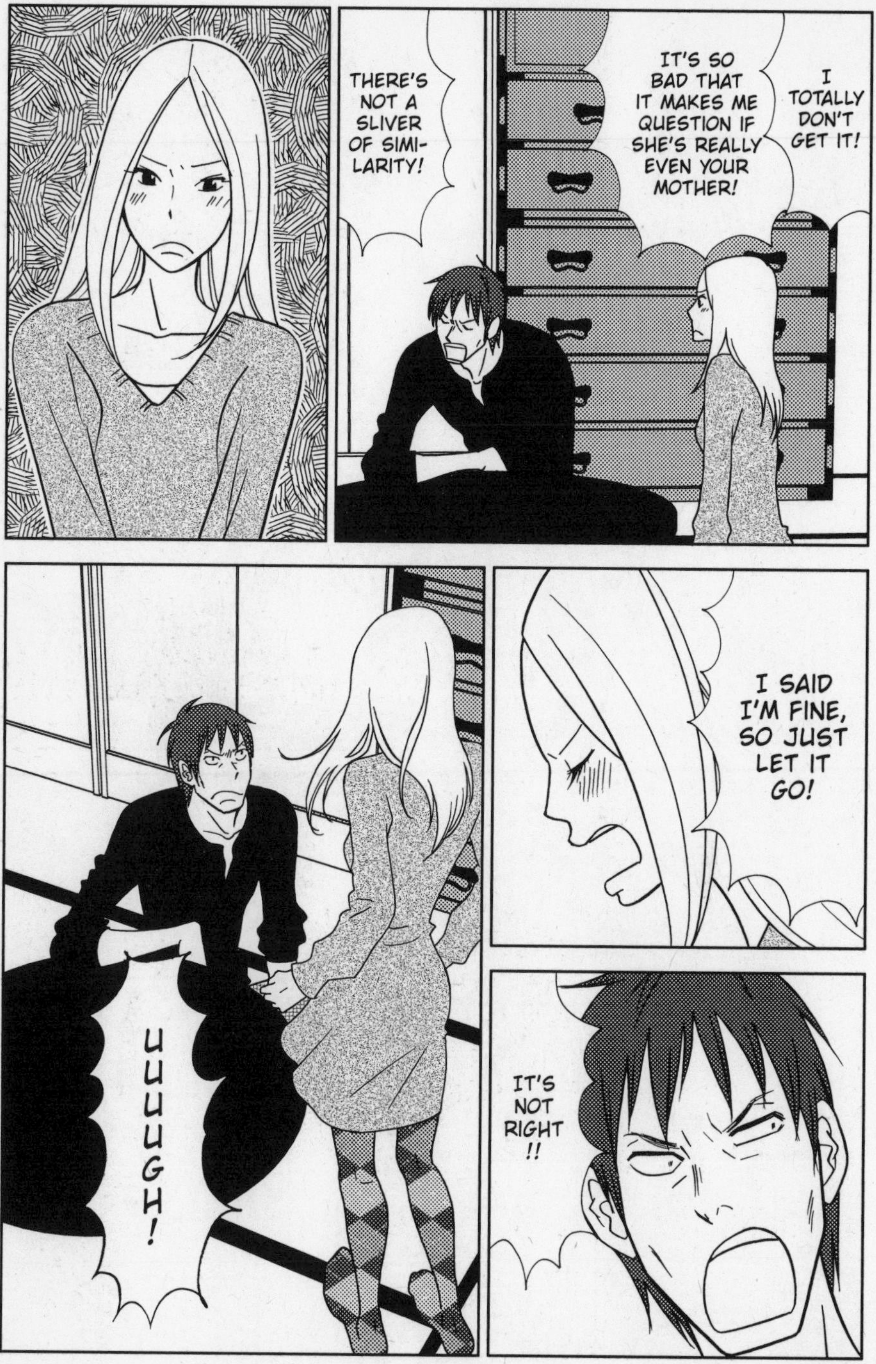
I TOTALLY DON'T GET IT!
IT'S SO BAD THAT IT MAKES ME QUESTION IF SHE'S REALLY EVEN YOUR MOTHER!
THERE'S NOT A SLIVER OF SIMI-LARITY!
I SAID I'M FINE, SO JUST LET IT GO!
IT'S NOT RIGHT!!
UUUUGH!

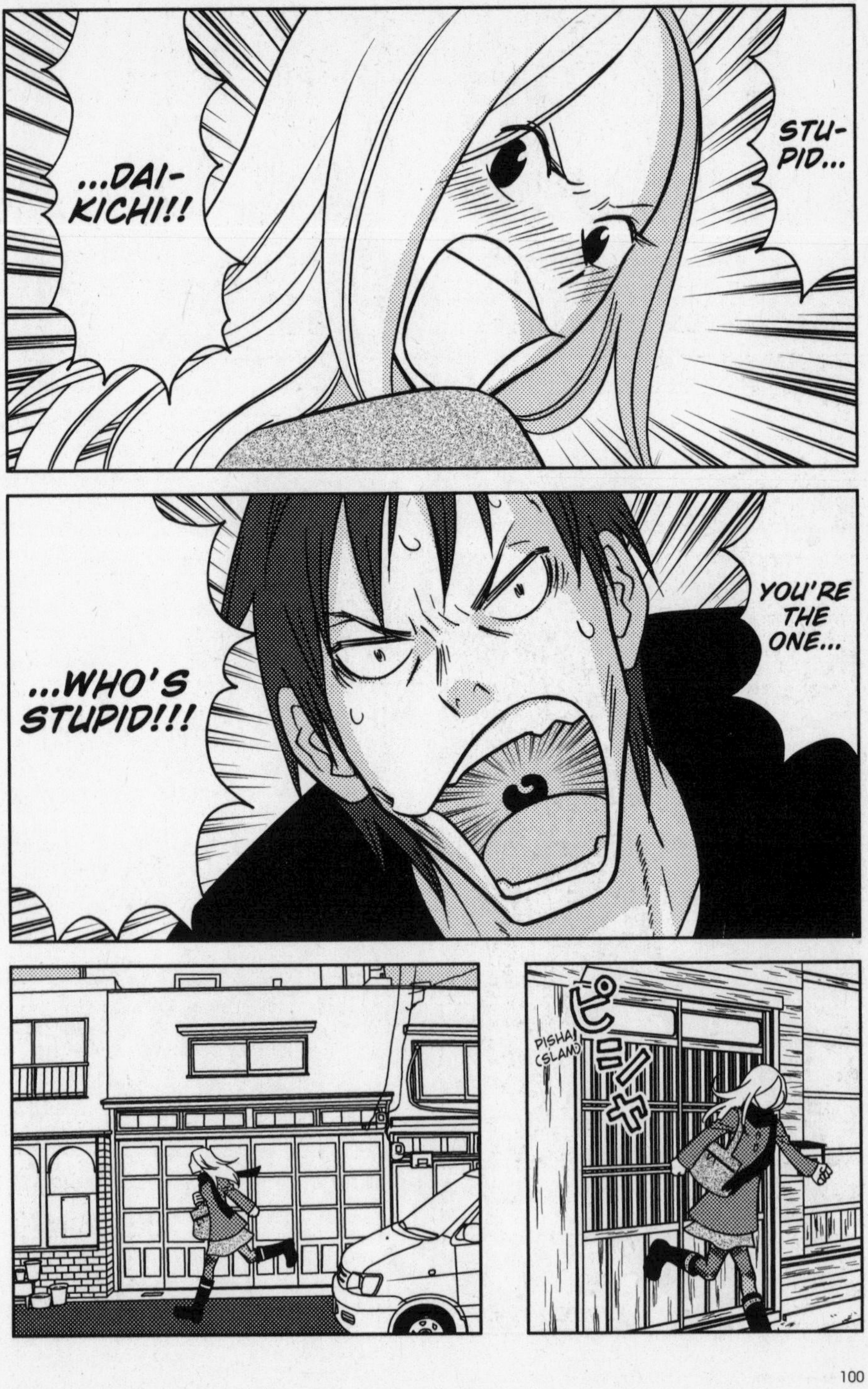
STU-PID...
...DAI-KICHI!!
YOU'RE THE ONE...
...WHO'S STUPID!!!
ピシャ
PISHA (SLAM)

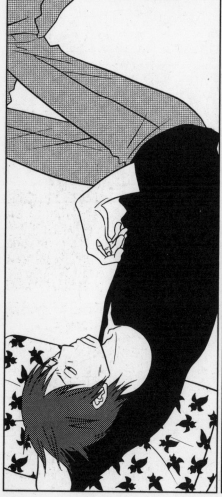

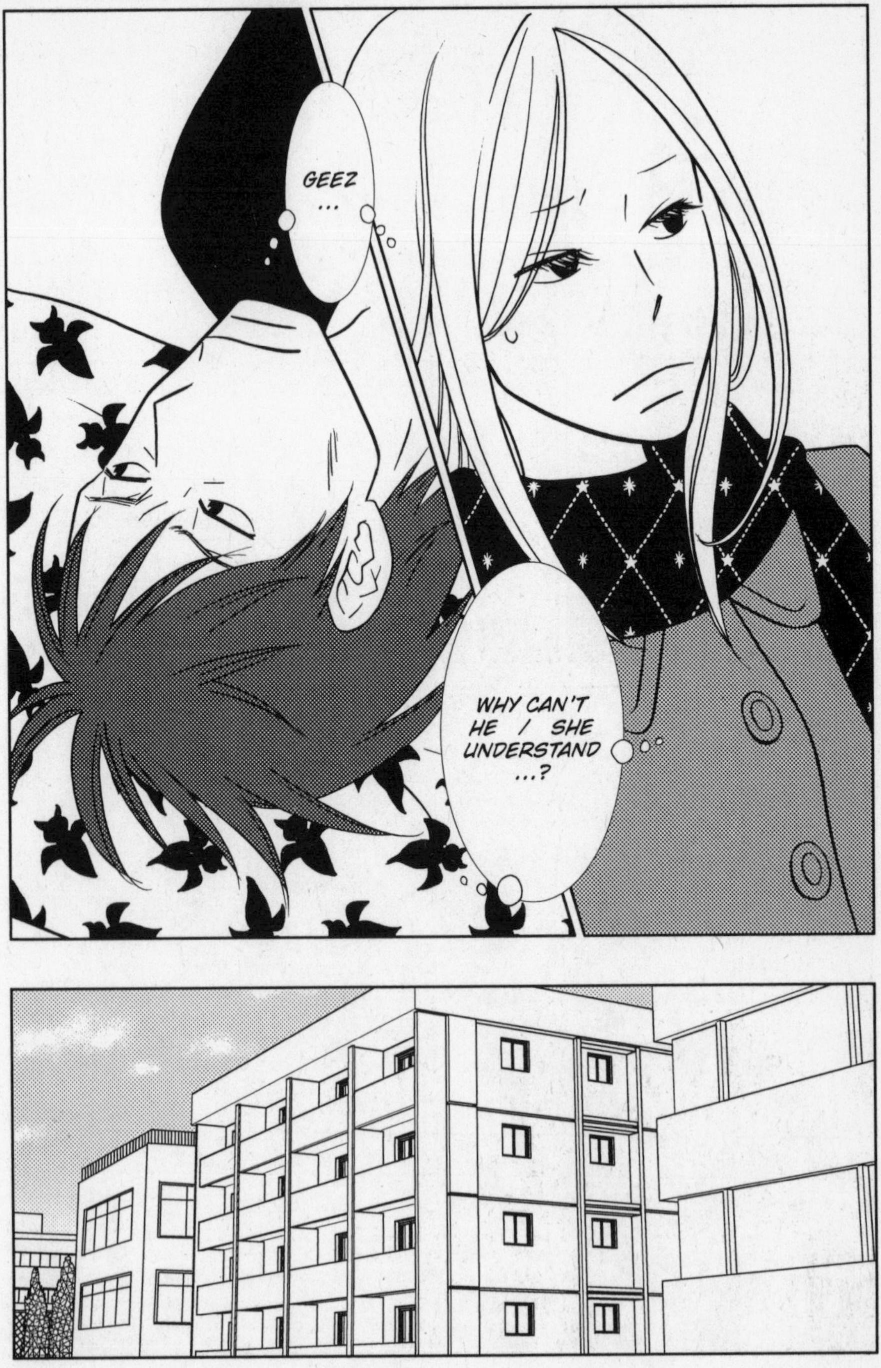
GEEZ ...
WHY CAN'T HE / SHE UNDERSTAND ...?

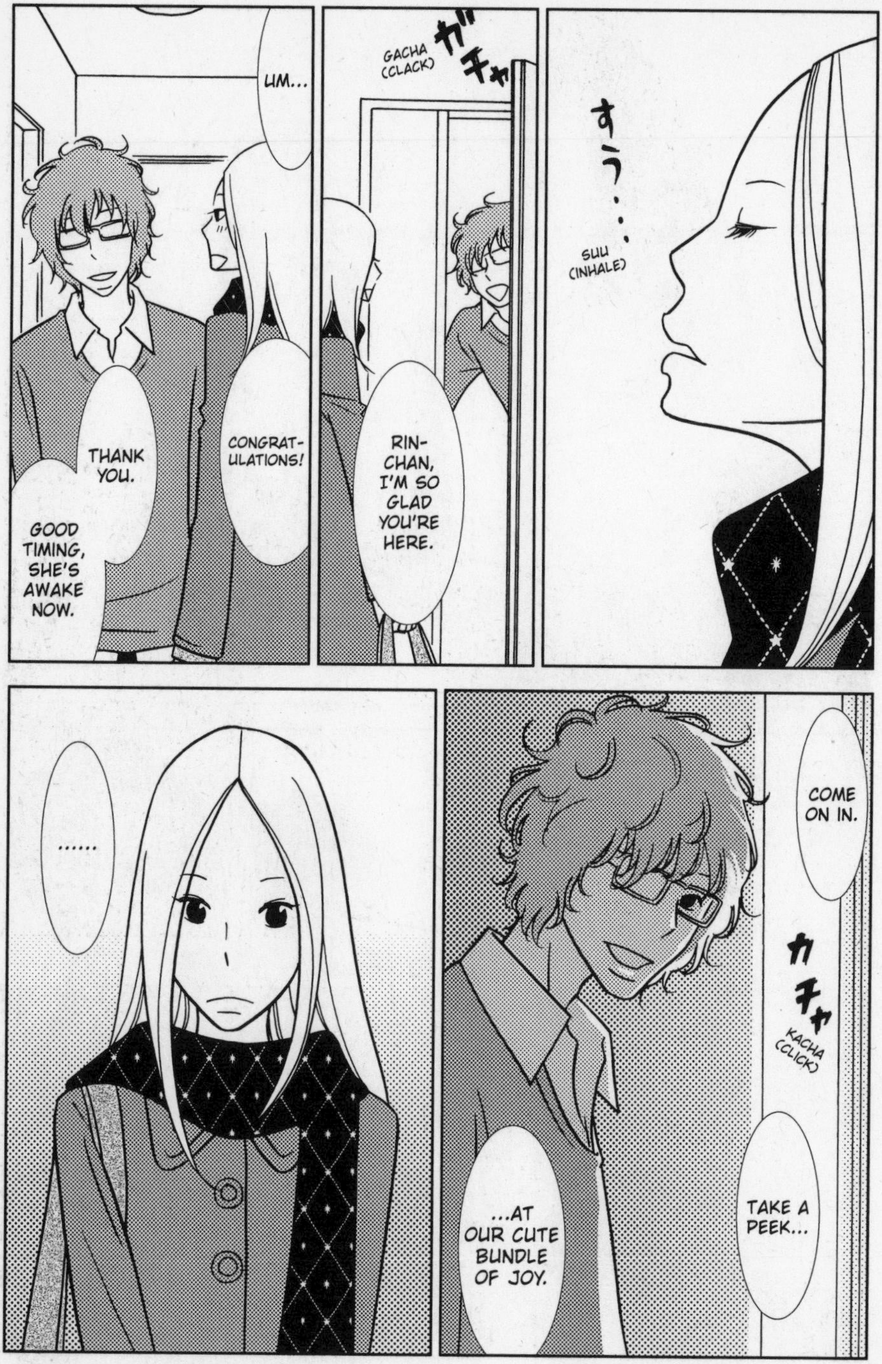
すぅ・・・
SUU (INHALE)
ガチャ
GACHA (CLACK)
RIN-CHAN, I'M SO GLAD YOU'RE HERE.
UM...
CONGRAT-ULATIONS!
THANK YOU.
GOOD TIMING, SHE'S AWAKE NOW.
COME ON IN.
カチャ
KACHA (CLICK)
TAKE A PEEK...
...AT OUR CUTE BUNDLE OF JOY.
......

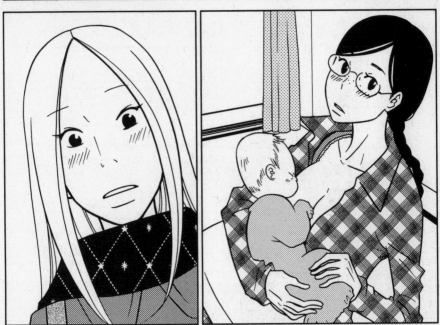

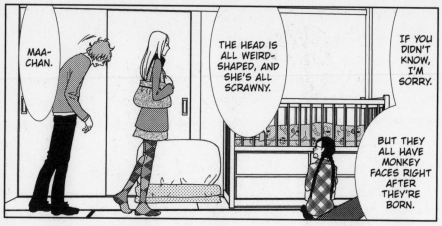

IF YOU DIDN'T KNOW, I'M SORRY.
BUT THEY ALL HAVE MONKEY FACES RIGHT AFTER THEY'RE BORN.
THE HEAD IS ALL WEIRD-SHAPED, AND SHE'S ALL SCRAWNY.
MAA-CHAN.
SO CUTE ...
COME OVER, AND TAKE A LOOK.
OKAY.

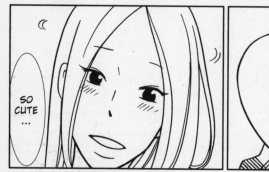

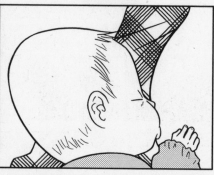

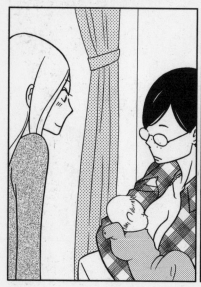

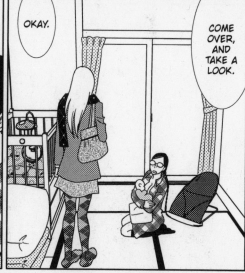

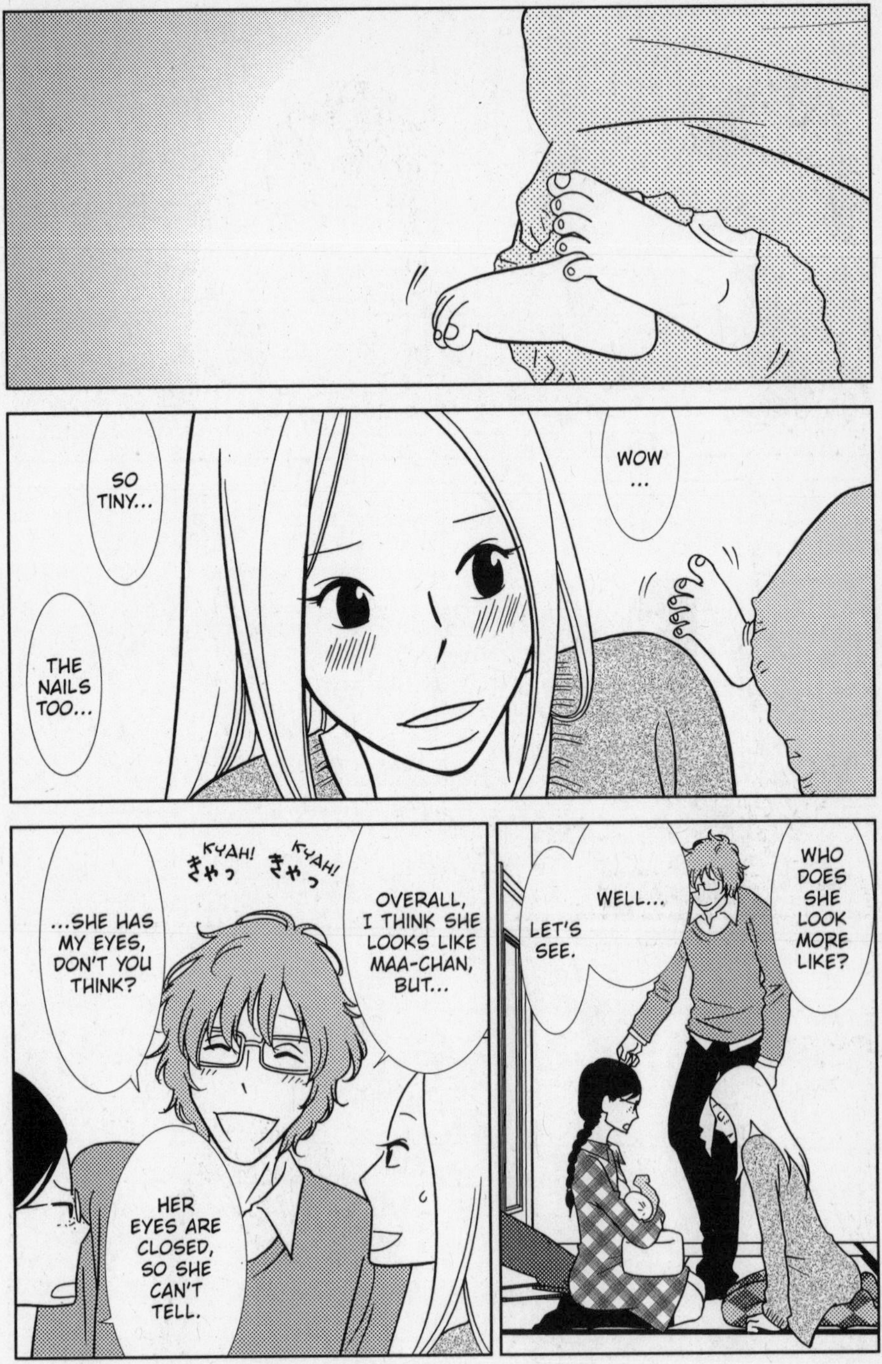
WOW ...
SO TINY...
THE NAILS TOO...
WHO DOES SHE LOOK MORE LIKE?
WELL...
LET'S SEE.
OVERALL, I THINK SHE LOOKS LIKE MAA-CHAN, BUT...
KYAH! きゃっ
KYAH! きゃっ
...SHE HAS MY EYES, DON'T YOU THINK?
HER EYES ARE CLOSED, SO SHE CAN'T TELL.

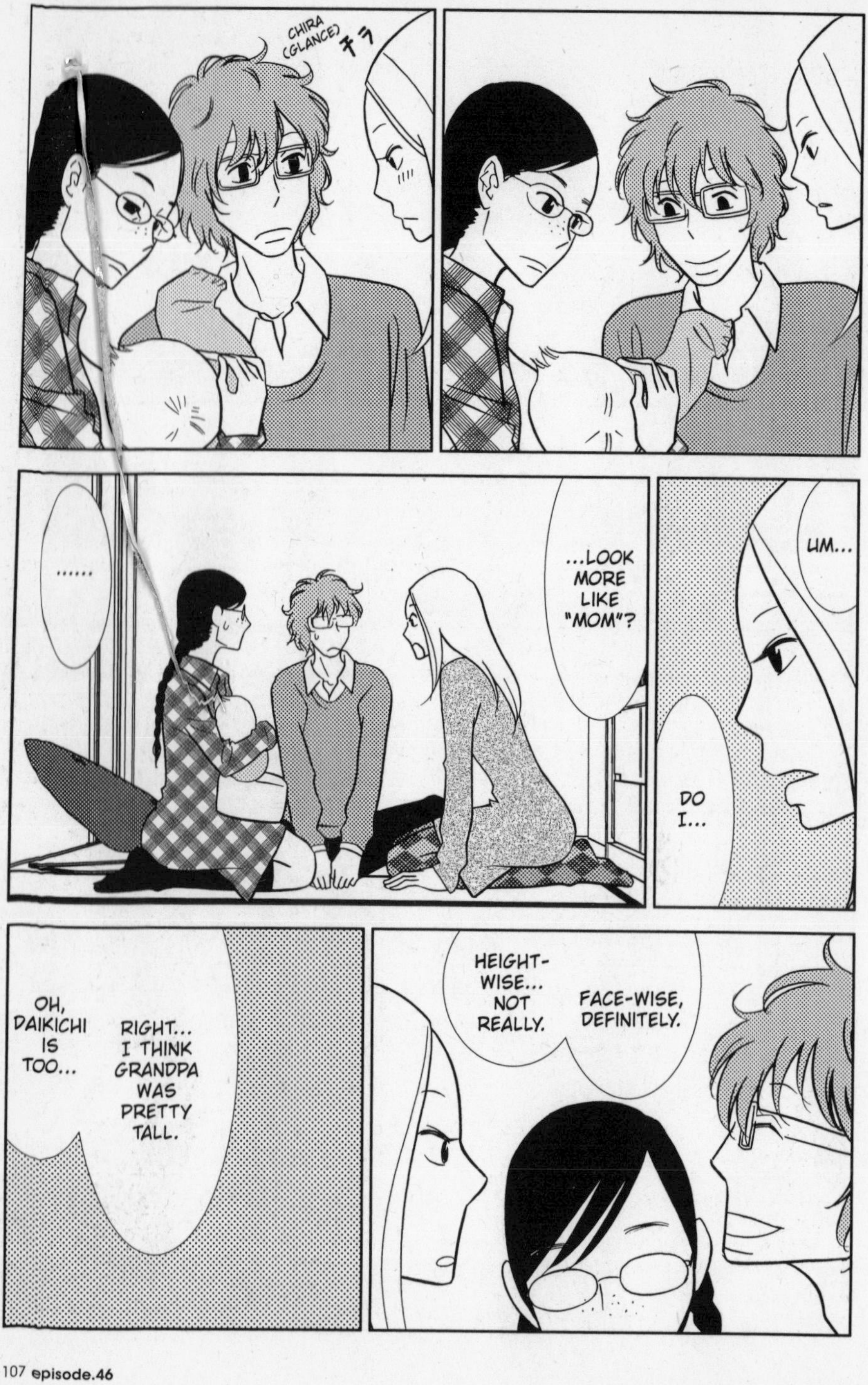
CHIRA (GLANCE) チラ
UM...
DO I...
...LOOK MORE LIKE "MOM"?
......
FACE-WISE, DEFINITELY.
HEIGHT-WISE... NOT REALLY.
RIGHT... I THINK GRANDPA WAS PRETTY TALL.
OH, DAIKICHI IS TOO...

I'D NEVER GIVEN IT ANY THOUGHT BEFORE.
IT'S FUN...
SHE'S PROBABLY LIKE YOU IN SOME WAYS TOO, RIN-CHAN.
OH, IT'S ALMOST TIME FOR HER MILK.
OKAY ...
WHOA! RIN-CHAN, YOU'RE REALLY GOOD AT THIS!
OH...
I HAVE A RELATIVE WITH A LITTLE BABY.
AND I LOVE BABIES, SO WHENEVER I VISIT, I HELP TAKE CARE OF HER...

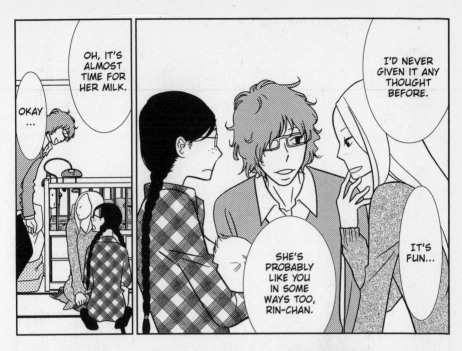

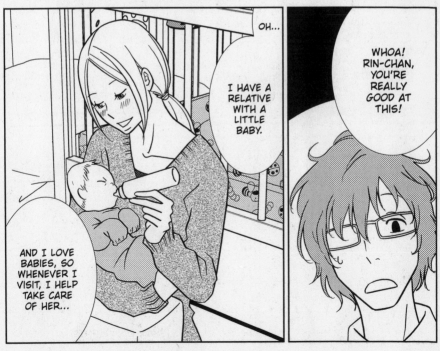

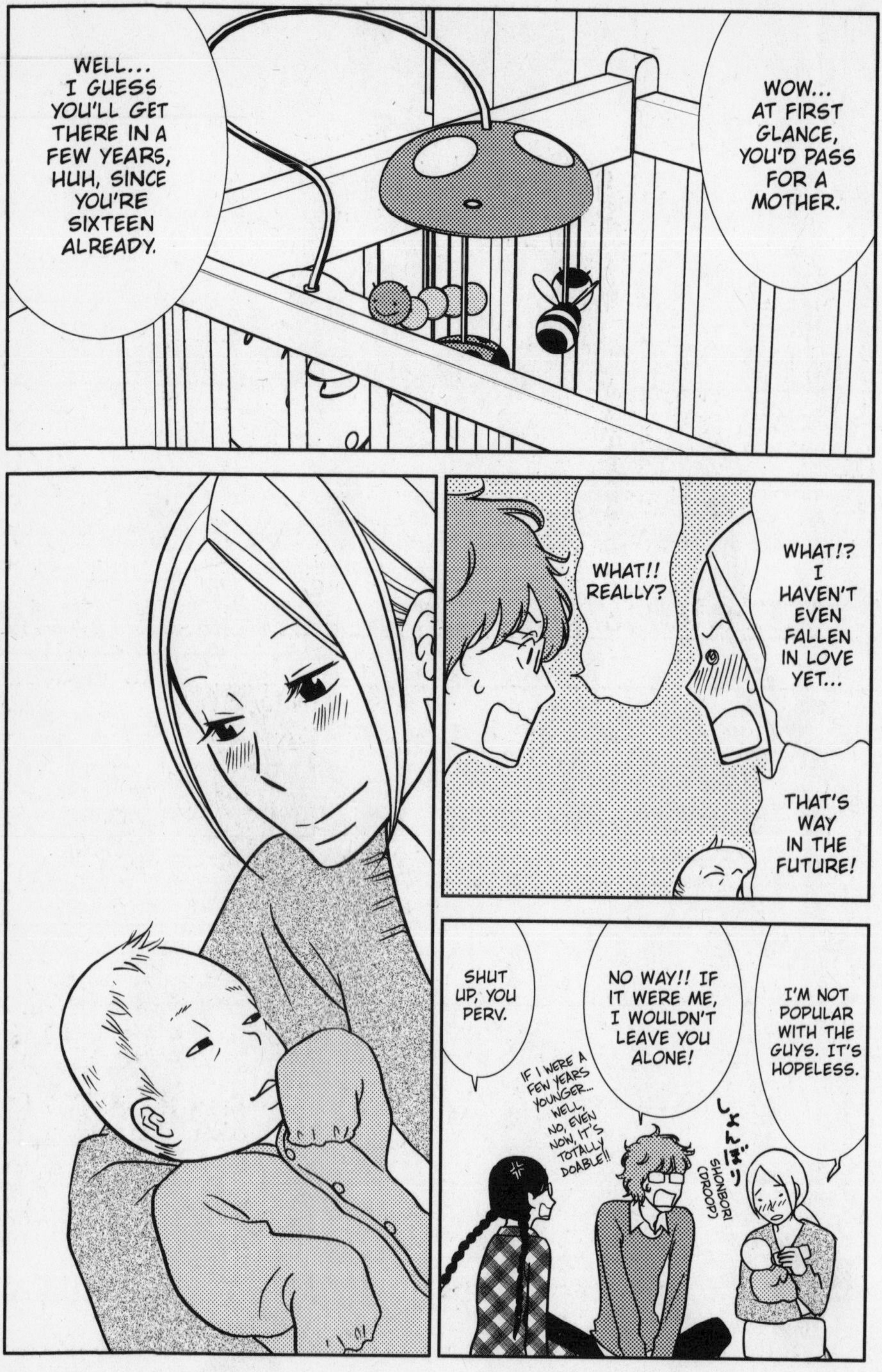

WOW... AT FIRST GLANCE, YOU'D PASS FOR A MOTHER.
WELL... I GUESS YOU'LL GET THERE IN A FEW YEARS, HUH, SINCE YOU'RE SIXTEEN ALREADY.
WHAT!? I HAVEN'T EVEN FALLEN IN LOVE YET...
WHAT!! REALLY?
THAT'S WAY IN THE FUTURE!
I'M NOT POPULAR WITH THE GUYS. IT'S HOPELESS.
しょんぼり
SHONBORI (DROOP)
NO WAY!! IF IT WERE ME, I WOULDN'T LEAVE YOU ALONE!
IF I WERE A FEW YEARS YOUNGER... WELL, NO, EVEN NOW, IT'S TOTALLY DOABLE!!
SHUT UP, YOU PERV.

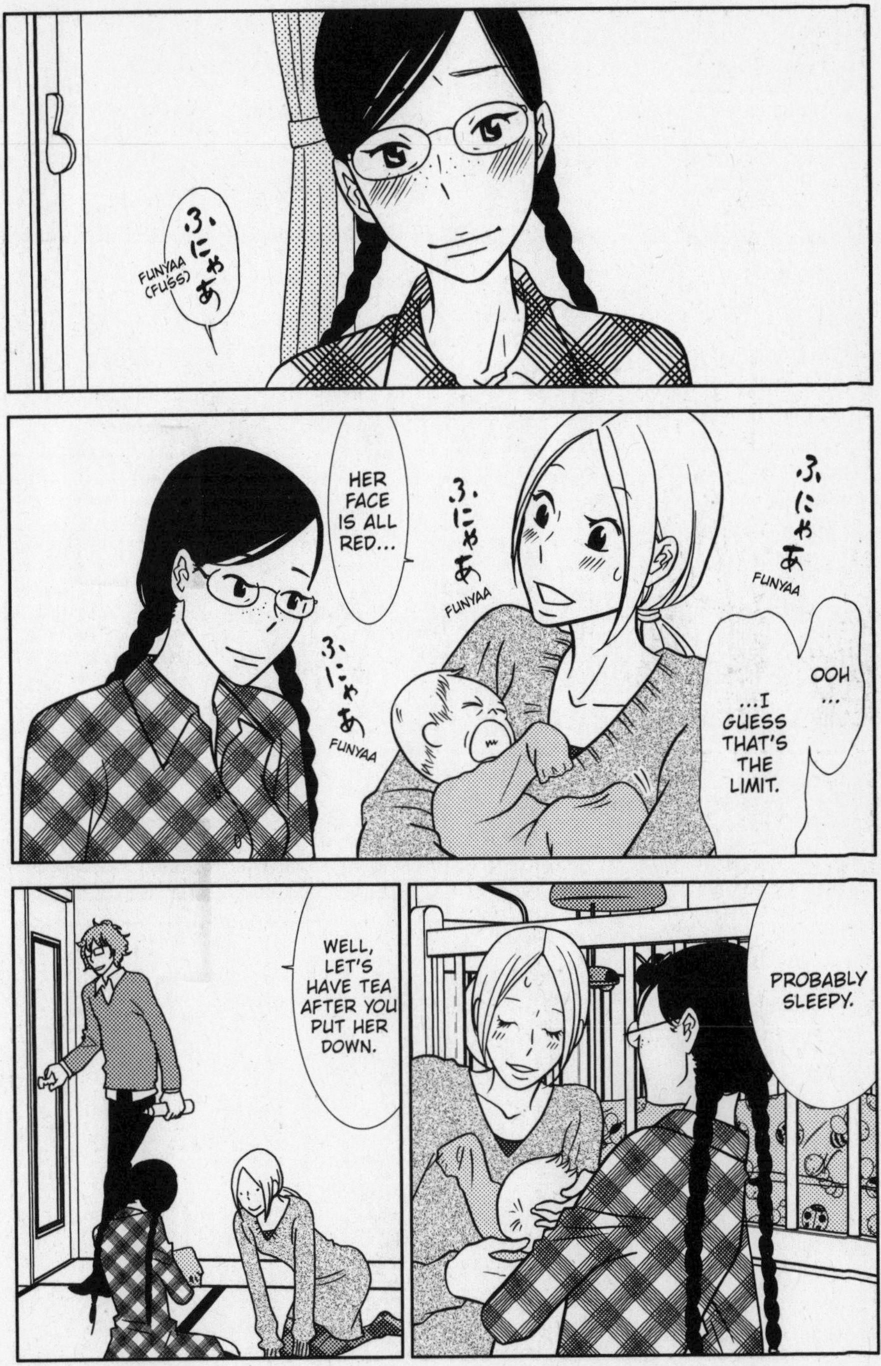
ふにゃあ
FUNYAA (FUSS)
ふにゃあ
FUNYAA
OOH...
...I GUESS THAT'S THE LIMIT.
ふにゃあ
FUNYAA
HER FACE IS ALL RED...
ふにゃあ
FUNYAA
PROBABLY SLEEPY.
WELL, LET'S HAVE TEA AFTER YOU PUT HER DOWN.

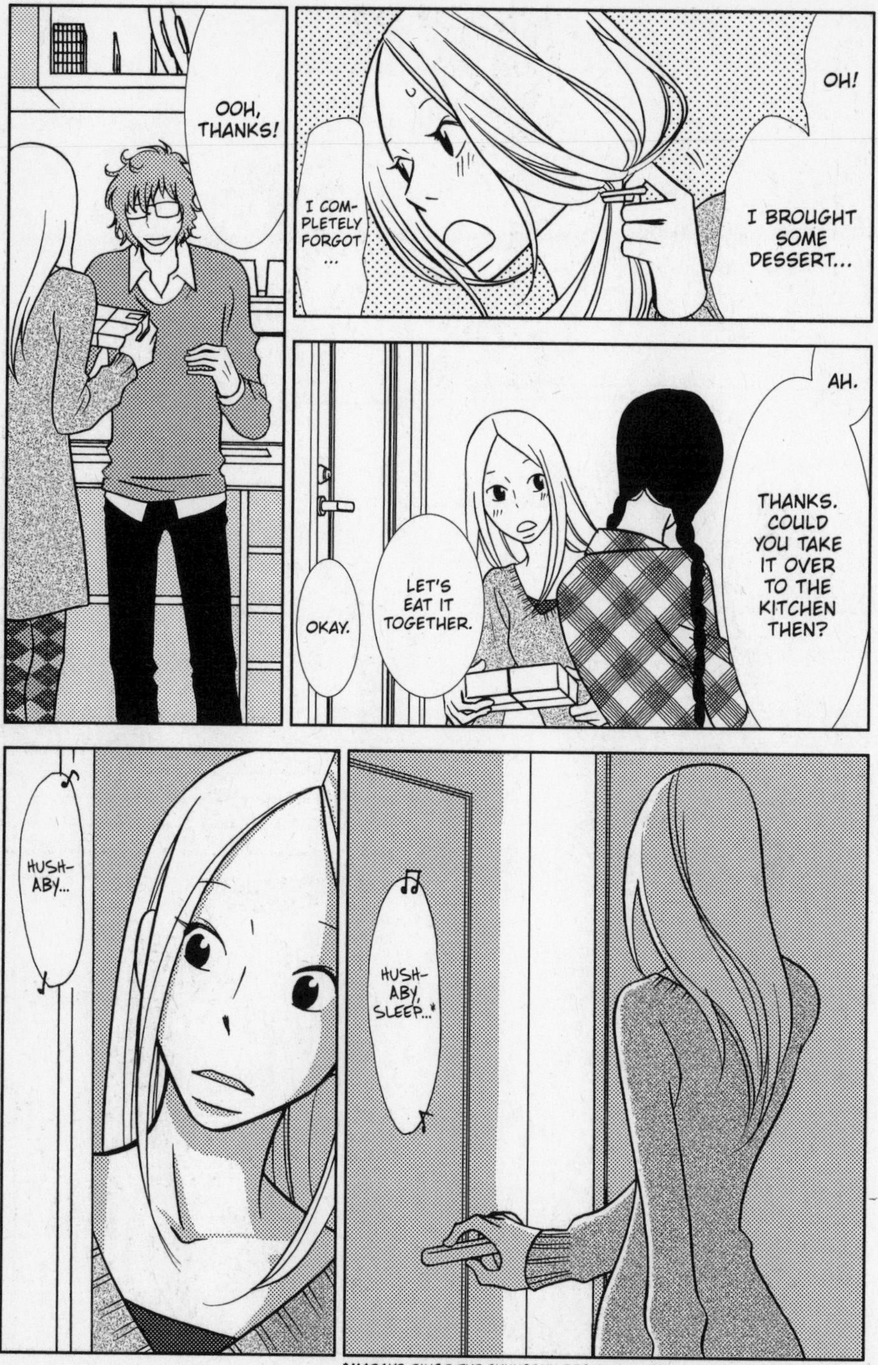
OH!
I BROUGHT SOME DESSERT...
I COMPLETELY FORGOT...
AH.
THANKS. COULD YOU TAKE IT OVER TO THE KITCHEN THEN?
LET'S EAT IT TOGETHER.
OKAY.
OOH, THANKS!
HUSH-ABY, SLEEP...*
HUSH-ABY...

*MASAKO SINGS THE CHUUGOKU REGION LULLABY, A TRADITIONAL LULLABY AND FOLK SONG.

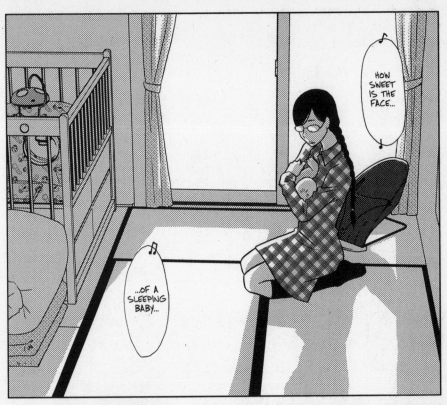

HOW SWEET IS THE FACE...
...OF A SLEEPING BABY...
IT WAS LIKE...
...A LULLABY...
...BUT WHISPERED.
AWAKE ...
...AND CRYING BABY...
AND THE SWEET SCENT...
...OF A BABY?
HUSH-ABY, SLEEP...

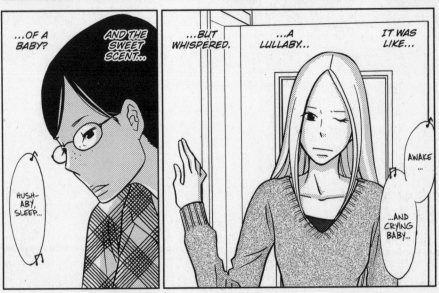

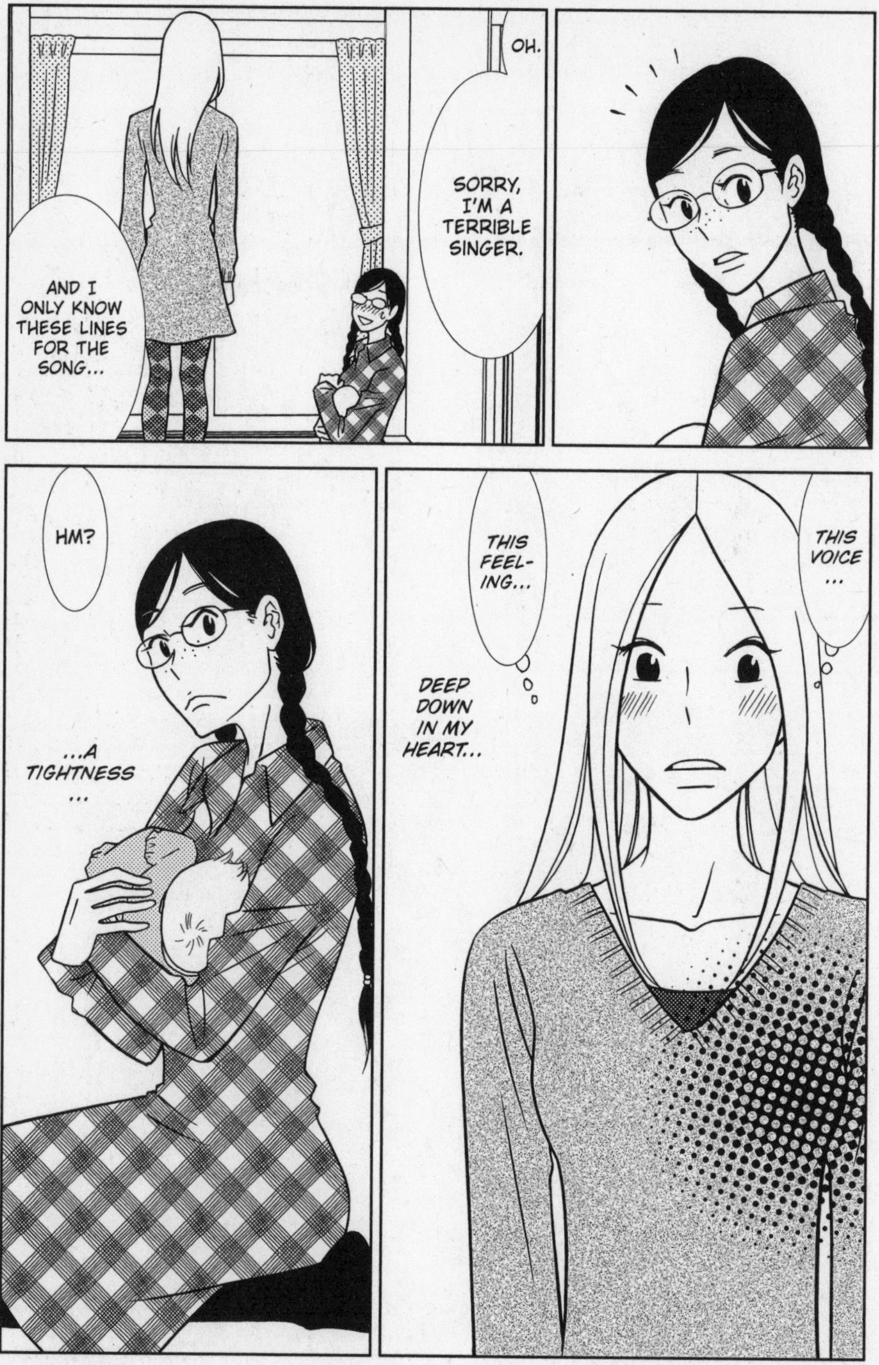
OH.
SORRY, I'M A TERRIBLE SINGER.
AND I ONLY KNOW THESE LINES FOR THE SONG...
THIS VOICE...
THIS FEEL-ING...
DEEP DOWN IN MY HEART...
HM?
...A TIGHTNESS...

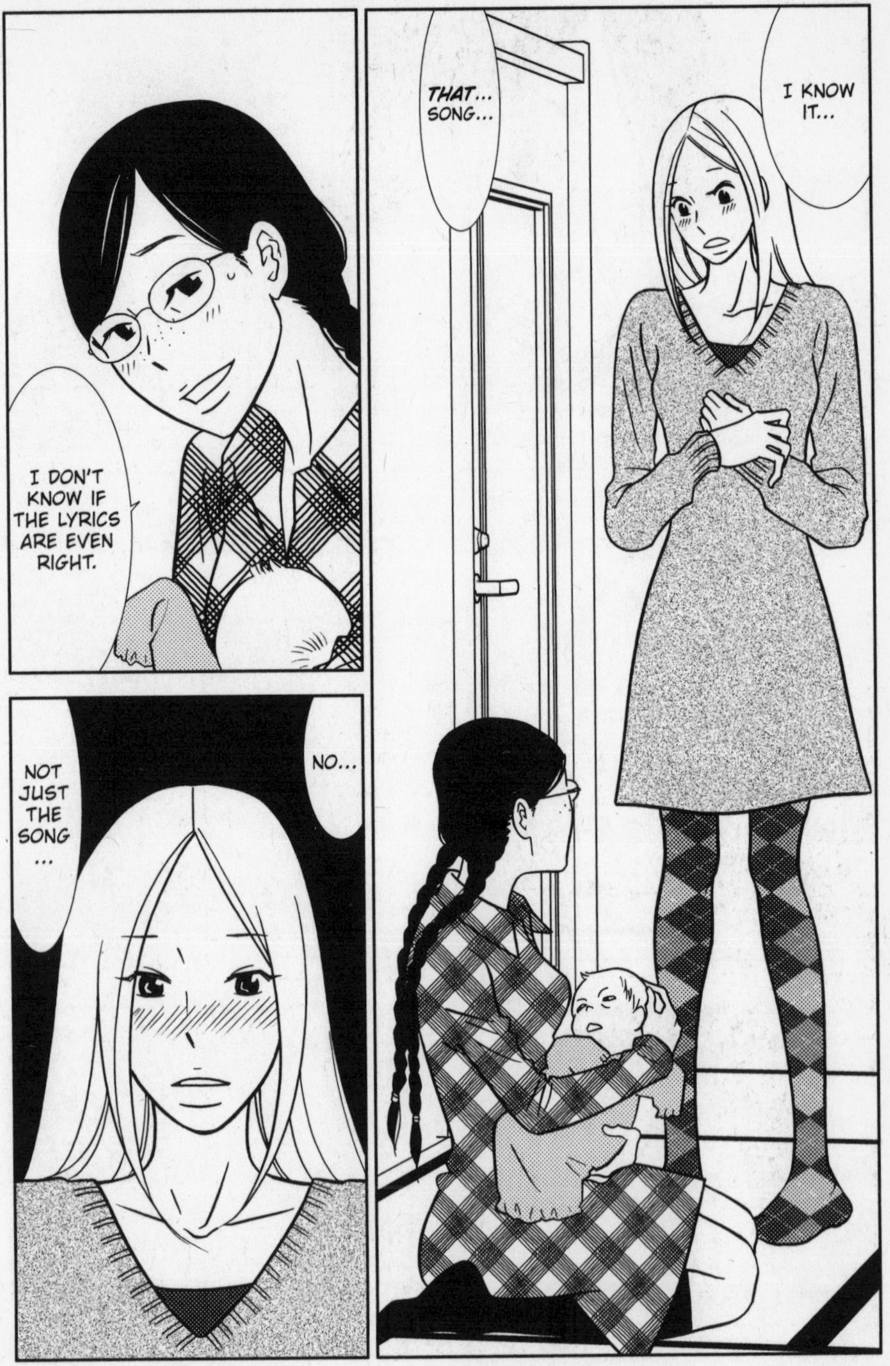
I KNOW IT...
THAT... SONG...
I DON'T KNOW IF THE LYRICS ARE EVEN RIGHT.
NO...
NOT JUST THE SONG ...

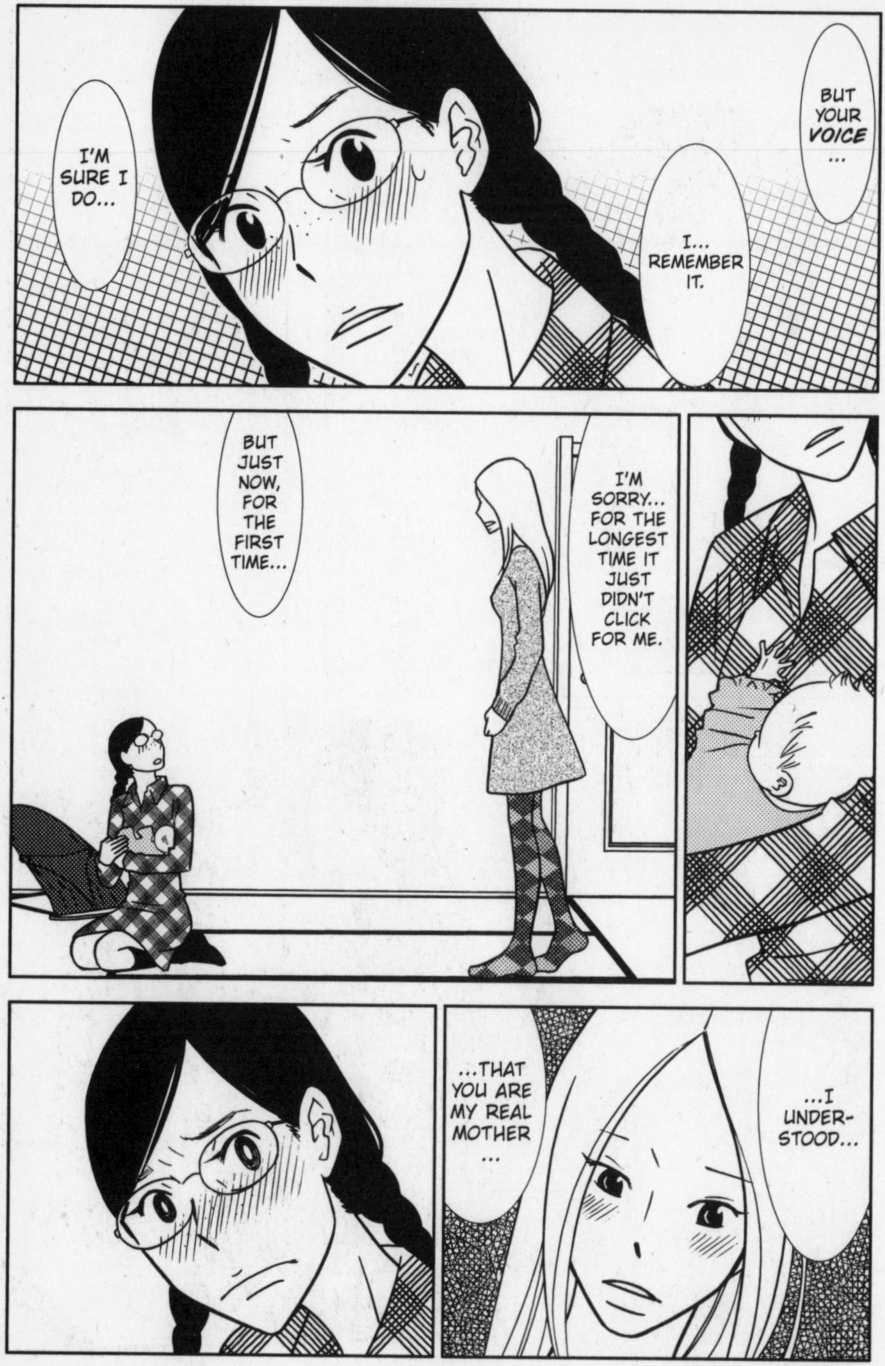
BUT YOUR VOICE ...
I... REMEMBER IT.
I'M SURE I DO...
I'M SORRY... FOR THE LONGEST TIME IT JUST DIDN'T CLICK FOR ME.
BUT JUST NOW, FOR THE FIRST TIME...
...I UNDERSTOOD...
...THAT YOU ARE MY REAL MOTHER ...

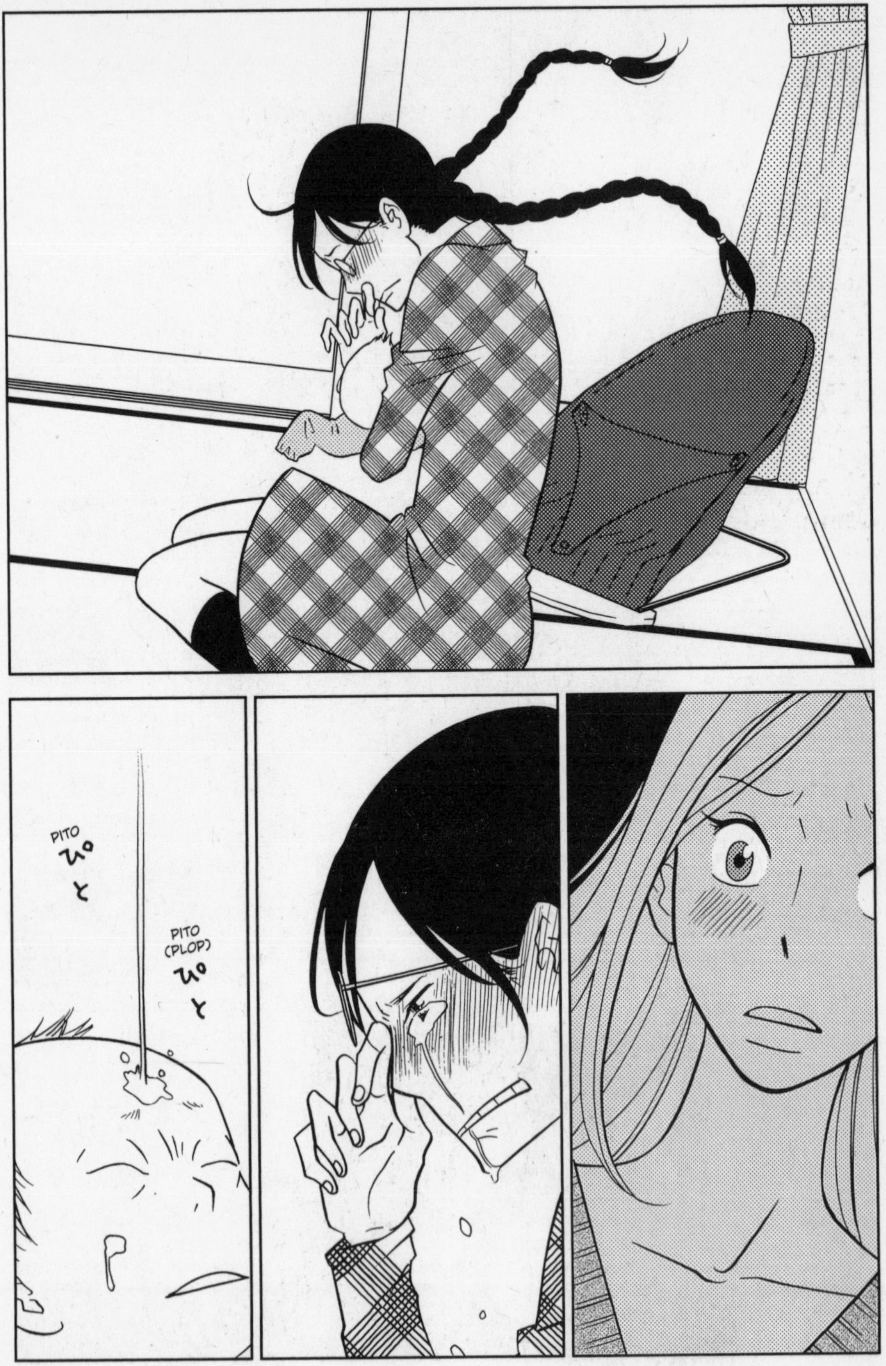
PITO
ぴと
PITO
(PLOP)
ぴと

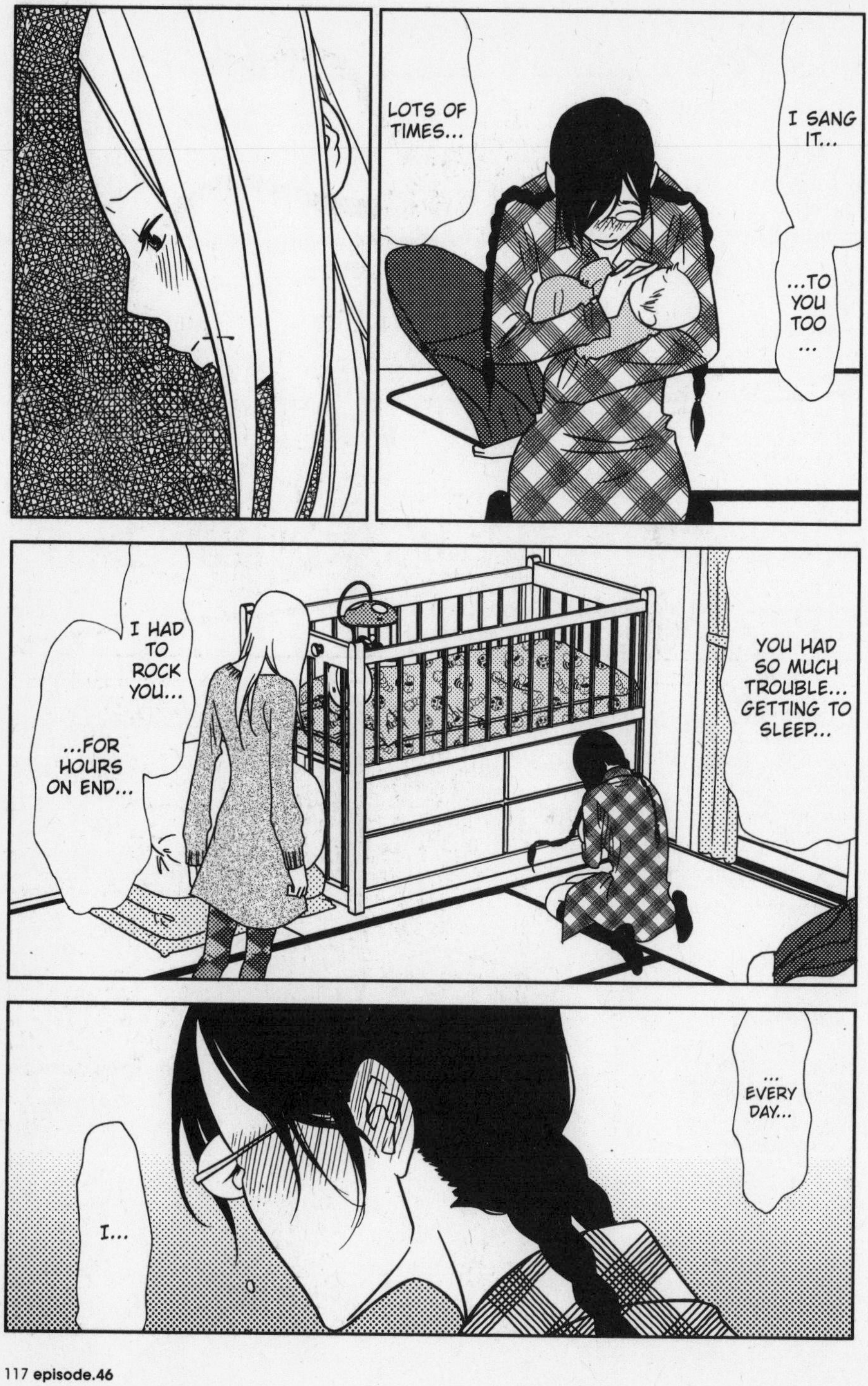
I SANG IT...
...TO YOU TOO ...
LOTS OF TIMES...
YOU HAD SO MUCH TROUBLE... GETTING TO SLEEP...
I HAD TO ROCK YOU...
...FOR HOURS ON END...
... EVERY DAY...
I...

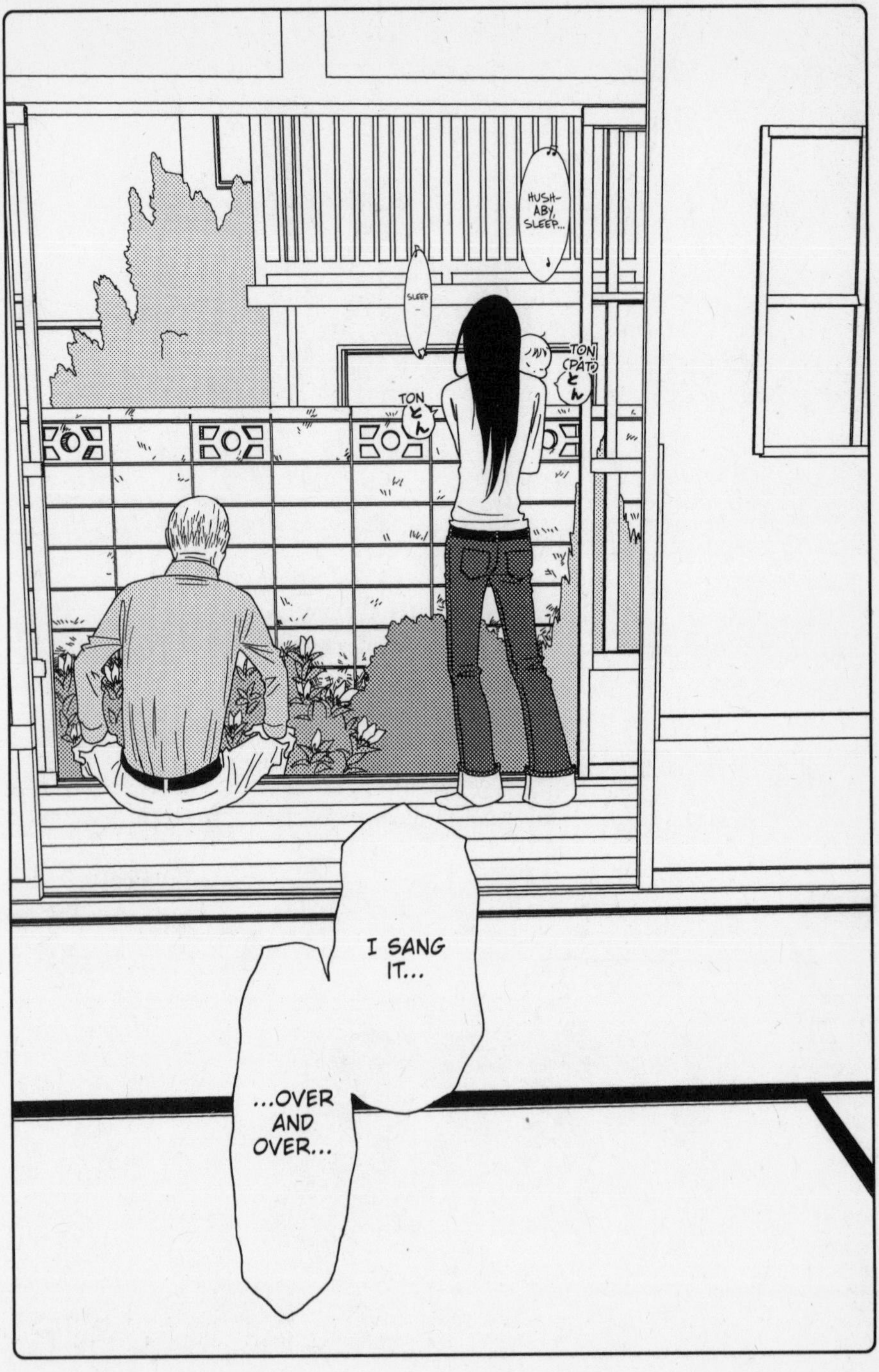
HUSH-ABY, SLEEP...
TON (PAT) とん
SLEEP —
TON とん
I SANG IT...
...OVER AND OVER...

BUNNY**DROP**

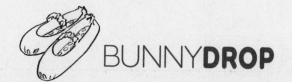

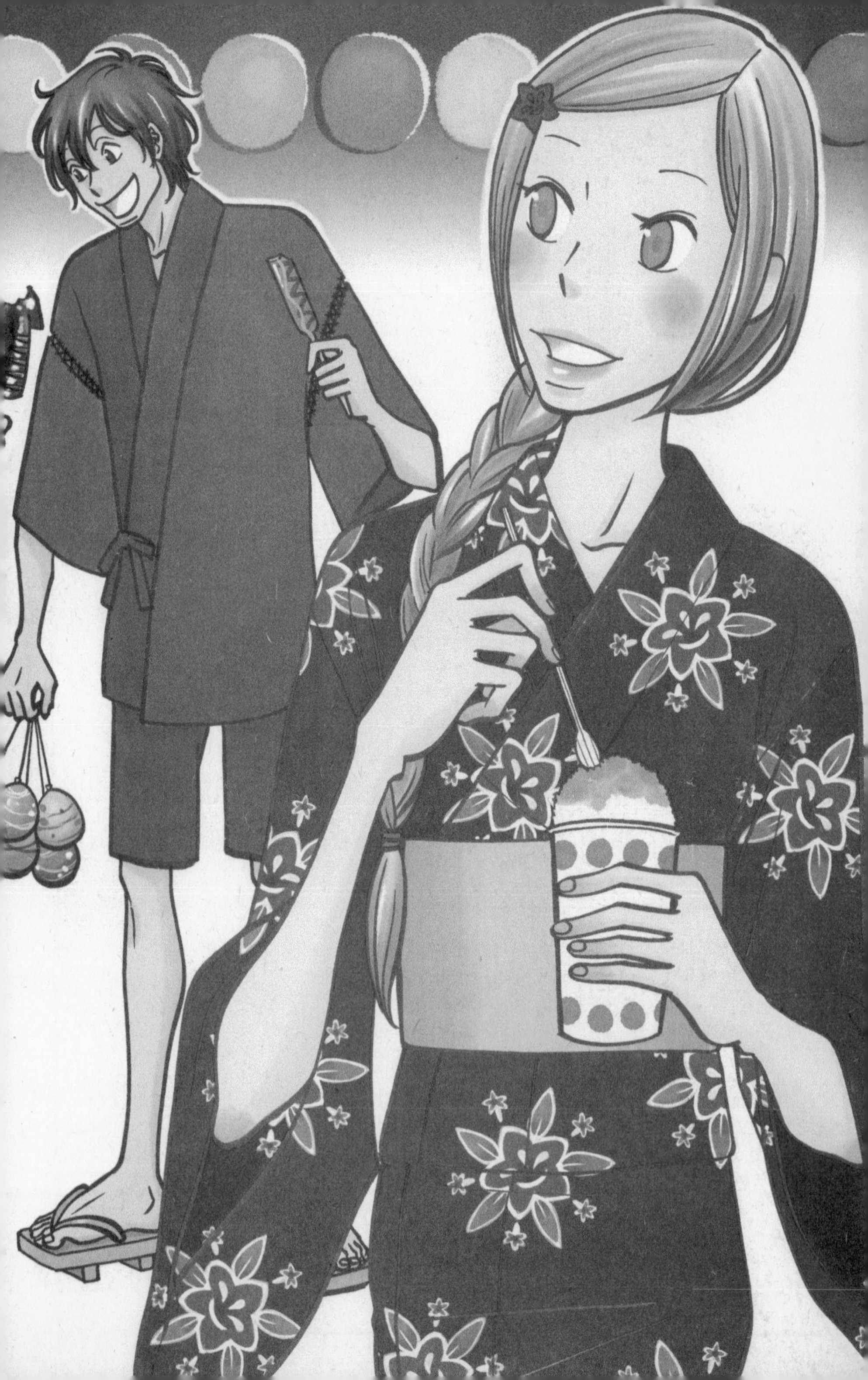

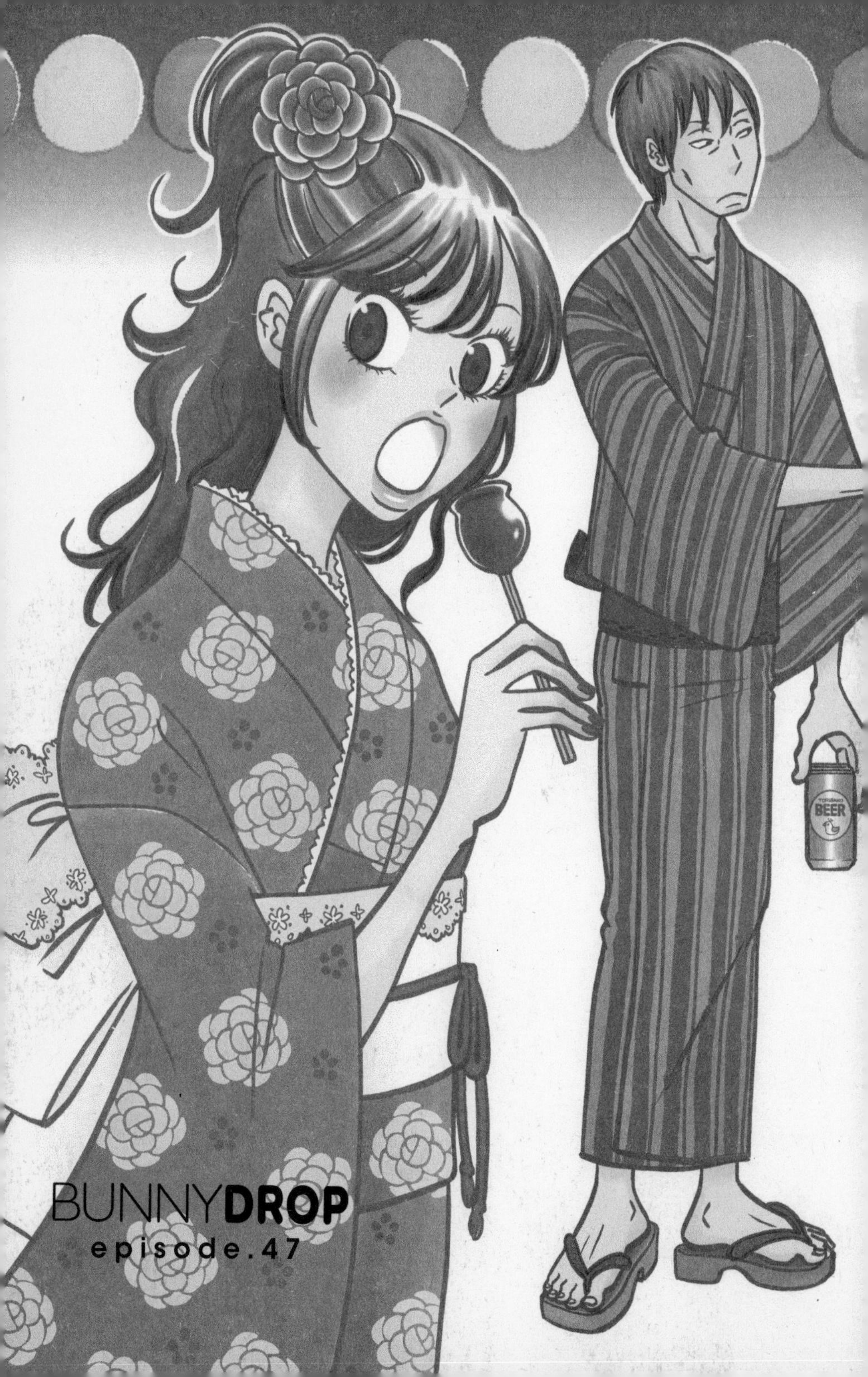
BEER
BUNNYDROP
episode.47

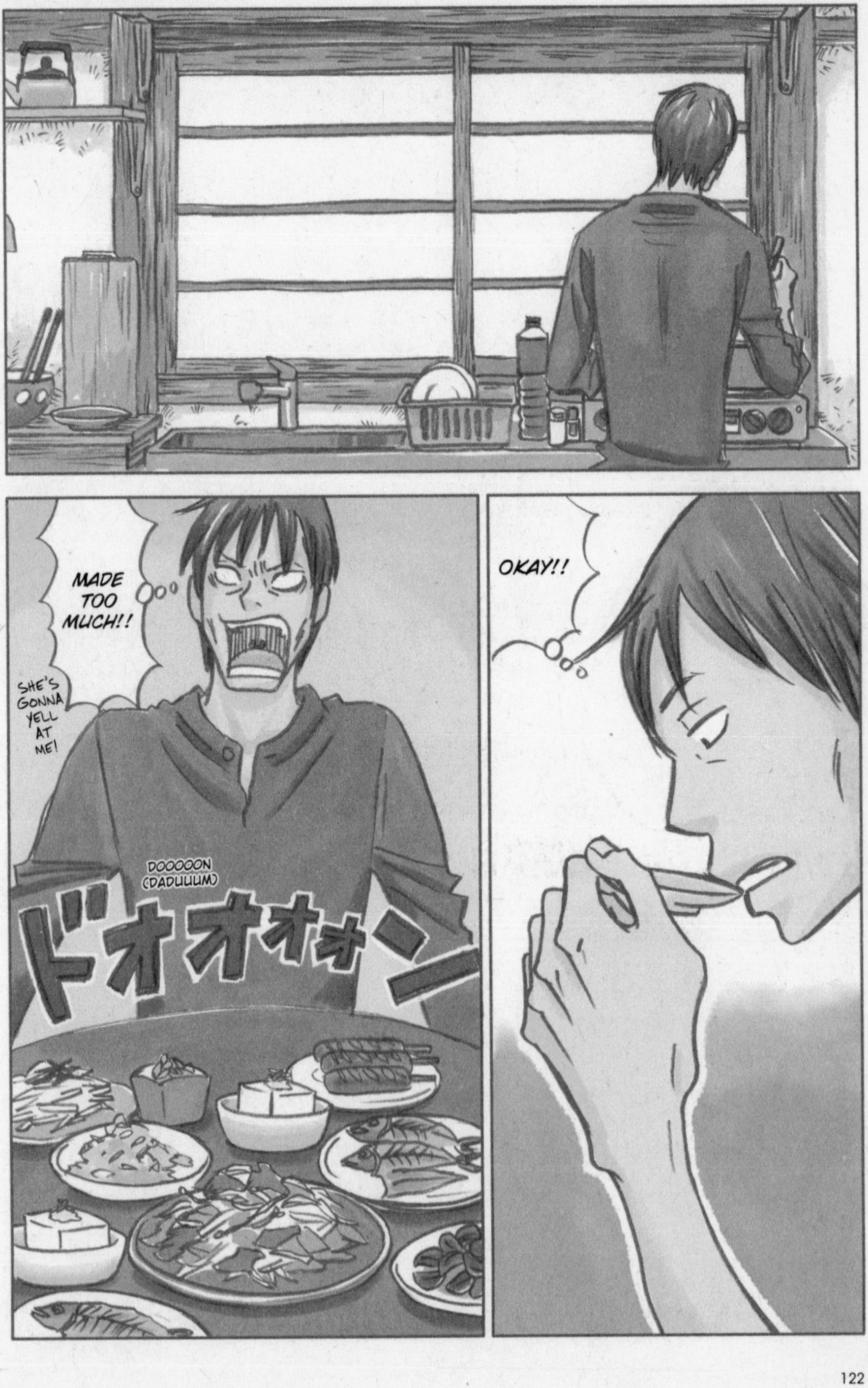
OKAY!!
MADE TOO MUCH!!
SHE'S GONNA YELL AT ME!
DOOOOON (DADUUUM)
ドオオオォン

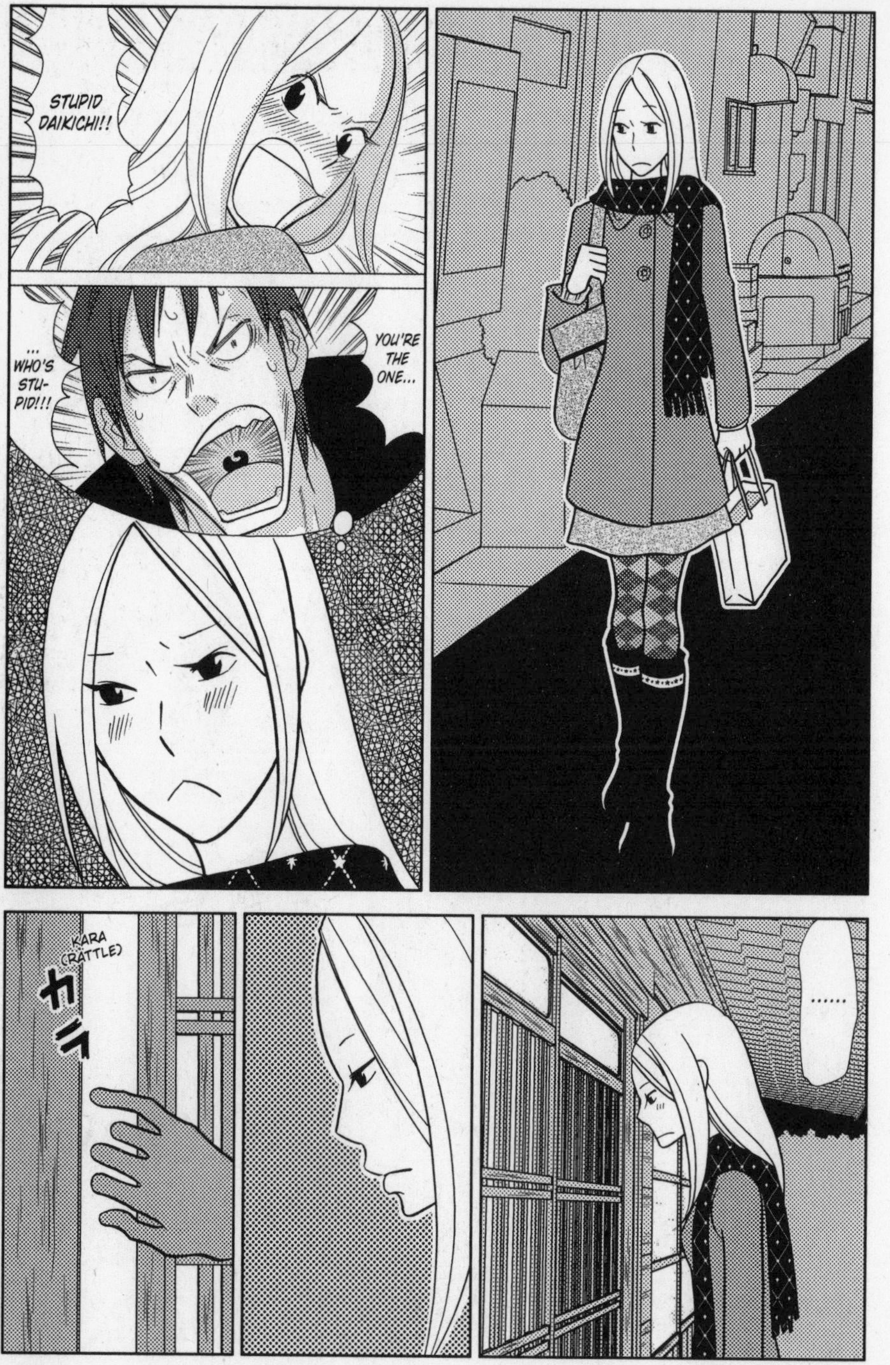
STUPID DAIKICHI!!
YOU'RE THE ONE...
... WHO'S STU-PID!!!
......
カラ
KARA (RATTLE)

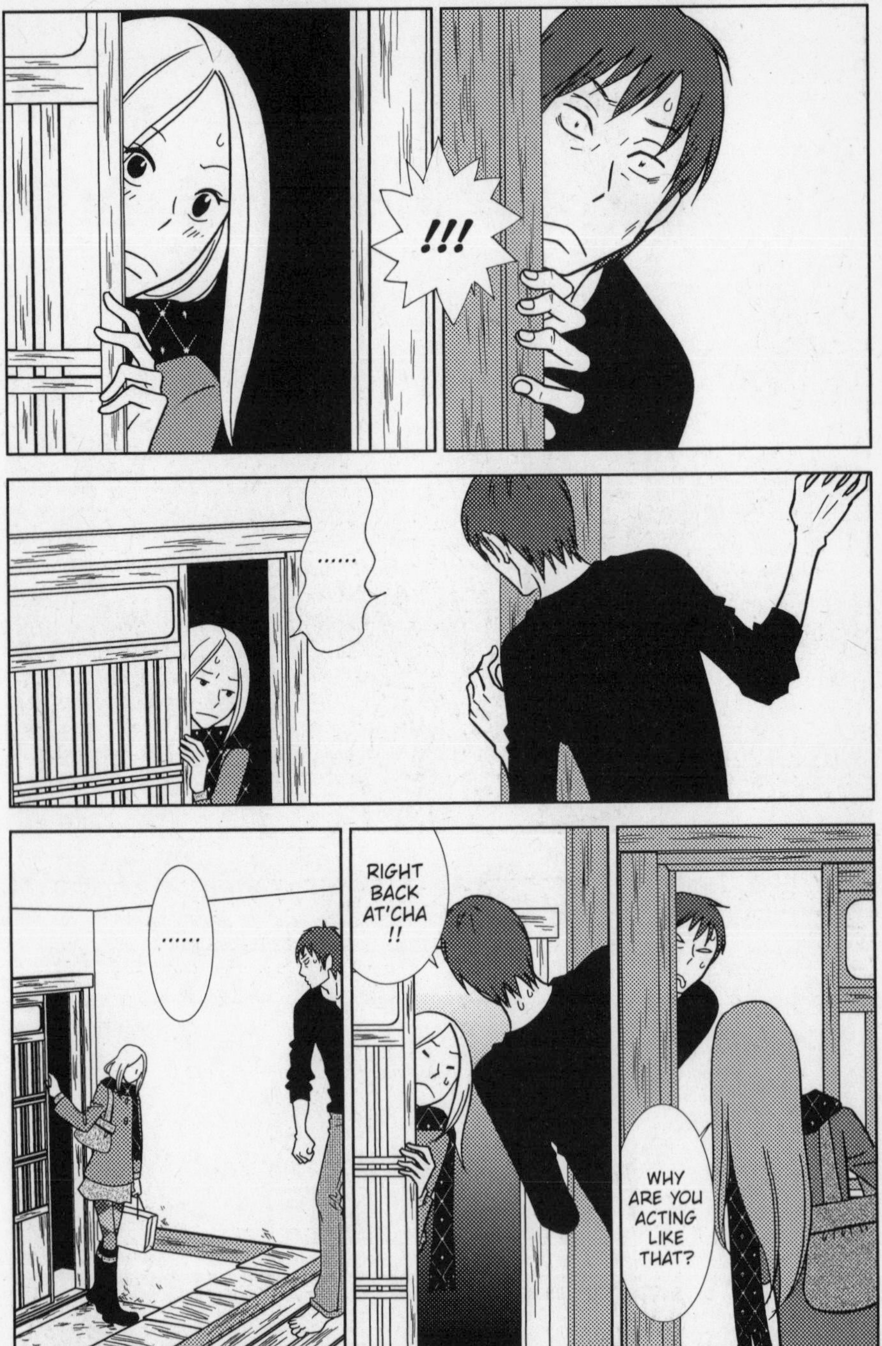
!!!
......
WHY ARE YOU ACTING LIKE THAT?
RIGHT BACK AT'CHA !!
......

PACKAGE: SHUUMAI DUMPLINGS

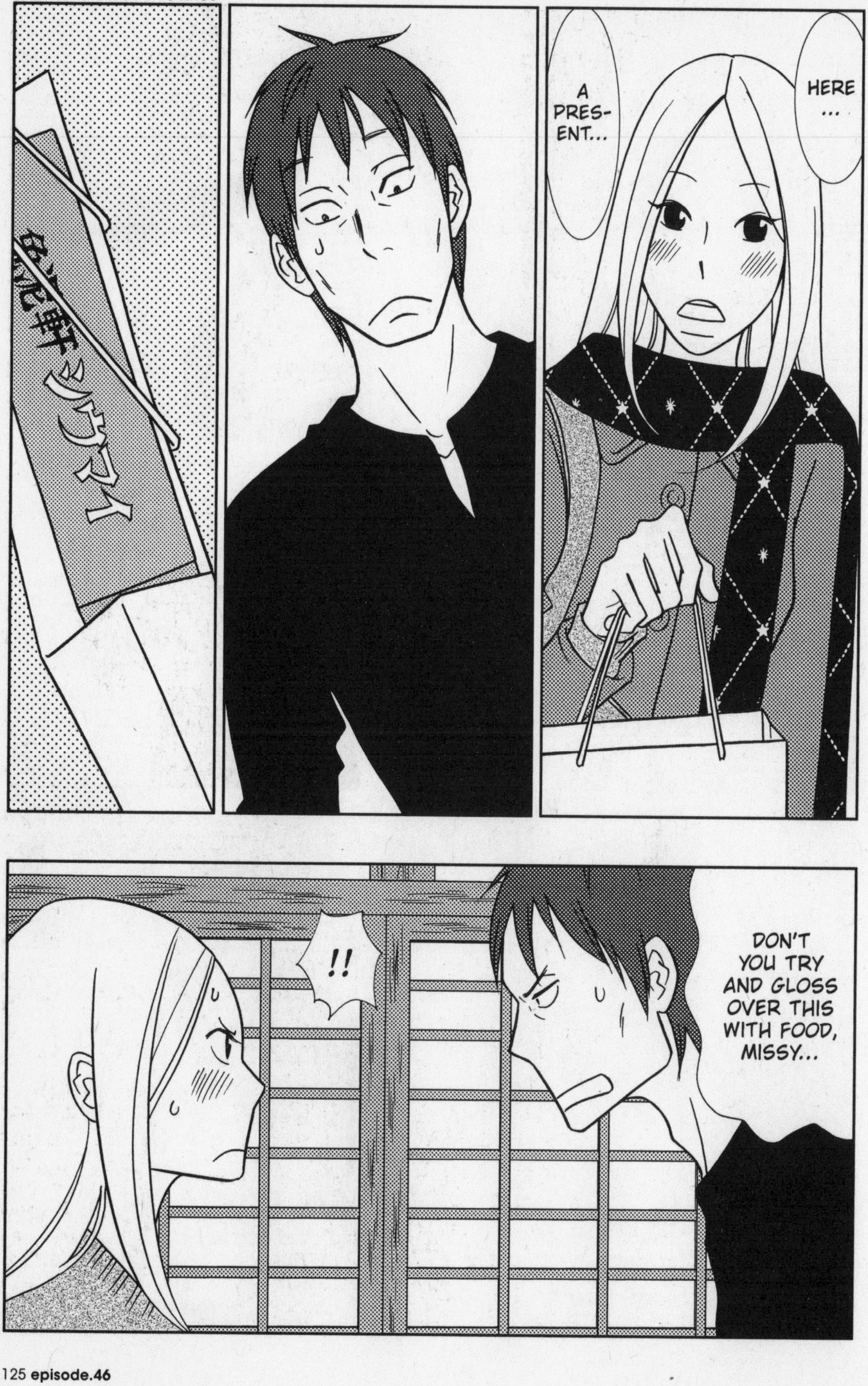
HERE ...
A PRESENT...
シウマイ
DON'T YOU TRY AND GLOSS OVER THIS WITH FOOD, MISSY...
!!

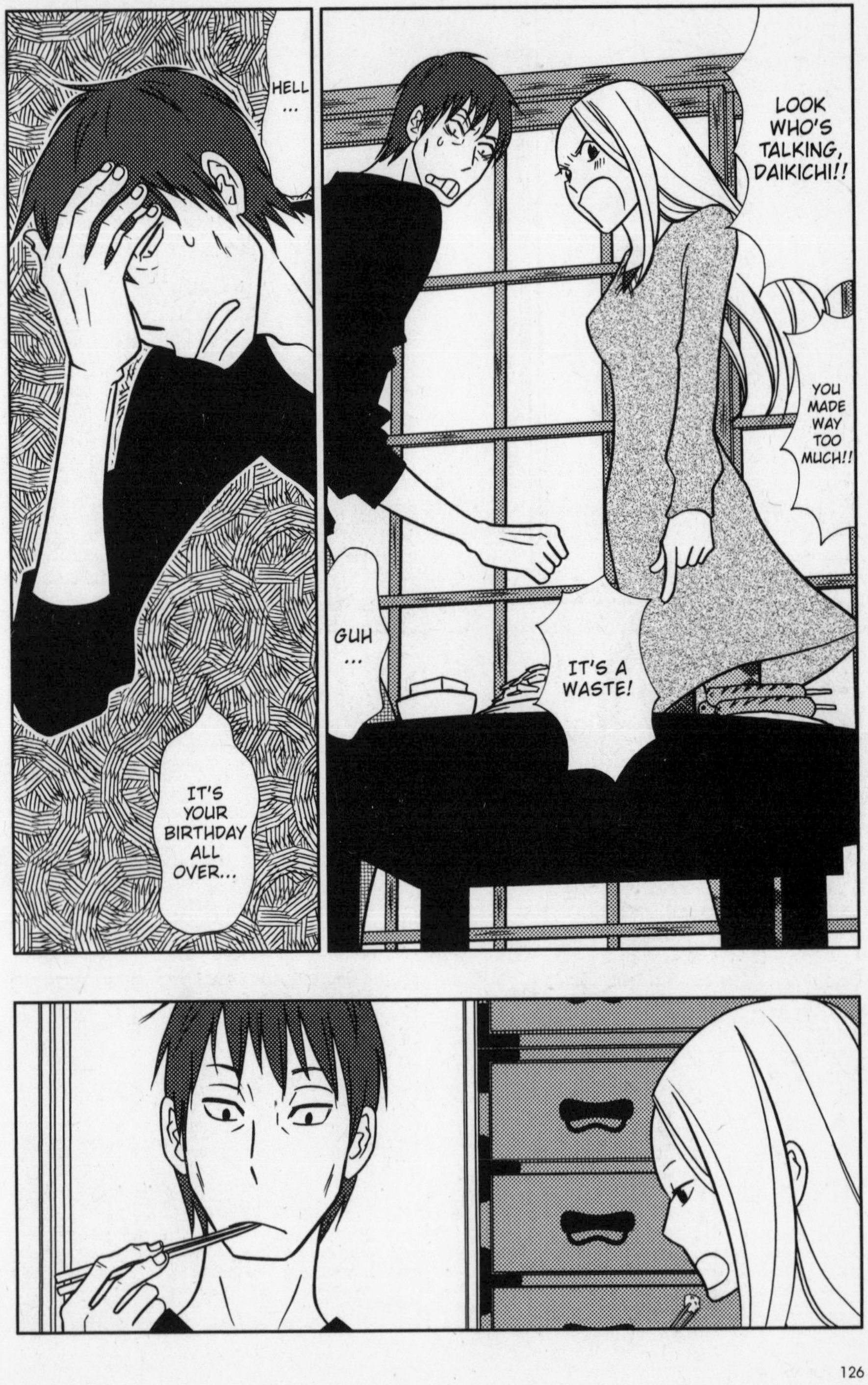
LOOK WHO'S TALKING, DAIKICHI!!
YOU MADE WAY TOO MUCH!!
IT'S A WASTE!
GUH ...
HELL ...
IT'S YOUR BIRTHDAY ALL OVER...

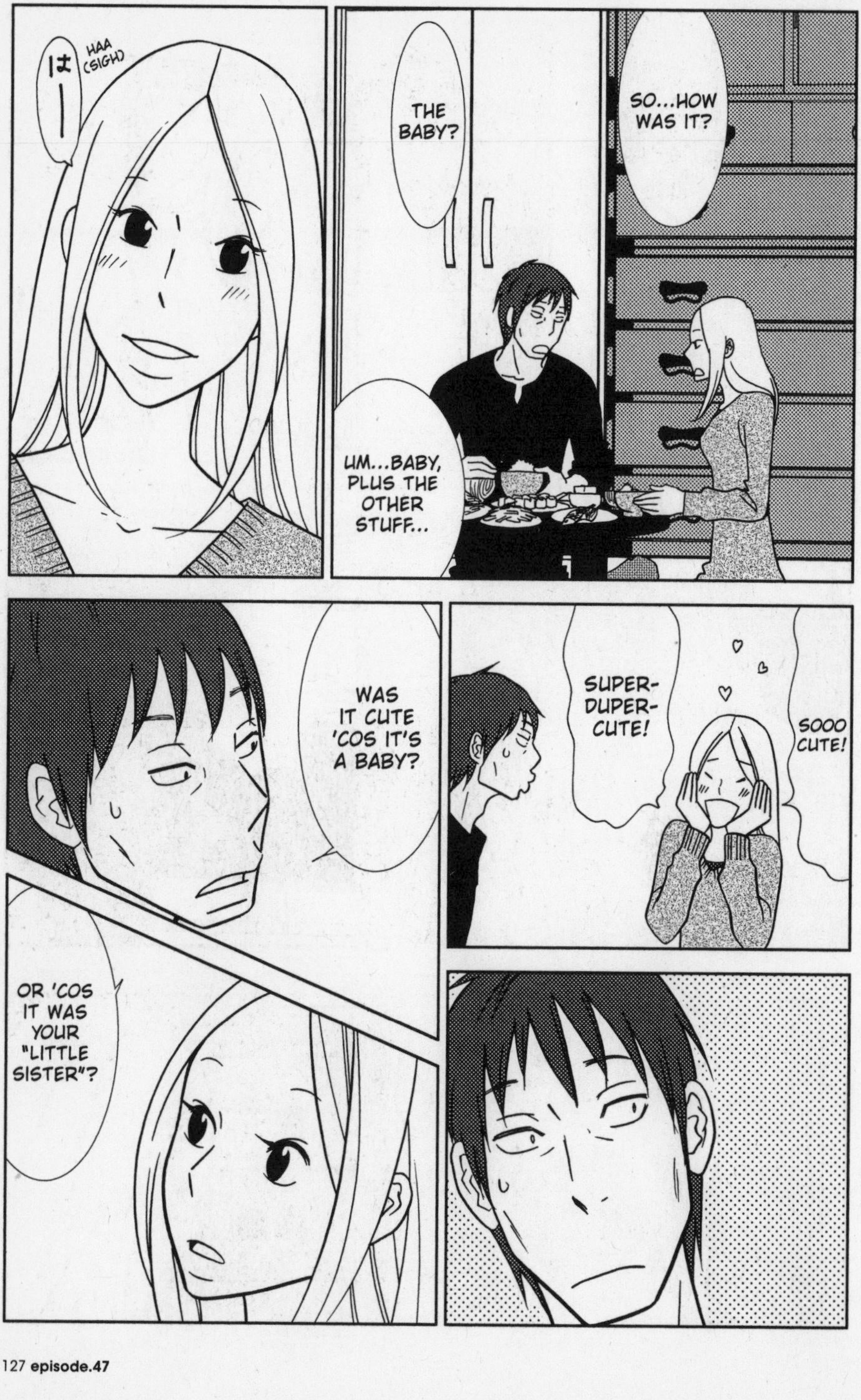
SO...HOW WAS IT?
THE BABY?
UM...BABY, PLUS THE OTHER STUFF...
はー
HAA (SIGH)
SOOO CUTE!
SUPER-DUPER-CUTE!
WAS IT CUTE 'COS IT'S A BABY?
OR 'COS IT WAS YOUR "LITTLE SISTER"?

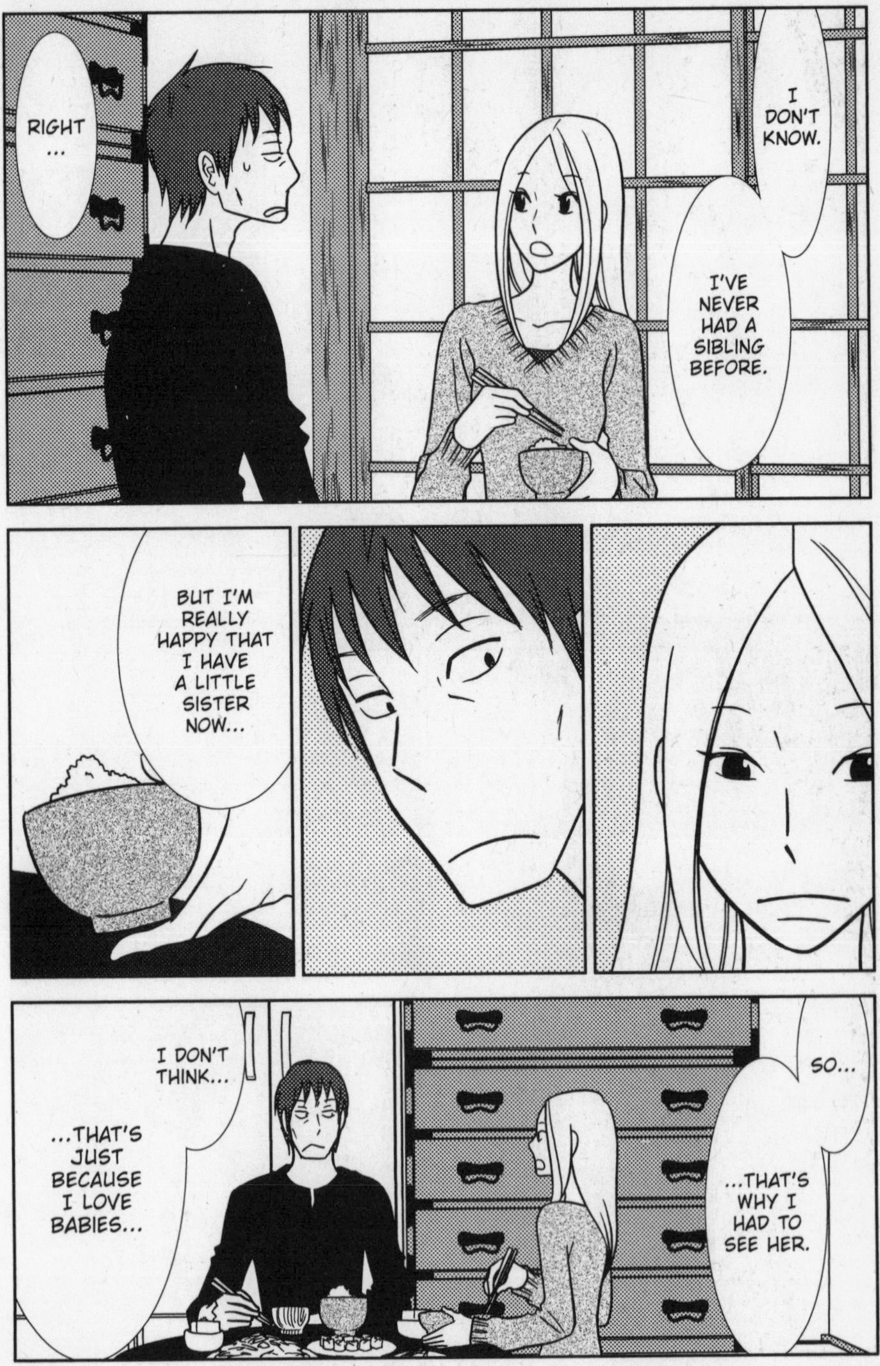
I DON'T KNOW.
I'VE NEVER HAD A SIBLING BEFORE.
RIGHT ...
BUT I'M REALLY HAPPY THAT I HAVE A LITTLE SISTER NOW...
SO...
...THAT'S WHY I HAD TO SEE HER.
I DON'T THINK...
...THAT'S JUST BECAUSE I LOVE BABIES...

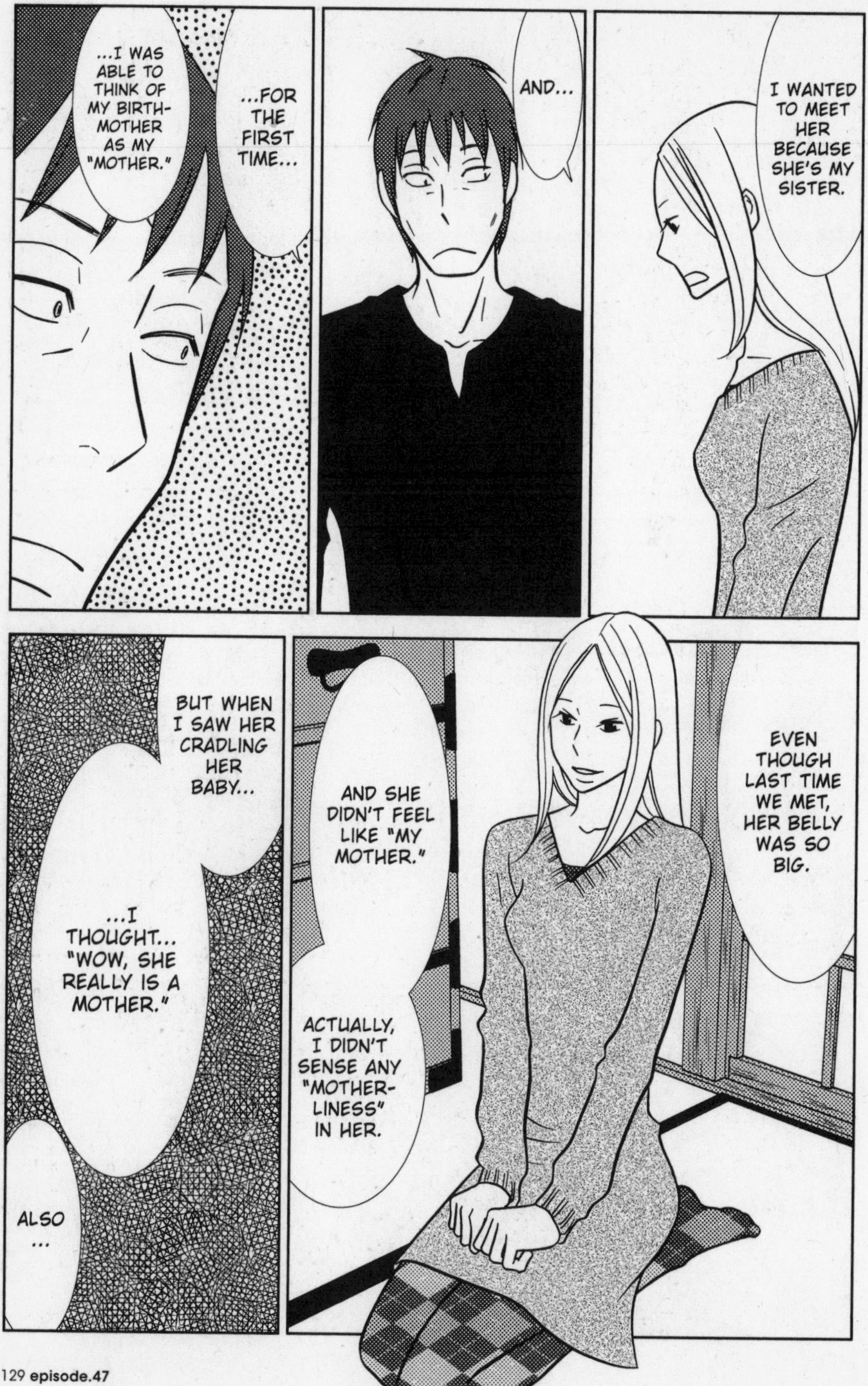
I WANTED TO MEET HER BECAUSE SHE'S MY SISTER.
AND...
...I WAS ABLE TO THINK OF MY BIRTH-MOTHER AS MY "MOTHER."
...FOR THE FIRST TIME...
EVEN THOUGH LAST TIME WE MET, HER BELLY WAS SO BIG.
AND SHE DIDN'T FEEL LIKE "MY MOTHER."
ACTUALLY, I DIDN'T SENSE ANY "MOTHER-LINESS" IN HER.
BUT WHEN I SAW HER CRADLING HER BABY...
...I THOUGHT... "WOW, SHE REALLY IS A MOTHER."
ALSO ...

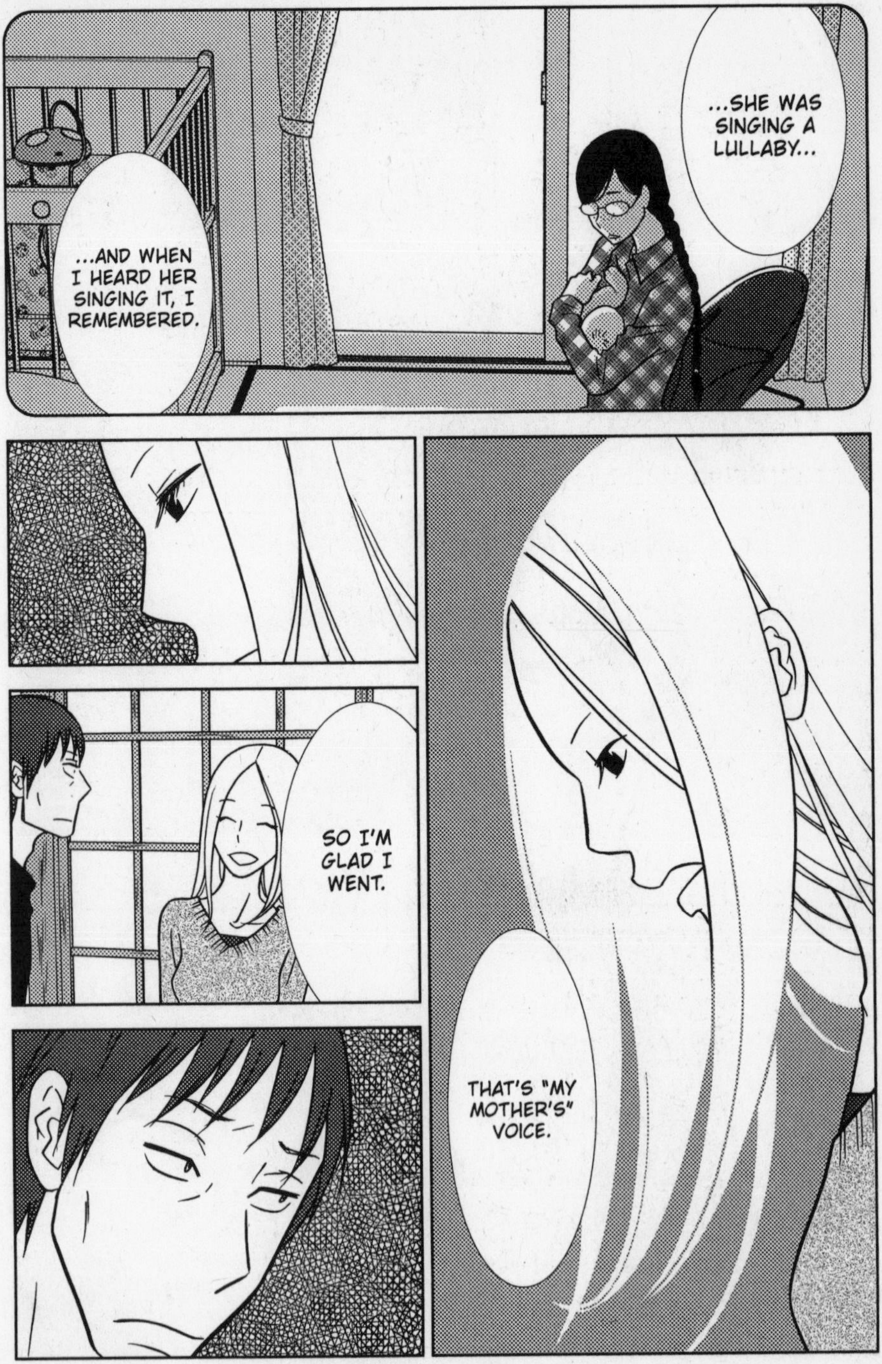
...SHE WAS SINGING A LULLABY...
...AND WHEN I HEARD HER SINGING IT, I REMEMBERED.
THAT'S "MY MOTHER'S" VOICE.
SO I'M GLAD I WENT.

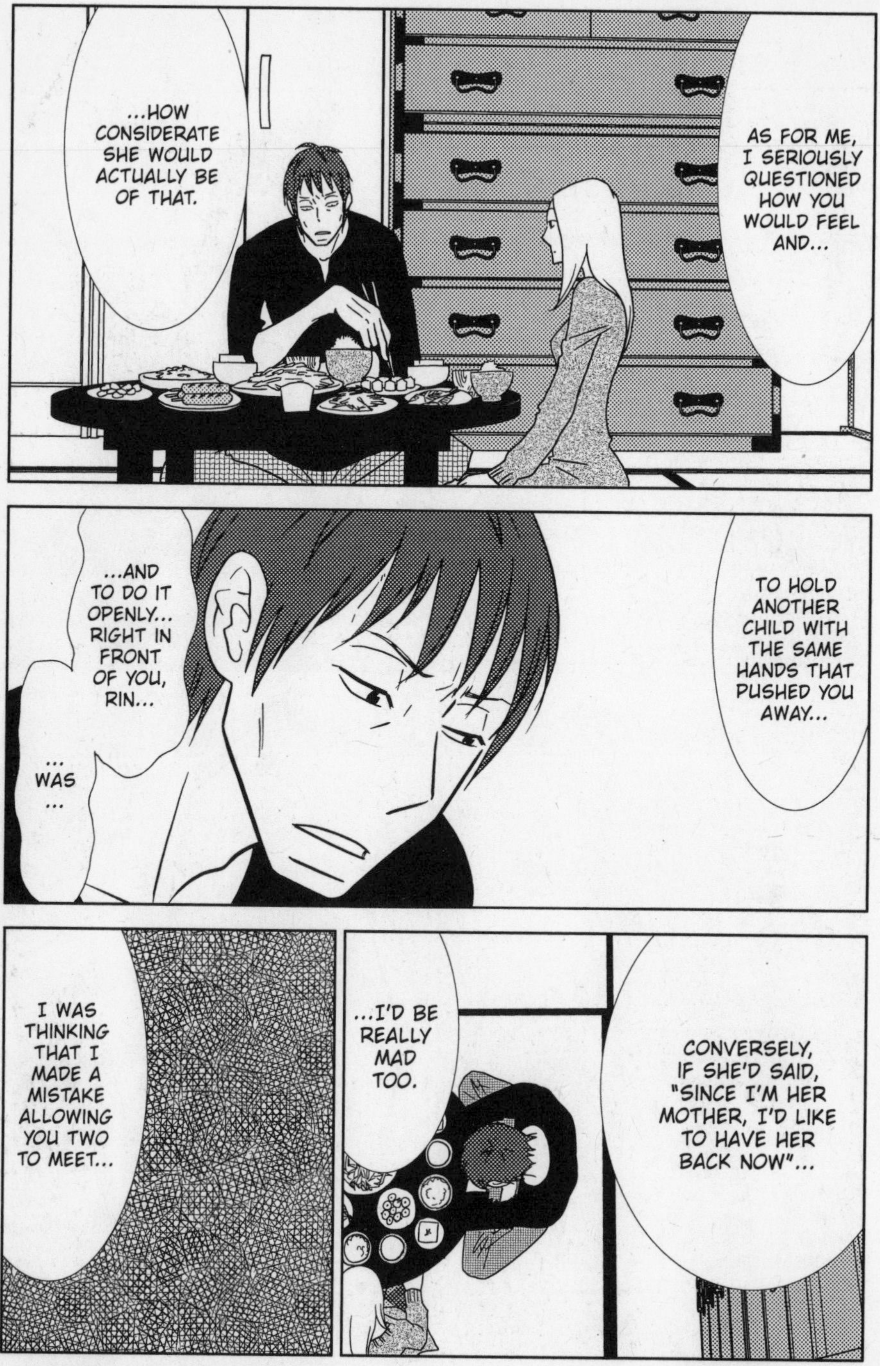
AS FOR ME, I SERIOUSLY QUESTIONED HOW YOU WOULD FEEL AND...
...HOW CONSIDERATE SHE WOULD ACTUALLY BE OF THAT.
TO HOLD ANOTHER CHILD WITH THE SAME HANDS THAT PUSHED YOU AWAY...
...AND TO DO IT OPENLY... RIGHT IN FRONT OF YOU, RIN...
... WAS ...
CONVERSELY, IF SHE'D SAID, "SINCE I'M HER MOTHER, I'D LIKE TO HAVE HER BACK NOW"...
...I'D BE REALLY MAD TOO.
I WAS THINKING THAT I MADE A MISTAKE ALLOWING YOU TWO TO MEET...

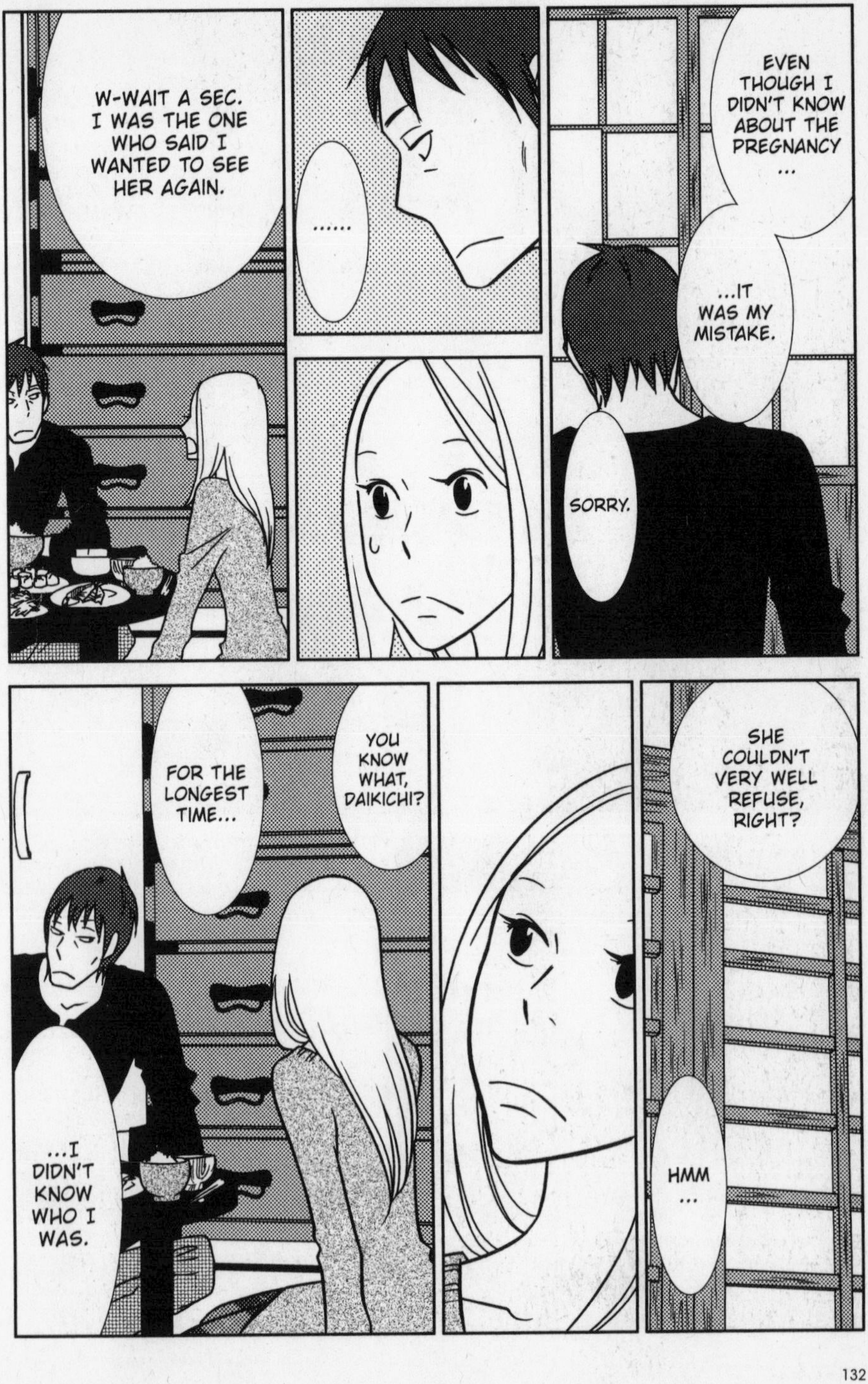
EVEN THOUGH I DIDN'T KNOW ABOUT THE PREGNANCY ...
...IT WAS MY MISTAKE.
SORRY.
......
W-WAIT A SEC. I WAS THE ONE WHO SAID I WANTED TO SEE HER AGAIN.
SHE COULDN'T VERY WELL REFUSE, RIGHT?
HMM ...
YOU KNOW WHAT, DAIKICHI?
FOR THE LONGEST TIME...
...I DIDN'T KNOW WHO I WAS.

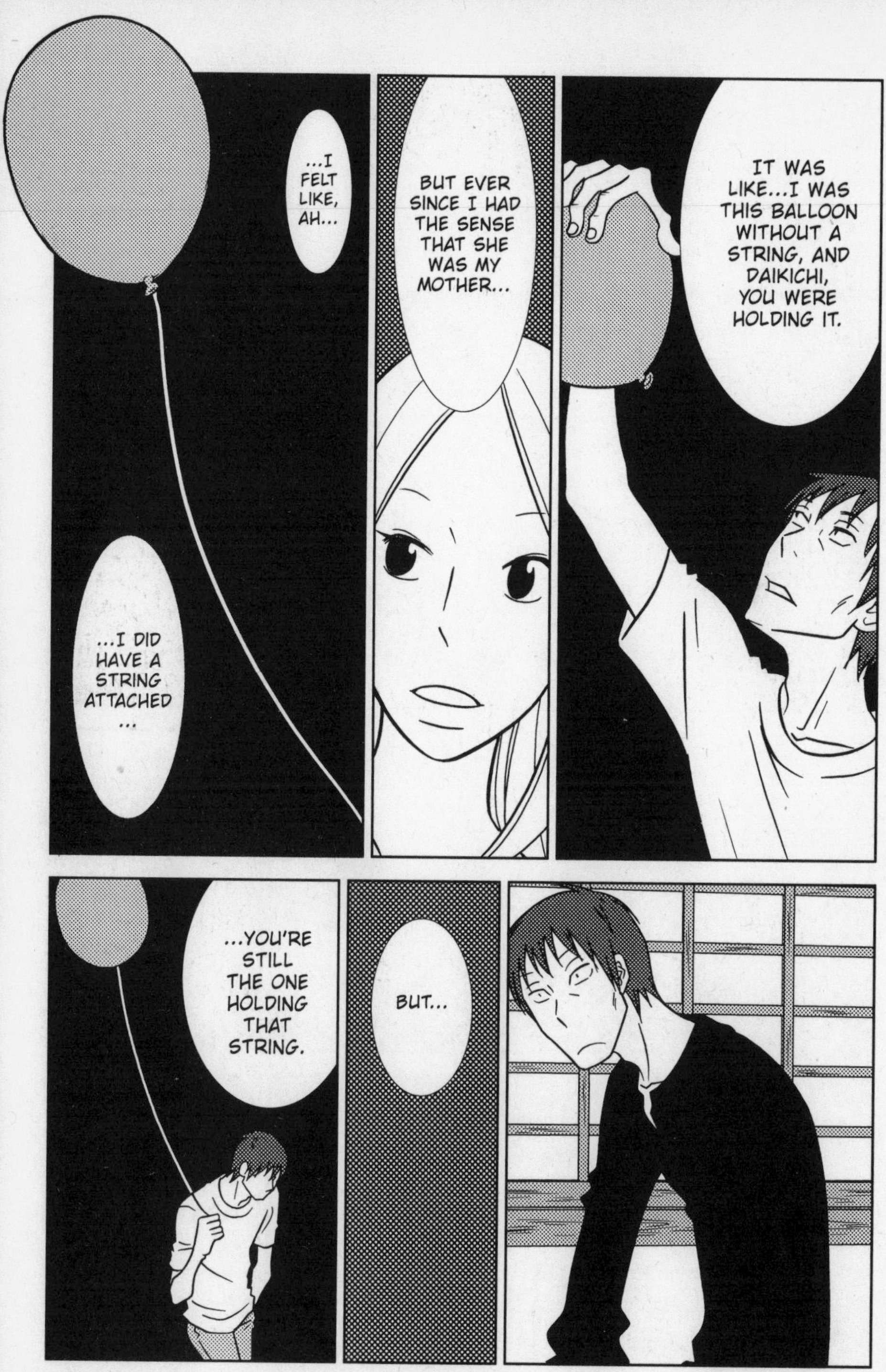
IT WAS LIKE...I WAS THIS BALLOON WITHOUT A STRING, AND DAIKICHI, YOU WERE HOLDING IT.
BUT EVER SINCE I HAD THE SENSE THAT SHE WAS MY MOTHER...
...I FELT LIKE, AH...
...I DID HAVE A STRING ATTACHED...
BUT...
...YOU'RE STILL THE ONE HOLDING THAT STRING.

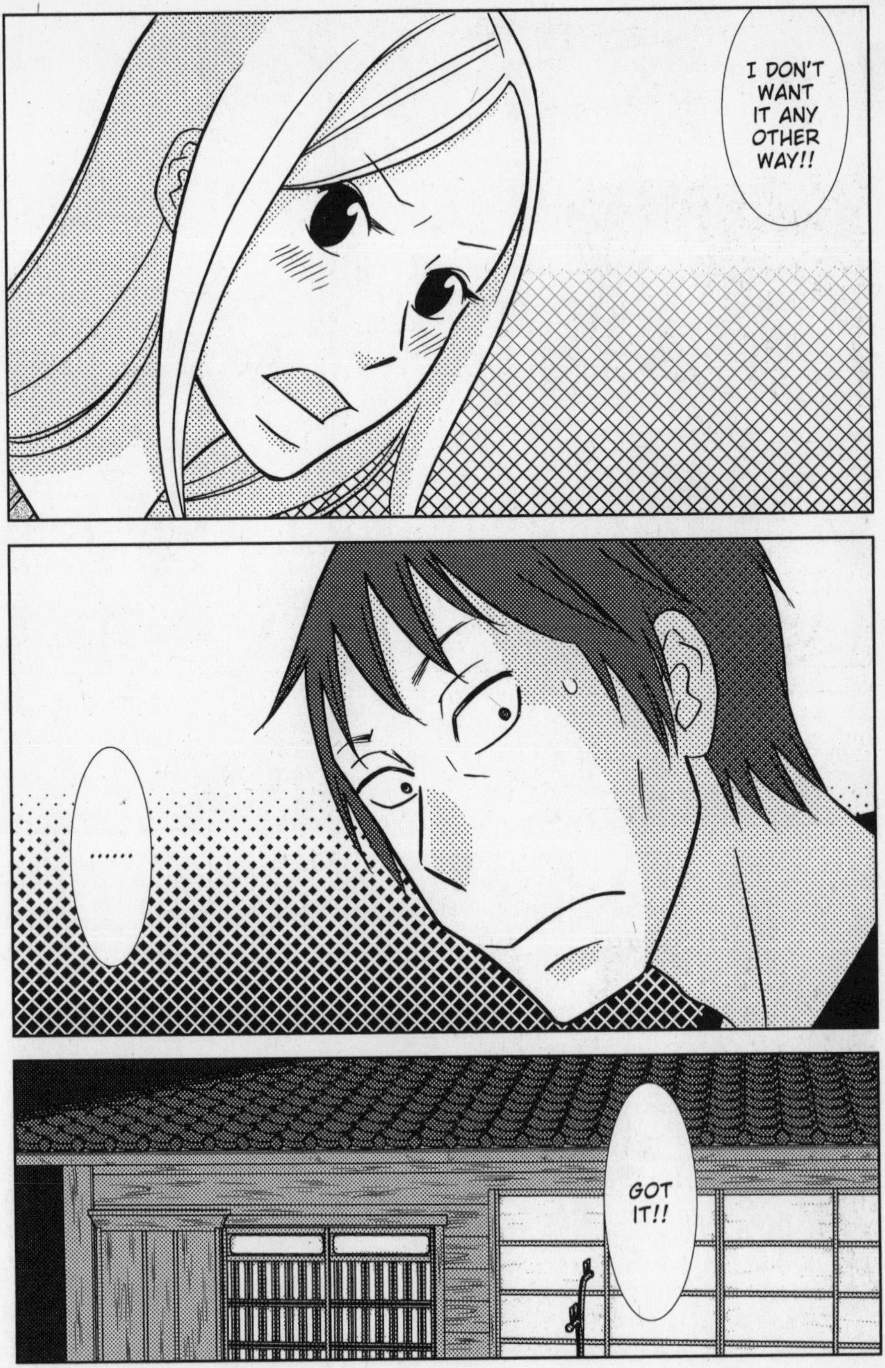
I DON'T WANT IT ANY OTHER WAY!!
......
GOT IT!!

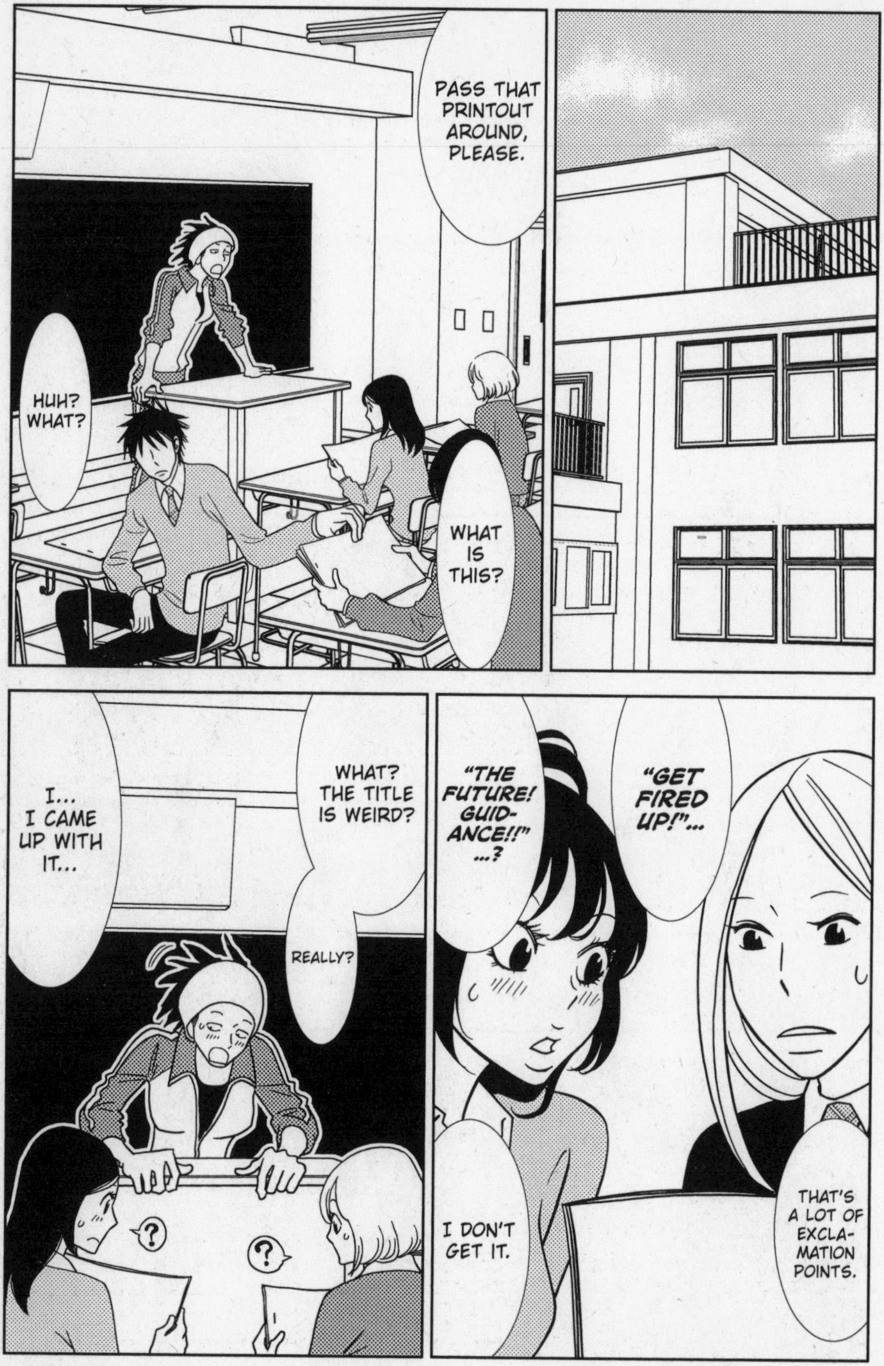
PASS THAT PRINTOUT AROUND, PLEASE.
WHAT IS THIS?
HUH? WHAT?
"GET FIRED UP!"...
"THE FUTURE! GUID-ANCE!!" ...?
THAT'S A LOT OF EXCLA-MATION POINTS.
I DON'T GET IT.
WHAT? THE TITLE IS WEIRD?
REALLY?
I... I CAME UP WITH IT...

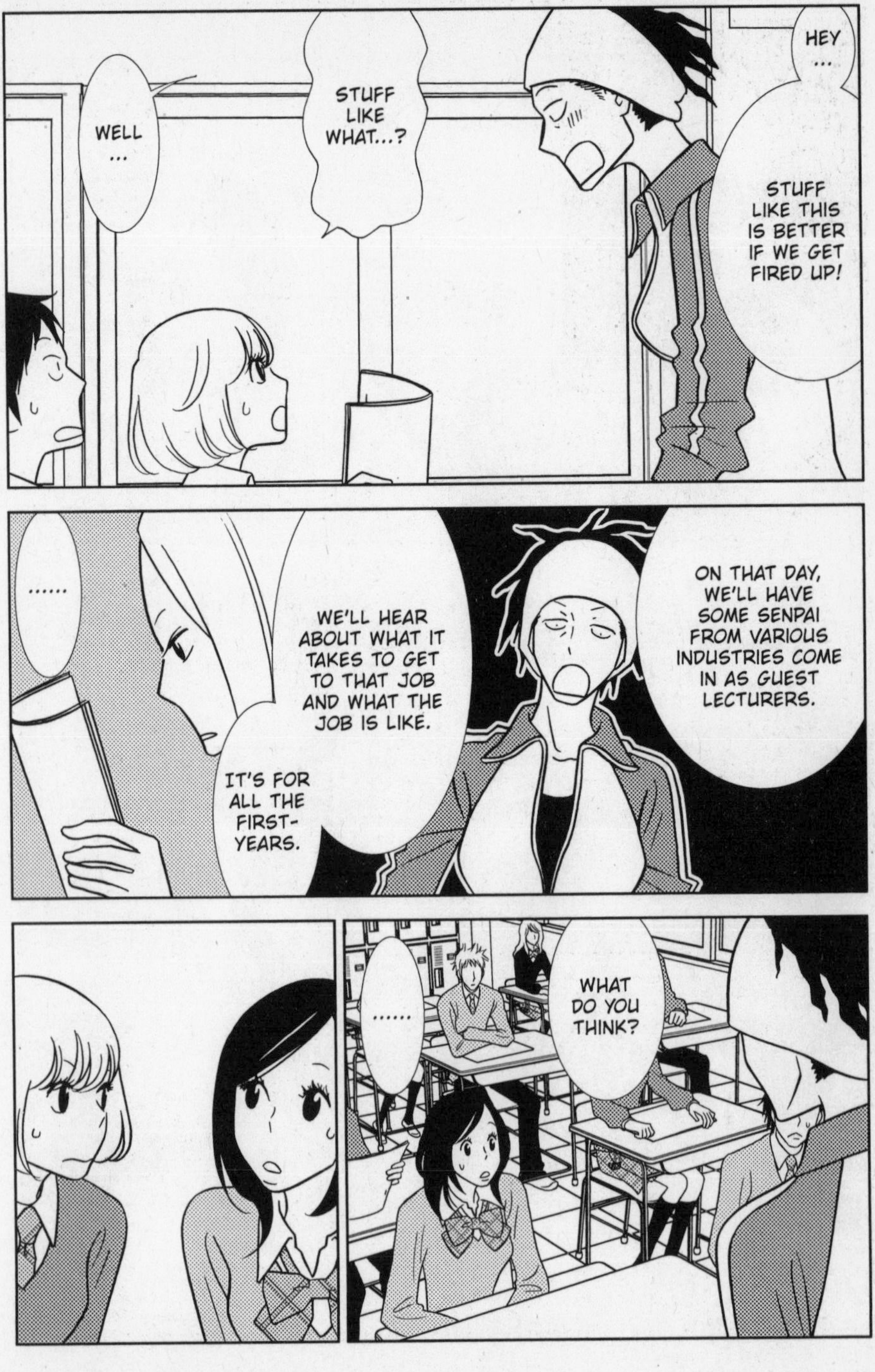
HEY ...
STUFF LIKE THIS IS BETTER IF WE GET FIRED UP!
STUFF LIKE WHAT...?
WELL ...
ON THAT DAY, WE'LL HAVE SOME SENPAI FROM VARIOUS INDUSTRIES COME IN AS GUEST LECTURERS.
WE'LL HEAR ABOUT WHAT IT TAKES TO GET TO THAT JOB AND WHAT THE JOB IS LIKE.
IT'S FOR ALL THE FIRST-YEARS.
......
WHAT DO YOU THINK?
......

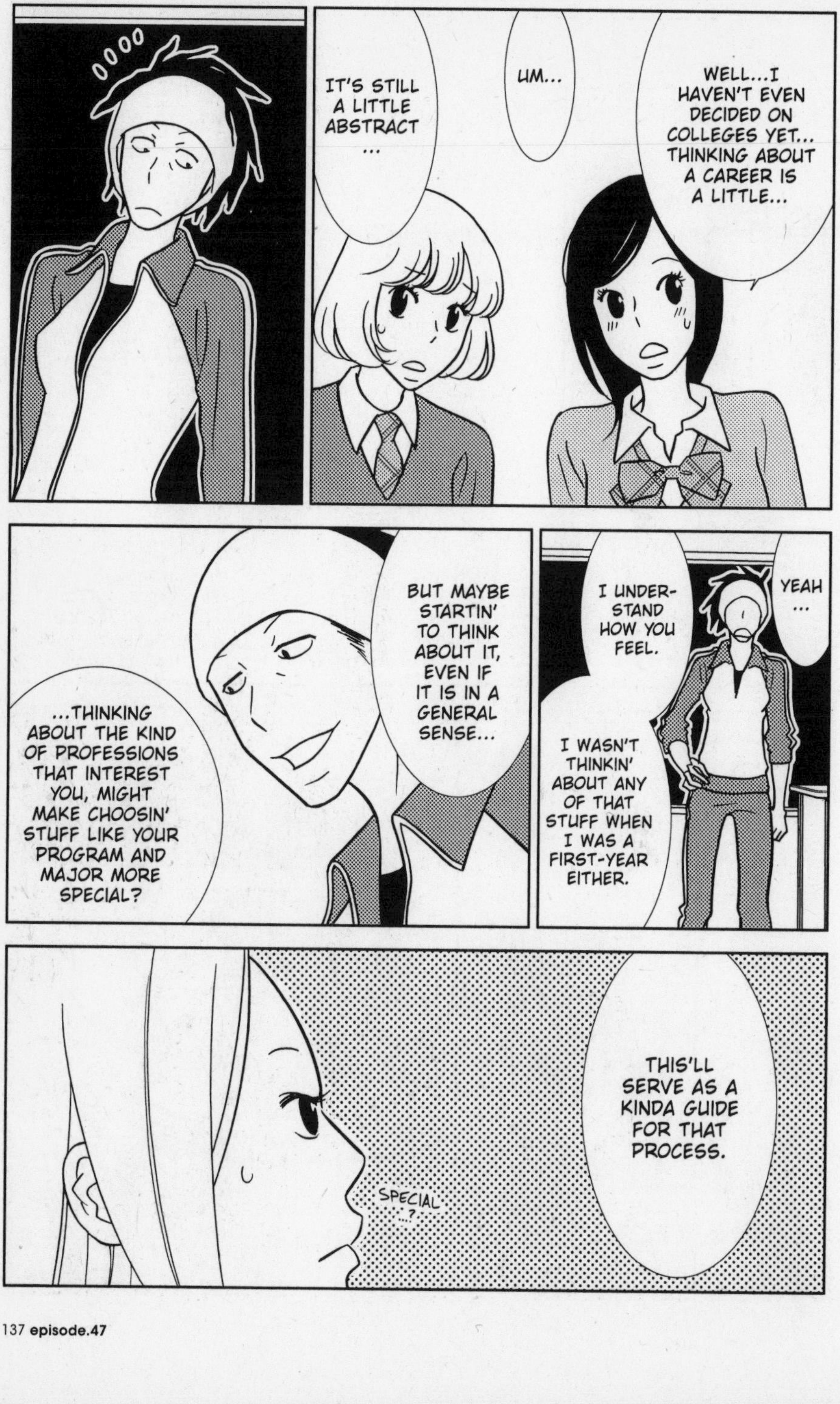
WELL...I HAVEN'T EVEN DECIDED ON COLLEGES YET... THINKING ABOUT A CAREER IS A LITTLE...
UM...
IT'S STILL A LITTLE ABSTRACT ...
YEAH ...
I UNDER-STAND HOW YOU FEEL.
I WASN'T THINKIN' ABOUT ANY OF THAT STUFF WHEN I WAS A FIRST-YEAR EITHER.
BUT MAYBE STARTIN' TO THINK ABOUT IT, EVEN IF IT IS IN A GENERAL SENSE...
...THINKING ABOUT THE KIND OF PROFESSIONS THAT INTEREST YOU, MIGHT MAKE CHOOSIN' STUFF LIKE YOUR PROGRAM AND MAJOR MORE SPECIAL?
THIS'LL SERVE AS A KINDA GUIDE FOR THAT PROCESS.
SPECIAL ...?

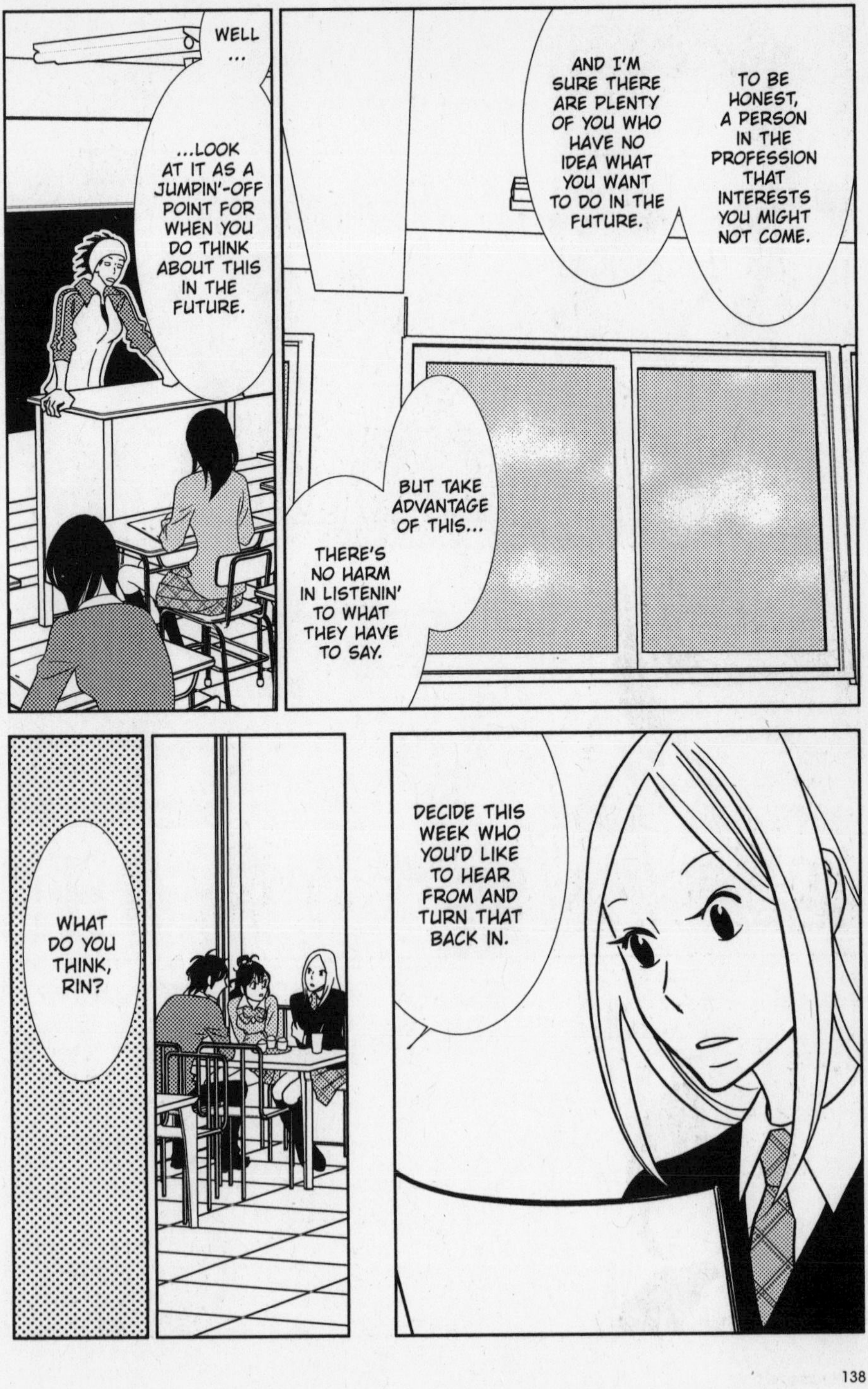
TO BE HONEST, A PERSON IN THE PROFESSION THAT INTERESTS YOU MIGHT NOT COME.
AND I'M SURE THERE ARE PLENTY OF YOU WHO HAVE NO IDEA WHAT YOU WANT TO DO IN THE FUTURE.
BUT TAKE ADVANTAGE OF THIS...
THERE'S NO HARM IN LISTENIN' TO WHAT THEY HAVE TO SAY.
WELL ...
...LOOK AT IT AS A JUMPIN'-OFF POINT FOR WHEN YOU DO THINK ABOUT THIS IN THE FUTURE.
DECIDE THIS WEEK WHO YOU'D LIKE TO HEAR FROM AND TURN THAT BACK IN.
WHAT DO YOU THINK, RIN?

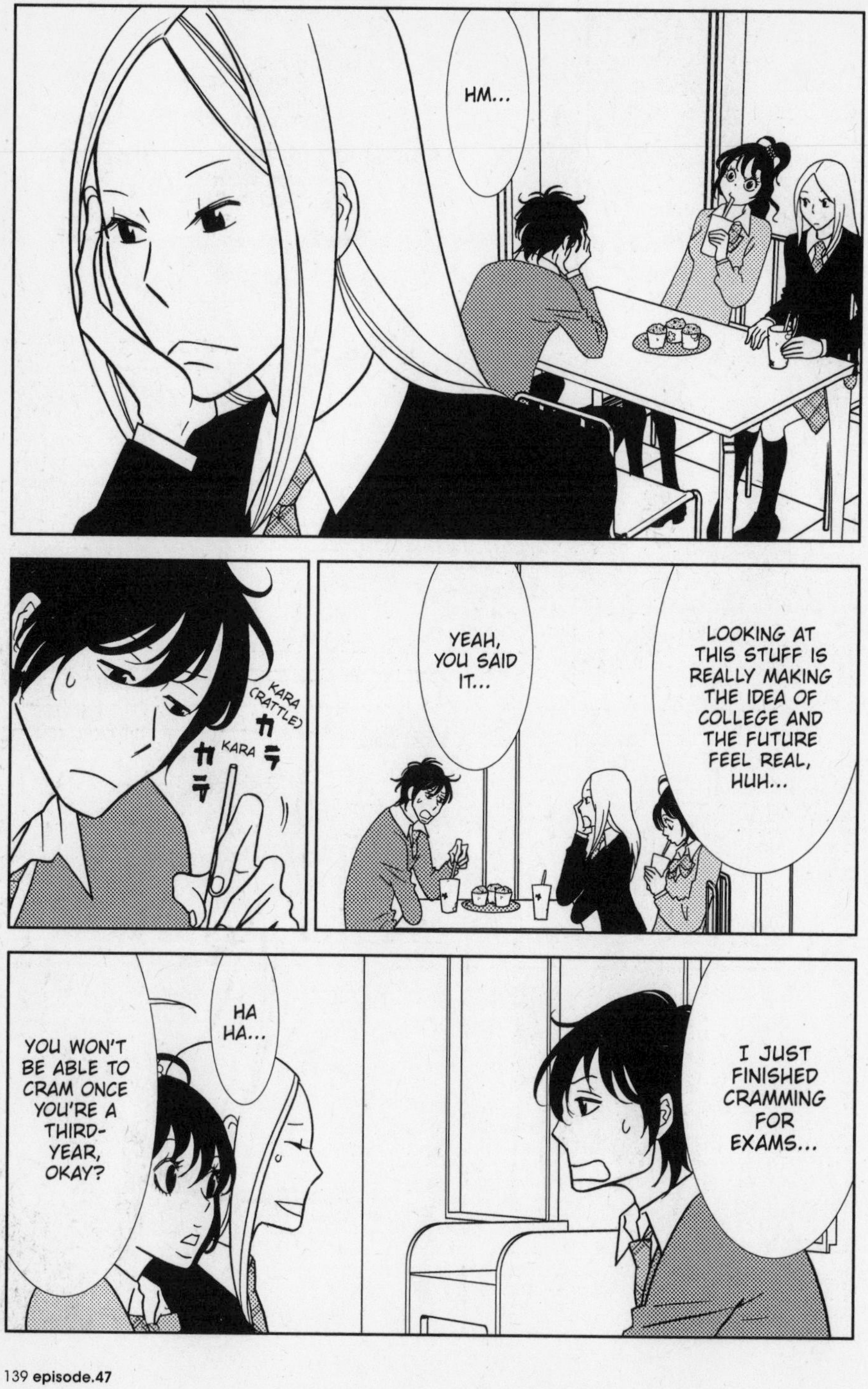
HM...
LOOKING AT THIS STUFF IS REALLY MAKING THE IDEA OF COLLEGE AND THE FUTURE FEEL REAL, HUH...
YEAH, YOU SAID IT...
KARA (RATTLE)
カラ
KARA
カラ
I JUST FINISHED CRAMMING FOR EXAMS...
HA HA...
YOU WON'T BE ABLE TO CRAM ONCE YOU'RE A THIRD-YEAR, OKAY?

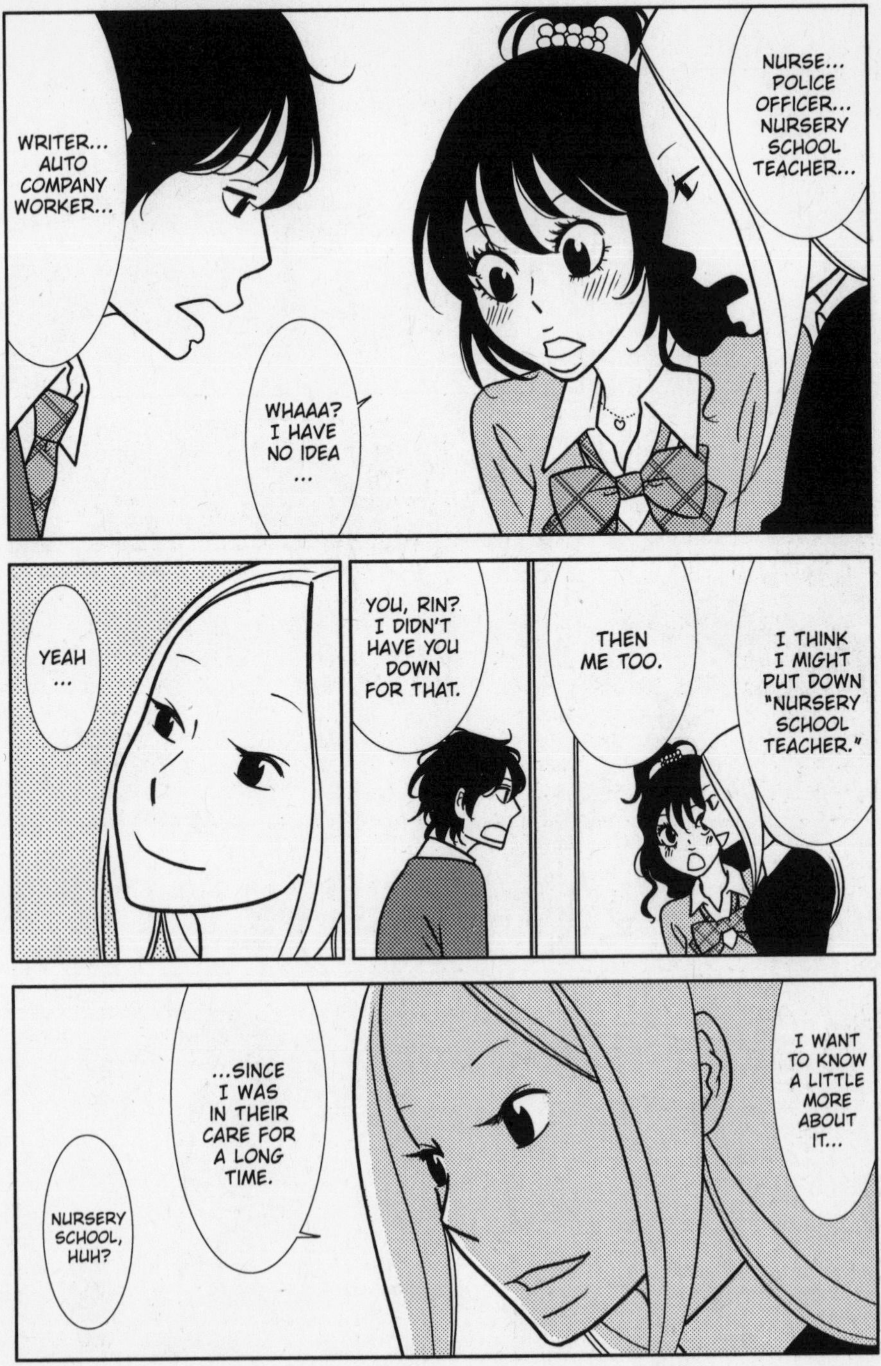
NURSE... POLICE OFFICER... NURSERY SCHOOL TEACHER...
WRITER... AUTO COMPANY WORKER...
WHAAA? I HAVE NO IDEA ...
I THINK I MIGHT PUT DOWN "NURSERY SCHOOL TEACHER."
THEN ME TOO.
YOU, RIN? I DIDN'T HAVE YOU DOWN FOR THAT.
YEAH ...
I WANT TO KNOW A LITTLE MORE ABOUT IT...
...SINCE I WAS IN THEIR CARE FOR A LONG TIME.
NURSERY SCHOOL, HUH?

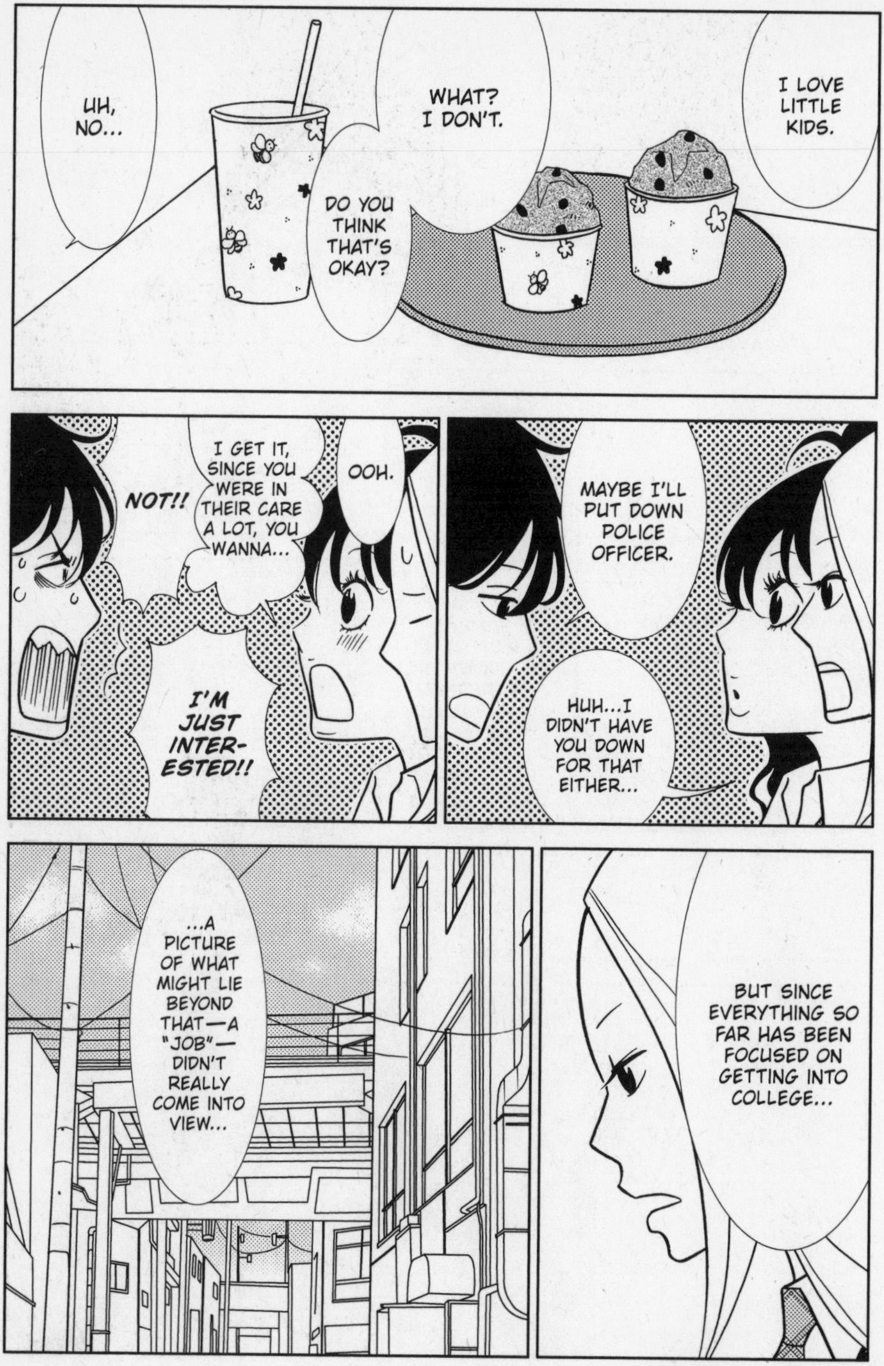
I LOVE LITTLE KIDS.
WHAT? I DON'T.
DO YOU THINK THAT'S OKAY?
UH, NO...
MAYBE I'LL PUT DOWN POLICE OFFICER.
HUH...I DIDN'T HAVE YOU DOWN FOR THAT EITHER...
OOH.
I GET IT, SINCE YOU WERE IN THEIR CARE A LOT, YOU WANNA...
NOT!!
I'M JUST INTERESTED!!
BUT SINCE EVERYTHING SO FAR HAS BEEN FOCUSED ON GETTING INTO COLLEGE...
...A PICTURE OF WHAT MIGHT LIE BEYOND THAT—A "JOB"—DIDN'T REALLY COME INTO VIEW...

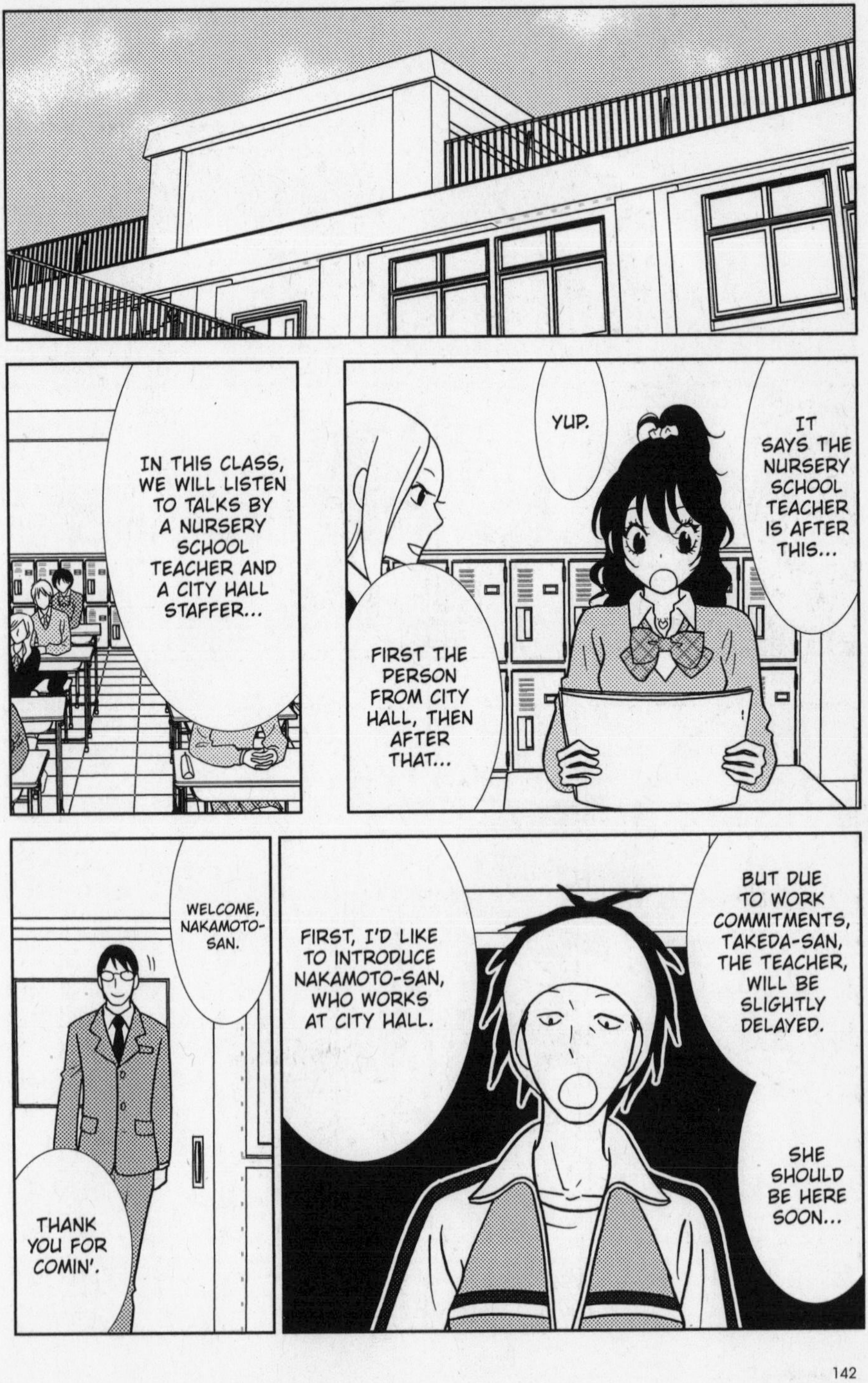
IT SAYS THE NURSERY SCHOOL TEACHER IS AFTER THIS...
YUP.
FIRST THE PERSON FROM CITY HALL, THEN AFTER THAT...
IN THIS CLASS, WE WILL LISTEN TO TALKS BY A NURSERY SCHOOL TEACHER AND A CITY HALL STAFFER...
BUT DUE TO WORK COMMITMENTS, TAKEDA-SAN, THE TEACHER, WILL BE SLIGHTLY DELAYED.
SHE SHOULD BE HERE SOON...
FIRST, I'D LIKE TO INTRODUCE NAKAMOTO-SAN, WHO WORKS AT CITY HALL.
WELCOME, NAKAMOTO-SAN.
THANK YOU FOR COMIN'.

GARA
(RATTLE)
ガラ‥

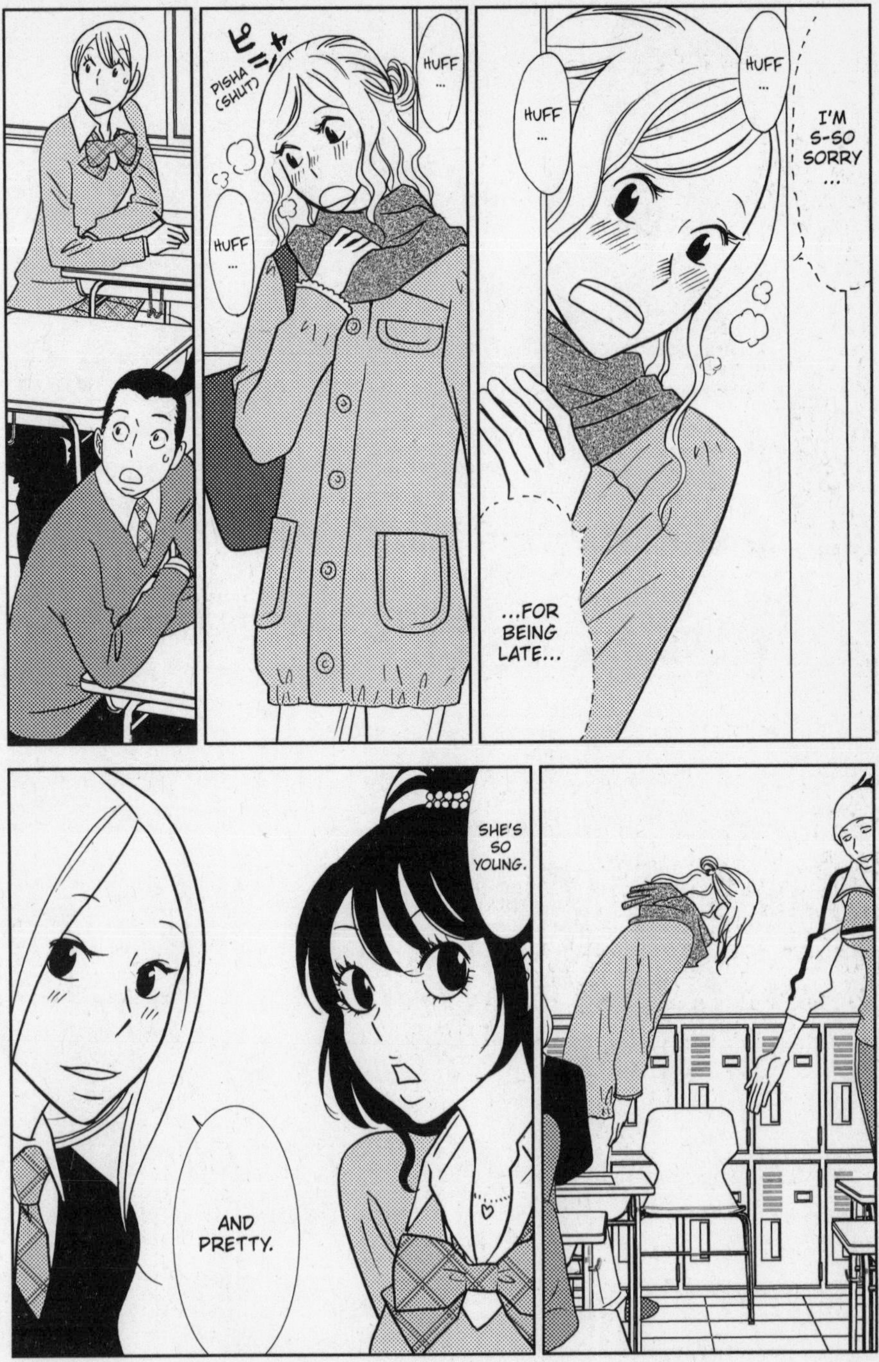
HUFF ...
HUFF ...
I'M S-SO SORRY ...
...FOR BEING LATE...
HUFF ...
ピシャ
PISHA (SHUT)
HUFF ...
SHE'S SO YOUNG.
AND PRETTY.

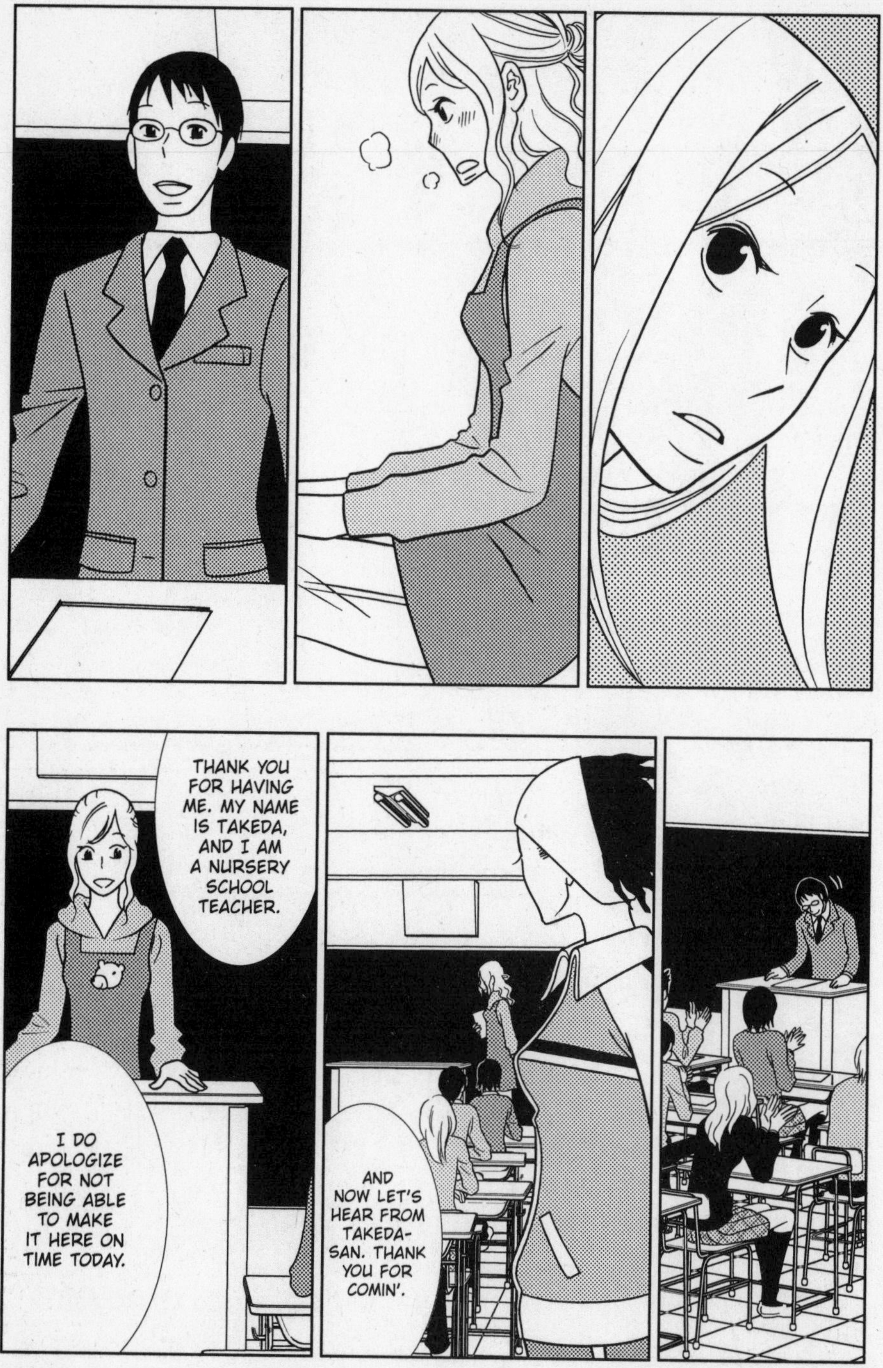
AND NOW LET'S HEAR FROM TAKEDA-SAN. THANK YOU FOR COMIN'.
THANK YOU FOR HAVING ME. MY NAME IS TAKEDA, AND I AM A NURSERY SCHOOL TEACHER.
I DO APOLOGIZE FOR NOT BEING ABLE TO MAKE IT HERE ON TIME TODAY.

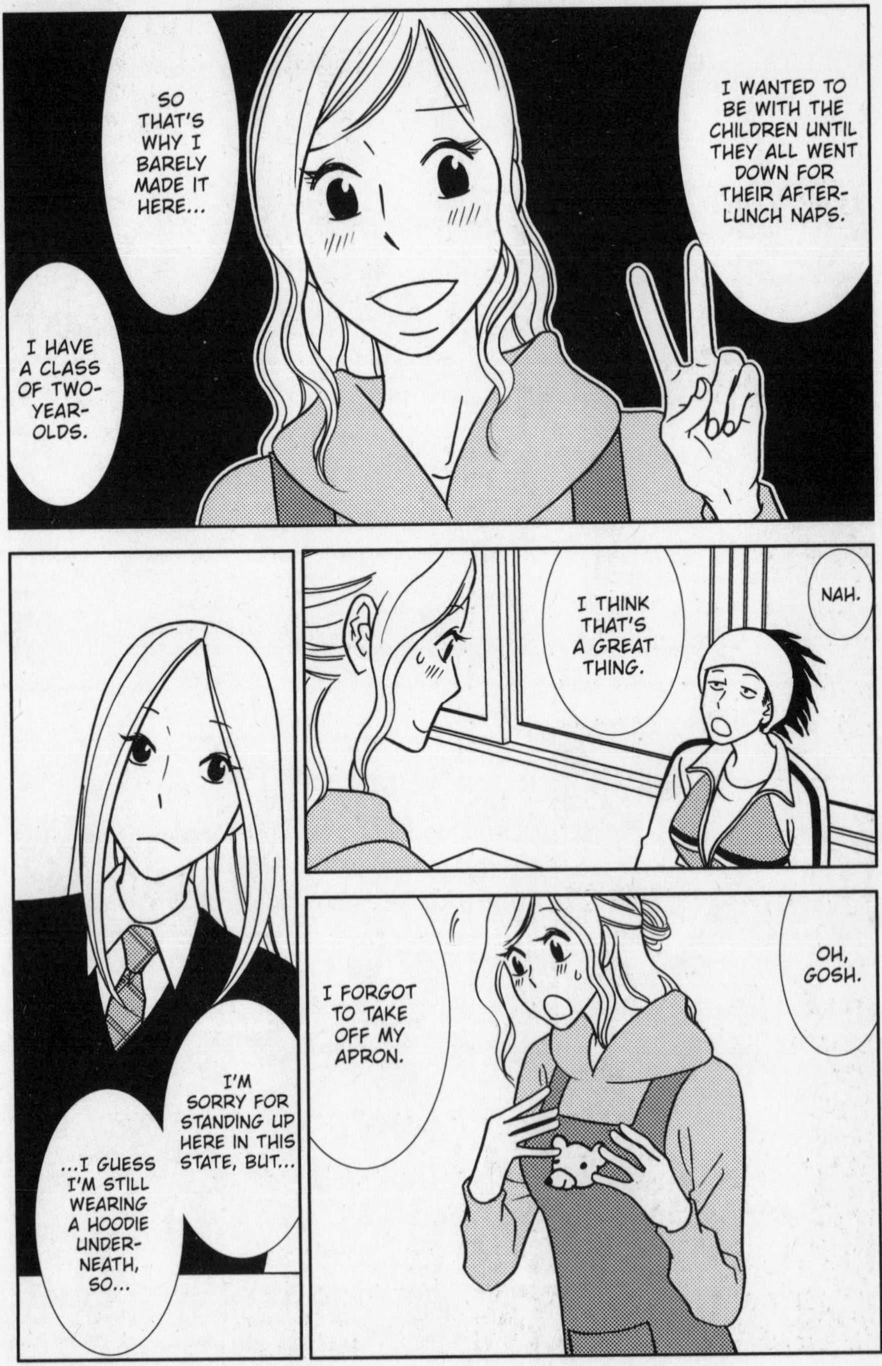
I WANTED TO BE WITH THE CHILDREN UNTIL THEY ALL WENT DOWN FOR THEIR AFTER-LUNCH NAPS.
SO THAT'S WHY I BARELY MADE IT HERE...
I HAVE A CLASS OF TWO-YEAR-OLDS.
NAH.
I THINK THAT'S A GREAT THING.
OH, GOSH.
I FORGOT TO TAKE OFF MY APRON.
I'M SORRY FOR STANDING UP HERE IN THIS STATE, BUT...
...I GUESS I'M STILL WEARING A HOODIE UNDER-NEATH, SO...

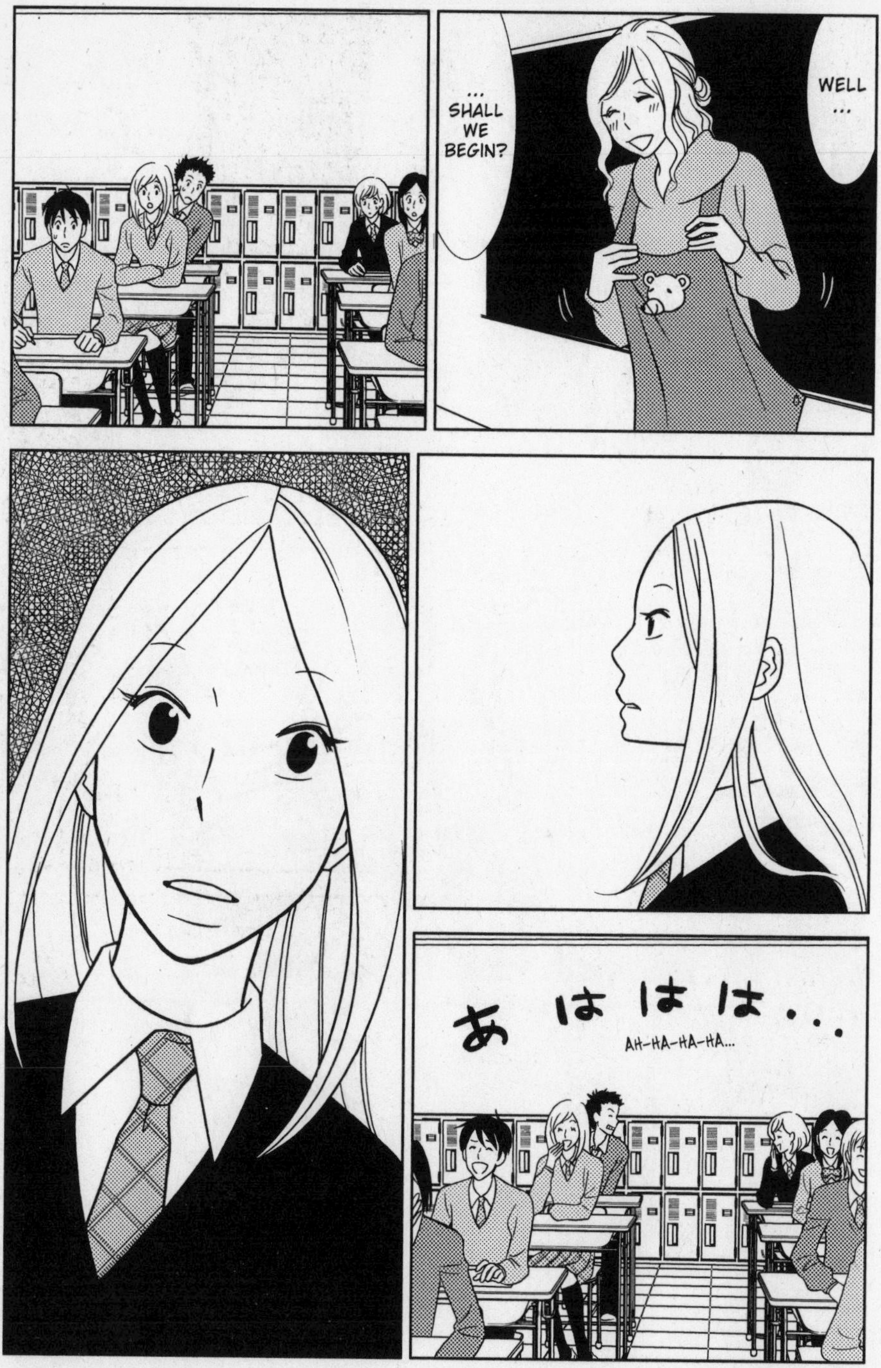
WELL ...
... SHALL WE BEGIN?
あははは...
AH-HA-HA-HA...

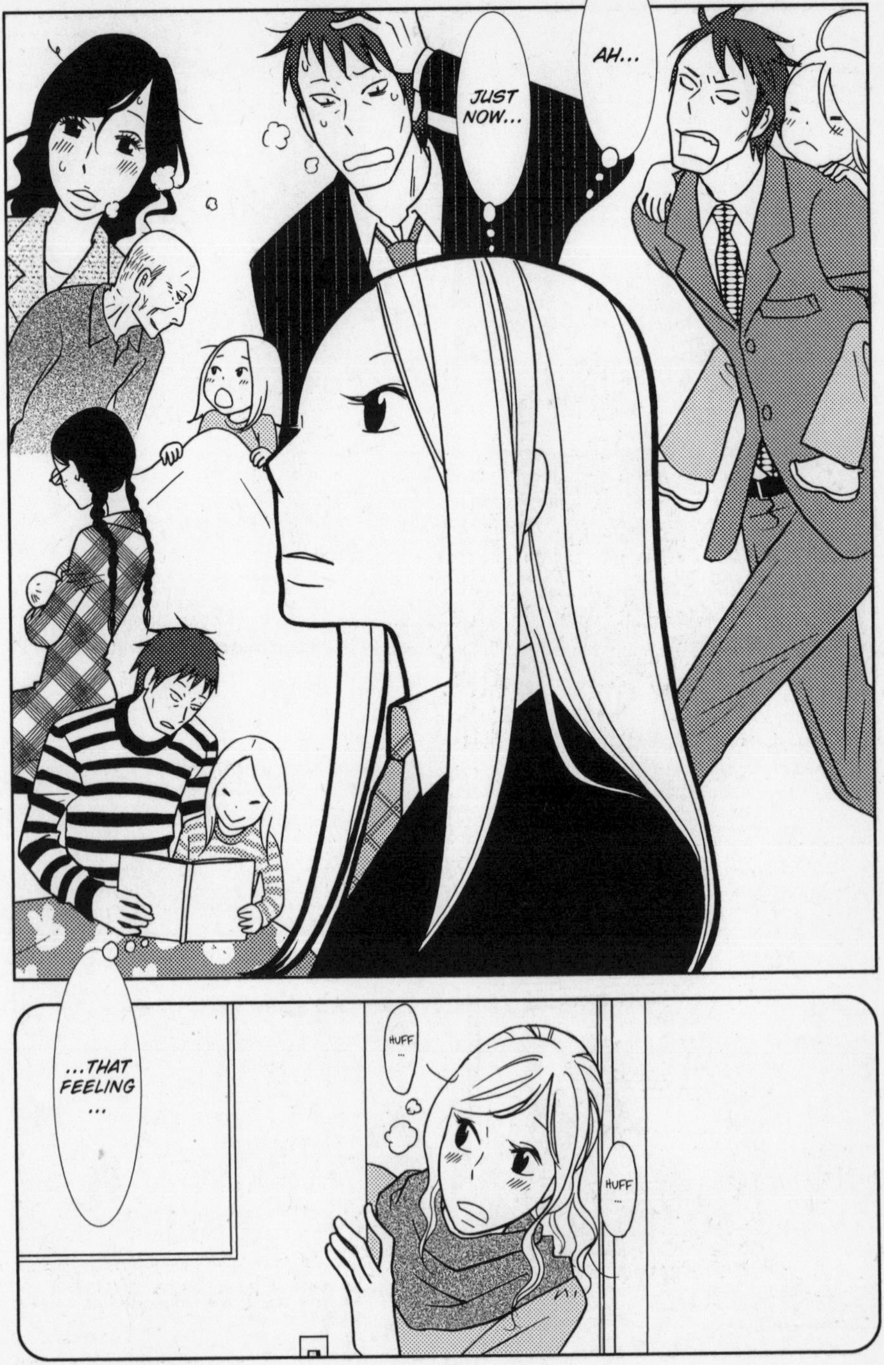
AH...
JUST NOW...
...THAT FEELING...
HUFF...
HUFF...

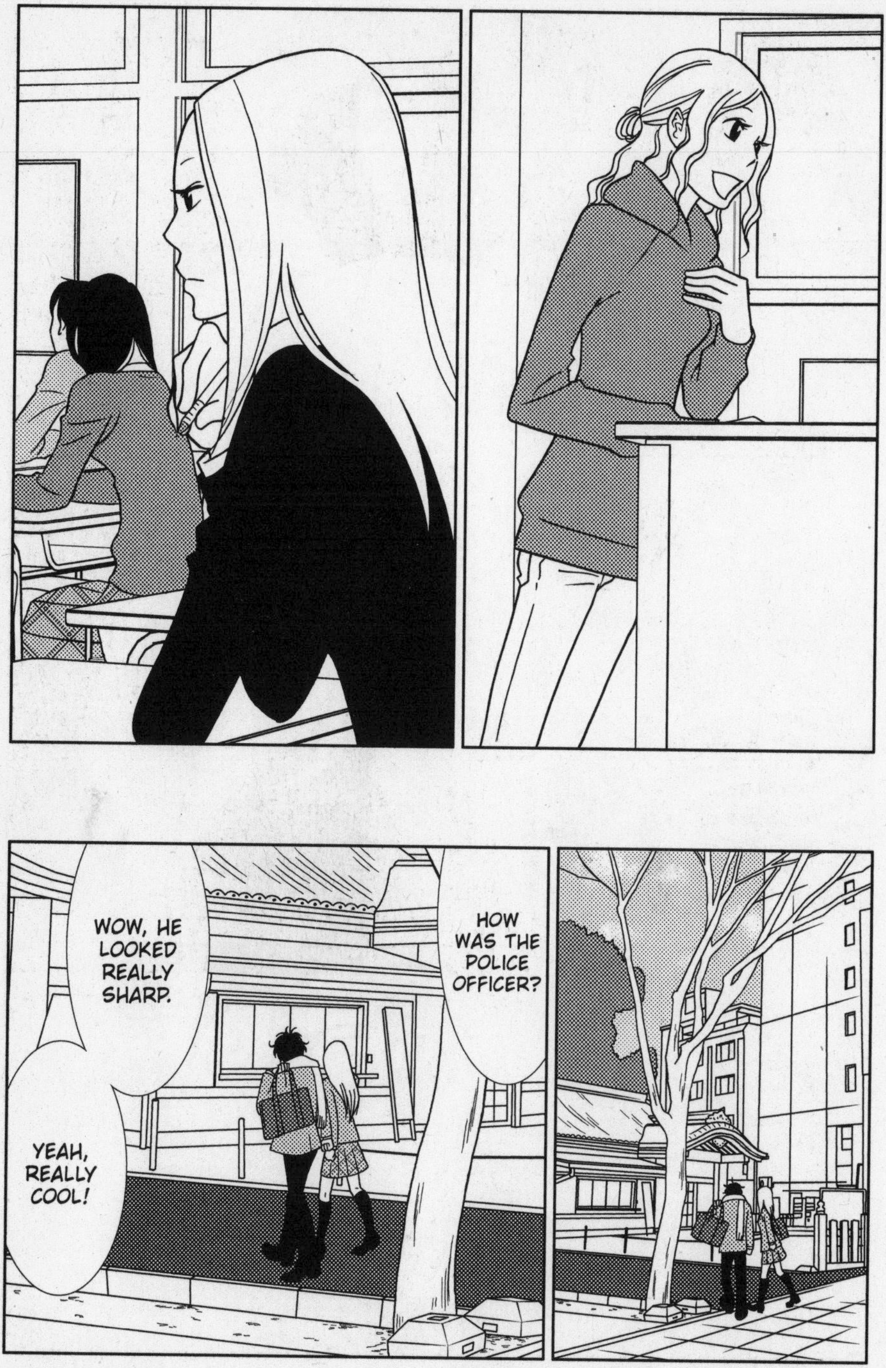
HOW WAS THE POLICE OFFICER?
WOW, HE LOOKED REALLY SHARP.
YEAH, REALLY COOL!

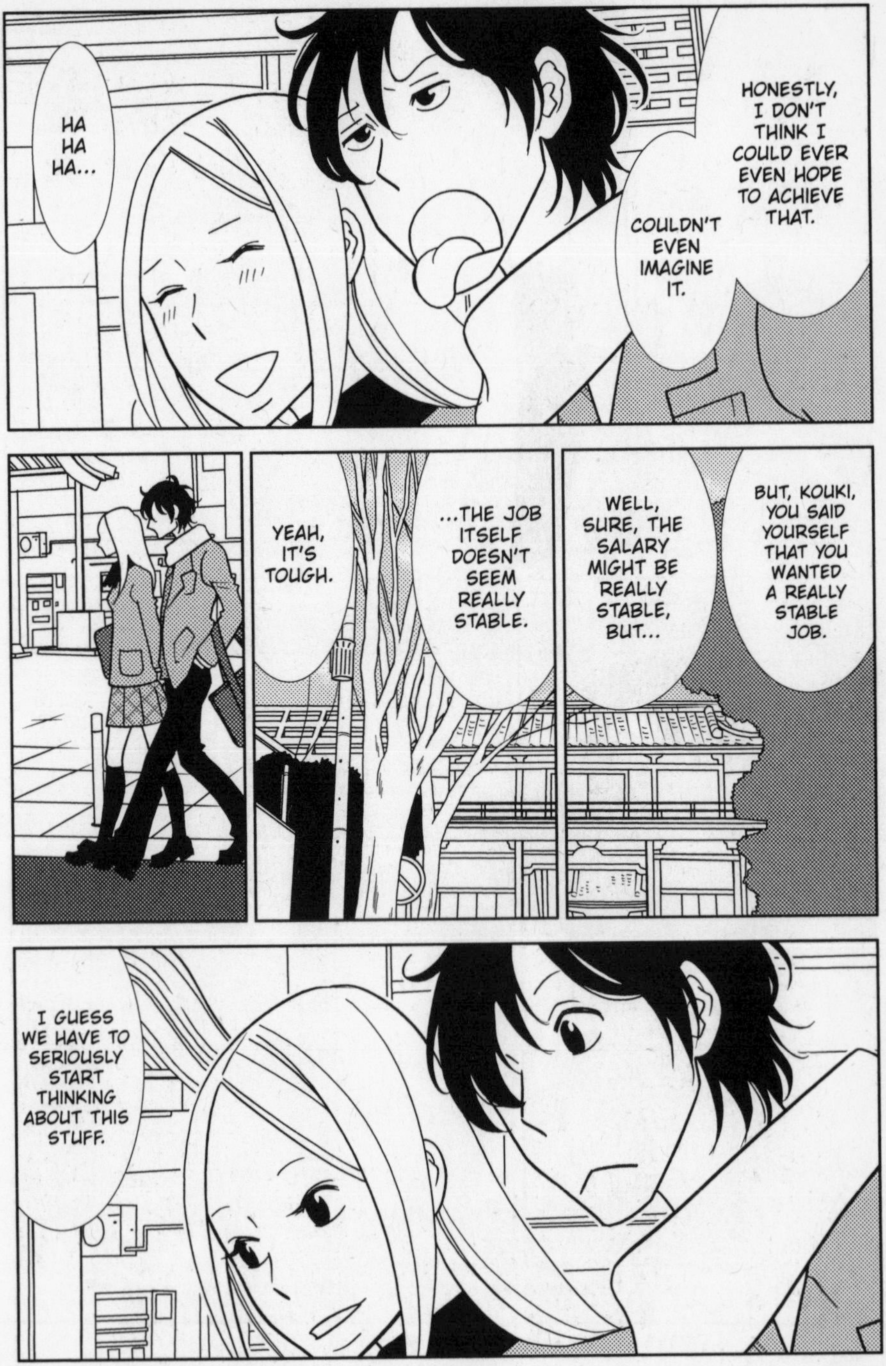
HONESTLY, I DON'T THINK I COULD EVER EVEN HOPE TO ACHIEVE THAT.
COULDN'T EVEN IMAGINE IT.
HA HA HA...
BUT, KOUKI, YOU SAID YOURSELF THAT YOU WANTED A REALLY STABLE JOB.
WELL, SURE, THE SALARY MIGHT BE REALLY STABLE, BUT...
...THE JOB ITSELF DOESN'T SEEM REALLY STABLE.
YEAH, IT'S TOUGH.
I GUESS WE HAVE TO SERIOUSLY START THINKING ABOUT THIS STUFF.

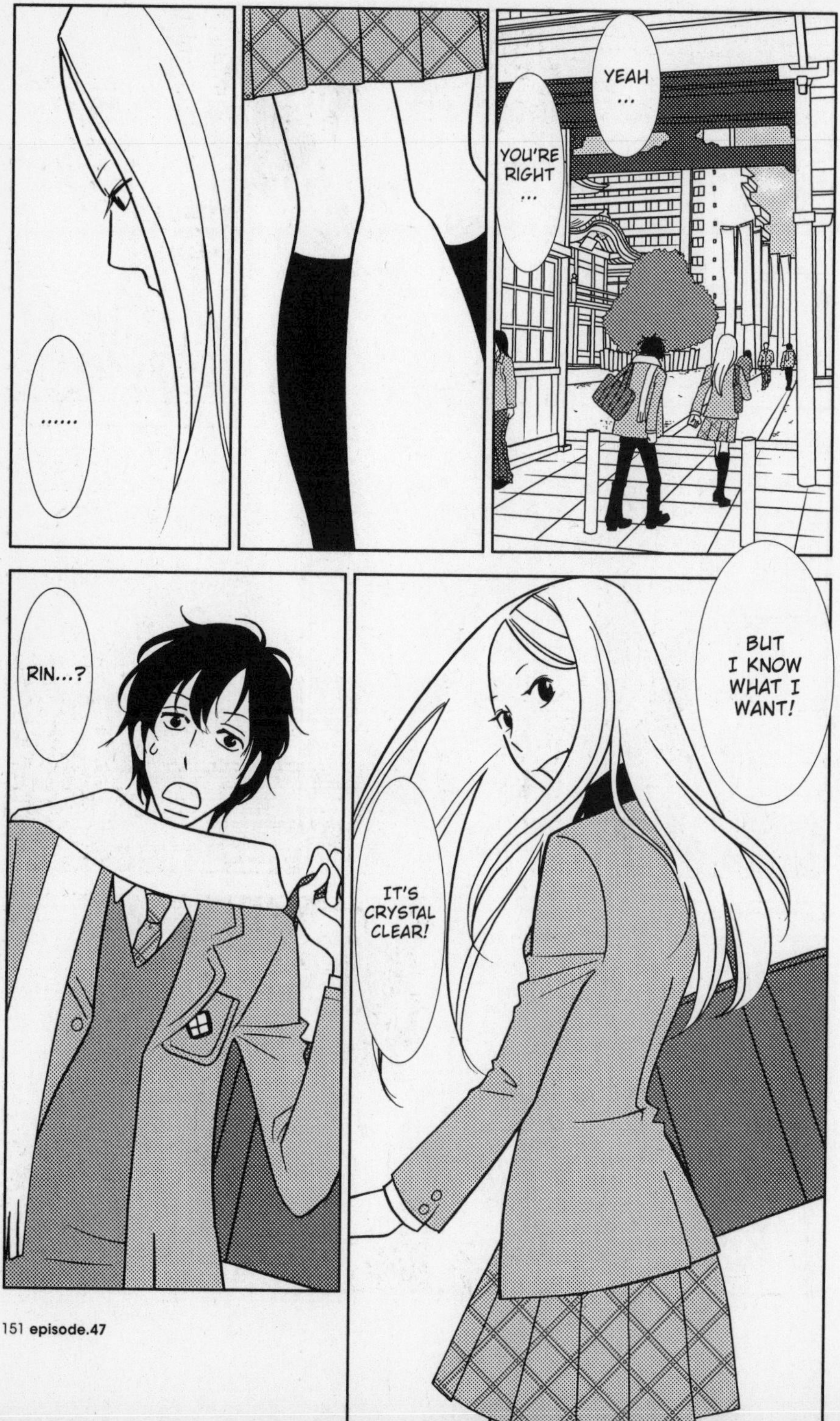
YEAH ...
YOU'RE RIGHT ...
......
BUT I KNOW WHAT I WANT!
IT'S CRYSTAL CLEAR!
RIN...?

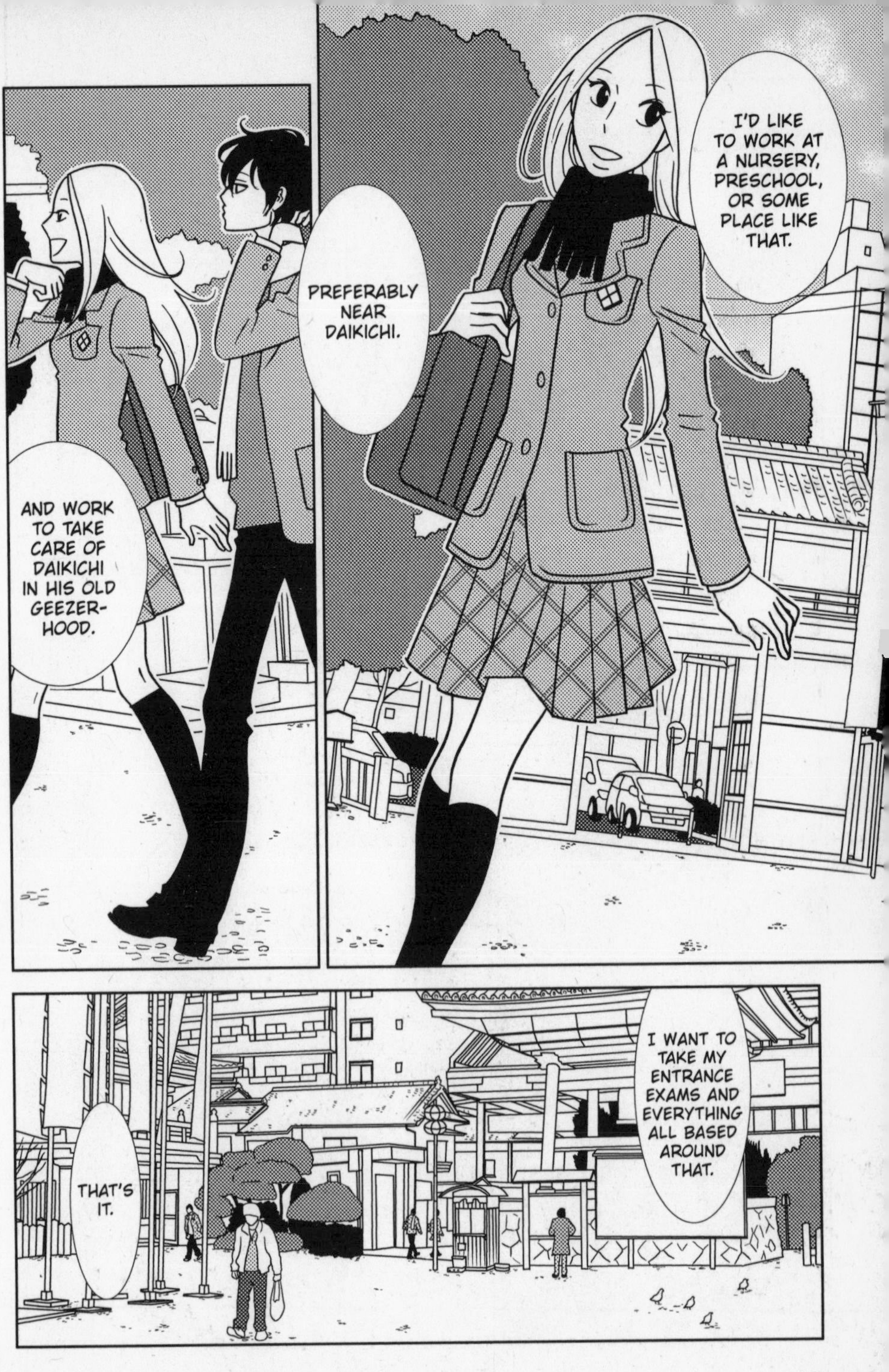
I'D LIKE TO WORK AT A NURSERY, PRESCHOOL, OR SOME PLACE LIKE THAT.
PREFERABLY NEAR DAIKICHI.
AND WORK TO TAKE CARE OF DAIKICHI IN HIS OLD GEEZER-HOOD.
I WANT TO TAKE MY ENTRANCE EXAMS AND EVERYTHING ALL BASED AROUND THAT.
THAT'S IT.

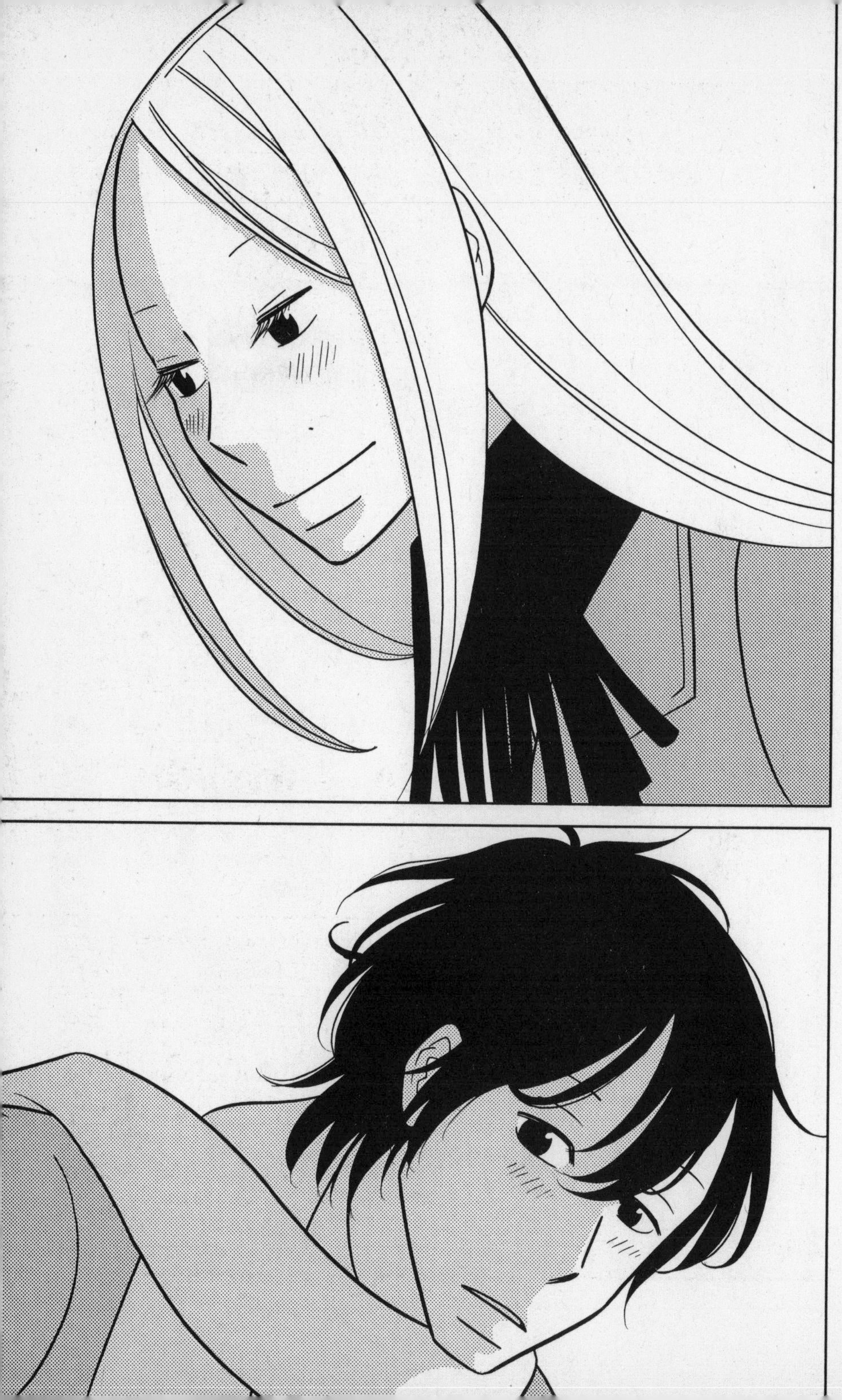

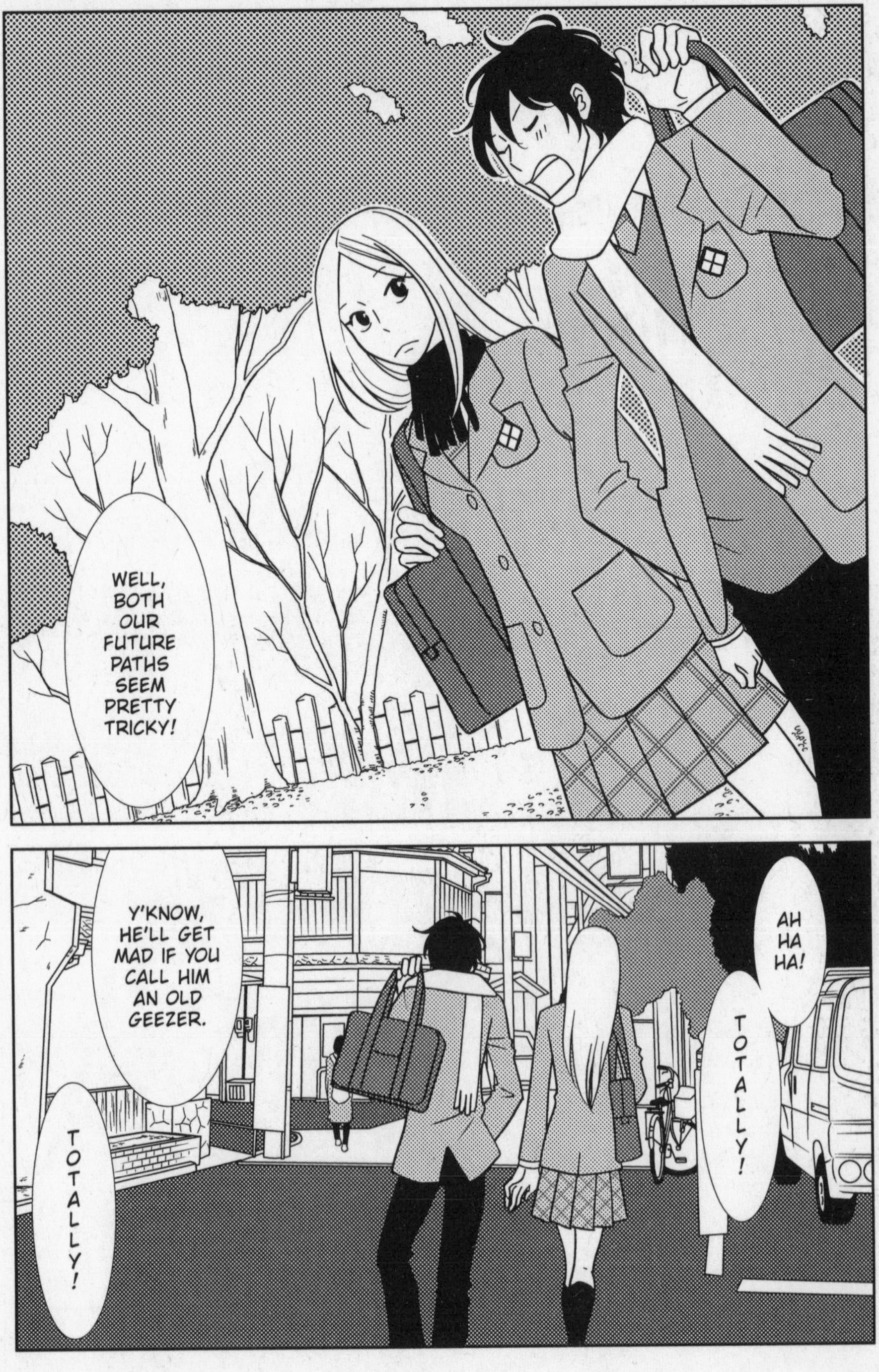
WELL, BOTH OUR FUTURE PATHS SEEM PRETTY TRICKY!
AH HA HA!
TOTALLY!
Y'KNOW, HE'LL GET MAD IF YOU CALL HIM AN OLD GEEZER.
TOTALLY!

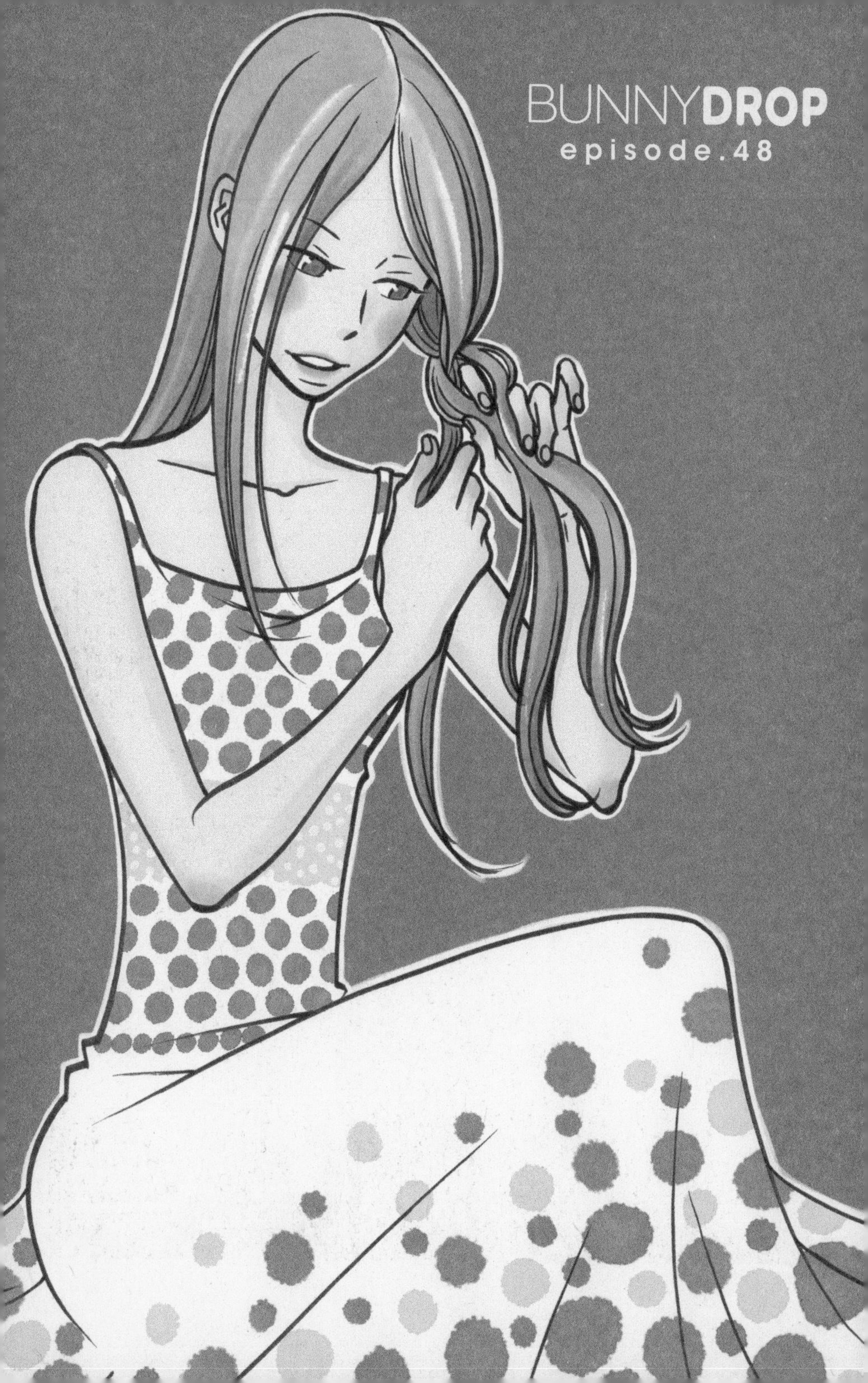
BUNNYDROP
episode.48

BUNNY**DROP**

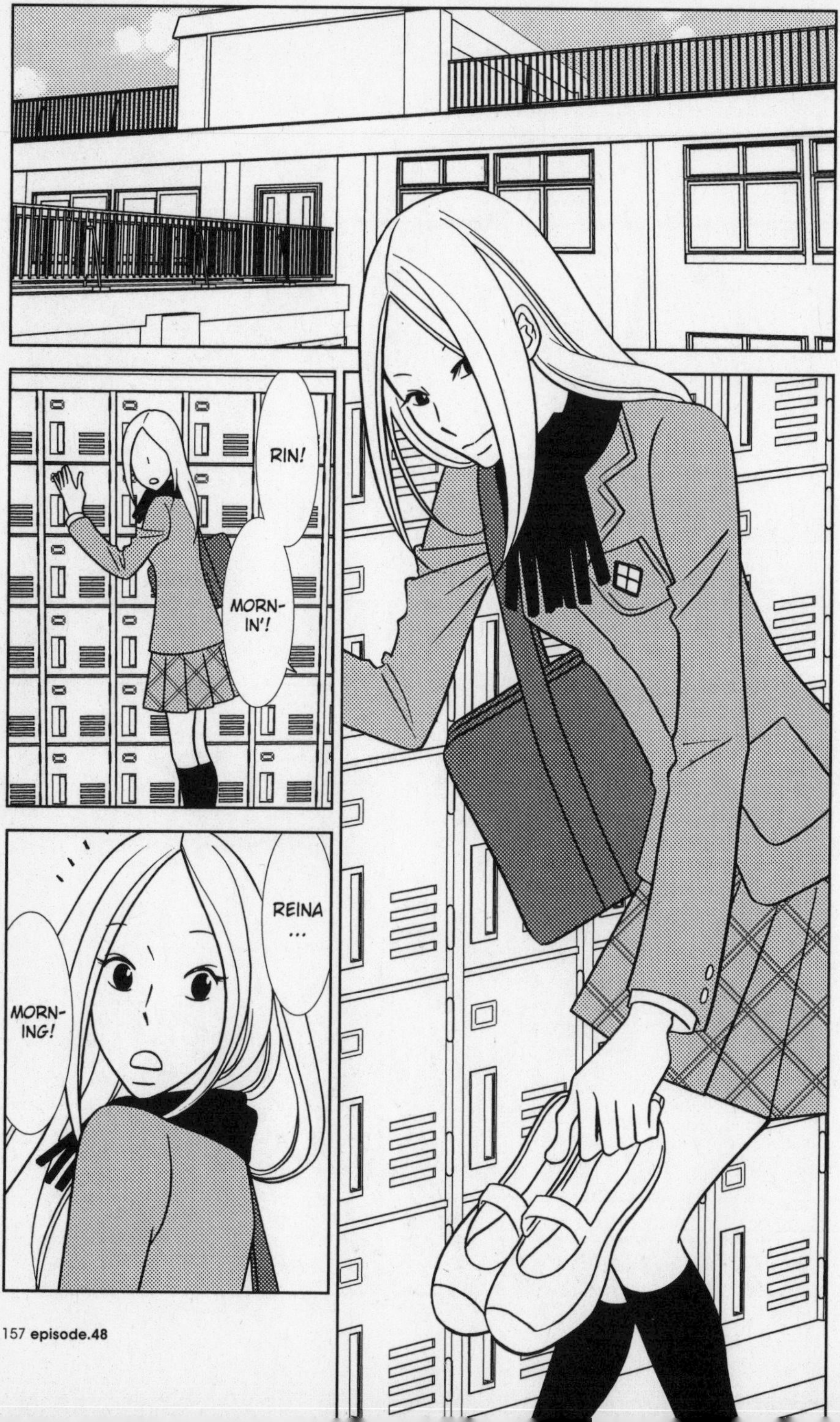
RIN!
MORN-IN'!
REINA ...
MORN-ING!

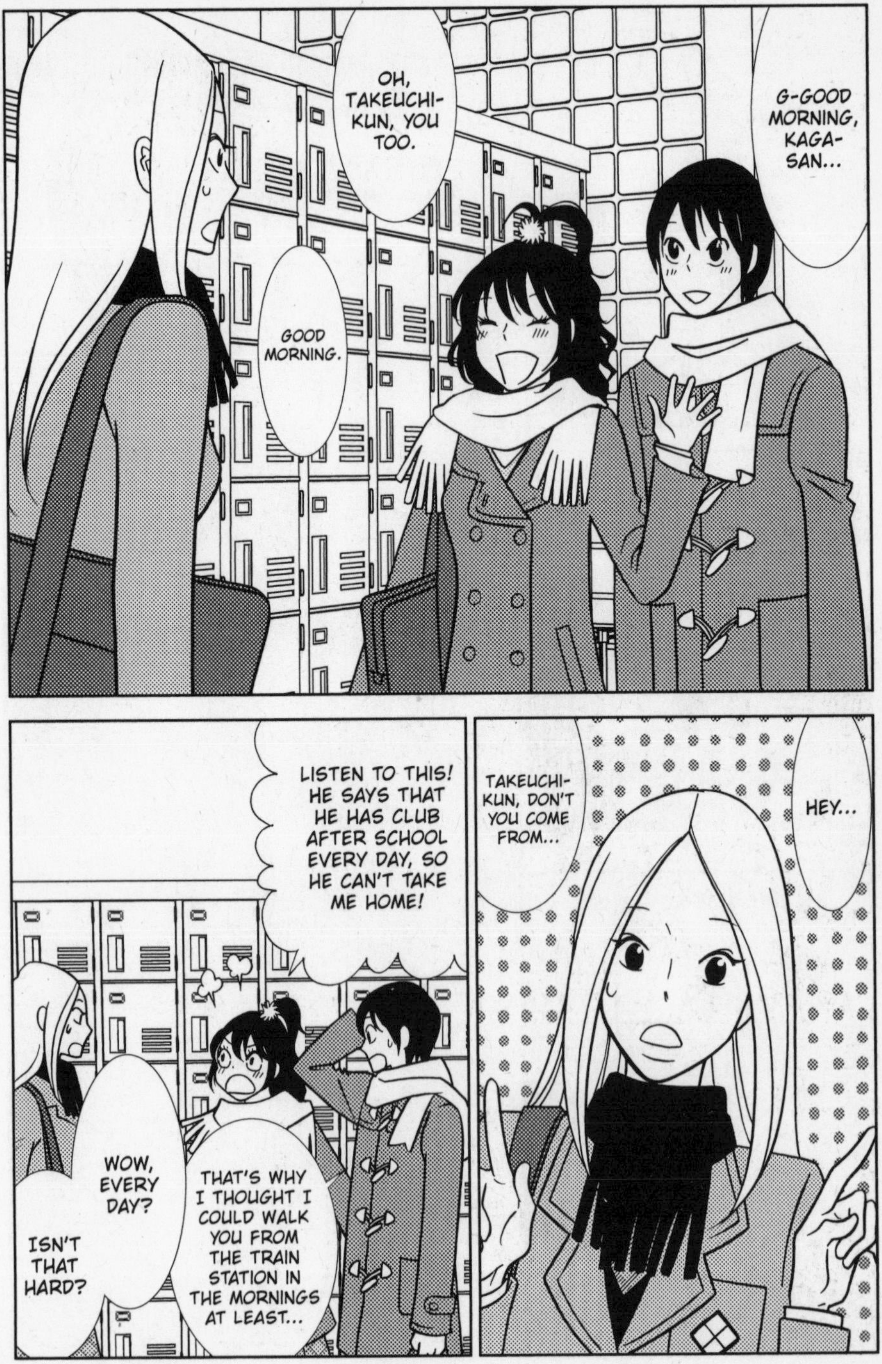
G-GOOD MORNING, KAGA-SAN...
OH, TAKEUCHI-KUN, YOU TOO.
GOOD MORNING.
HEY...
TAKEUCHI-KUN, DON'T YOU COME FROM...
LISTEN TO THIS! HE SAYS THAT HE HAS CLUB AFTER SCHOOL EVERY DAY, SO HE CAN'T TAKE ME HOME!
THAT'S WHY I THOUGHT I COULD WALK YOU FROM THE TRAIN STATION IN THE MORNINGS AT LEAST...
WOW, EVERY DAY?
ISN'T THAT HARD?

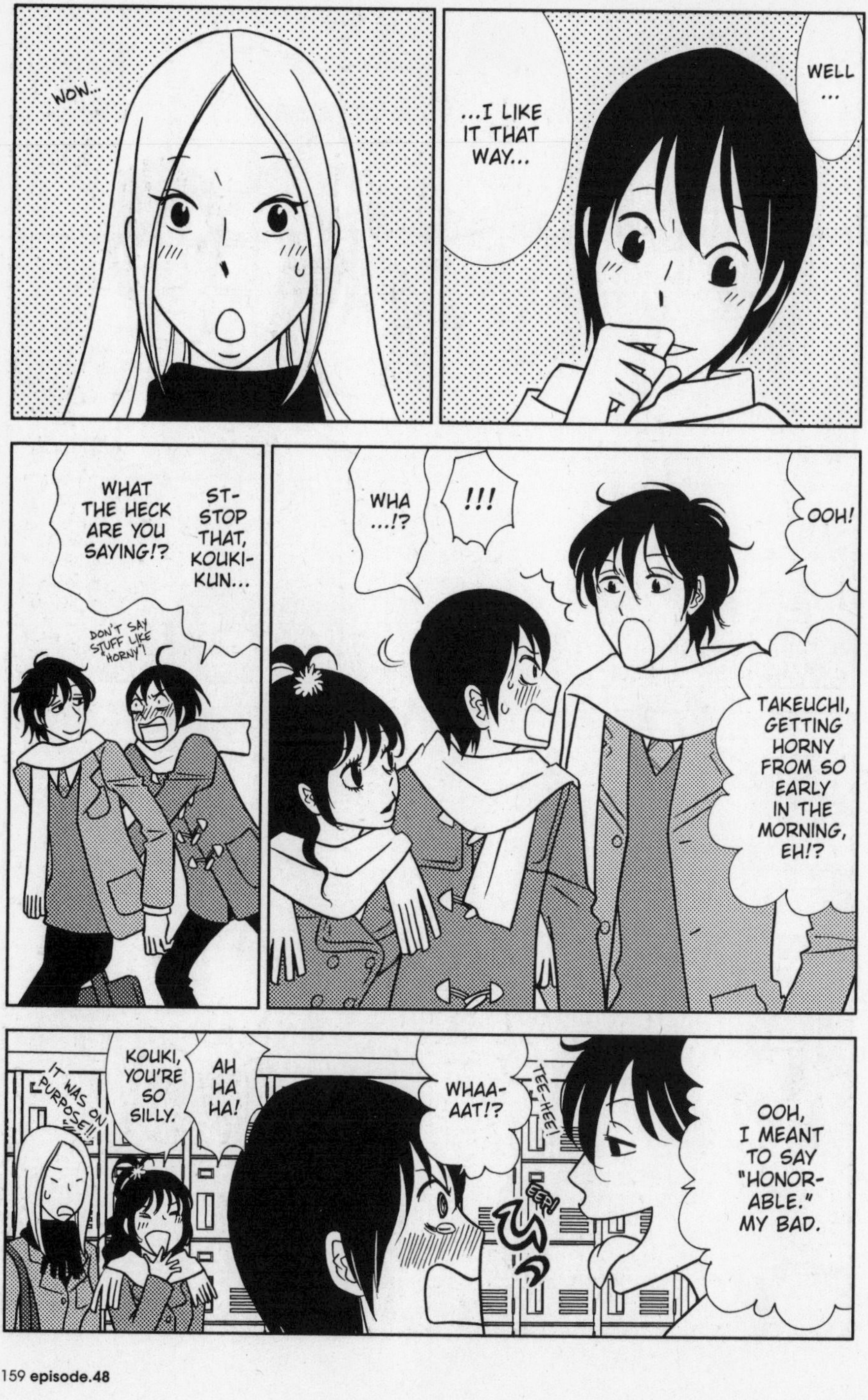
WELL ...
...I LIKE IT THAT WAY...
WOW...
OOH!
TAKEUCHI, GETTING HORNY FROM SO EARLY IN THE MORNING, EH!?
!!!
WHA ...!?
ST-STOP THAT, KOUKI-KUN...
WHAT THE HECK ARE YOU SAYING!?
DON'T SAY STUFF LIKE "HORNY"!
OOH, I MEANT TO SAY "HONORABLE." MY BAD.
TEE-HEE!
EEP!
WHAAA-AAT!?
AH HA HA!
KOUKI, YOU'RE SO SILLY.
IT WAS ON PURPOSE!!

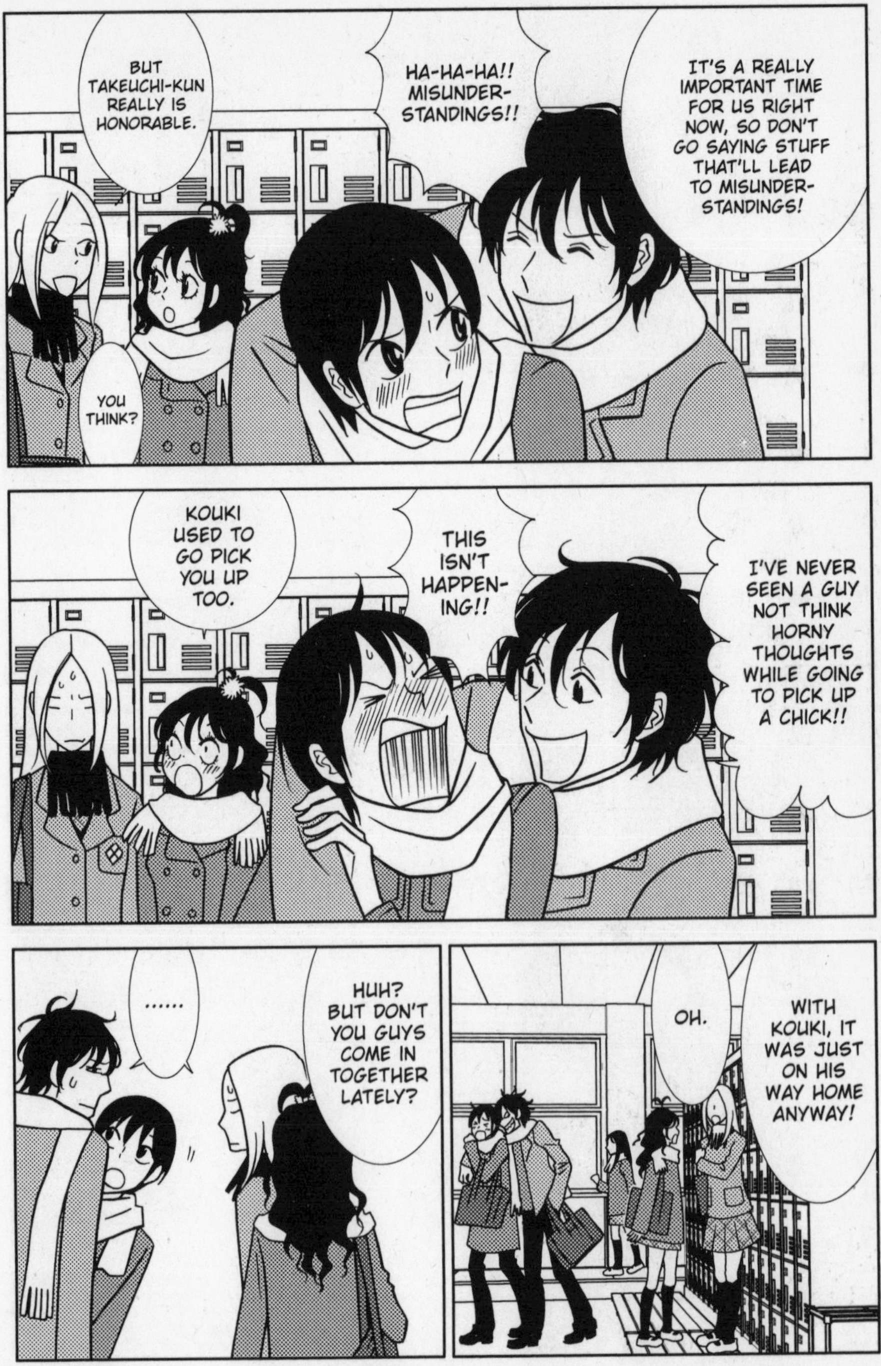
IT'S A REALLY IMPORTANT TIME FOR US RIGHT NOW, SO DON'T GO SAYING STUFF THAT'LL LEAD TO MISUNDER-STANDINGS!
HA-HA-HA!! MISUNDER-STANDINGS!!
BUT TAKEUCHI-KUN REALLY IS HONORABLE.
YOU THINK?
I'VE NEVER SEEN A GUY NOT THINK HORNY THOUGHTS WHILE GOING TO PICK UP A CHICK!!
THIS ISN'T HAPPEN-ING!!
KOUKI USED TO GO PICK YOU UP TOO.
WITH KOUKI, IT WAS JUST ON HIS WAY HOME ANYWAY!
OH.
HUH? BUT DON'T YOU GUYS COME IN TOGETHER LATELY?
......

1-F
STILL, I'M SO HAPPY FOR YOU, REINA.
ABOUT WHAT? TAKEUCHI-KUN?
YUP.
TAKEUCHI-KUN LOOKED HAPPY TOO.
OH, BUT I DON'T KNOW FOR SURE YET.
I FAILED ONCE BEFORE, SO I'M GONNA SEE HOW IT GOES FIRST.
WHAT?
BUT THAT WAS WITH A GUY YOU DIDN'T EVEN KNOW, SO THAT WAS INEVITABLE.
PLUS ...

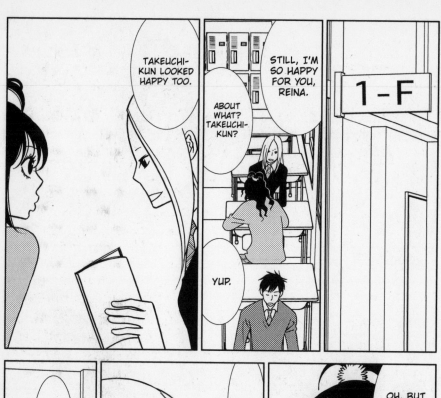

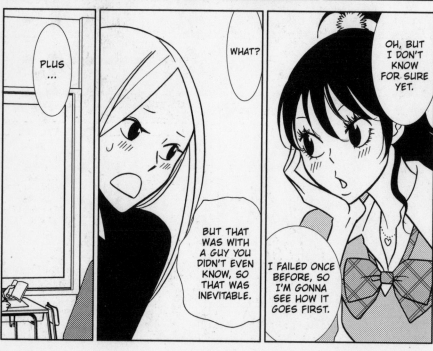

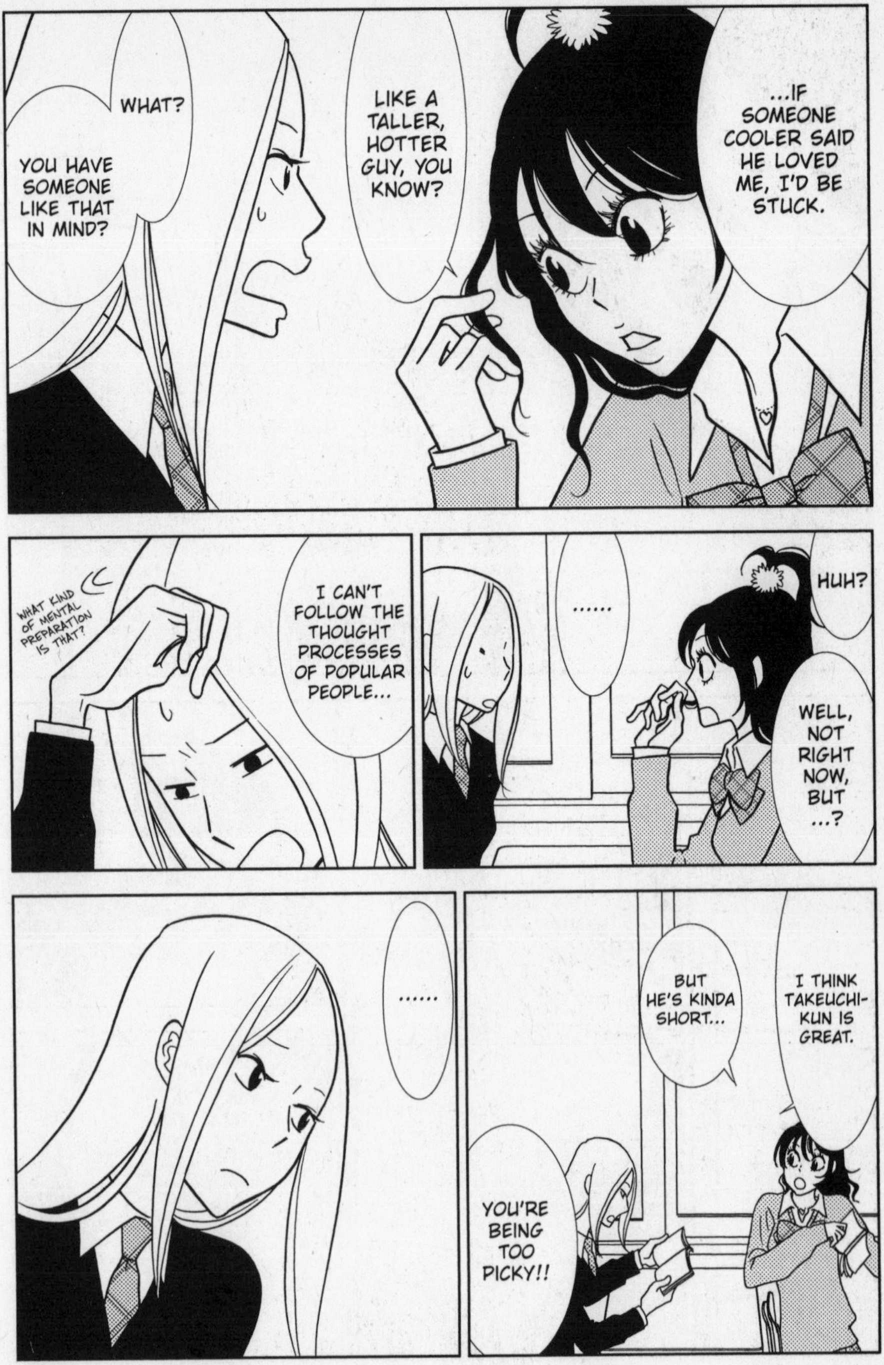
...IF SOMEONE COOLER SAID HE LOVED ME, I'D BE STUCK.
LIKE A TALLER, HOTTER GUY, YOU KNOW?
WHAT?
YOU HAVE SOMEONE LIKE THAT IN MIND?
HUH?
WELL, NOT RIGHT NOW, BUT ...?
......
I CAN'T FOLLOW THE THOUGHT PROCESSES OF POPULAR PEOPLE...
WHAT KIND OF MENTAL PREPARATION IS THAT?
I THINK TAKEUCHI-KUN IS GREAT.
BUT HE'S KINDA SHORT...
YOU'RE BEING TOO PICKY!!
......

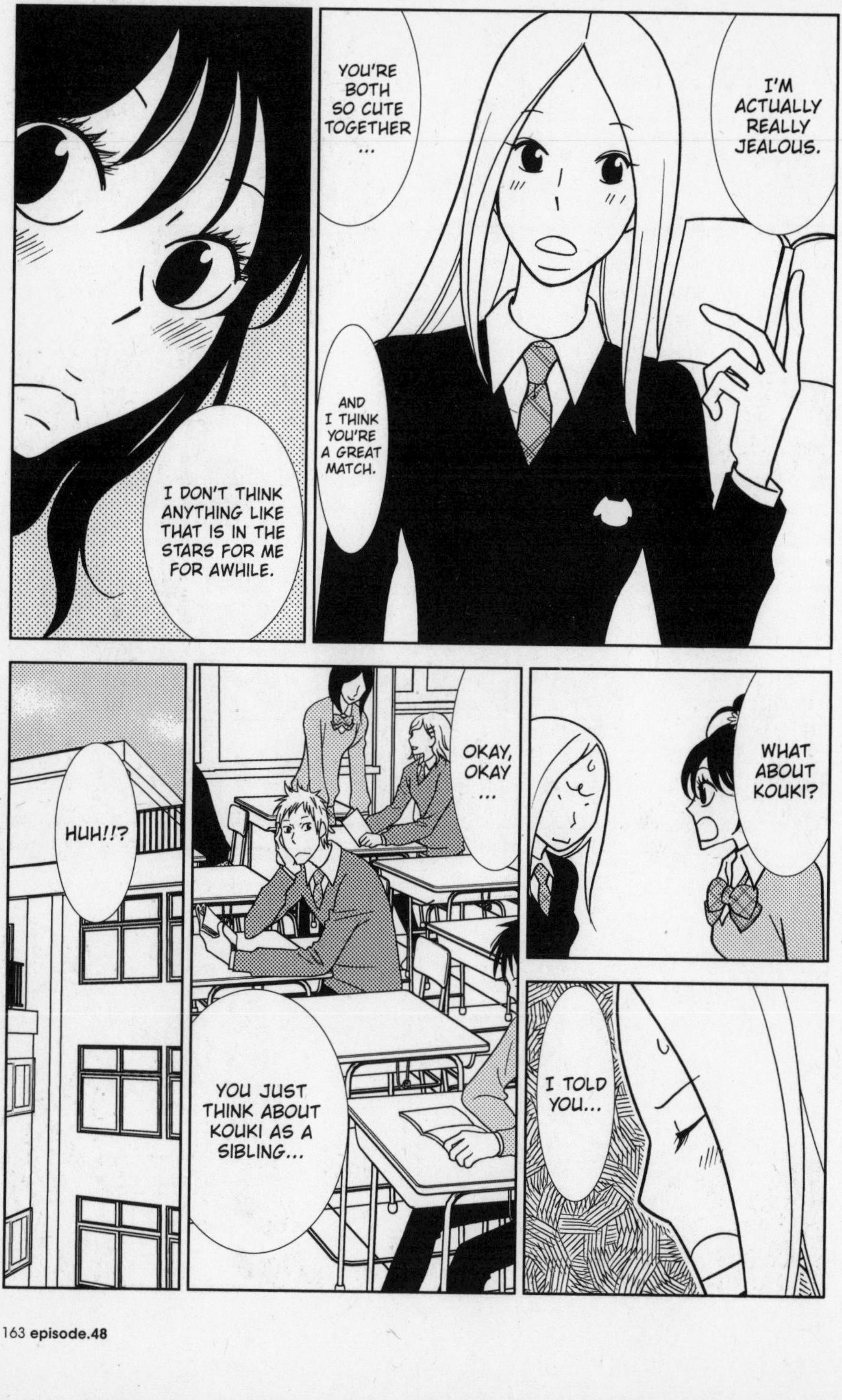
I'M ACTUALLY REALLY JEALOUS.
YOU'RE BOTH SO CUTE TOGETHER ...
AND I THINK YOU'RE A GREAT MATCH.
I DON'T THINK ANYTHING LIKE THAT IS IN THE STARS FOR ME FOR AWHILE.
WHAT ABOUT KOUKI?
I TOLD YOU...
OKAY, OKAY ...
YOU JUST THINK ABOUT KOUKI AS A SIBLING...
HUH!!?

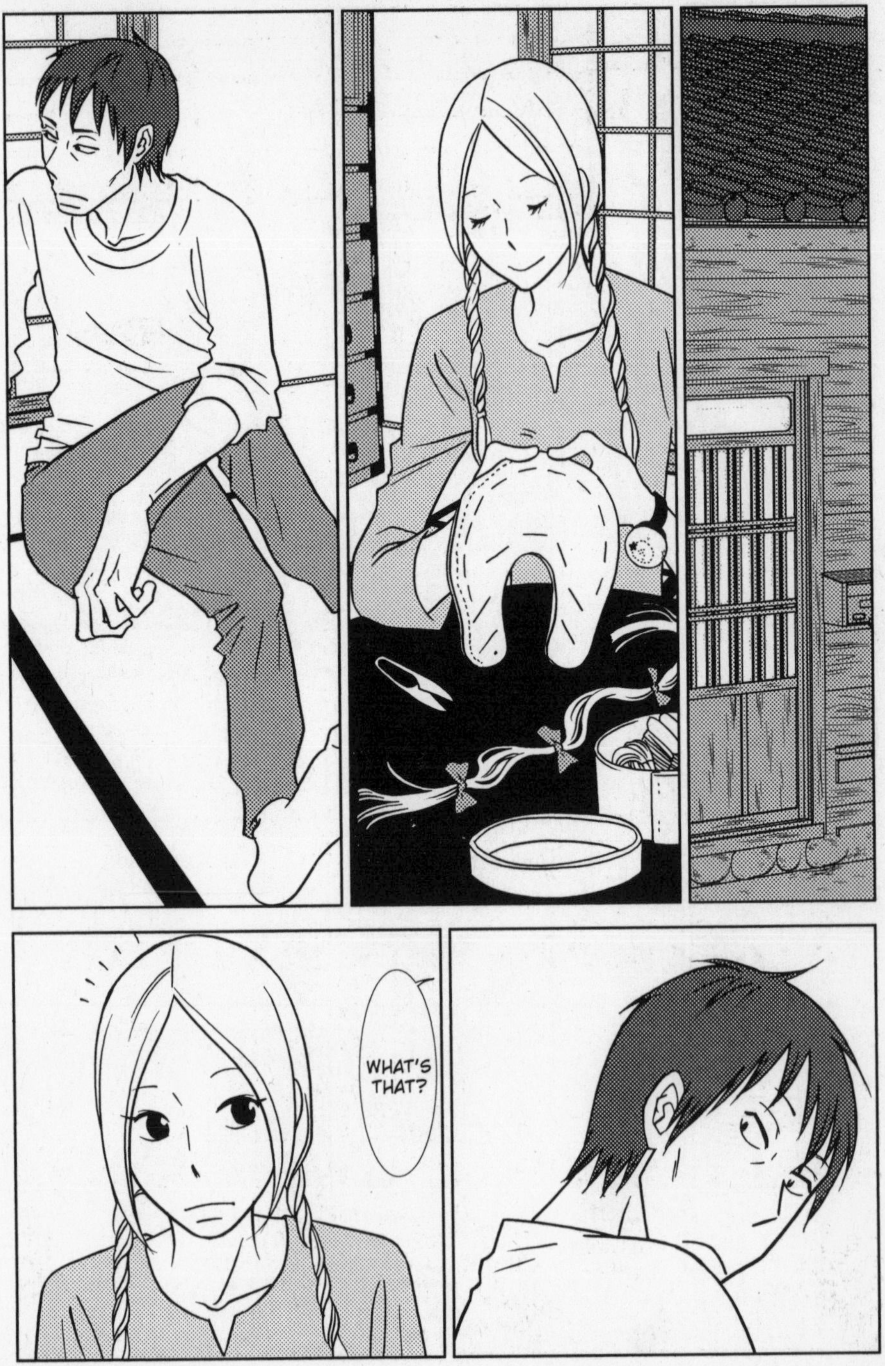
WHAT'S THAT?

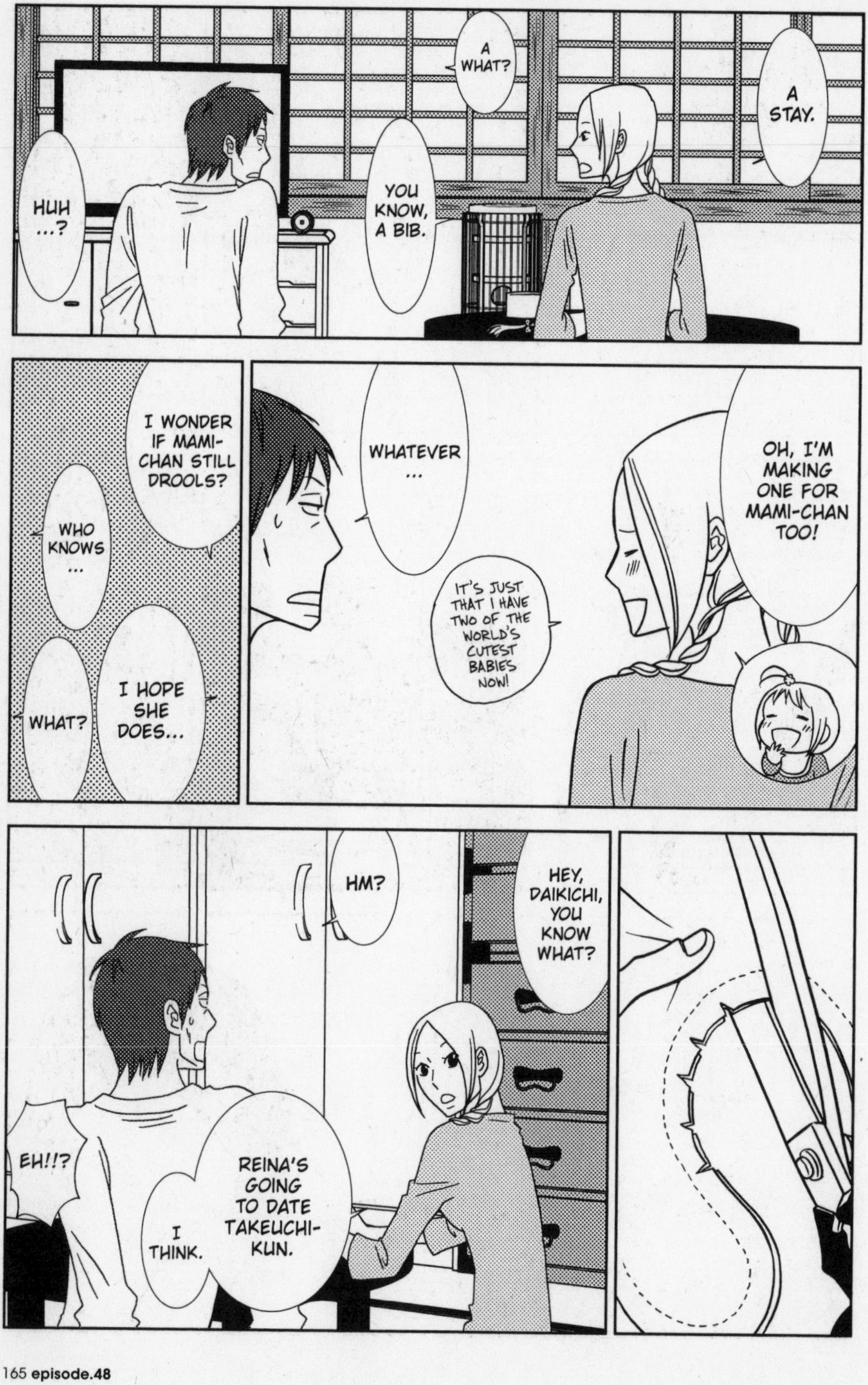
A STAY.
A WHAT?
YOU KNOW, A BIB.
HUH ...?
OH, I'M MAKING ONE FOR MAMI-CHAN TOO!
WHATEVER ...
IT'S JUST THAT I HAVE TWO OF THE WORLD'S CUTEST BABIES NOW!
I WONDER IF MAMI-CHAN STILL DROOLS?
WHO KNOWS ...
I HOPE SHE DOES...
WHAT?
HEY, DAIKICHI, YOU KNOW WHAT?
HM?
REINA'S GOING TO DATE TAKEUCHI-KUN.
I THINK.
EH!!?

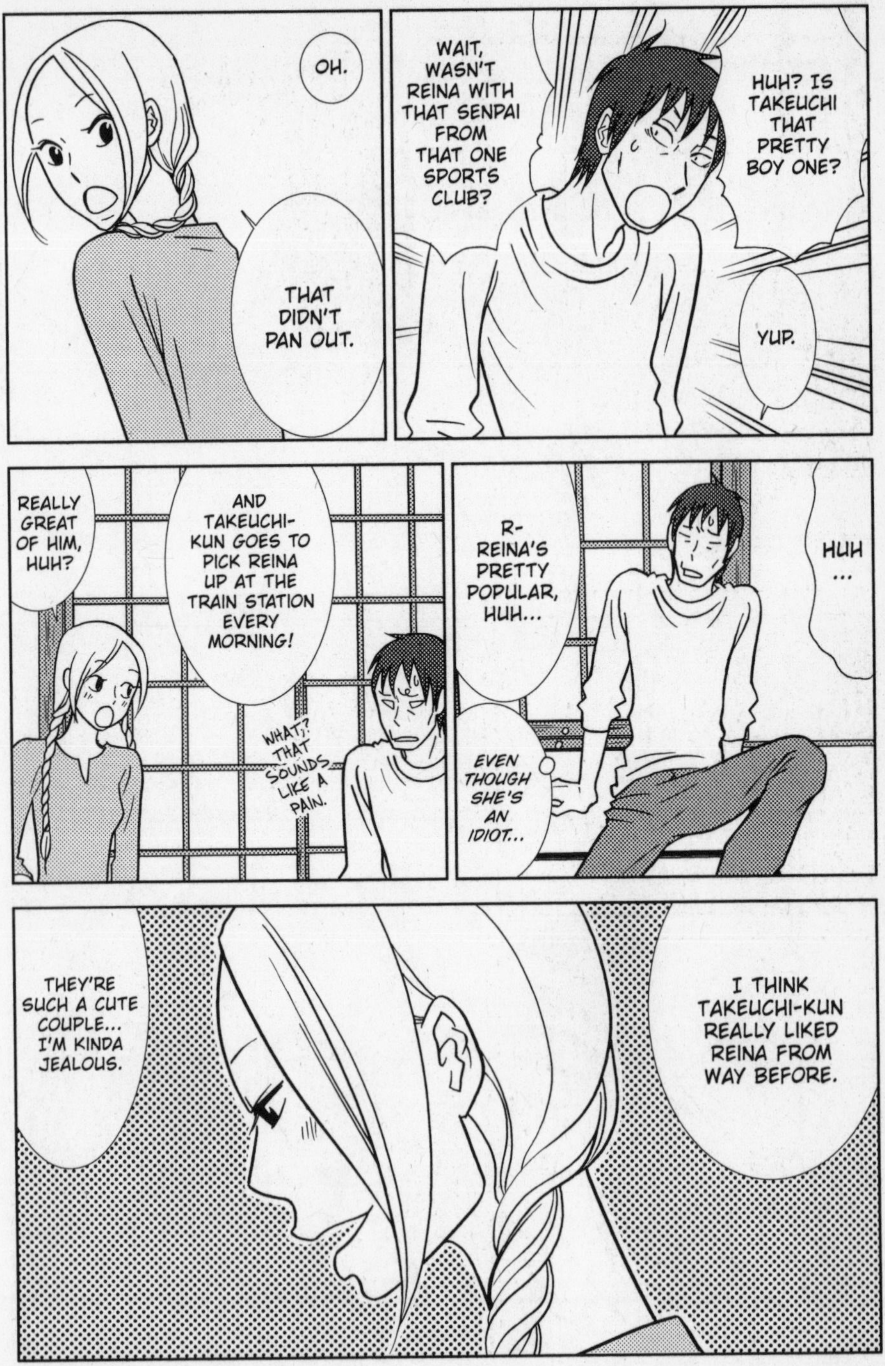
HUH? IS TAKEUCHI THAT PRETTY BOY ONE?
WAIT, WASN'T REINA WITH THAT SENPAI FROM THAT ONE SPORTS CLUB?
YUP.
OH.
THAT DIDN'T PAN OUT.
HUH ...
R-REINA'S PRETTY POPULAR, HUH...
EVEN THOUGH SHE'S AN IDIOT...
AND TAKEUCHI-KUN GOES TO PICK REINA UP AT THE TRAIN STATION EVERY MORNING!
REALLY GREAT OF HIM, HUH?
WHAT;? THAT SOUNDS LIKE A PAIN.
I THINK TAKEUCHI-KUN REALLY LIKED REINA FROM WAY BEFORE.
THEY'RE SUCH A CUTE COUPLE... I'M KINDA JEALOUS.

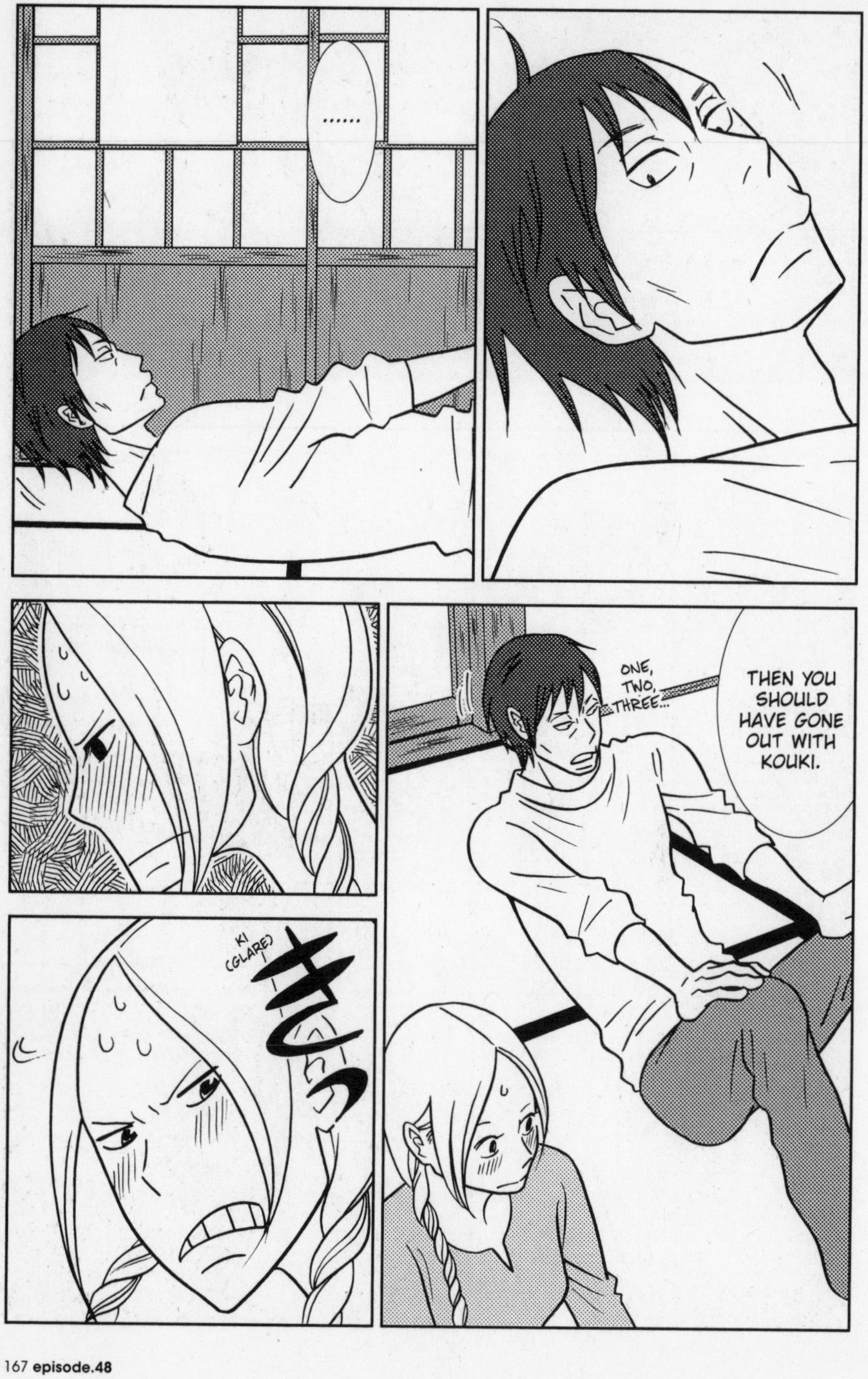
......
THEN YOU SHOULD HAVE GONE OUT WITH KOUKI.
ONE, TWO, THREE...
きっ
KI (GLARE)

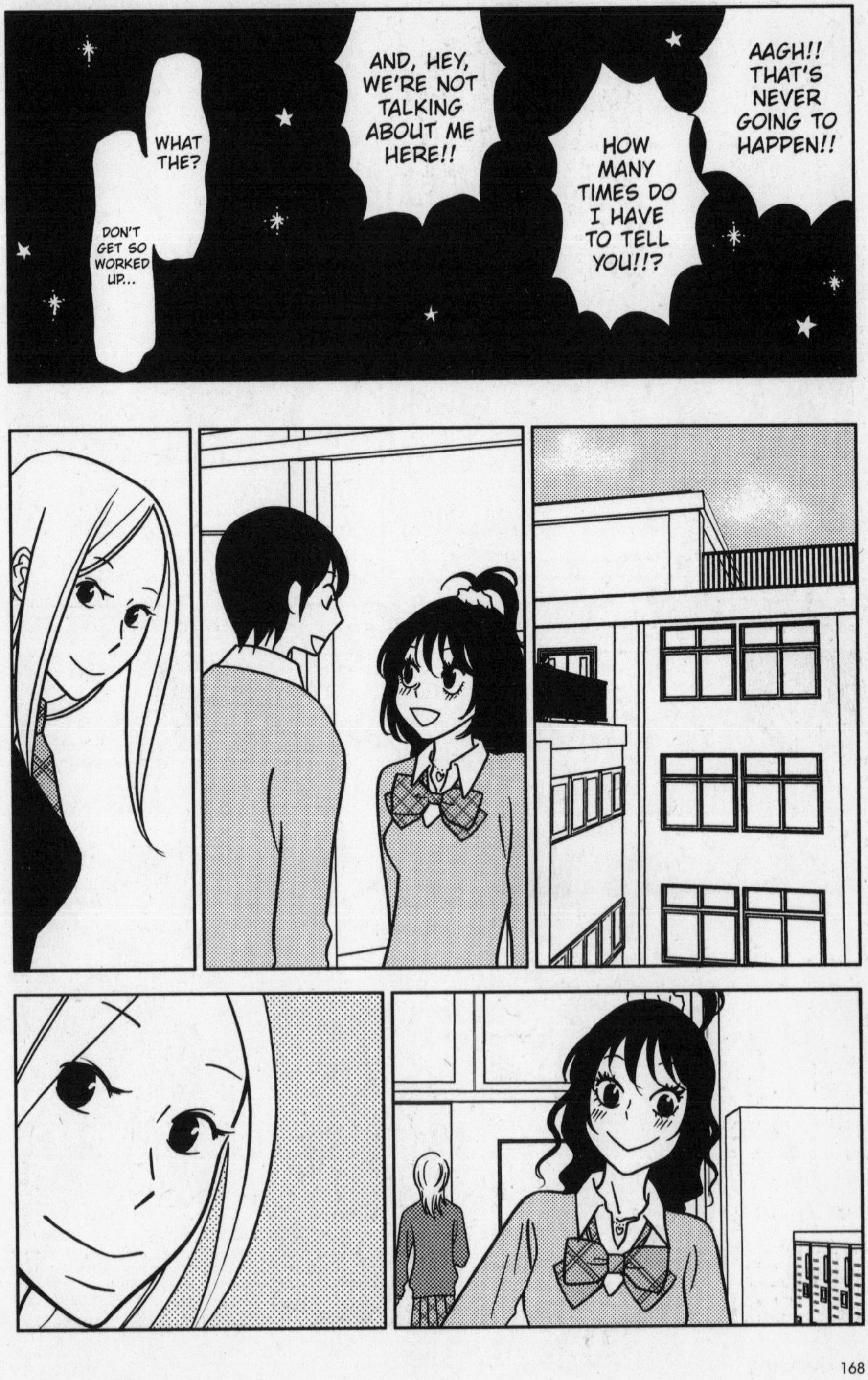
AAGH!! THAT'S NEVER GOING TO HAPPEN!!
HOW MANY TIMES DO I HAVE TO TELL YOU!!?
AND, HEY, WE'RE NOT TALKING ABOUT ME HERE!!
WHAT THE?
DON'T GET SO WORKED UP...

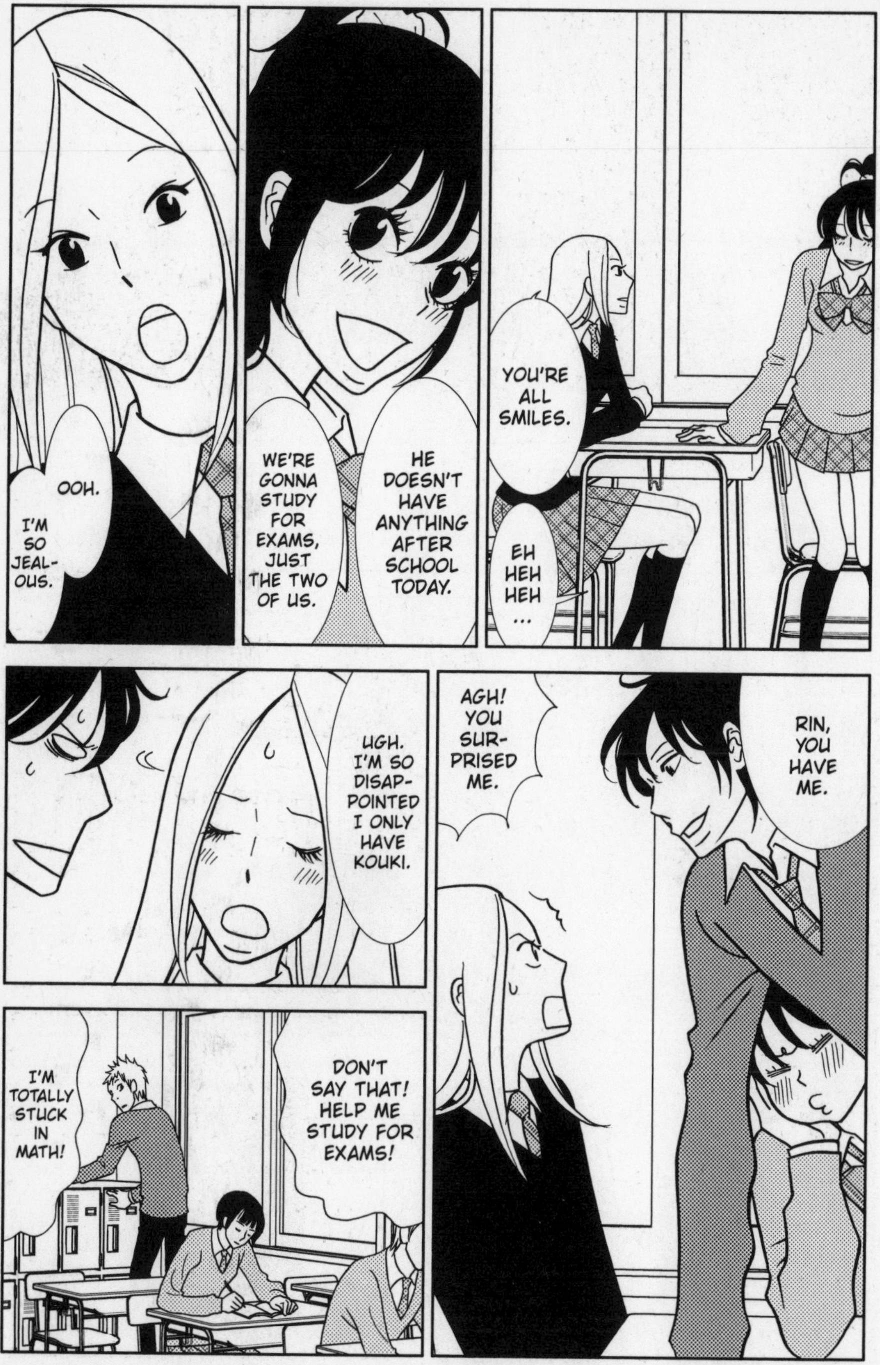
YOU'RE ALL SMILES.
EH HEH HEH ...
HE DOESN'T HAVE ANYTHING AFTER SCHOOL TODAY.
WE'RE GONNA STUDY FOR EXAMS, JUST THE TWO OF US.
OOH.
I'M SO JEAL-OUS.
RIN, YOU HAVE ME.
AGH! YOU SUR-PRISED ME.
UGH. I'M SO DISAP-POINTED I ONLY HAVE KOUKI.
DON'T SAY THAT! HELP ME STUDY FOR EXAMS!
I'M TOTALLY STUCK IN MATH!

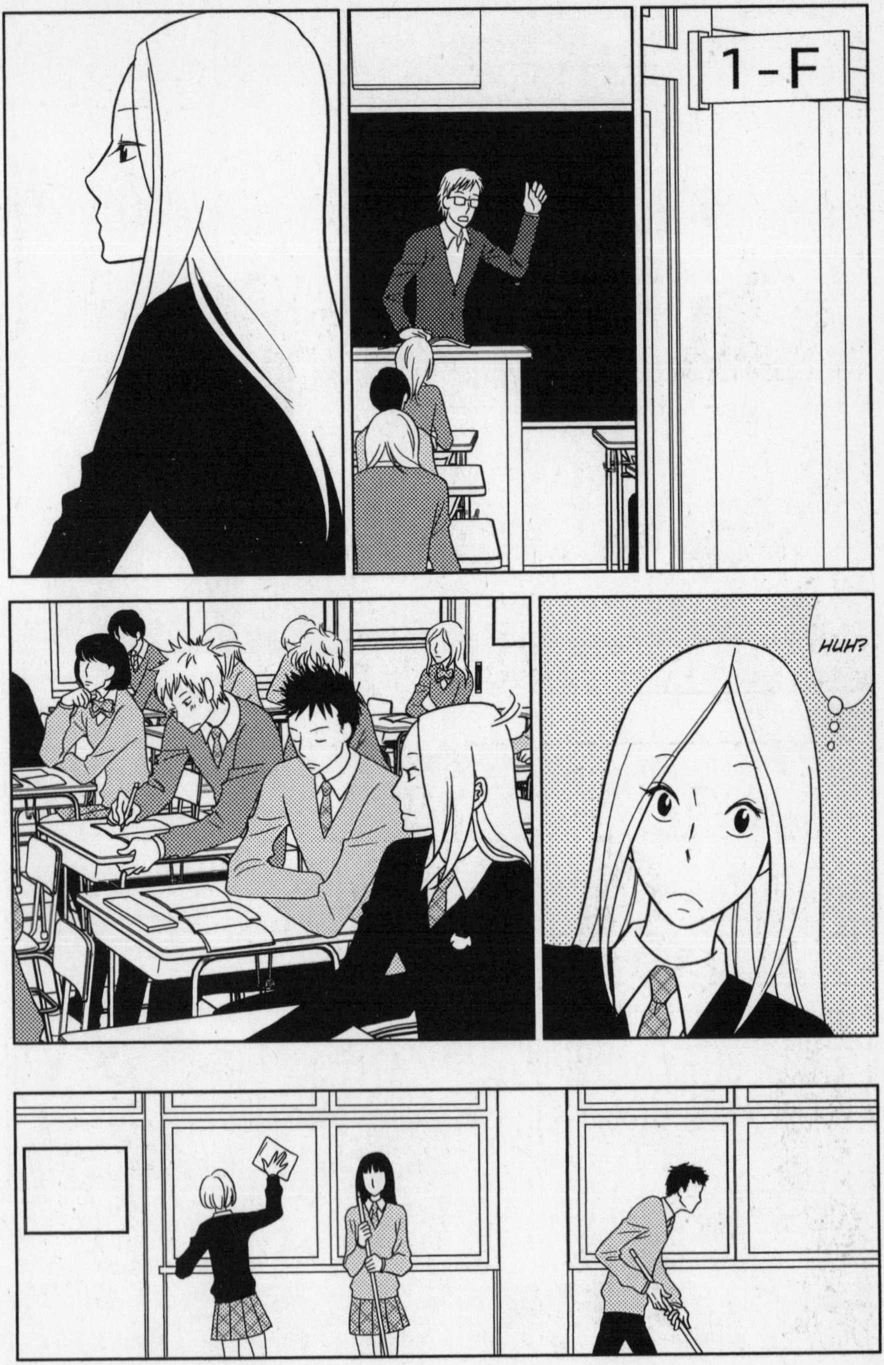
1-F
HUH?

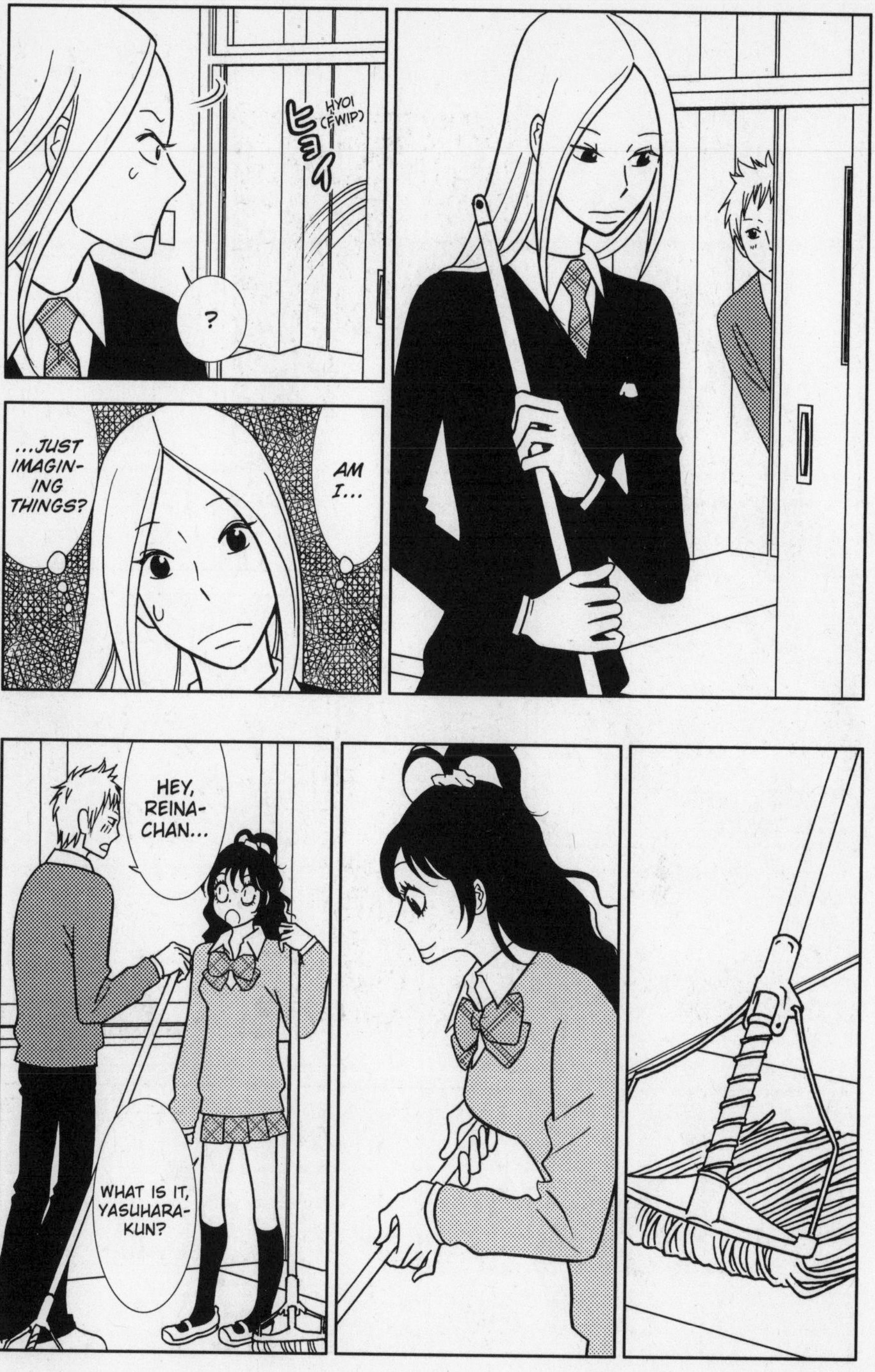
ヒョイ
HYOI (FWIP)
?
AM I...
...JUST IMAGINING THINGS?
HEY, REINA-CHAN...
WHAT IS IT, YASUHARA-KUN?

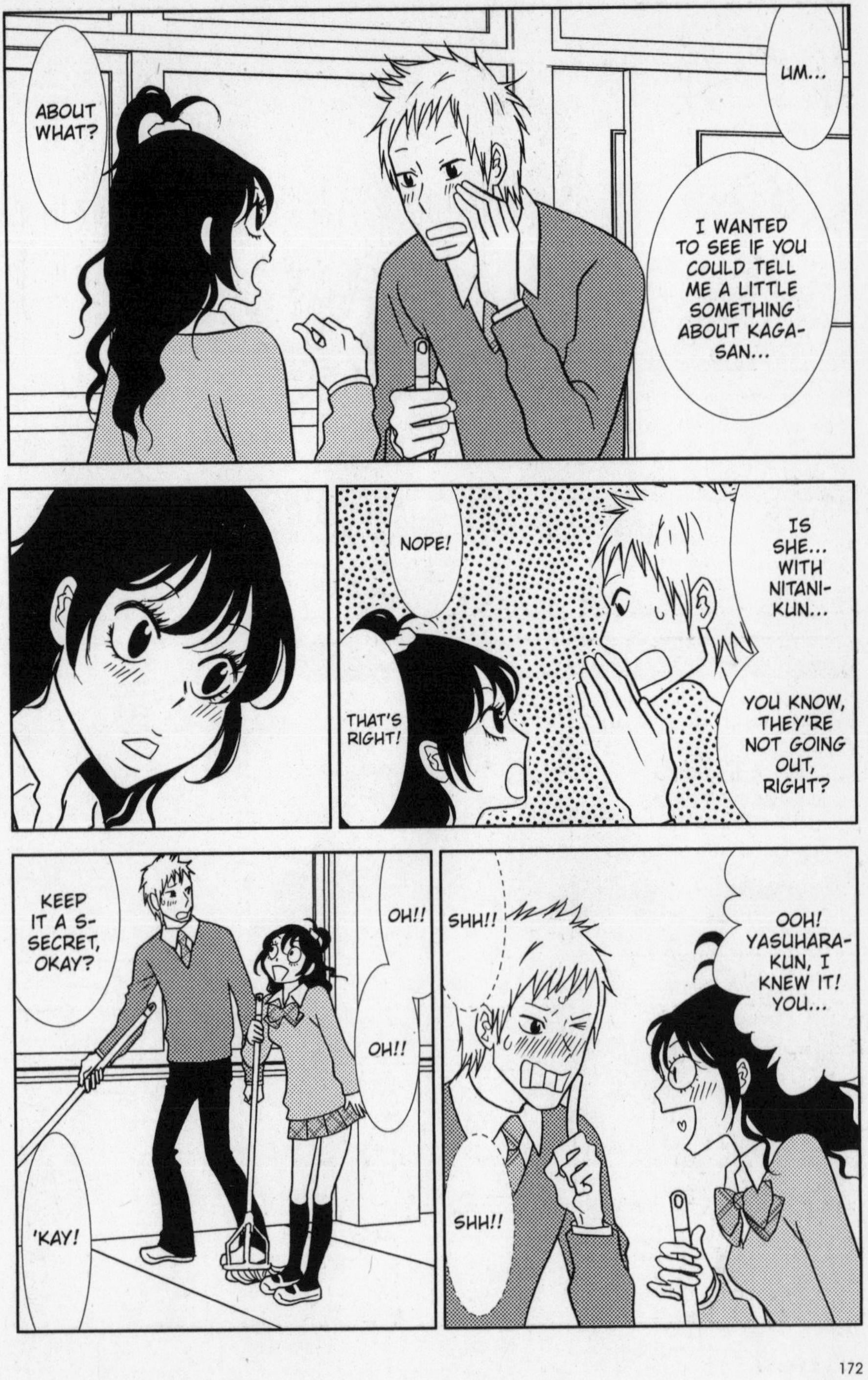
UM...
I WANTED TO SEE IF YOU COULD TELL ME A LITTLE SOMETHING ABOUT KAGA-SAN...
ABOUT WHAT?
IS SHE... WITH NITANI-KUN...
NOPE!
YOU KNOW, THEY'RE NOT GOING OUT, RIGHT?
THAT'S RIGHT!
OOH! YASUHARA-KUN, I KNEW IT! YOU...
SHH!!
SHH!!
OH!!
KEEP IT A S-SECRET, OKAY?
OH!!
'KAY!

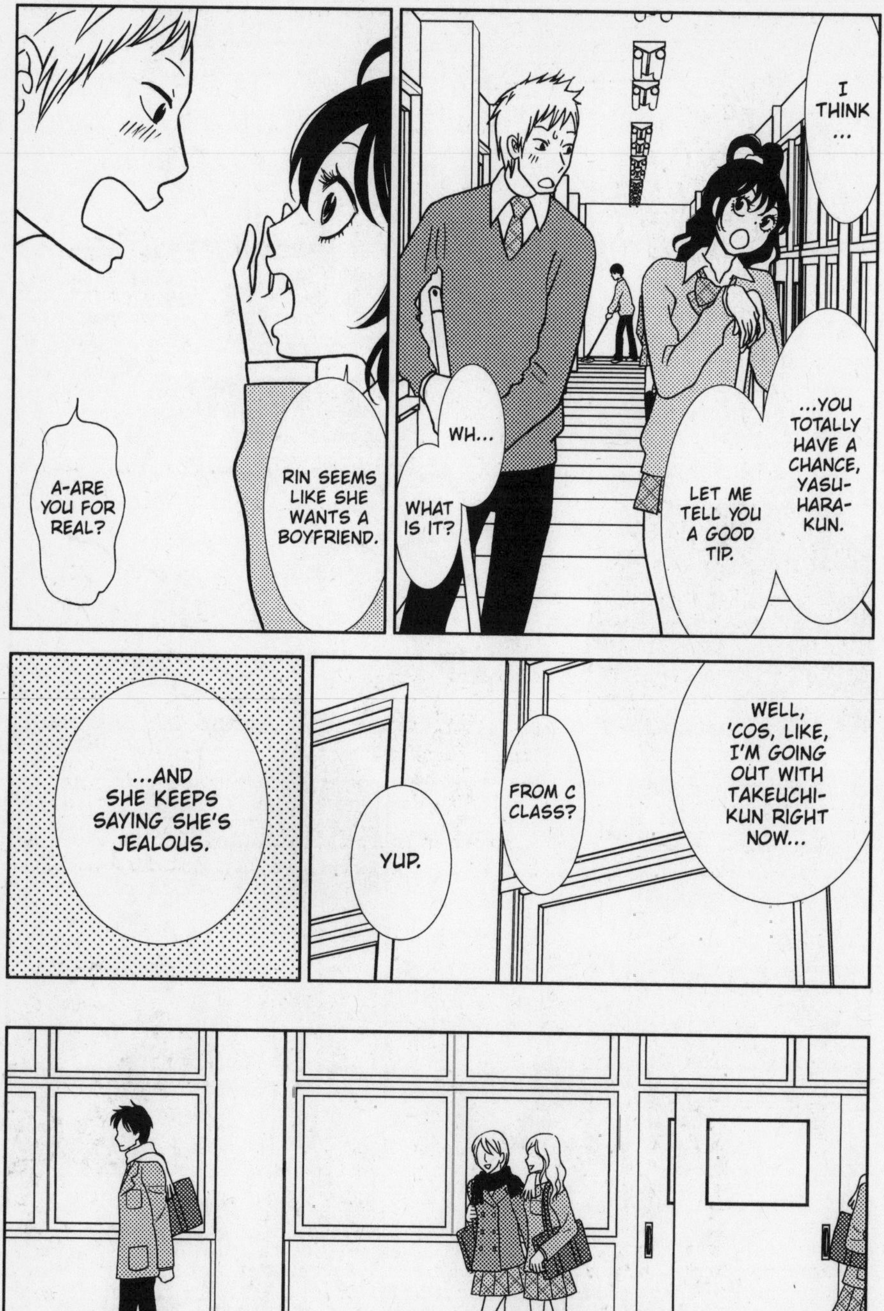
I THINK...
...YOU TOTALLY HAVE A CHANCE, YASU-HARA-KUN.
LET ME TELL YOU A GOOD TIP.
WH...
WHAT IS IT?
RIN SEEMS LIKE SHE WANTS A BOYFRIEND.
A-ARE YOU FOR REAL?
WELL, 'COS, LIKE, I'M GOING OUT WITH TAKEUCHI-KUN RIGHT NOW...
FROM C CLASS?
YUP.
...AND SHE KEEPS SAYING SHE'S JEALOUS.

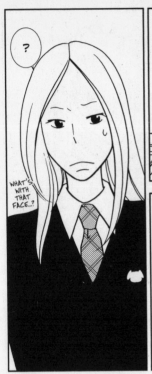

OH.
TAKEUCHI-KUN'S HERE.
BYE, RIN.
OKAY, BYE-BYE.
?
WHAT'S WITH THAT FACE...?
KAGA-SAN.
OH.
YASU-HARA-KUN.

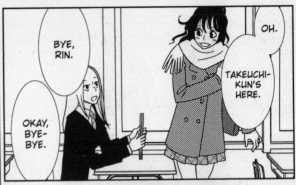

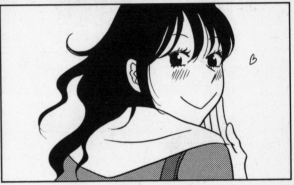

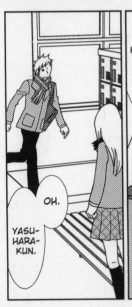

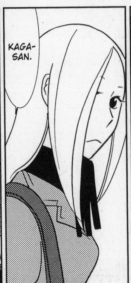

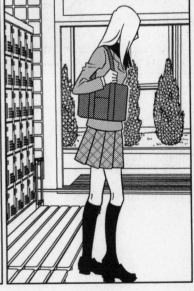

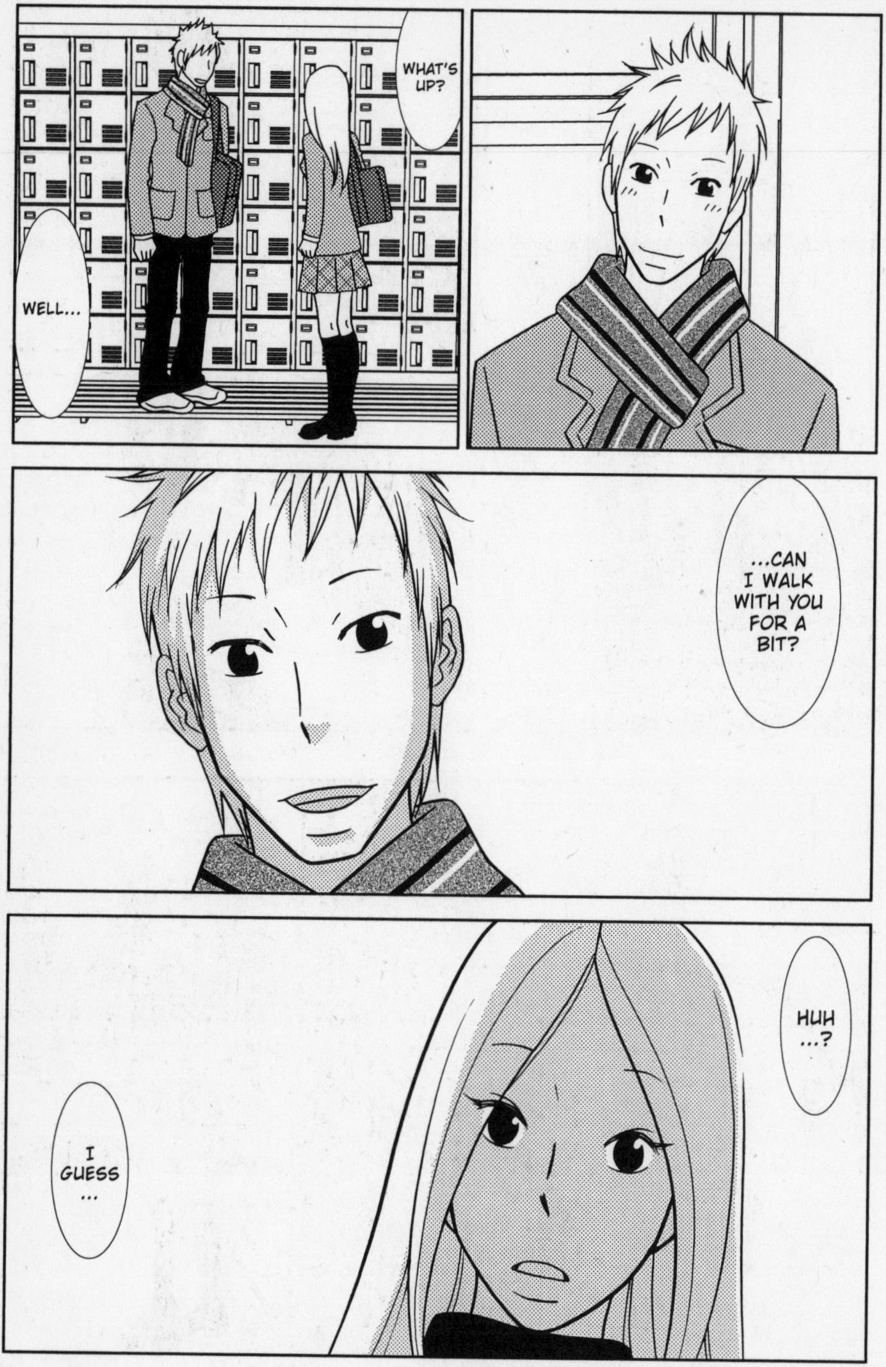
WHAT'S UP?
WELL...
...CAN I WALK WITH YOU FOR A BIT?
HUH ...?
I GUESS ...

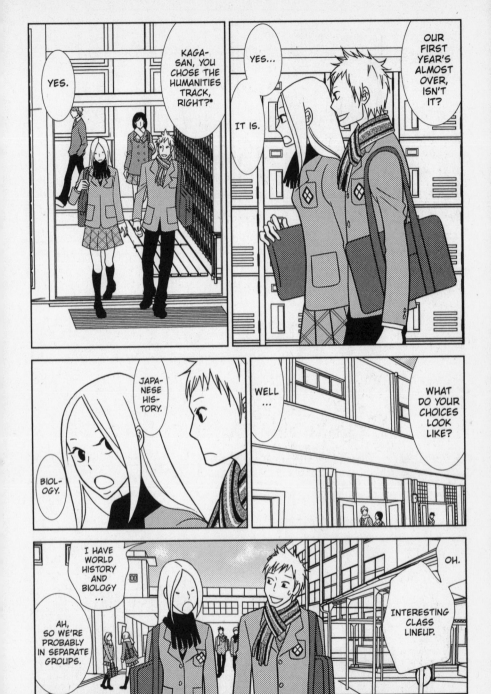

OUR FIRST YEAR'S ALMOST OVER, ISN'T IT?
YES...
IT IS.
KAGA-SAN, YOU CHOSE THE HUMANITIES TRACK, RIGHT?*
YES.
WHAT DO YOUR CHOICES LOOK LIKE?
WELL ...
JAPA-NESE HIS-TORY.
BIOL-OGY.
OH.
INTERESTING CLASS LINEUP.
I HAVE WORLD HISTORY AND BIOLOGY ...
AH, SO WE'RE PROBABLY IN SEPARATE GROUPS.

*STUDENTS IN ACADEMICALLY ORIENTED HIGH SCHOOLS ARE PLACED IN EITHER A HUMANITIES OR A SCIENCE TRACK BY THE MINISTRY OF EDUCATION, CULTURE, SPORTS, SCIENCE, AND TECHNOLOGY. TRACK PLACEMENT IS LARGELY DETERMINED BY THE STUDENTS THEMSELVES, BUT TEACHERS ALSO DISCOURAGE STUDENTS FROM SEEKING A TRACK THEY FEEL IS ABOVE THEIR LEVEL OF ACHIEVEMENT. THE AMOUNT OF MATH AND SCIENCE IN THE HUMANITIES TRACK IS CONSIDERABLY LESS THAN IN THE SCIENCE TRACK, BUT STUDENTS IN THE HUMANITIES MUST STILL PASS THE MINIMUM MINISTRY REQUIREMENTS.

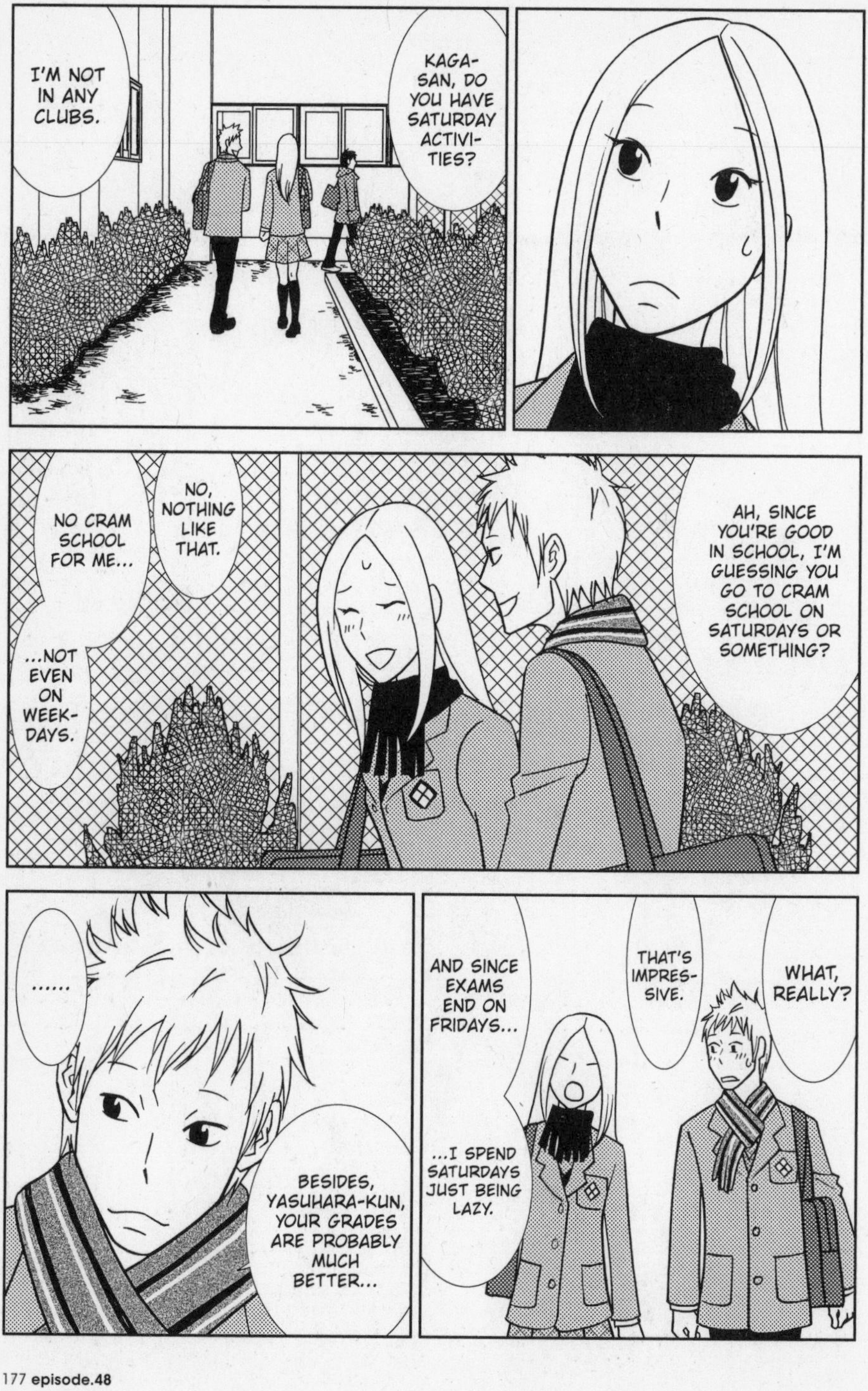
KAGA-SAN, DO YOU HAVE SATURDAY ACTIVITIES?
I'M NOT IN ANY CLUBS.
AH, SINCE YOU'RE GOOD IN SCHOOL, I'M GUESSING YOU GO TO CRAM SCHOOL ON SATURDAYS OR SOMETHING?
NO, NOTHING LIKE THAT.
NO CRAM SCHOOL FOR ME...
...NOT EVEN ON WEEK-DAYS.
WHAT, REALLY?
THAT'S IMPRES-SIVE.
AND SINCE EXAMS END ON FRIDAYS...
...I SPEND SATURDAYS JUST BEING LAZY.
......
BESIDES, YASUHARA-KUN, YOUR GRADES ARE PROBABLY MUCH BETTER...

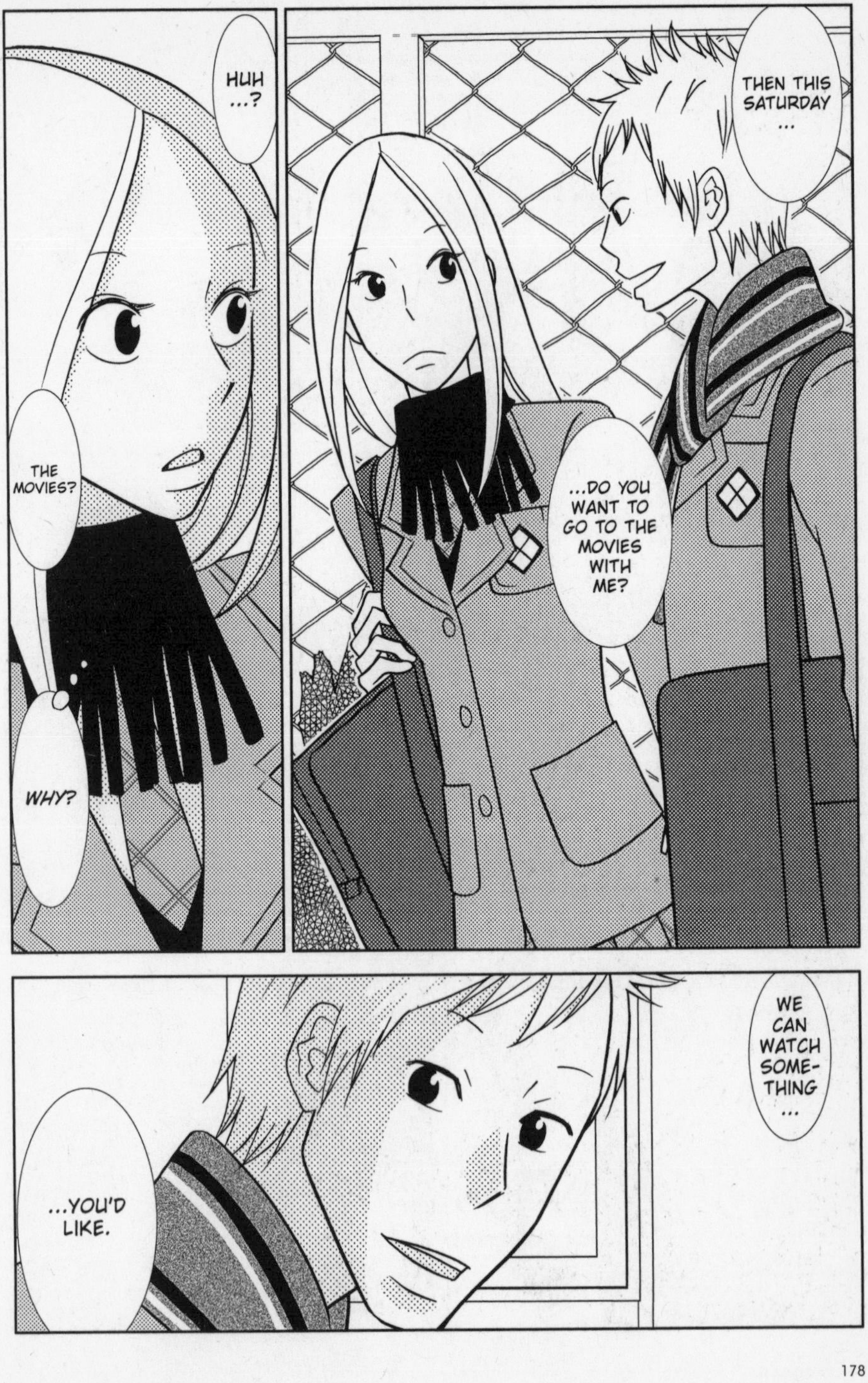
THEN THIS SATURDAY ...
...DO YOU WANT TO GO TO THE MOVIES WITH ME?
HUH ...?
THE MOVIES?
WHY?
WE CAN WATCH SOME-THING ...
...YOU'D LIKE.

WHAT?
I DON'T... UNDERSTAND.
WAIT... IS THIS ...

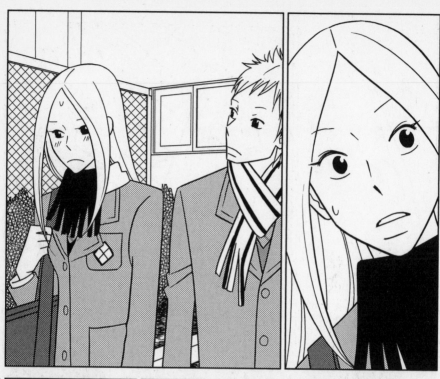

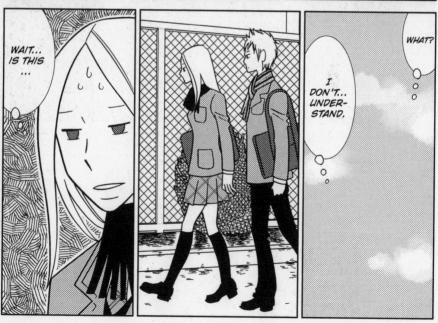

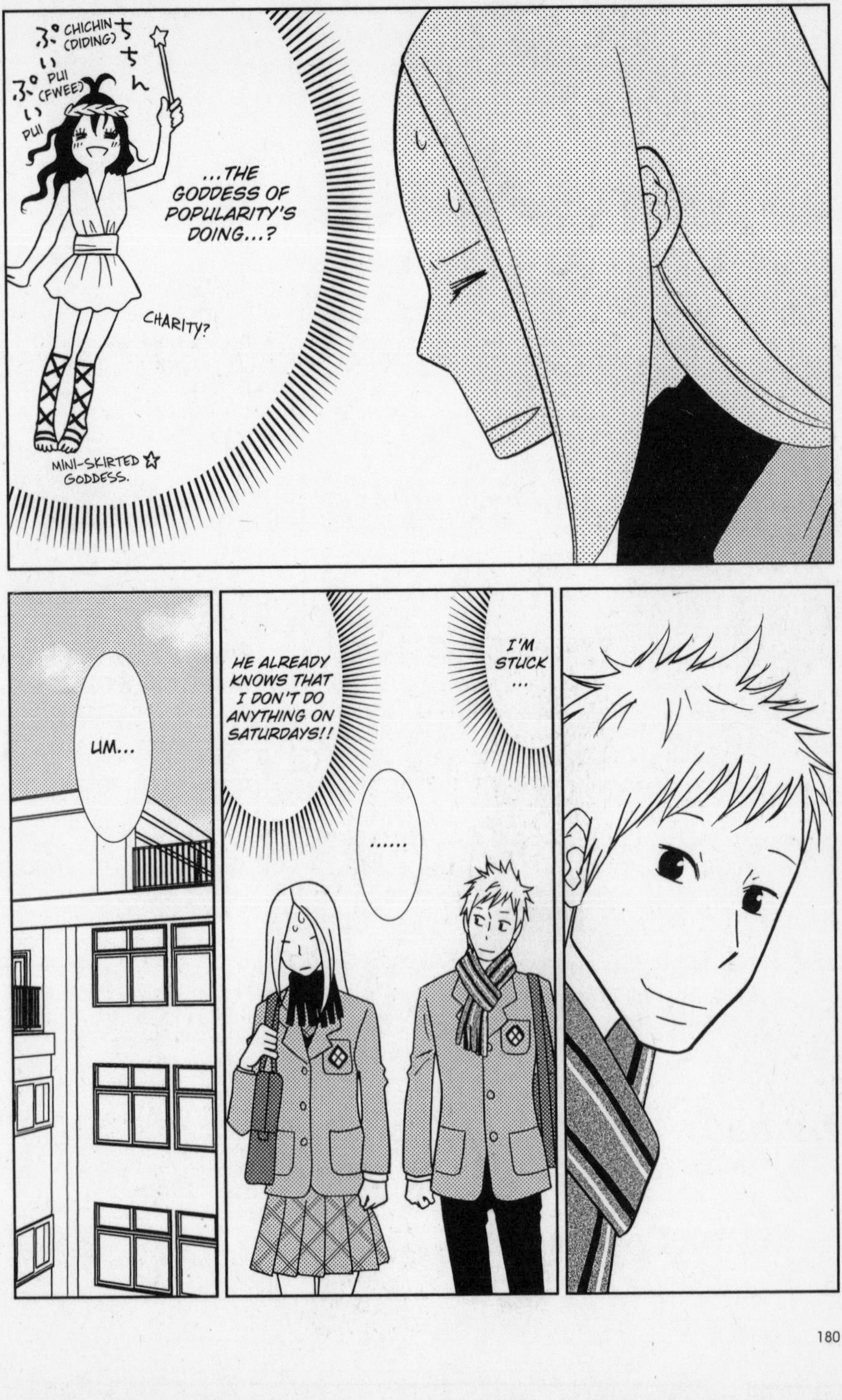
...THE GODDESS OF POPULARITY'S DOING...?
ちちん
CHICHIN (DIDING)
ぷい
PUI (FWEE)
ぷい
PUI
CHARITY?
MINI-SKIRTED ☆ GODDESS.
I'M STUCK...
HE ALREADY KNOWS THAT I DON'T DO ANYTHING ON SATURDAYS!!
......
UM...

BUNNY**DROP**
episode.49

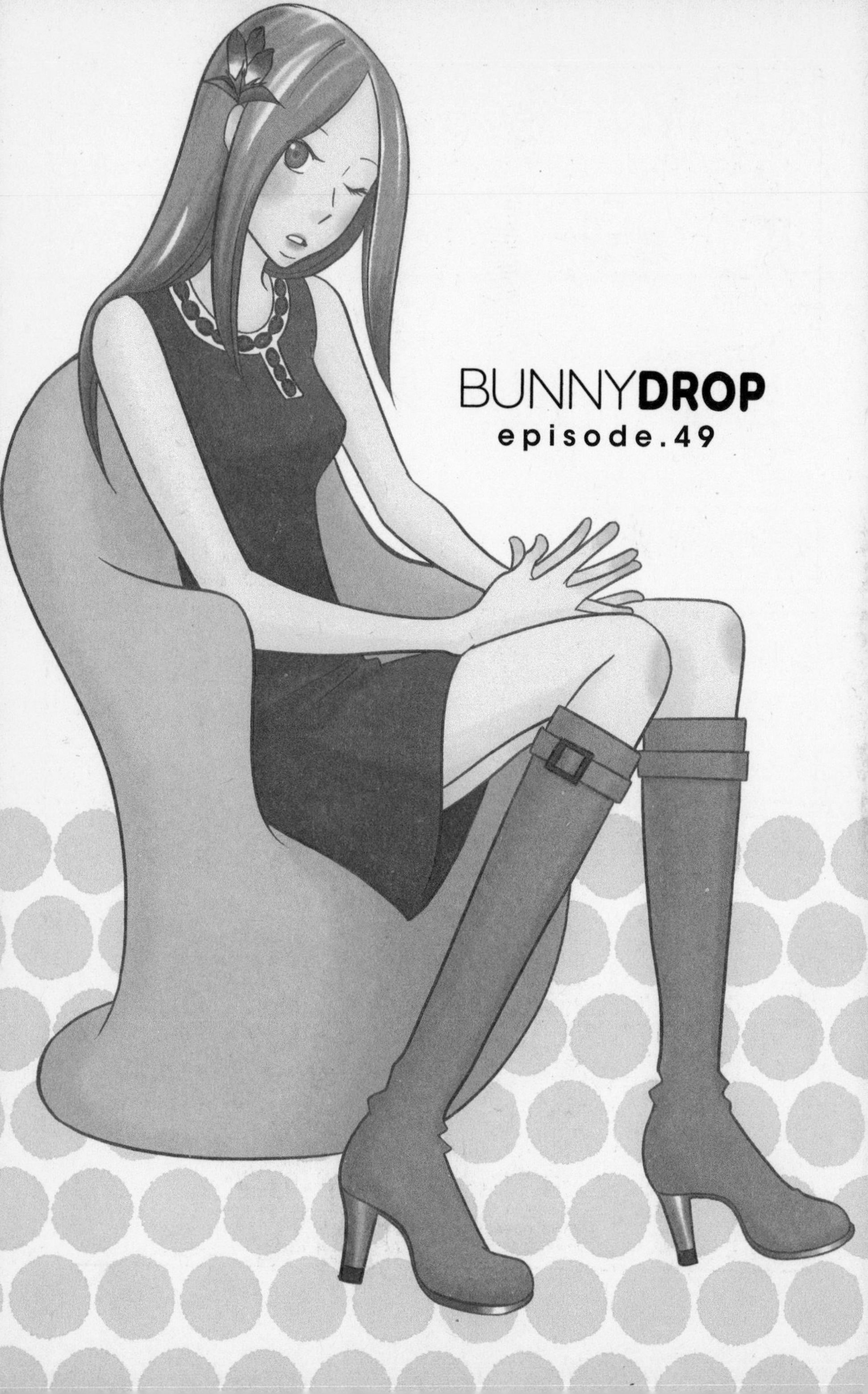

BUNNY**DROP**

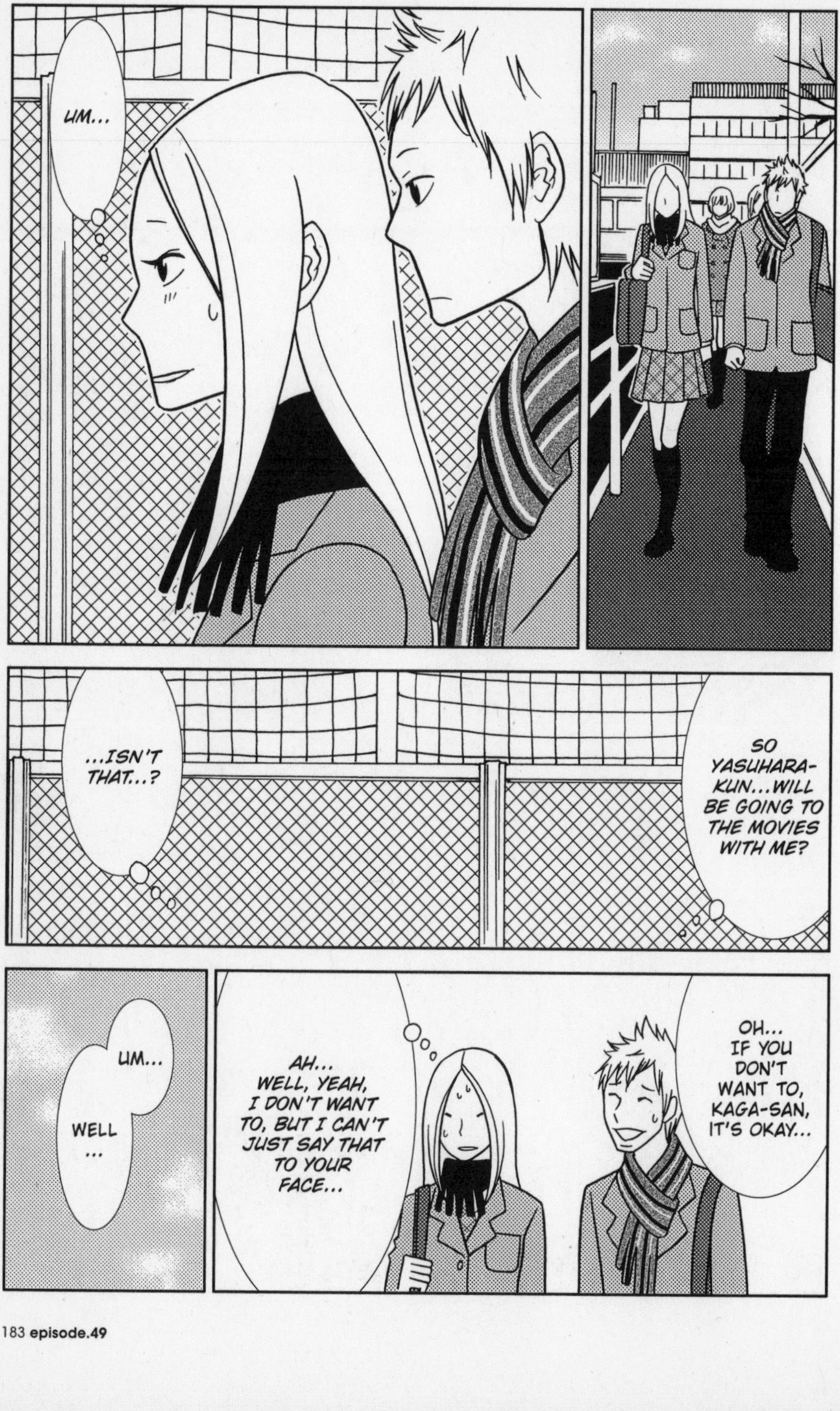
UM...
SO YASUHARA-KUN...WILL BE GOING TO THE MOVIES WITH ME?
...ISN'T THAT...?
OH... IF YOU DON'T WANT TO, KAGA-SAN, IT'S OKAY...
AH... WELL, YEAH, I DON'T WANT TO, BUT I CAN'T JUST SAY THAT TO YOUR FACE...
UM...
WELL ...

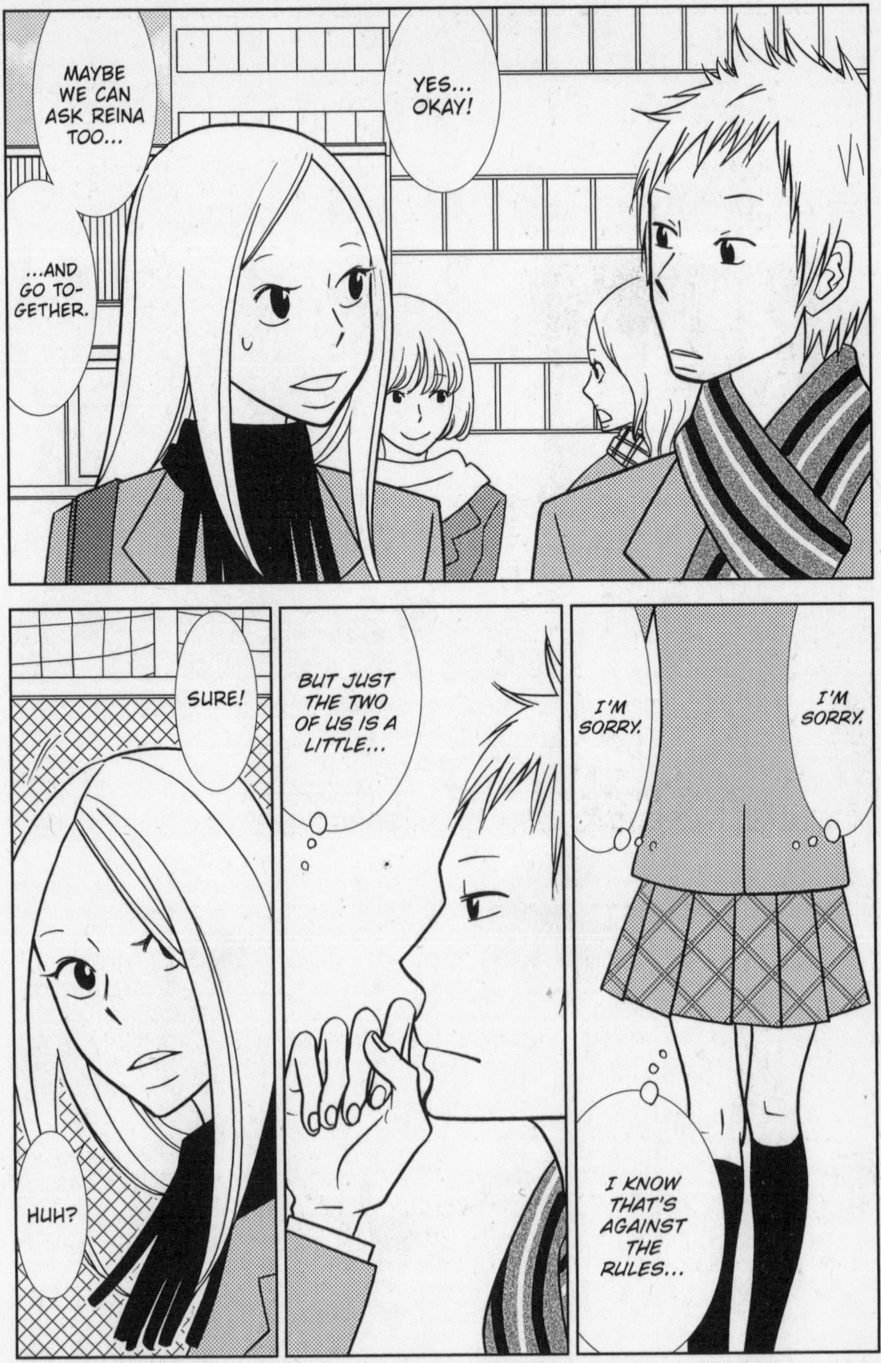
YES... OKAY!
MAYBE WE CAN ASK REINA TOO...
...AND GO TO-GETHER.
I'M SORRY.
I'M SORRY.
I KNOW THAT'S AGAINST THE RULES...
BUT JUST THE TWO OF US IS A LITTLE...
SURE!
HUH?

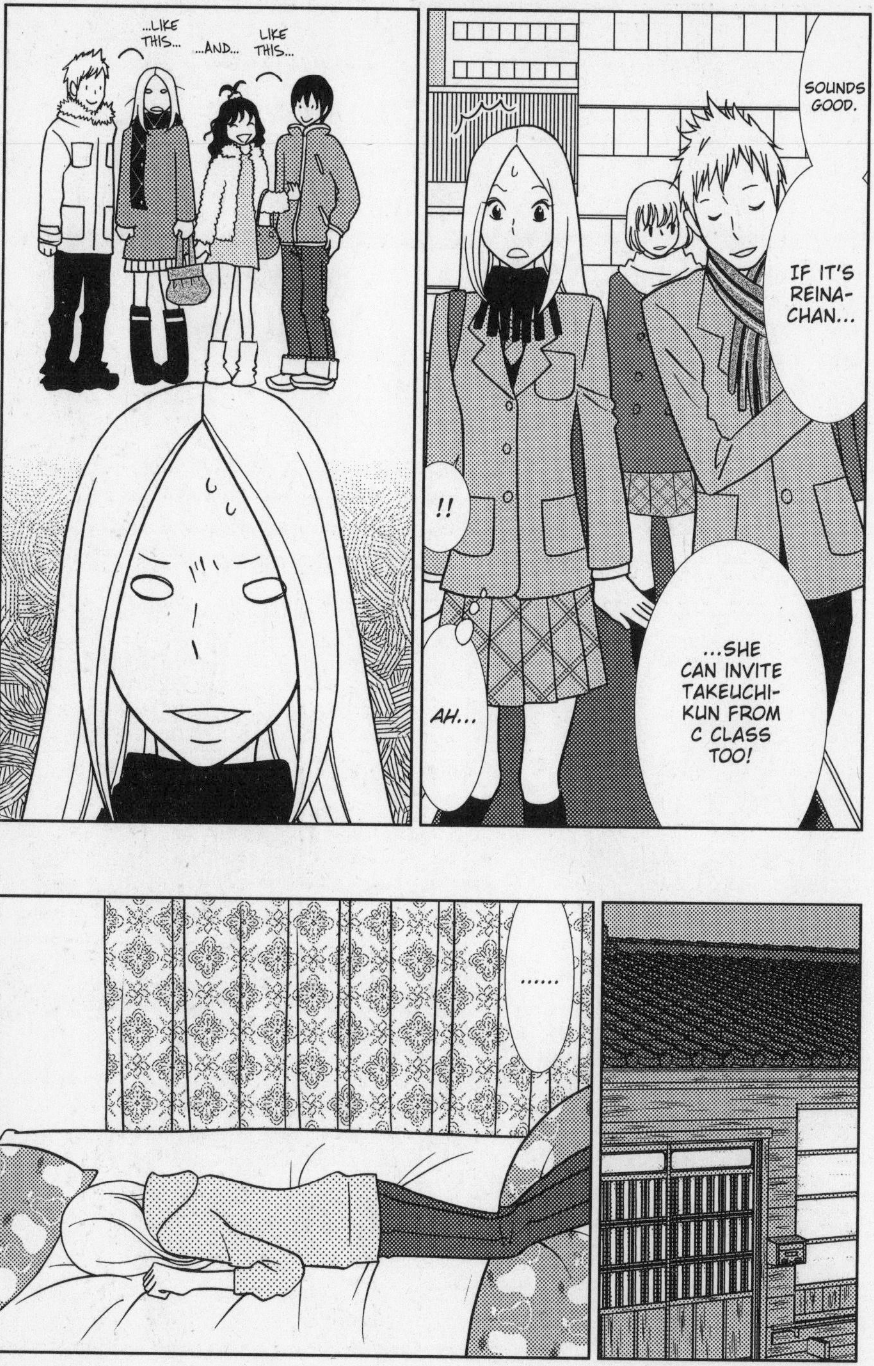
SOUNDS GOOD.
IF IT'S REINA-CHAN...
...SHE CAN INVITE TAKEUCHI-KUN FROM C CLASS TOO!
!!
AH...
LIKE THIS...
...AND...
...LIKE THIS...
......

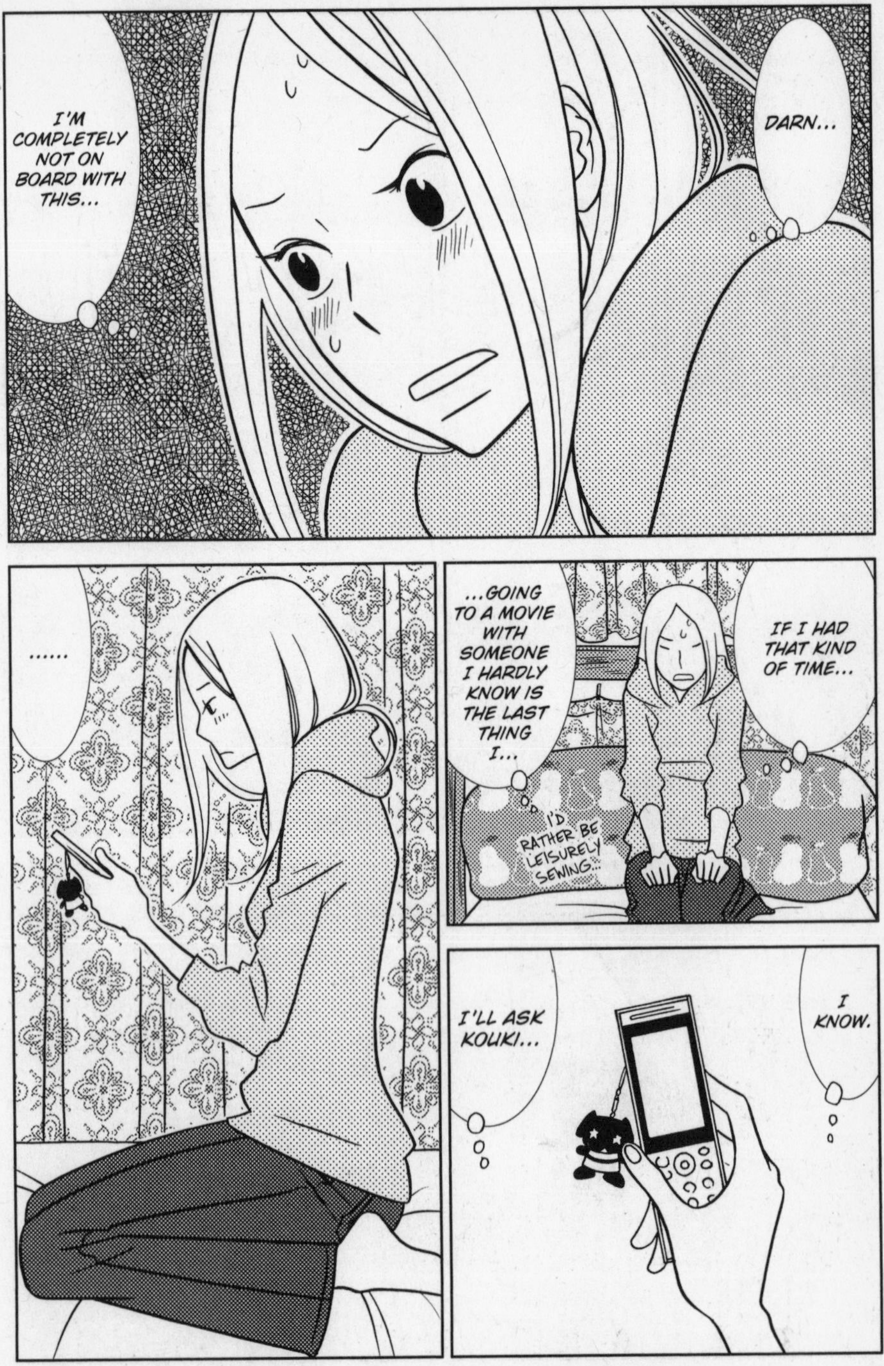
DARN...
I'M COMPLETELY NOT ON BOARD WITH THIS...
IF I HAD THAT KIND OF TIME...
...GOING TO A MOVIE WITH SOMEONE I HARDLY KNOW IS THE LAST THING I...
I'D RATHER BE LEISURELY SEWING...
I KNOW.
I'LL ASK KOUKI...
......

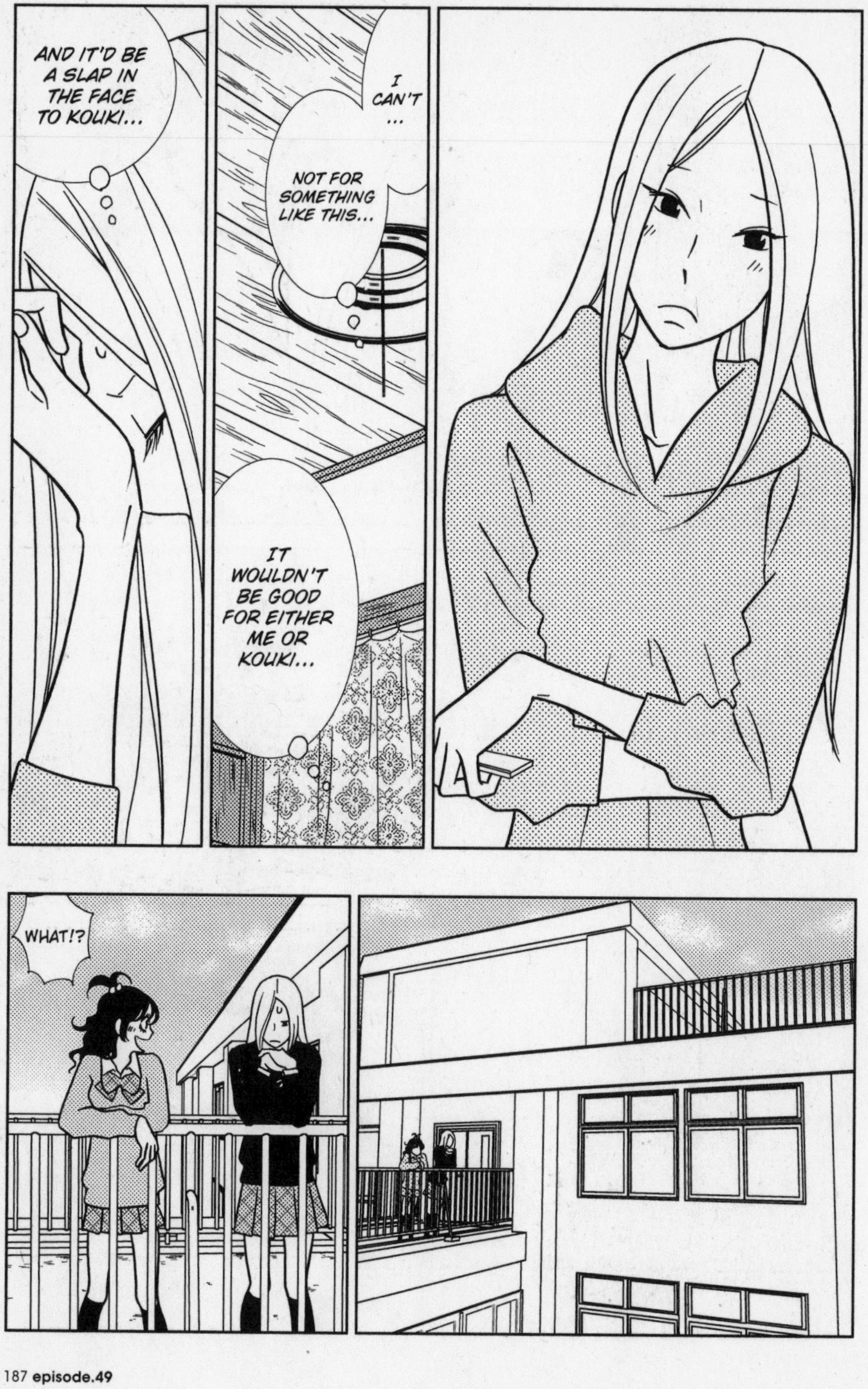
I CAN'T ...
NOT FOR SOMETHING LIKE THIS...
IT WOULDN'T BE GOOD FOR EITHER ME OR KOUKI...
AND IT'D BE A SLAP IN THE FACE TO KOUKI...
WHAT!?

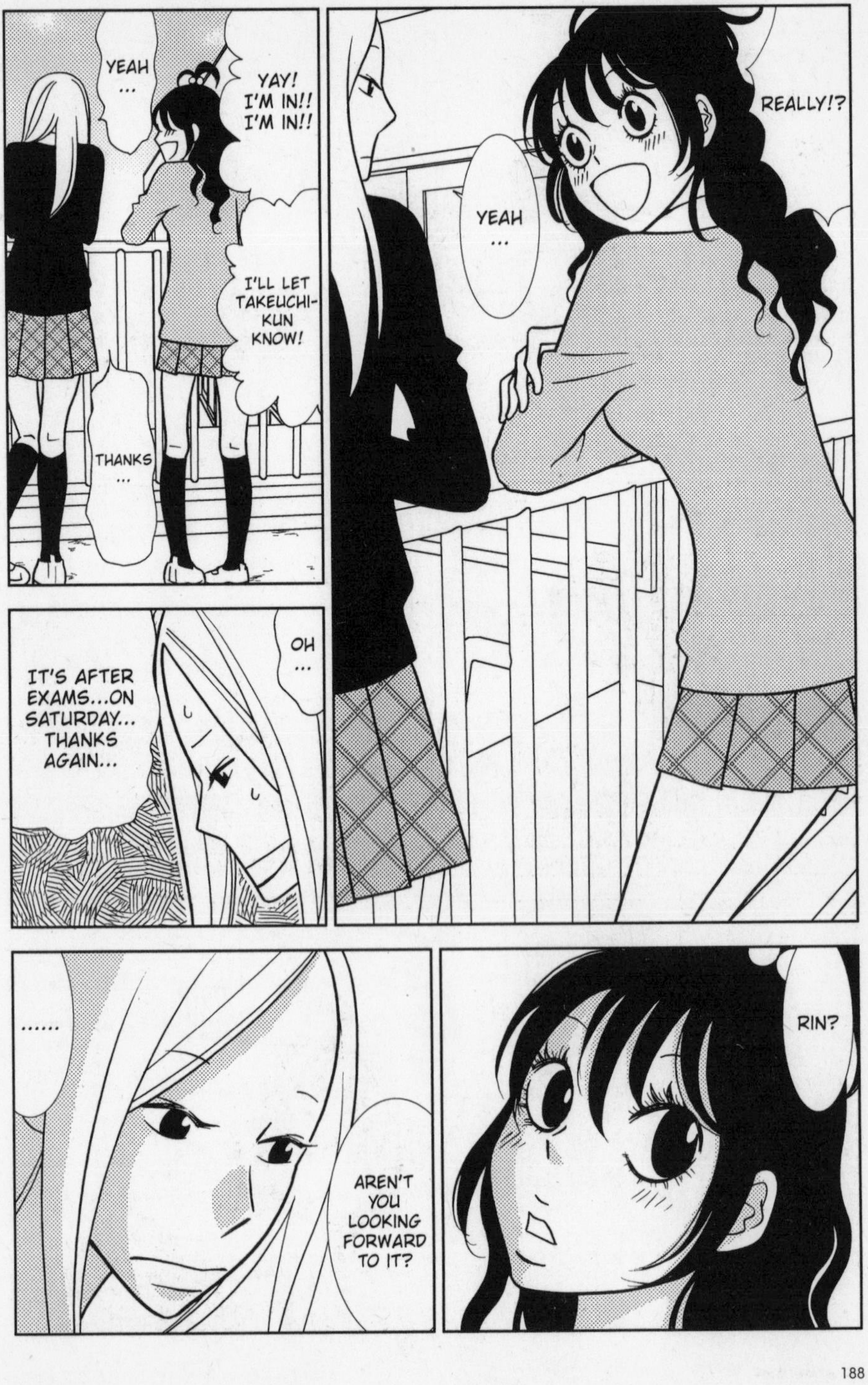
REALLY!?
YEAH ...
YAY! I'M IN!! I'M IN!!
YEAH ...
I'LL LET TAKEUCHI-KUN KNOW!
THANKS ...
OH ...
IT'S AFTER EXAMS...ON SATURDAY... THANKS AGAIN...
RIN?
......
AREN'T YOU LOOKING FORWARD TO IT?

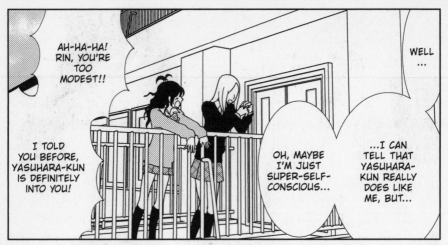

WELL ...
...I CAN TELL THAT YASUHARA-KUN REALLY DOES LIKE ME, BUT...
OH, MAYBE I'M JUST SUPER-SELF-CONSCIOUS...
AH-HA-HA! RIN, YOU'RE TOO MODEST!!
I TOLD YOU BEFORE, YASUHARA-KUN IS DEFINITELY INTO YOU!
WE DON'T EVEN KNOW MUCH ABOUT EACH OTHER...I DON'T SEE THE POINT...
WHAT?
YOU'LL NEVER HAVE A BOYFRIEND IF YOU KEEP SAYING STUFF LIKE THAT!
A BOY-FRIEND, HUH...
I DON'T KNOW IF I WANT SOMETHING LIKE THAT RIGHT NOW...
WHAT!?
I DON'T GET YOU!!

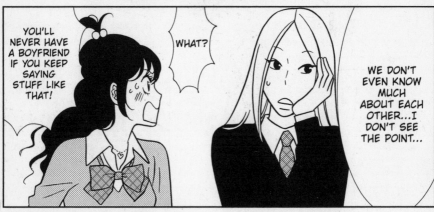

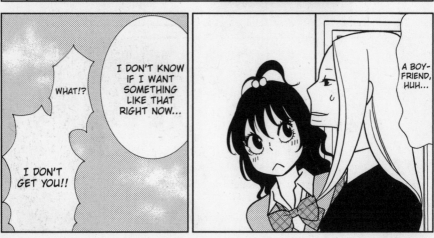

OH, A MOVIE?

WITH KOUKI?

...AND...

...TAKE-UCHI-KUN...

WITH REINA...

NOPE...

...A BOY FROM MY CLASS.

...AND...

BUT ISN'T THAT...?

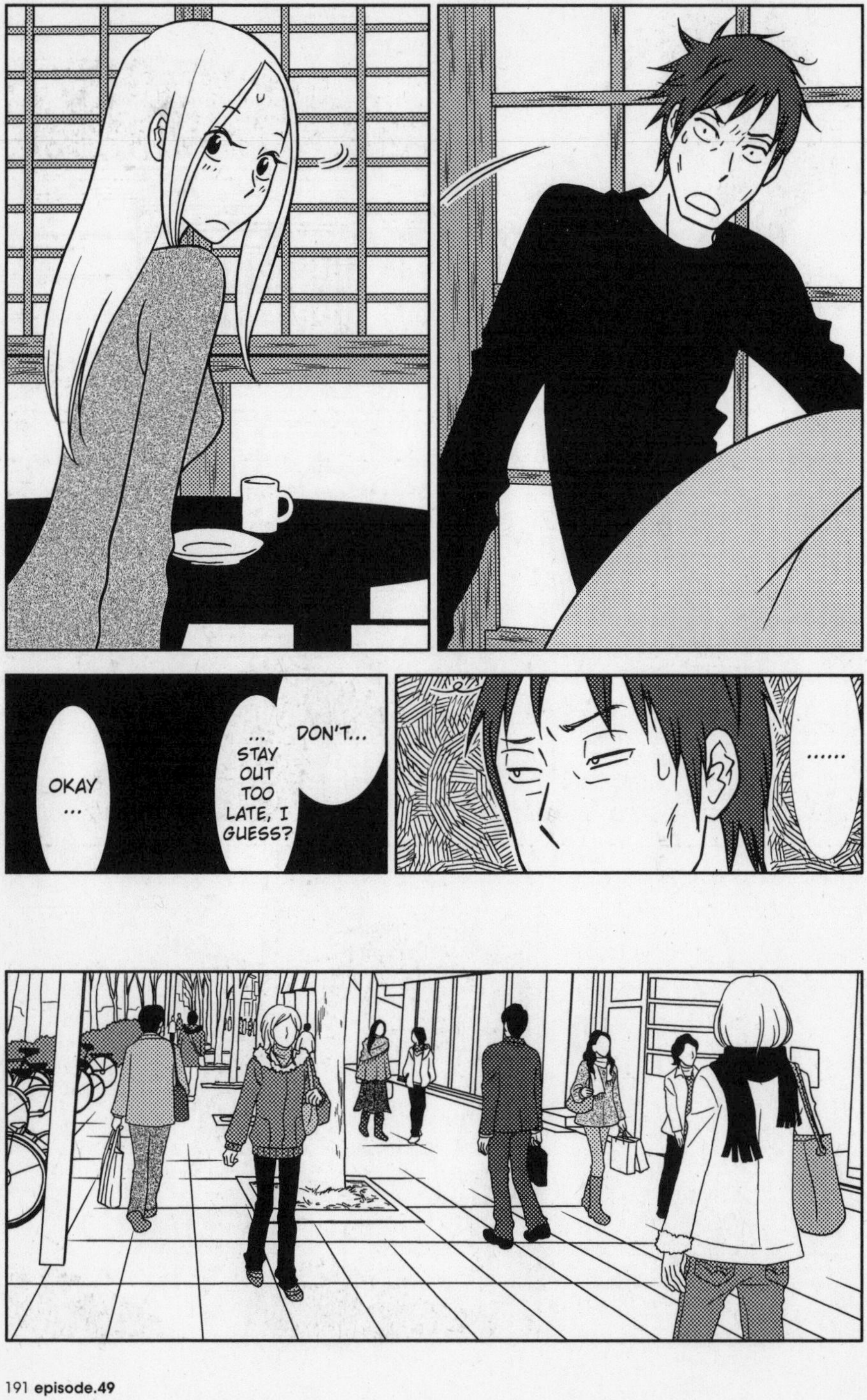
......
DON'T...
... STAY OUT TOO LATE, I GUESS?
OKAY ...

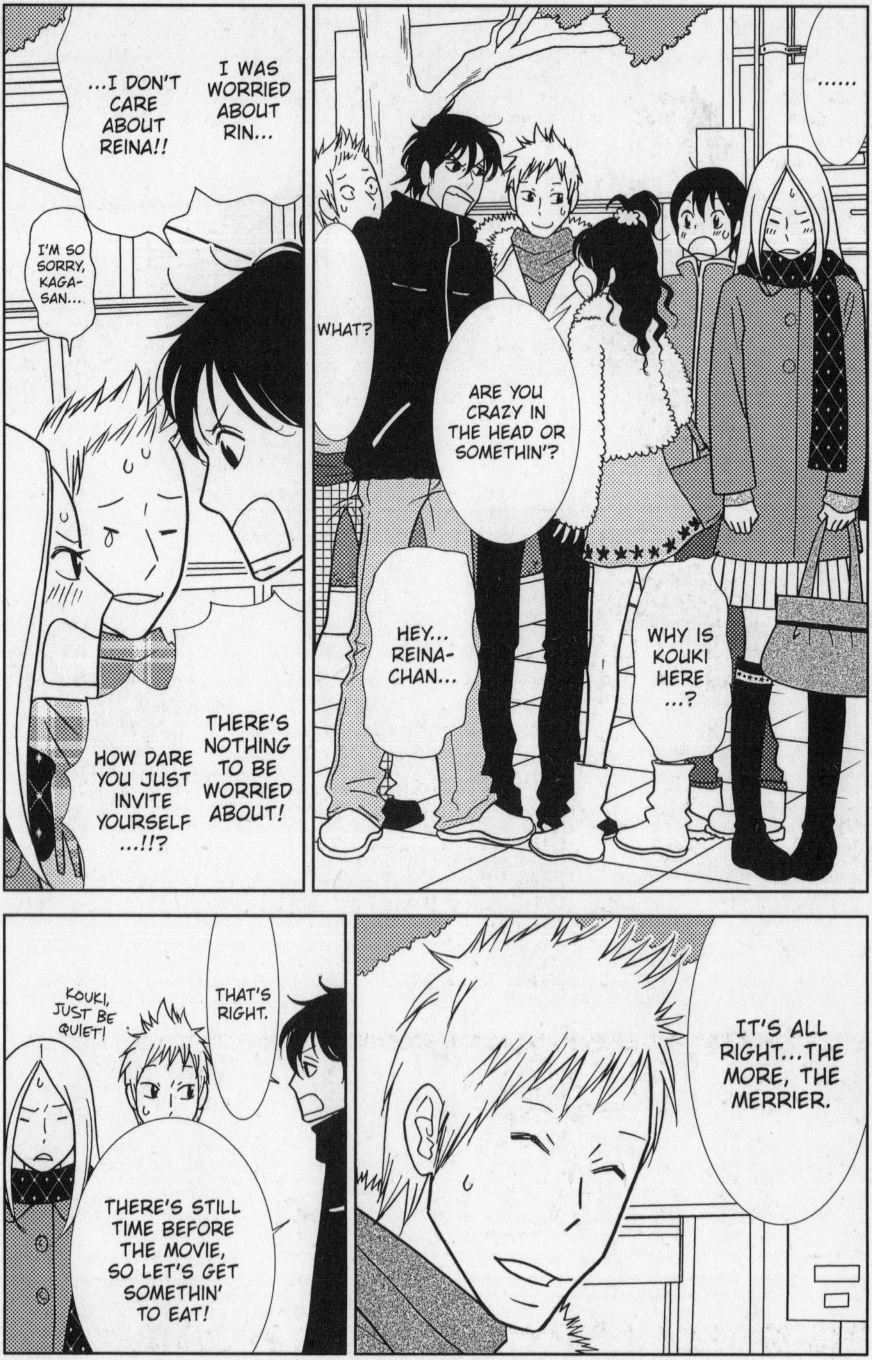
......
WHAT?
ARE YOU CRAZY IN THE HEAD OR SOMETHIN'?
WHY IS KOUKI HERE ...?
HEY... REINA-CHAN...
I WAS WORRIED ABOUT RIN...
...I DON'T CARE ABOUT REINA!!
I'M SO SORRY, KAGA-SAN...
THERE'S NOTHING TO BE WORRIED ABOUT!
HOW DARE YOU JUST INVITE YOURSELF ...!!?
IT'S ALL RIGHT...THE MORE, THE MERRIER.
THAT'S RIGHT.
KOUKI, JUST BE QUIET!
THERE'S STILL TIME BEFORE THE MOVIE, SO LET'S GET SOMETHIN' TO EAT!

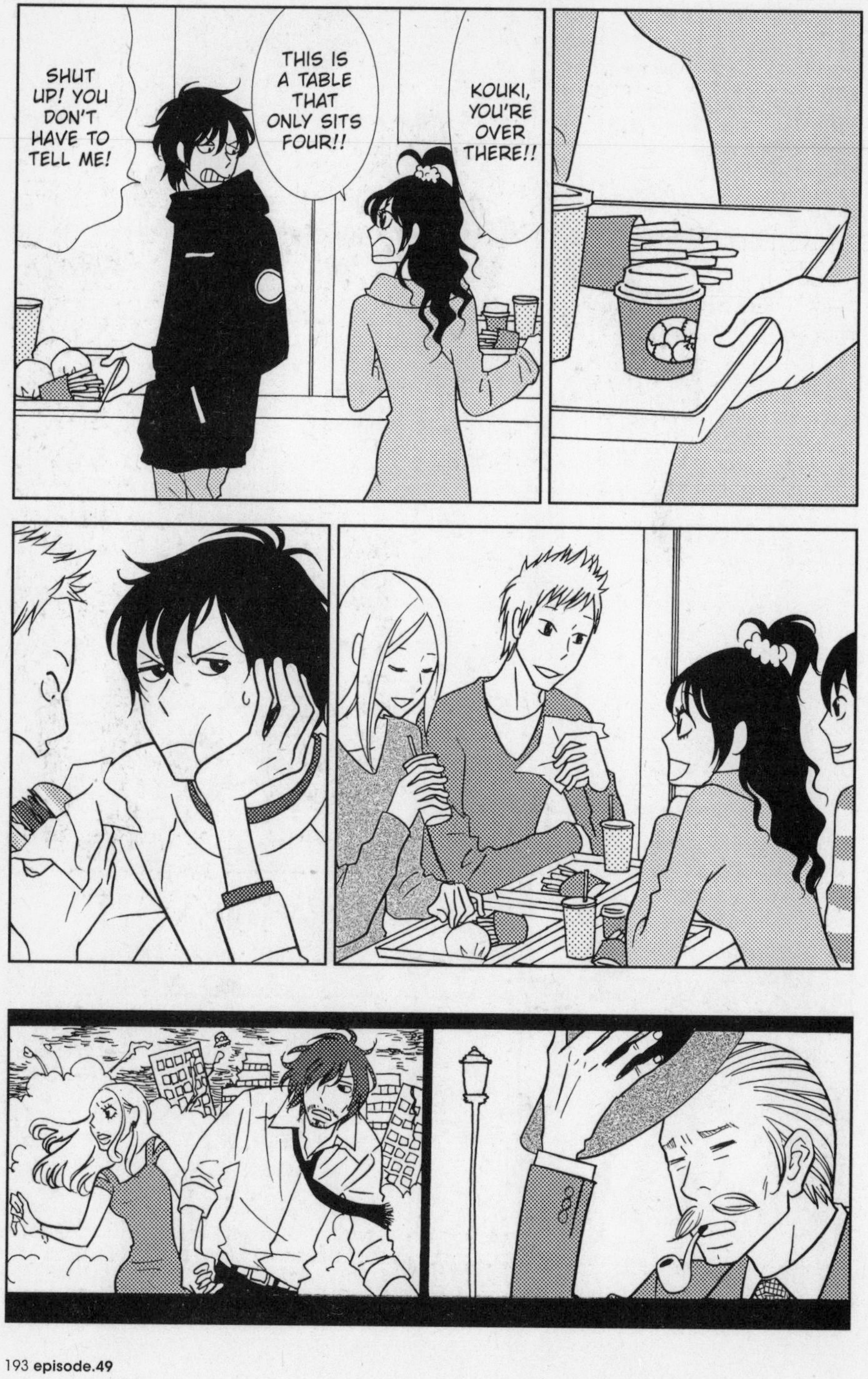
KOUKI, YOU'RE OVER THERE!!
THIS IS A TABLE THAT ONLY SITS FOUR!!
SHUT UP! YOU DON'T HAVE TO TELL ME!

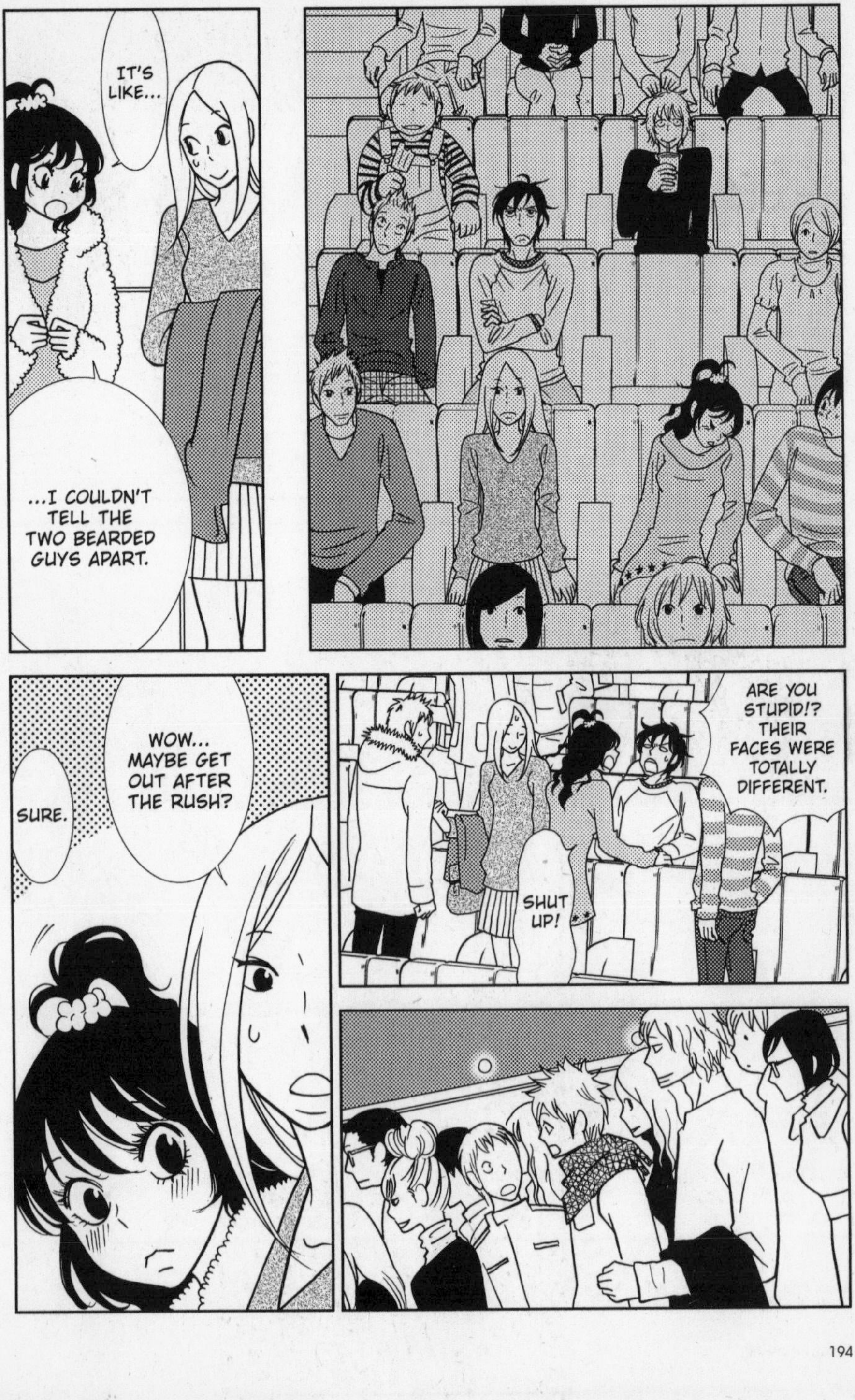
IT'S LIKE...
...I COULDN'T TELL THE TWO BEARDED GUYS APART.
ARE YOU STUPID!? THEIR FACES WERE TOTALLY DIFFERENT.
SHUT UP!
WOW... MAYBE GET OUT AFTER THE RUSH?
SURE.

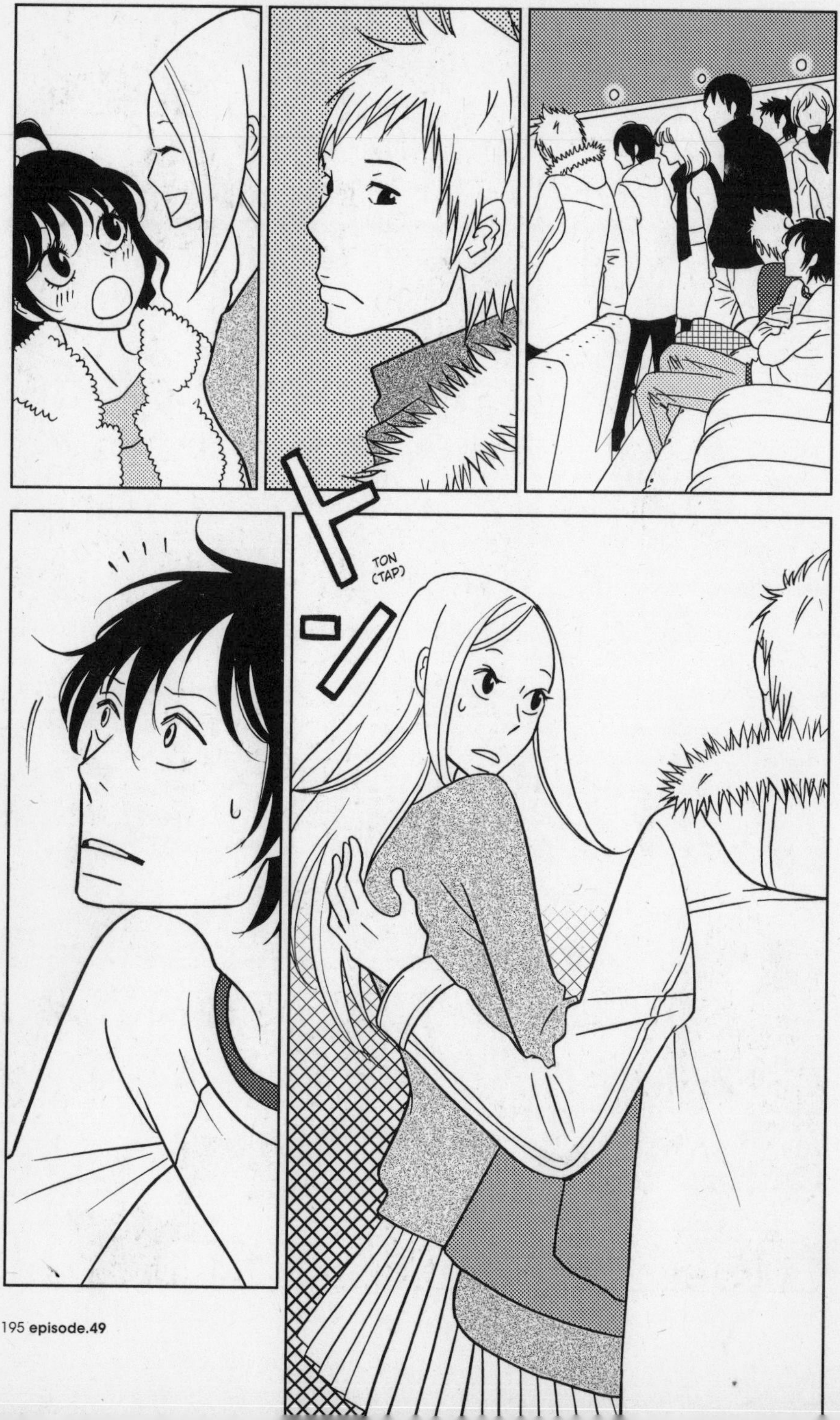
TON
(TAP)

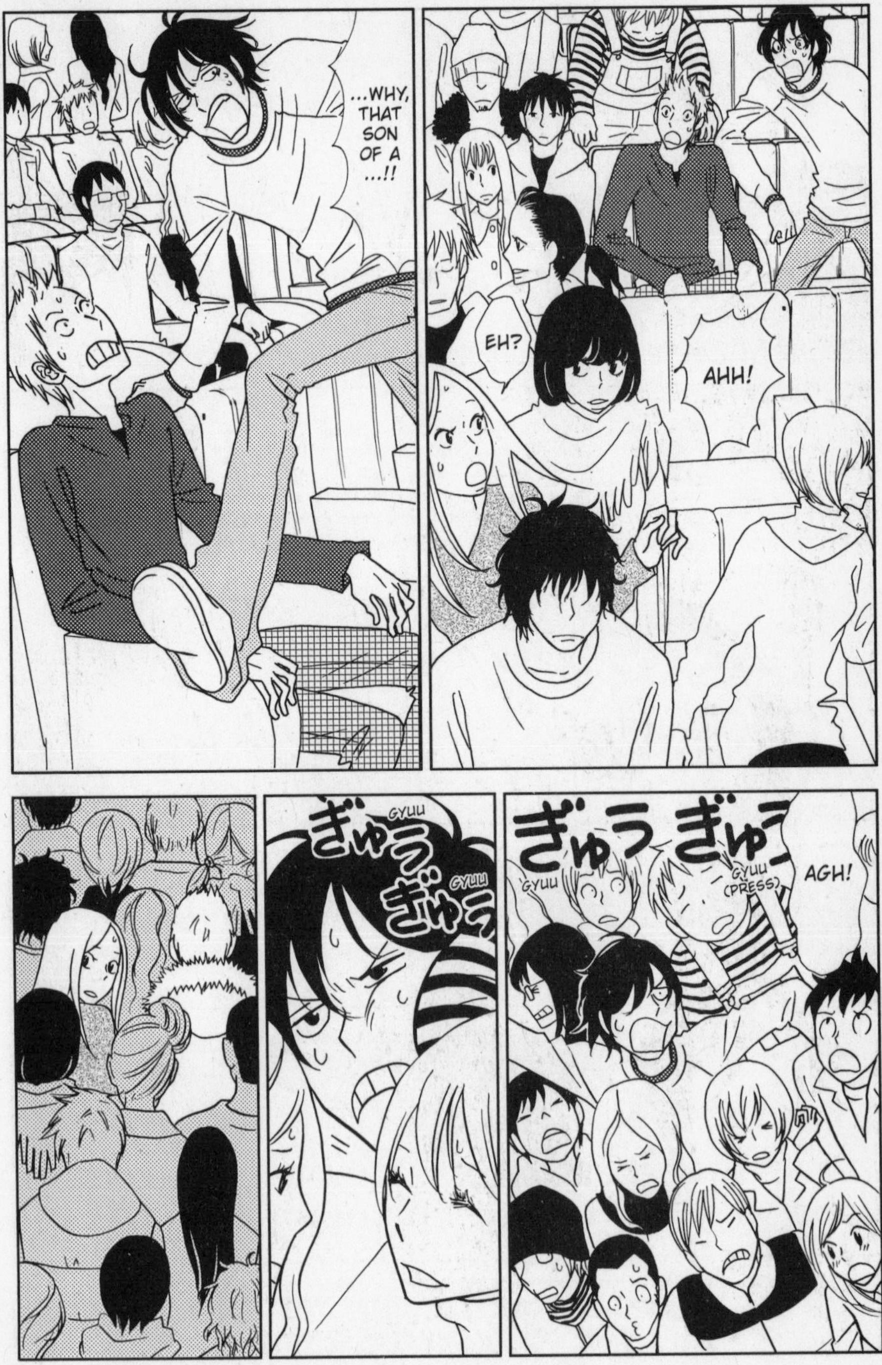
AHH!
EH?
...WHY, THAT SON OF A ...!!
ぎゅう GYUU
ぎゅう GYUU (PRESS)
AGH!
ぎゅう GYUU
ぎゅう GYUU

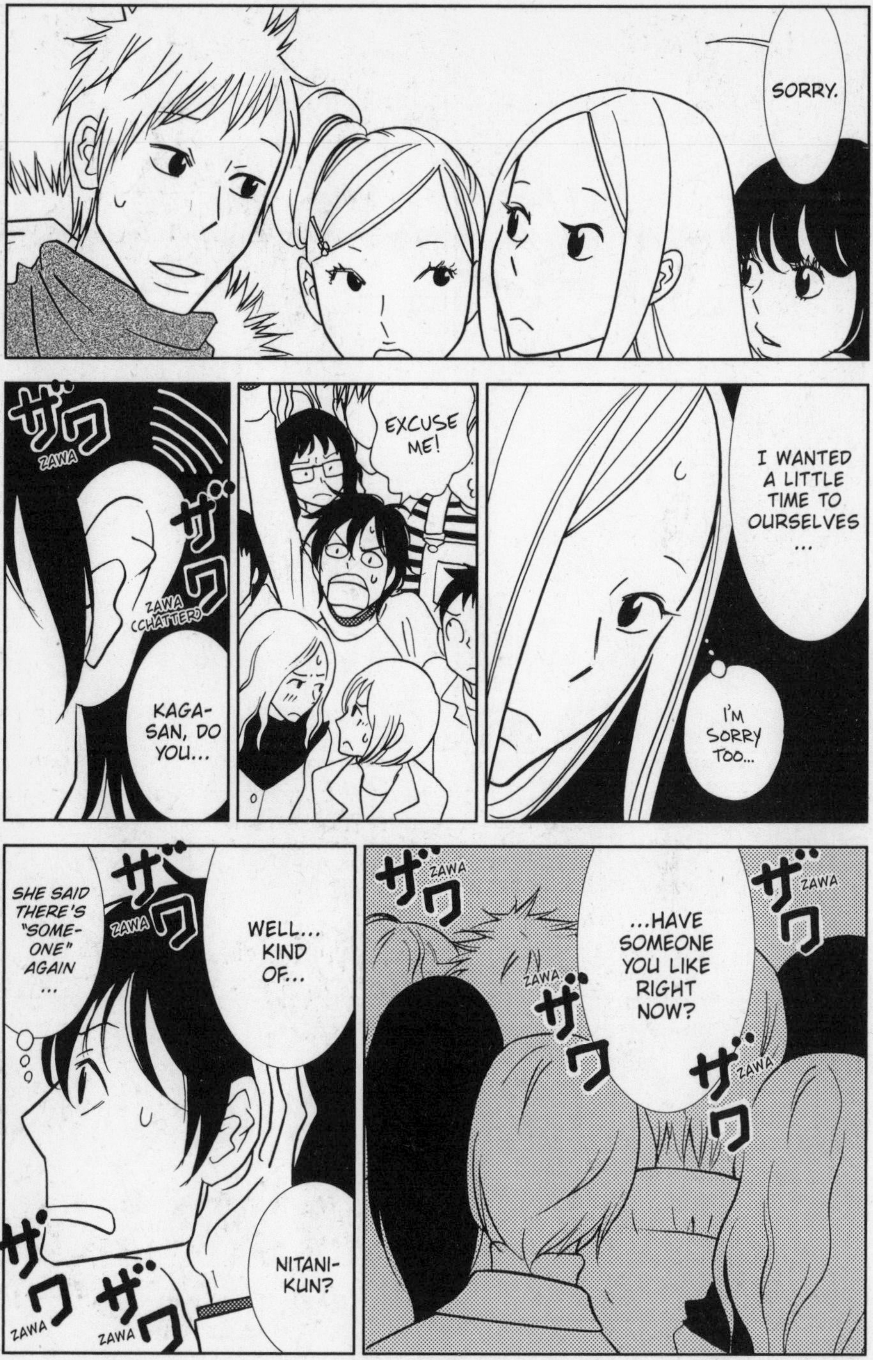
SORRY.
I WANTED A LITTLE TIME TO OURSELVES ...
I'M SORRY TOO...
EXCUSE ME!
ザワ
ZAWA
ザワ
ZAWA (CHATTER)
KAGA-SAN, DO YOU...
ザワ
ZAWA
...HAVE SOMEONE YOU LIKE RIGHT NOW?
ザワ
ZAWA
ザワ
ZAWA
ザワ
ZAWA
WELL... KIND OF...
ザワ
ZAWA
SHE SAID THERE'S "SOME-ONE" AGAIN ...
NITANI-KUN?
ザワ
ZAWA
ザワ
ZAWA

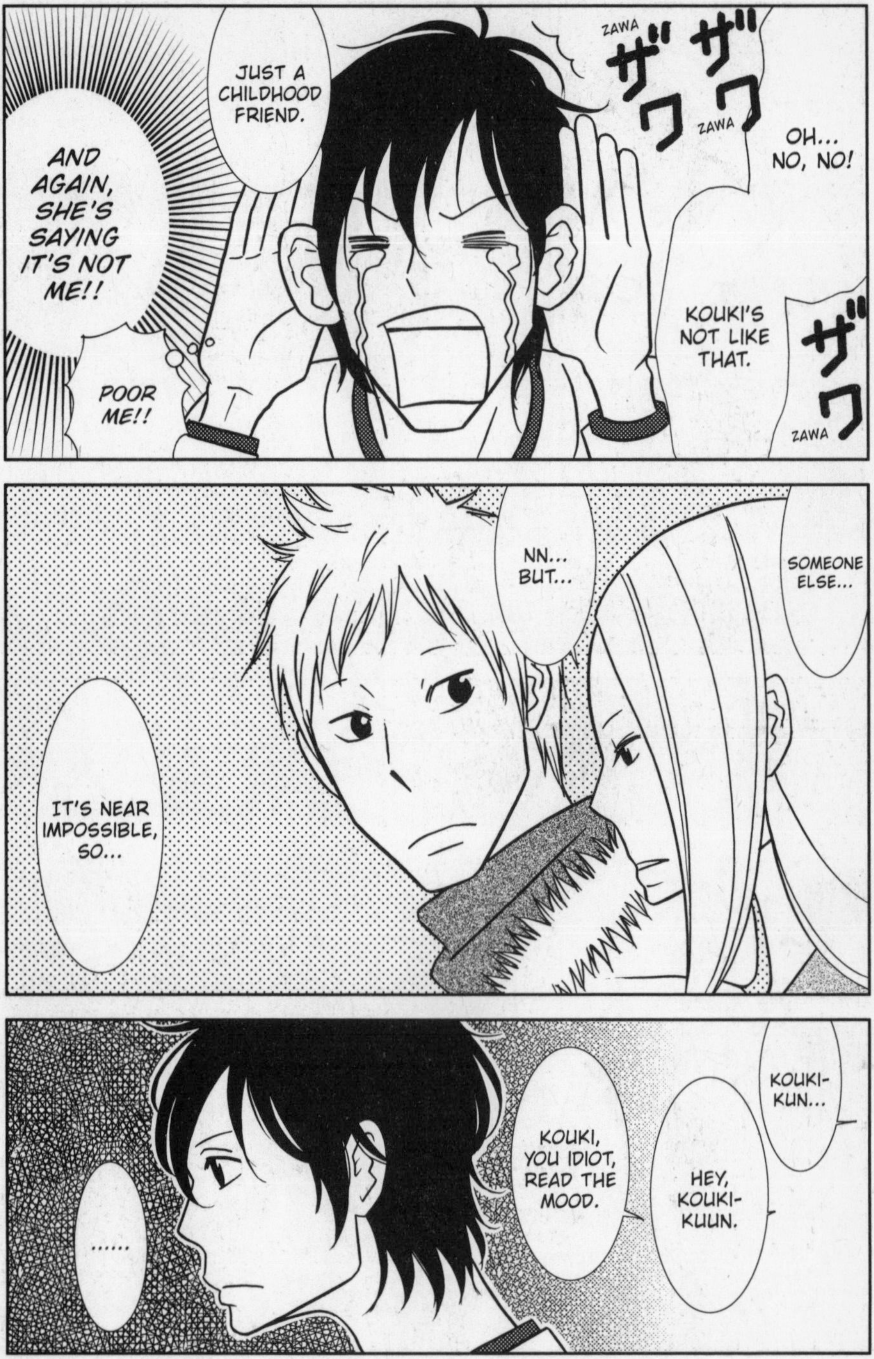
ザワ
ZAWA
ザワ
ZAWA
OH... NO, NO!
ザワ
ZAWA
KOUKI'S NOT LIKE THAT.
JUST A CHILDHOOD FRIEND.
AND AGAIN, SHE'S SAYING IT'S NOT ME!!
POOR ME!!
SOMEONE ELSE...
NN... BUT...
IT'S NEAR IMPOSSIBLE, SO...
KOUKI-KUN...
HEY, KOUKI-KUUN.
KOUKI, YOU IDIOT, READ THE MOOD.
......

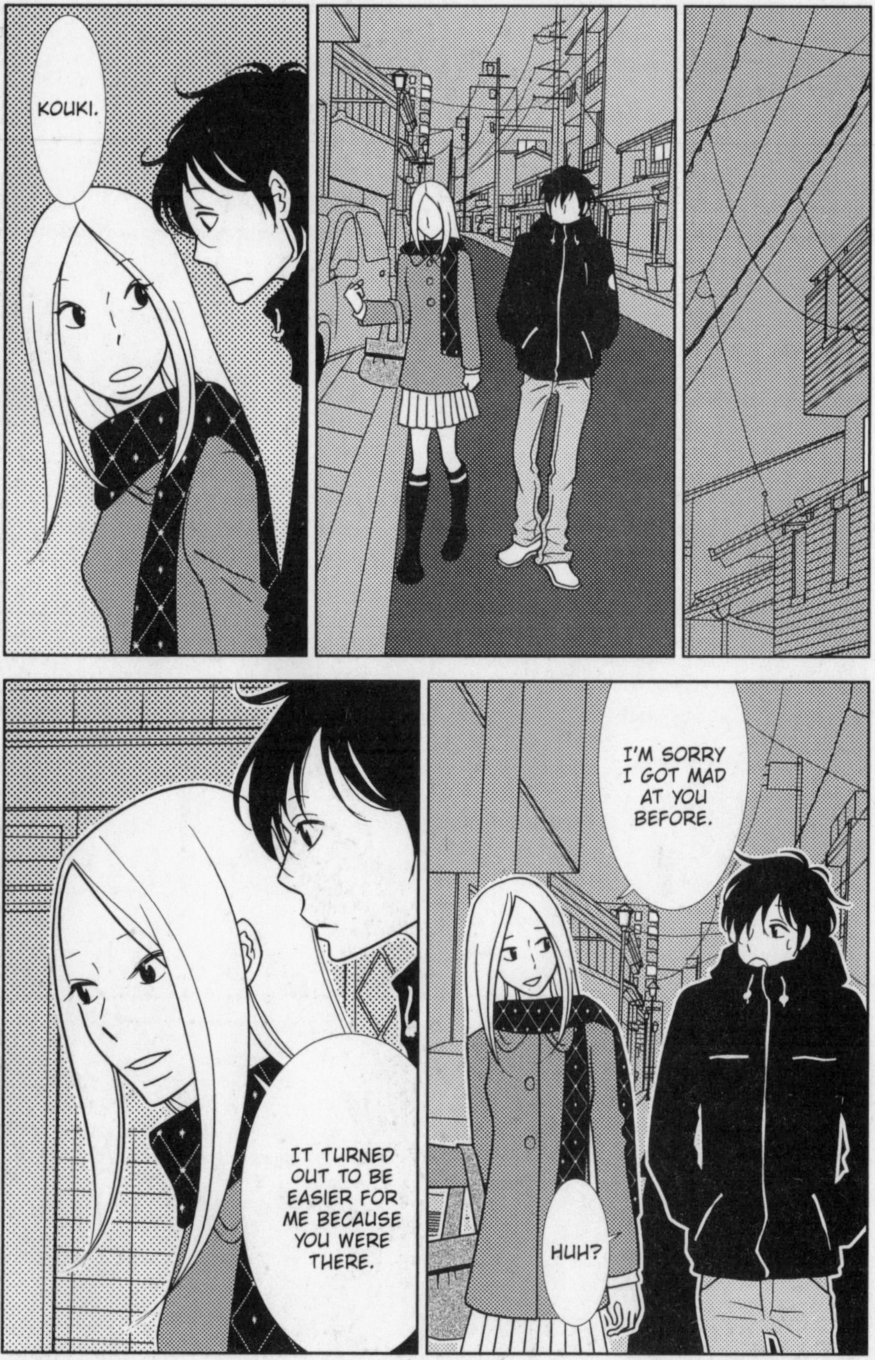
KOUKI.
I'M SORRY I GOT MAD AT YOU BEFORE.
HUH?
IT TURNED OUT TO BE EASIER FOR ME BECAUSE YOU WERE THERE.

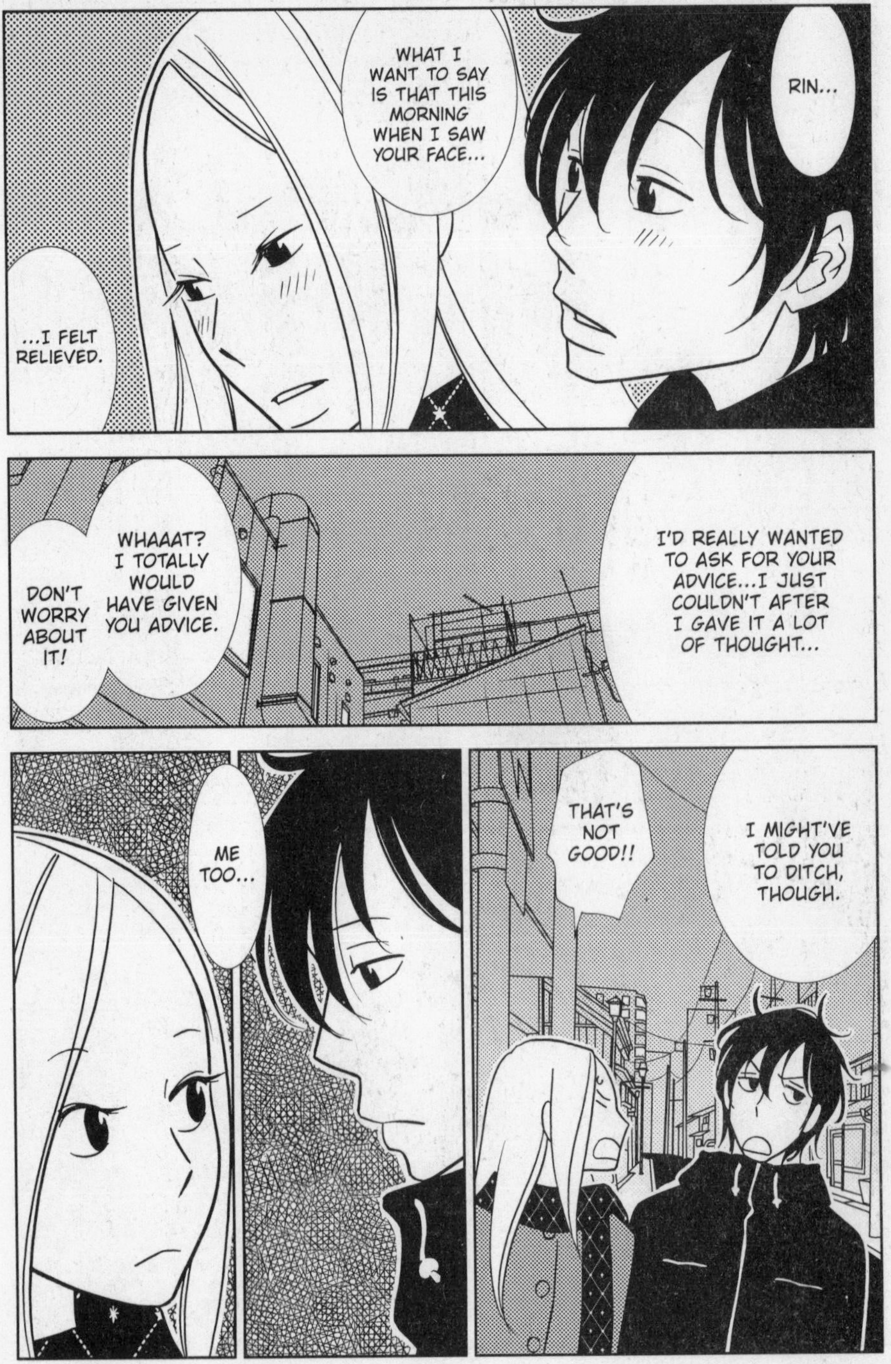
RIN...
WHAT I WANT TO SAY IS THAT THIS MORNING WHEN I SAW YOUR FACE...
...I FELT RELIEVED.
I'D REALLY WANTED TO ASK FOR YOUR ADVICE...I JUST COULDN'T AFTER I GAVE IT A LOT OF THOUGHT...
WHAAAT? I TOTALLY WOULD HAVE GIVEN YOU ADVICE.
DON'T WORRY ABOUT IT!
I MIGHT'VE TOLD YOU TO DITCH, THOUGH.
THAT'S NOT GOOD!!
ME TOO...

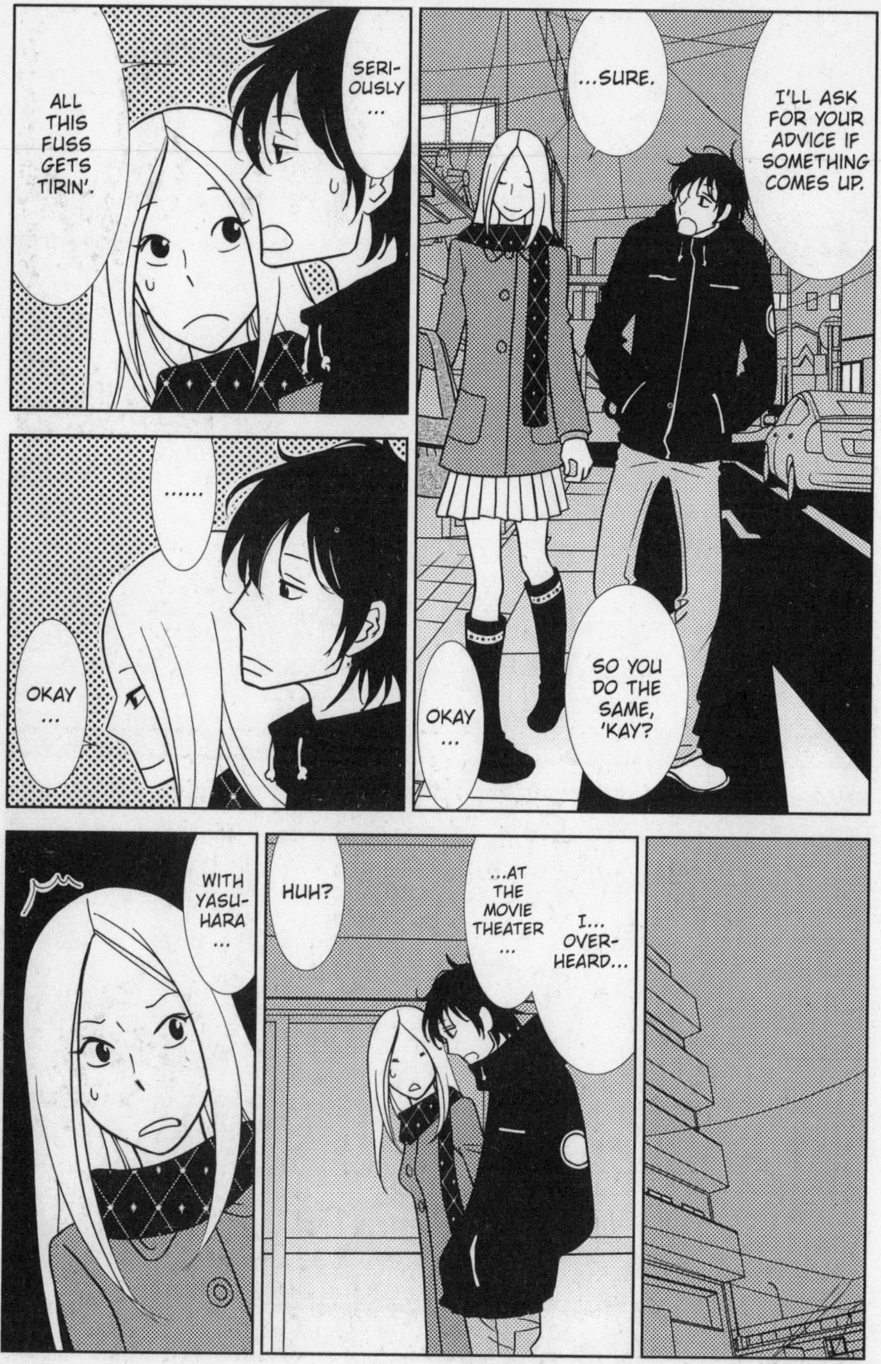
I'LL ASK FOR YOUR ADVICE IF SOMETHING COMES UP.
...SURE.
SO YOU DO THE SAME, 'KAY?
OKAY ...
SERI-OUSLY ...
ALL THIS FUSS GETS TIRIN'.
......
OKAY ...
I... OVER-HEARD...
...AT THE MOVIE THEATER ...
HUH?
WITH YASU-HARA ...

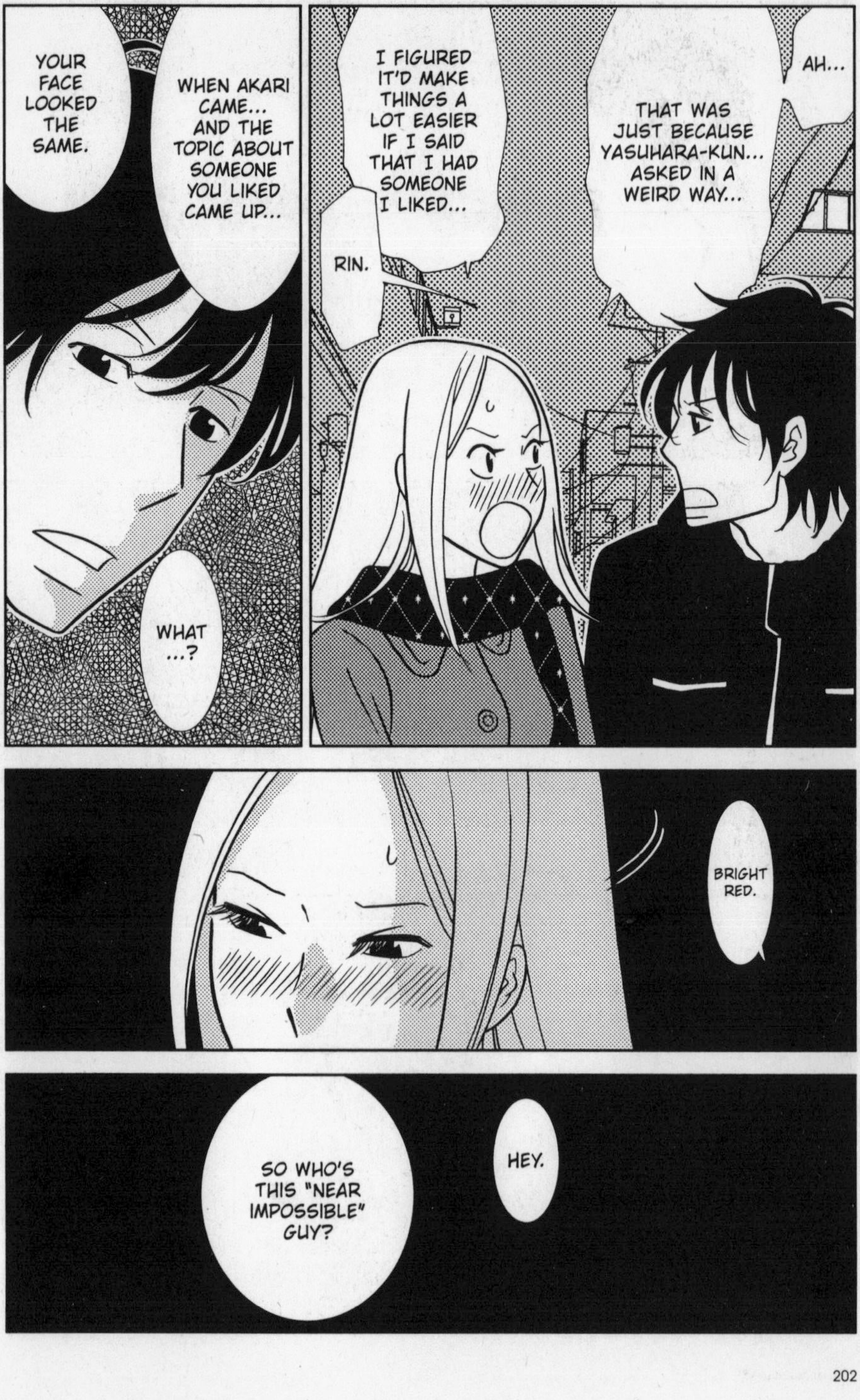
AH...
THAT WAS JUST BECAUSE YASUHARA-KUN... ASKED IN A WEIRD WAY...
I FIGURED IT'D MAKE THINGS A LOT EASIER IF I SAID THAT I HAD SOMEONE I LIKED...
RIN.
WHEN AKARI CAME... AND THE TOPIC ABOUT SOMEONE YOU LIKED CAME UP...
YOUR FACE LOOKED THE SAME.
WHAT ...?
BRIGHT RED.
HEY.
SO WHO'S THIS "NEAR IMPOSSIBLE" GUY?

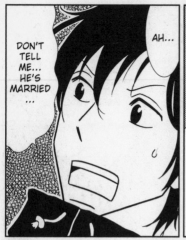

A GUY WITH A GIRL-FRIEND?
NO...
NOT LIKE THAT...
NOT A TEACHER!?
NO!!
AH...
DON'T TELL ME... HE'S MARRIED...
N-NO, NOT MARRIED!
ガラッ
GARA (RATTLE)
NOT MARRIED!!
......
NOT MARRIED, BUT IS HE AN ADULT...?
A...
AH, RIN!!
HEY, DAIKICHI!
I TOLD YOU TO GET BACK BEFORE IT GOT DARK!!
YOU'RE LATE!!

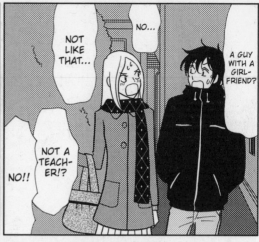

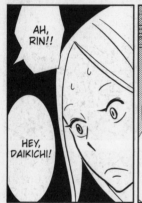

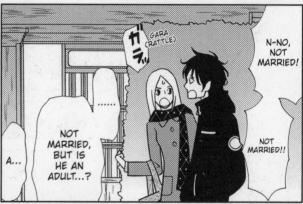

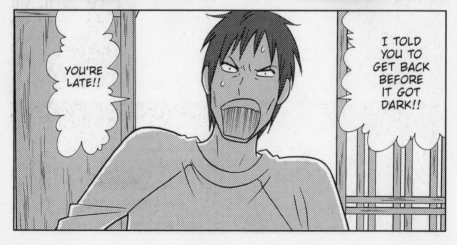

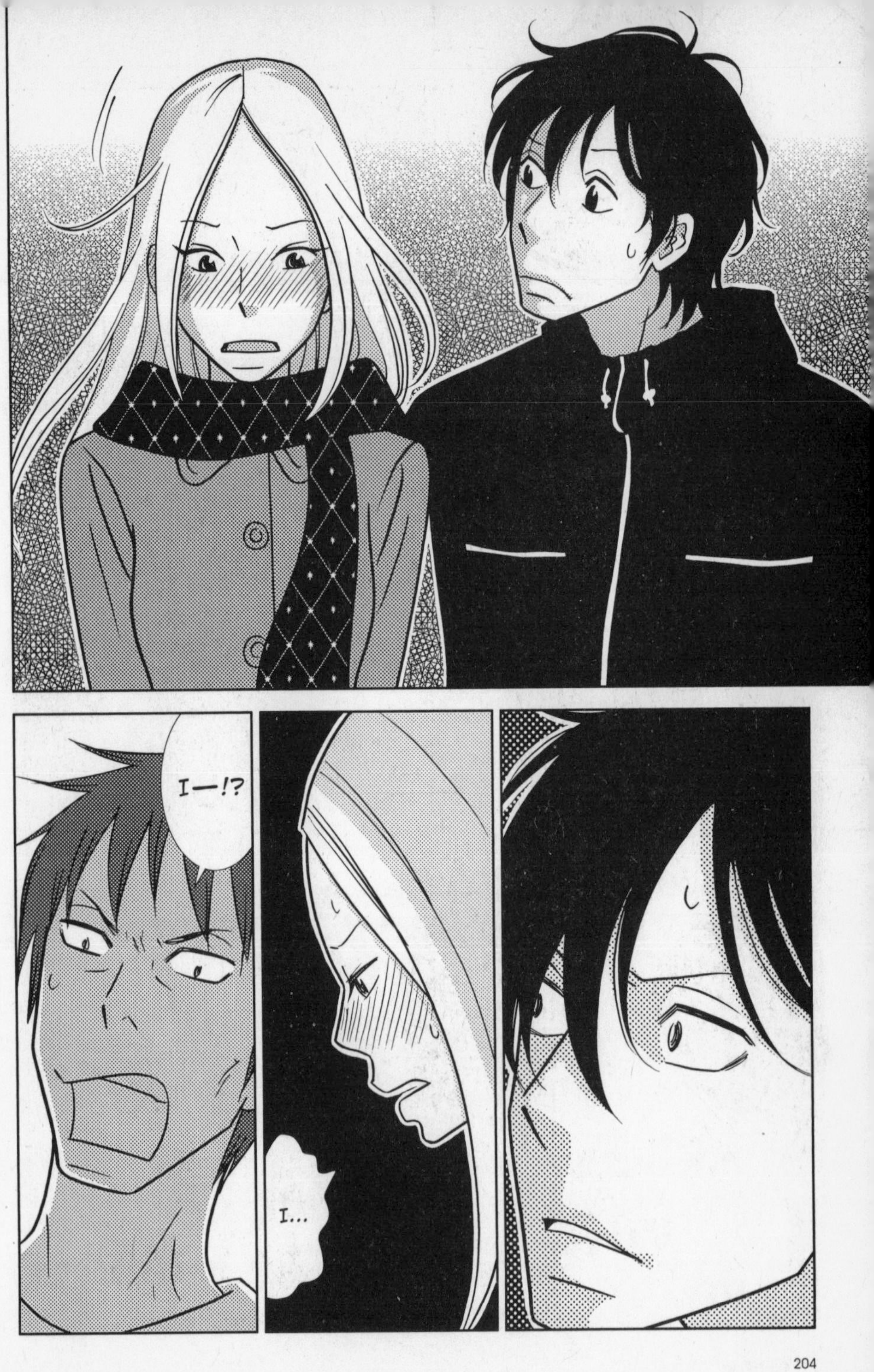
I...
I—!?

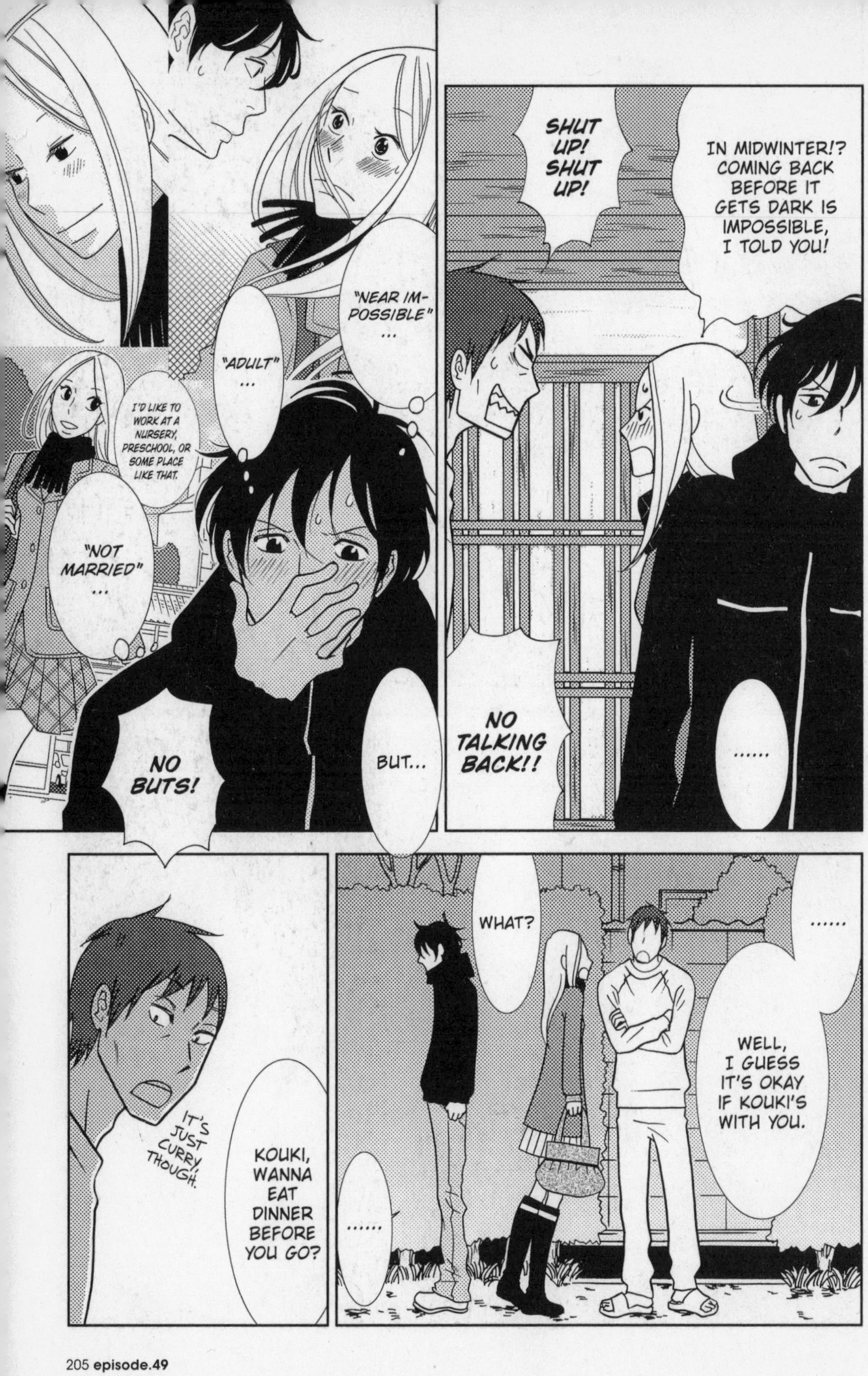
IN MIDWINTER!? COMING BACK BEFORE IT GETS DARK IS IMPOSSIBLE, I TOLD YOU!
SHUT UP! SHUT UP!
......
NO TALKING BACK!!
"NEAR IMPOSSIBLE"...
"ADULT"...
I'D LIKE TO WORK AT A NURSERY, PRESCHOOL, OR SOME PLACE LIKE THAT.
"NOT MARRIED"...
BUT...
NO BUTS!
......
WHAT?
WELL, I GUESS IT'S OKAY IF KOUKI'S WITH YOU.
......
KOUKI, WANNA EAT DINNER BEFORE YOU GO?
IT'S JUST CURRY THOUGH.

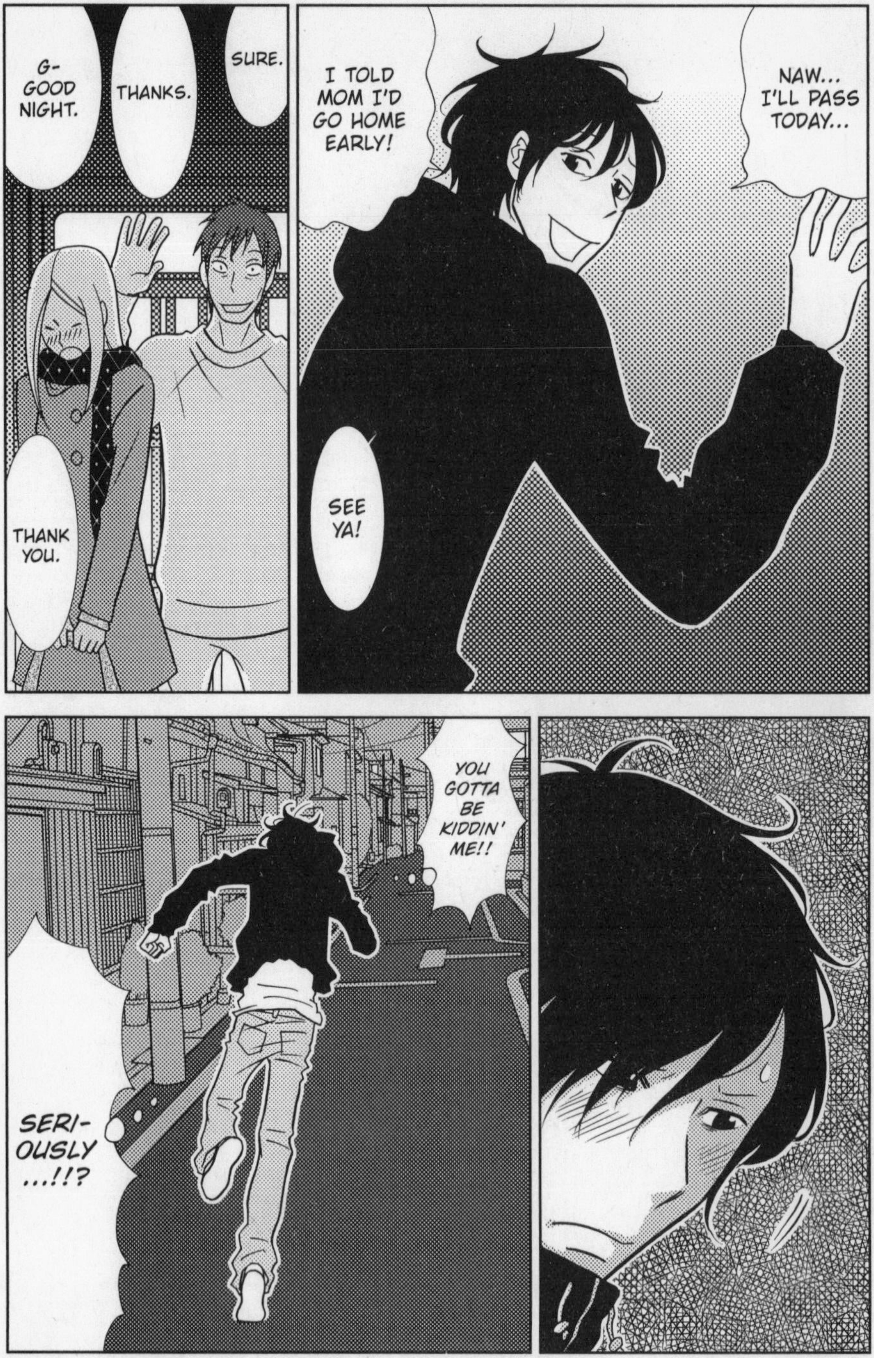
NAW... I'LL PASS TODAY...
I TOLD MOM I'D GO HOME EARLY!
SEE YA!
SURE.
THANKS.
G-GOOD NIGHT.
THANK YOU.
YOU GOTTA BE KIDDIN' ME!!
SERI-OUSLY ...!!?

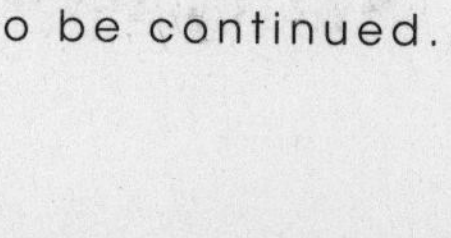

to be continued...

BUNNY DROP 8

YUMI UNITA

Translation: Kaori Inoue   •   Lettering: Alexis Eckerman

BUNNY DROP Vol. 8 © 2010 by Yumi Unita. All rights reserved. First
published in Japan in 2010 by SHODENSHA PUBLISHING CO., LTD.,
Tokyo. English translation rights in USA, Canada, and UK arranged with
SHODENSHA PUBLISHING CO., LTD. and Hachette Book Group through
Tuttle-Mori Agency, Inc., Tokyo.

Translation © 2013 by Hachette Book Group, Inc.

Yen Press
Hachette Book Group
237 Park Avenue, New York, NY 10017

www.HachetteBookGroup.com
www.YenPress.com

Yen Press is an imprint of Hachette Book Group, Inc. The Yen Press name
and logo are trademarks of Hachette Book Group, Inc.

First Yen Press Edition: April 2013

ISBN: 978-0-316-21722-4

10 9 8 7 6 5 4 3 2 1

BVG

Printed in the United States of America